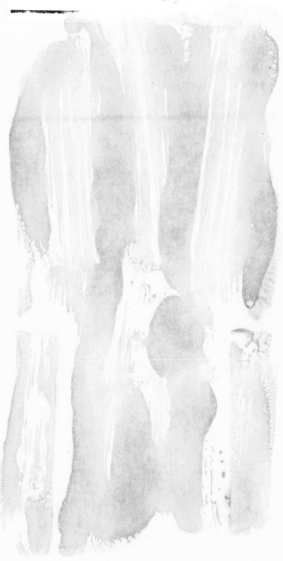

DATE DU

EARLY
AMERICAN CHILDREN'S BOOKS

Early American Children's Books

BY

A. S. W. ROSENBACH

With Bibliographical Descriptions of the Books
in his Private Collection

Foreword by
A. EDWARD NEWTON

DOVER PUBLICATIONS, INC.
NEW YORK

This Dover edition, first published in 1971, is an
unabridged republication of the work originally published by The Southworth Press, Portland, Maine, in
1933. Seven plates (those facing pages 197, 226, 227,
232, 238, 286 and 287) were in color in the original
edition and are here reproduced in black and white.

International Standard Book Number: 0-486-22467-8
Library of Congress Catalog Card Number: 77-150808

Manufactured in the United States of America
Dover Publications, Inc.
180 Varick Street
New York, N. Y. 10014

TO THE MEMORY OF

MY UNCLE

MOSES POLOCK

FOREWORD

THE *old adage, that a man's character can be told by the company he keeps, suggests also that his character may be told by the books that he collects, but it fails utterly if applied to Dr. A. S. W. Rosenbach and the books in this collection. Here is a man midway, I should say, between his first childhood and his second, who has for years devoted his enormous resources and his scanty leisure to the collecting of Early American Children's Books. When I say enormous resources, I do not refer merely to his wealth: I have in mind chiefly his magnetic qualities, and I use this word literally—meaning thereby his power to draw to himself whatever books he wishes; for the moment a rare or scarce book is discovered, the discoverer's first impulse is to 'take it to the Doctor', whether he wants to know what it is or to dispose of it.*

I have known my Rosy, the world's Dr. Rosenbach, the man who, when he enters the auction room, causes other book-buyers to shake in their

Foreword

shoes,—I have known this man, I say, intimately for half his lifetime and I never discovered in him any inordinate love of children. Had he such love he surely would have given hostages to fortune and raised a family, like the rest of us. I suspect him of being a coward and I can imagine him as a child doing almost anything but singing, 'Here we go round the mulberry bush' or playing 'London Bridge is falling down,' or doing any of those things which I am sure I did when I was a small boy. I can imagine him playing at kissing games with but little skill until he became a man, when, trampling upon his diffident nature, he sought the instructions of the ablest masters and applied himself with 'rigor' to the game. I can, however, very easily imagine him with a book—a boy with a book in a corner in which he might not be disturbed, busily engaged in pouring into his inexhaustible memory fictions and facts and dates in X quantities, to be brought out many years later just when and as wanted.

Foreword

I should be sorry if I have suggested that Dr. Rosenbach is an unlovely character. His parents, I am sure, loved him and were proud of him; his brother, Philip, loves him, I feel certain, but does not fear him as does the rest of the world; whereas, Rosy loves his brother Phil, and I suspect, fears him too, as a properly brought up younger brother should. Here, then, is an enigma: here is a man as learned as a Chinese Mandarin, a man with a knowledge of languages the very sight of which is disturbing, a man of affairs bearing heavy business burdens and responsibilities, a man who, when he is not in London or Paris buying books, or in New York or Philadelphia or Chicago or Los Angeles selling them, is, one is usually informed by his secretary, 'down at Corson's Inlet —fishing.' 'I'd rather fish than do anything else,' Rosy tells his friends. Such, then, is the man who has—out of the corner of his eye, as it were— made this amazing collection of Early American Children's Books. And caused it to be catalogued

Foreword

and printed in this admirable format. And do not think, Gentle Reader, that I use this word 'admirable' inadvisedly: I have been 'in' on this publication from the first.

I have several times said, and I have been criticised for saying that no bookseller has ever before enjoyed so unique a position as does Dr. Rosenbach today. His own private library is a very distinguished one: this collection is but a small, a very small and relatively unimportant part of it. Indeed, if Dr. Rosenbach were not the Napoleon of Booksellers, he would be known as having one of the choicest small libraries in America. In the auction-rooms of London, Paris, New York, or wherever fine books are selling, he is expected to hold his own against all comers, who sometimes act as a unit against him. He must have in his mind not only the tens of thousands of tricky points and dates of such European books as the American collector is interested in, but the whole range of Americana—using that word in its broadest sense—as

Foreword

well, of which the average European bookseller knows little or nothing.

As I have before suggested, no amount of nerve or learning would enable a man to achieve Dr. Rosenbach's unique position without a memory trained almost beyond belief in what might be called the mechanics of his trade. Boswell tells us that 'it was Dr. Johnson's habit, when asked a question, to repeat the question aloud: "Why, Sir, as to the good or evil of card-playing,—" thinking, meantime, which side of the argument he would take.' In like manner, the Doctor when asked a question will almost invariably say, 'I don't know the date of the first book printed in Mexico,' all the time turning the question over in his mind and, in a moment, giving you the answer—correctly, and in some detail.

These Children's Books, then, having afforded relaxation for a mind tuned by circumstance to concert pitch, have served their purpose: possession is the grave of bliss. I will not say that the moment

Foreword

one has a book that moment it ceases to interest one, but rather that the moment one has one rare book, one wants another one, until at last one turns one's attention to something else. So it is with the Doctor. It may be that there are no more worlds to conquer, or the worlds are not worth conquering. In a collection of this kind one begins as early as one can: in this case with 1682 and comes down to 1836. After that, collecting is not the sport of the angler with rod and fly, but of the crabber with a net. And when it is realized how flimsy, how easily destroyed children's books were, and are, and what destructive tendencies lurk in the little brains and hands of the best trained child, the wonder is that so many books have been preserved.

I know the question you would now ask me and I will answer it—as Andy sometimes answers Amos, 'Yes and no, rather more no than yes.' 'No, the collection is not for sale in whole or in part, for love or for money, now or at any other time.' 'But the Doctor will not live forever' I can hear you

Foreword

say. Certainly all great collectors have, in the past, died, sooner or later, but later rather than sooner, as collecting tends to longevity, and it may indeed be that Rosy, who has broken so many precedents may break this one also and live forever. But I hope not, for upon his arrival in the Elysium Fields I shall be there, sitting on the fence surrounding those same fields waiting for him, eager to hear the latest reports on 'This Book-Collecting Game',—and who can give them in such detail and with such authority as Rosy? But 'Yes' to your other question: the collection can be seen. In John Ashhurst's; that is to say, in the Free Library of Philadelphia, where it has been on exhibition for a long time past and is likely to be for a long time to come.

Of the individual books in this collection, I, knowing nothing, shall say nothing,—and by the way, this excellent rule is too frequently neglected by editors and commentators. I have been limited by the terms of my commission from the Publisher

Foreword

to say a few words on behalf of my friend, the Collector. The Books speak for themselves, or perhaps the Doctor may be persuaded to speak for them.

A. EDWARD NEWTON

Contents

List of Illustrations

List of Illustrations

List of Illustrations

List of Illustrations

List of Illustrations

List of Illustrations

List of Illustrations

Introduction

THE assembling of this collection of Early American Children's Books has covered a period of almost one hundred years. My interest in it was inherited from my uncle, Moses Polock, who was born in Philadelphia in 1817, and who started the collection about 1835, when employed as clerk to M'Carty & Davis, a firm of Philadelphia publishers and book dealers, who had at that time a large stock of American juveniles, passed down to them from former owners of the business. I am fortunate in possessing a series of ledgers and letter books of the old firm, which contain an enormous quantity of correspondence with contemporary authors and publishers. These letters provide valuable source material for the history of the American book trade, and much new and interesting data relating to the literature of the nursery.

Jacob Johnson, the founder of the firm, was a Quaker, who established himself in the book business at 147 Market Street, Philadelphia about the year 1780. He early became interested in the publication of children's books, for which he acquired so much fame that in the course of time the activities of his House were confined almost exclusively to the production of books of this class. The business grew rapidly, and Johnson eventually found himself unable to carry it alone. About the year 1808, therefore, he invited a Quaker named Benjamin Warner to become a partner in the business, and the firm of Johnson and Warner continued the publication of children's books from the same address.

About twenty years later the firm was taken over by M'Carty & Davis, who thereby acquired a remarkable collection of juvenile

Introduction

publications. It became the duty of my uncle to sort and arrange these books, which he found so extremely interesting that he was eventually inspired with the happy idea of himself forming a collection of American children's books, an inspiration which has had far reaching effects on my own life, for in 1900 he gave his collection to me and thus started me in what has proved to be one of the most exciting and interesting hobbies of my career.

My uncle's collection formed an excellent nucleus, for not only did I obtain from him in their original condition, a large number of the publications of his predecessors in his own firm (he had eventually acquired the business of M'Carty & Davis), but also some extremely valuable examples of early American juvenilia, such for instance as the *Legacy for Children*, an excessively rare volume published in 1717 by Andrew Bradford in Philadelphia.

Since my uncle's death the riding of this hobby has led me a most exciting chase in every part of this country, and even in Europe, the chase having been rewarded as a rule with highly satisfactory results, and rarely turning out to be the kind known as 'wild goose.' Sometimes my friends have given me tips where rarities could be found, occasionally I have come across treasures by accident, and still others I have bought either in book stores, or after keen competition at auction, with the result that today I have a comprehensive collection of American and English juveniles, ranging in rarity, if I may be allowed my uncle's terminology, from 'rare' to 'infernally rare.'

Children's books have such a many-sided appeal that they are strangely satisfying to the collector. Not only do they have as much scholarly and bibliographical interest as books in other fields, but more than any class of literature they reflect the minds

Introduction

of the generation that produced them. Hence no better guide to the history and development of any country can be found than its juvenile literature. For as that eminent philosopher and novelist, and at the same time successful publisher and writer of children's books, William Godwin, once pointed out to Charles Lamb, *it is children that read children's books, when they read, but it is parents who choose them.*

Children are naturally destructive, and from time immemorial have realized that the purpose of books was to provide them with a 'feast' of reason, if not a flow of soul. They have always taken a strange delight in the flavor of printer's ink, have nibbled at the pages and sampled the bindings of the books provided for them so that the wonder is that any specimens of early American children's books are in existence today. The more popular a book, the greater the possibilities of destruction, for as it passed in turn to each new member of a family the more meals would be taken from it, and the fewer copies would be likely to be preserved intact, with the result that whole editions of books written and published for the young have entirely disappeared.

One pleasant result of this otherwise deplorable circumstance is that any collector of children's books is almost bound to find himself the happy possessor of a number of unique volumes. I have been extremely fortunate in this respect, and the accompanying catalogue contains descriptions of a large number of books which to the best of my knowledge are the sole surviving evidences of their editions, and of many others which have been preserved in only one or two copies. Obviously it is not always possible to state definitely that a volume is unique, particularly

Introduction

in the field of children's books where comparatively little census work has been done, although fortunately the number of special bibliographies is increasing steadily.

In 1682, the date of the printing of *The Rule of the New-Creature*, the earliest book in this collection, the whole of the intellectual activity of the New England Colonies was in the hands of the puritanical clergy, men of the calibre of Cotton Mather, and it is not therefore a matter of surprise that the books printed at that time had a strongly religious bias. Children were brought up on the principle that they were not *born to live, but born to dye* and the literature provided for them was with the definite purpose of teaching them how they should die in a befitting manner. Nor were they left under any illusions as to their ultimate destination after the due accomplishment of a *pious death*. They were taught in their books that a *Hell of Eternal Fire* or the *Blackness of Darkness forever* were merely some of the minor horrors that almost inescapably awaited them. Witness Mr. Cotton Mather himself, in *A Family well Ordered*, who amongst other horrible warnings tells the children that *If by Undutifulness to your Parents, you incur the Curse of God, it won't be Long before you go down into Obscure Darkness, even, into Utter Darkness: God has Reserv'd for you the Blackness of Darkness for ever*. A child brought up on such teaching might well go about in dread of *witches and other night fears* and of the *bug that flieth by night*, and any other horrors his imagination could conjure.

All the early spiritual guides were extremely popular, and were read almost out of existence. My copy of the 1682 edition of *The Rule of the New-Creature*, published in Boston by Mary Avery, the first woman publisher in New England, appears to be the only

Introduction

surviving copy of the second edition of that work. The first edition of this famous book has also completely disappeared save for a copy recently discovered in the library of the American Antiquarian Society at Worcester. Similarly the edition printed in Boston, 1684, of John Cotton's *Spiritual Milk for Boston Babes* seems to have survived in one copy only. Incidentally it may be remarked that if this was milk the unfortunate Babes might well have hoped to remain on a diet of pap forever.

However, in the art of dying, as in that of living, example was thought to be better than precept, and the children of New England were therefore forced to read, mark, learn and inwardly digest the morbid accounts of the long drawn out illnesses and dying speeches of numbers of children who died pious deaths at an early age.

Among the numerous books of this class, two of the most interesting are indigenous to this country, namely Benjamin Colman's *A Devout Contemplation On the Meaning of Divine Providence, in the Early Death of Pious and Lovely Children. Preached upon the Sudden and Lamented Death of Mrs. Elizabeth Wainwright. Who Departed this Life, April the 8th, 1714. Having just compleated the Fourteenth Year of Her Age*, printed in Boston by John Allen, for Joanna Perry, in 1714, and the still more famous *A Legacy for Children, being Some of the Last Expressions, and Dying Sayings, of Hannah Hill, Junr. Of the City of Philadelphia, in the Province of Pennsilvania, in America, Aged Eleven Years and near Three Months. The Third Eddition*, printed in Philadelphia by Andrew Bradford, 1717. My copy of Colman's book belonged to Judith Sewall, the daughter of the famous Chief Justice Sewall, whose Diary has given us such a heartrending pic-

Introduction

ture of child life of the day; it has her childish signature in several places and other marks of her ownership. The title-page and preliminary leaves are plentifully besprinkled with thick black mourning lines, and the address to the children of the town asks such pointed questions as *Children, do you Pray to God daily for your Precious and Immortal Souls? Will you not be put upon doing so by this Example? May you not die so suddenly as not to have time to pray at last?* Hannah Hill, Junr., the heroine of *A Legacy for Children*, seems to have been a more tiresome little prig than Elizabeth Wainwright. *She was very Importunate in requesting her Parents freely to give her up to the Will of God, saying, It would be better both for them and her, so to do. And when she thought to have prevail'd, Now (said she) I am Easy in Mind. Then asked her Father for a piece of Silver (which he gave her) and after she had held it and looked at it a little while, return'd it to him again, saying, Now I give it to thee freely, for it was mine, because thou gavest it me. Thereby Intimating herself God's Gift to them and her Example therein, for their Resigning her to him again Chearfully.*

By far the most popular book in this class, however, was an importation from England written by James Janeway, a non-conformist divine, and entitled *A Token for Children. Being an Exact Account of the Conversion, Holy and Exemplary Lives, and Joyful Deaths of several young Children.* This book was introduced into America in 1700 and was not only frequently reprinted, but was the inspiration for numerous imitations. The earliest edition in my collection is that printed by Franklin and Hall in Philadelphia in 1749, and, as far as I know, my own copy and one in the Boston Public Library are the only two examples of this edition extant.

Introduction

The children described by Janeway are even more obnoxious than Hannah Hill, Junr. and Elizabeth Wainwright. A typical example is that of *A Certain little Child, whose Mother had dedicated him to the Lord in her Womb, when he could not speak plain.* This forward infant died when he was five or six years old, but during his short lifetime *He was very fearful of wicked Company, and would often beg of God to keep him from it. . . . He abhorred Lying with his Soul. . . . He loved to go to School, that he might learn something of God,* which he did in *Lessens,* thereby proving that the Gryphon may have been right after all. On the arrival of this book in America in 1700 Cotton Mather added the *Token for the Children of New England,* containing the descriptions of the pious deaths of several young people in this country, including a member of his own family. The most famous of Mr. Mather's contributions concerns Elizabeth Butcher, the young lady who, *When she was about Two Years and half Old; as she lay in the Cradle, she would ask her self that Question, What is my corrupt Nature? and would make Answer again to her self, It is empty of Grace, bent unto Sin, and only to Sin, and that continually. She took great Delight in learning her Catechism, and would not willingly go to Bed without saying some Part of it.*

In spite of the apparent impossibility of these stories, we cannot dismiss them lightly as mere exaggerations. The remembrance of Daisy Ashford, who in our own era produced that sublime masterpiece *The Young Visiters* when only nine years old, would be sufficient to give us pause before asserting that Hannah Hill, Junr. would have been incapable, at the advanced age of eleven years and three months, of offering grave and pithy council to her elders, if not her betters. We have only too much reason to fear that

Introduction

these accounts of Puritan children may have been founded on fact. We know from Judge Sewall's Diary and other sources that babies were *given up to God in the Womb* and it is comforting to think that so many of them survived to a wicked old age.

In his *Juvenile Letters*, Boston, 1803, Caleb Bingham, a famous New England schoolmaster, shows us how eminently suitable Janeway's book was considered for the children of the day. In a letter addressed to his sister Lucy, young Samuel Thoughtful writes: *You remember you told me, that when I had learned the "Young Lady's Accidence" by heart, you would make me a present. I hope it will be a book. I like book presents the best of any. Simeon Sobriety tells me that the "Token for Children" is a choice book, giving an account of good children. I like to read about good children, that I may learn to grow better myself.* To which Sister Lucy replies: *The "Token for Children" I shall send you with pleasure. The author of that work was a zealous promotor of religion; and spared no pains in persuading children to become virtuous and happy.*

It is difficult to say exactly how much the Bible itself was forced upon the children of the early days. We know that Timothy Dwight, the author of that rare pamphlet relating to Yale College, *A Valedictory Address*, 1776, could read his Bible before he was four years old, and in view of Janeway's *Token* and other books of the kind, are relieved to know that he lived to the reasonable age of sixty-five years. In 1763 Andrew Steuart of Philadelphia published a Bible for children, the first edition especially for children printed in America, which apparently had a great success for it is now practically extinct. This was followed by numerous abridgements which were made additionally attractive to children by being published in *Thumb Bible* size and illustrated

Introduction

with woodcuts. The original *Thumb Bible* was a metrical version by
John Taylor, the Water Poet, which achieved great popularity in
this country, and copies of any edition are now extremely difficult
to find. In the earlier editions this book was entitled *Verbum Sempiternum*, and the language in which it is written is certainly pithy,
if not grave, as witness the opening lines of the book of Genesis:

> Jehovah here of nothing all things makes
>   And Man, the chief of all, his God forsakes.
> Yet by th' Almighty's Mercy 'twas decreed,
>   Heav'ns Heir should satisfy for Man's misdeed.
>
> Men now live long, but do not act aright,
>   For which the flood destroys them all but eight,
> Noah, his wife, their sons, with those they wed
>   The rest all perish'd in that watery bed.

A frequently reprinted metrical version of the New Testament was entitled *The History of the Holy Jesus*, and doubtless the
children enjoyed the doggerel verse:

> The Wise Men from the East do come,
>   Led by a shining Star,
> And offer to the new-born King,
>   Frankincense, Gold and Myrrh.
>
> Which Herod hears, and wrathful grows,
>   And now by Heav'n's Decree,
> Joseph and Mary and her Son,
>   Do into Egypt flee.
>
> The bloody Wretch, enrag'd to think
>   Christ's Death he could not gain,
> Commands that Infants all about
>   Bethlehem should be slain.

Introduction

Later the teaching of the Bible was made more attractive by means of puzzle pictures or rebuses, and several interesting *hieroglyphick* bibles were issued.

Verse was always found to be an easy way of persuading a child to assimilate biblical and moral instruction, and numerous books of religious poems were issued during the puritan period. We cannot imagine the sensitive child acquiring much comfort from some of the poems, and we tremble to think the devastating effect such lines as

> My days will quickly end, and I must lie
> Broyling in flames to all Eternity

may have had on the nerves of a child brought up on Hannah Hill, Junr., or Janeway's *Token*. These lines are from the earliest book of poems in this collection, entitled *War with the Devil*, by Benjamin Keach, an English divine, and printed in New York by William Bradford about 1707. It may have given the children some consolation to know that the author suffered imprisonment, fines and the pillory for his teaching.

Another book of poems of the period was entitled *Some Excellent Verses for the Education of Youth* written by that famous author and publisher, Nathaniel Crouch who preferred to be known as Richard (or Robert) Burton. My copy of this edition, printed by Bartholomew Green in Boston, 1708, belonged to the aforementioned Judith Sewall, and we can picture the poor child learning by heart

> Though I am Young, yet I may Die
> And hasten to Eternity:
> There is a dreadful fiery Hell,
> Where Wicked ones must always dwell

Introduction

from the *Verses for Little Children* contained in that book. So eminently suited were these *Verses* considered for the little ones that the poem was included in almost every edition of the New England Primer, which was also brightened with such rhymes as

> I in the burying place may see
> Graves shorter far than I

and

> Our days begin with trouble here,
> Our life is but a span.

One of the most popular books of religious poems was the famous *Divine and Moral Songs* of Dr. Watts. This book was highly recommended by Cotton Mather and the clergy, and was reprinted innumerable times. In fact no opportunity was ever lost for forcing these poems on the attention of the children, and selections from them were almost invariably used by printers to fill up the blank pages at the end of any nursery book on no matter what subject.

The views of Dr. Watts on hell and punishment were true to form:

> There is a dreadful hell,
>   And everlasting pains;
> There sinners must with devils dwell,
>   In darkness, fire, and chains.

and

> The Lord delights in them that speak
> The words of truth; but ev'ry liar
> Must have his portion in the lake
> That burns with brimstone and with fire.

To the present day reader, many of the sentiments of Dr. Watts are so extraordinarily unchristian in spirit, and so unutterably

Introduction

smug in expression that their great popularity is one of the best
guides to our understanding the mental outlook of the time:

> Not more than others I deserve,
>> Yet God hath giv'n me more;
> For I have food while others starve,
>> Or beg from door to door.

These poems had a long lived popularity, and some of the verses
have been known to goad the children of the nineteenth century
to desperation. Even today quarrelsome children are apt to be reminded that

> Birds in their little nests agree;
>> And 'tis a shameful sight,
> When children of one family
>> Fall out, and chide, and fight.

and

> Let dogs delight to bark and bite,
>> For God hath made them so;
> Let bears and lions growl and fight,
>> For 'tis their nature too.

though there is no question that the inspired misprint in the first
edition *For 'tis their nature to* has done much to prolong the
popularity of this verse.

The beautiful Cradle Hymn is not without a taint of smugness,
but nevertheless must have been strangely comforting to the little
readers:

> Hush, my dear, lie still and slumber,
>> Holy angels guard thy bed,
> Heavenly blessings without number
>> Gently falling on thy head.

It can be presumed that every New England child knew this poem
by heart, for it was given a place in the New England Primer,

Introduction

the most important book in the eighteenth-century nursery.

Much has been written about this famous book, the authorship of which has been ascribed to Benjamin Harris, a London bookseller, who suffered the pillory in 1681 for printing a *Protestant Petition*, and who came to Boston in 1686. The earliest issue of the American New England Primer extant is that printed by S. Kneeland and T. Green in Boston, 1727, though many earlier editions have apparently completely disappeared, and Mr. Charles F. Heartman estimates that the number printed between the years 1680 and 1830 must have been over six million. This book was the first to provide the children with religious education in a form in which they could assimilate it. The backbone of its teaching was *The Shorter Catechism of the Assembly of Divines at Westminster*, which every child was made to learn by heart. The New England Primer made a praiseworthy attempt to hold the attention of the children by the introduction of pictures; the martyrdom of John Rogers, which formed an essential part of the primer, was invariably illustrated by a crude cut, and the alphabet couplets placed near the beginning of every edition were always accompanied by naive illustrations.

One of these, that for the letter C, is significant in that it provides us with the hope that the children's lives may not have been entirely black, but that they may have learned from their mothers the frivolous rhymes of their own girlhood. C stands for cat, exemplified by the couplet

The cat will play
And after slay

the usual illustration for which is a cat playing a fiddle to dancing mice. This idea is obviously taken from the poem *High diddle*

Introduction

diddle, *The Cat and the Fiddle,* in *Mother Goose's Melodies,* of which the first American edition was not printed until about 1785, a considerably later date than the cat and the fiddle illustrations in the New England Primer.

This popular book must not be confused with the Royal Primer, a much less austere production, which was originally printed in London by the famous John Newbery. I am fortunate in owning the sole surviving copy of each of the first two editions of the Royal Primer printed in America, the one by James Chattin in Philadelphia, 1753, and the other by W. M'Alpine in Boston, 1768.

The minds and manners of the children were not sacrificed to their souls and the importance of knowing how to live well in order to be able to die well, was duly recognized, with the result that numerous school books of all kinds, including spellers, Latin grammars, instructions in the art of letter-writing, schools of good manners, and other educational works were constantly being produced. These books are all exceedingly valuable today for the light they throw on the manners, customs, grammar, pronunciation and so forth of the period.

One of the most interesting of the early secular primers is the *Instructions for Right Spelling* by George Fox, the famous founder of the Society of Friends. The first American edition of this book was published by Reynier Jansen in Philadelphia in 1702, and the second by Benjamin Franklin in 1737 in the same city. Mr. Fox's book is full of interesting information to the present day scholar. Among his *Directions for true spelling and writing English Words, which are alike in sound, yet unlike in their significations,* are Ask *the Carpenter for his* Ax; *If he leave not* Cough-

Introduction

ing, *he will soon be put in a* Coffin; *His* Chaps *were full of* Chops; *A* Kennel *for Dogs, sweep the* Channel *clean; A* sound *Body may fall into a* Swoon; *He* shoots 3 *Arrows; He has* 3 Sutes *of Apparel, and* 3 Suits *in Law;* and other equally surprising examples. The pronunciation of the word *neither* would have been no guide to nationality in the days of Mr. Fox, for he pronounced it *nether* —*It is* neither *thee nor I can lift the* nether *millstone.*

The code of manners instilled into the colonial children is surprisingly the same as the code today, and the Schools of Good Manners could still be studied with profit. Table manners are always interesting: *Grease not thy fingers or napkin more than necessity requires.—Spit not, cough not, nor blow thy nose at the table, if it may be avoided; but if there be necessity, do it aside, and without much noise.—Lean not thy elbow on the table, or on the back of the chair.—Stuff not thy mouth so as to fill thy cheeks, be content with smaller mouthfuls.—Smell not of thy meat nor put it to thy nose; turn it not the other side upward to view it upon thy plate.—Gnaw not bones at the table but clean them with thy knife (unless they be very small ones) and hold them not with a whole hand, but with two fingers.—Drink not nor speak with anything in thy mouth.*

In spite of the hardness of the times, however, human nature being what it is, a certain amount of frivolity could not be suppressed, to the great distress of the earnest spiritual leaders. We can well suspect the puritan mothers of having taught their children *High diddle diddle* and the other old nursery rhymes, for we know that they frequently so far forgot themselves as to buy books and ballads from chapmen and peddlers. In Cotton Mather's Diary, under the date September 27, 1713 is the entry:

Introduction

I am informed that the Minds and Manners of many people about the Countrey are much corrupted by foolish Songs and Ballads, which the Hawkers and Peddlars carry into all parts of the Countrey. By way of antidote, I would procure poetical Compositions full of Piety, and such as may have a Tendency to advance Truth and Goodness, to be published, and scattered into all Corners of the Land. These may be an extract of some, from the excellent Watts's Hymns.

As we have seen, the excellent Watts's Hymns were published in more editions than almost any book, so we can conclude that the reverend gentleman's words had their due effect.

The chapbooks which were such a source of consternation to Mr. Mather were probably popular with both parents and children, and have become extremely difficult to find at the present day. Boston was an important city in the history of early chapbook literature, and many of the leading printers and publishers issued books of this class, including Thomas and John Fleet, Andrew Barclay and the famous Isaiah Thomas, who produced *The Prodigal Daughter*, remarkable for its curious woodcuts, which, signed I.T., were probably by the printer himself.

Good times were in store for the children and they were soon to cease being treated as small sized adults, and to be provided with books printed especially for their edification and amusement. The idea had already taken root, and several printers in Boston had put out charming little juvenile books.

In 1761 Andrew Barclay had published an edition of *Tom Thumb's Play-Book*, an edition which had great significance in the history of children's literature, for it was the *Prentice's Token* of Isaiah Thomas, a fact of considerable moment in view of the interest later to be taken by that great printer in the production of

Introduction

books for the nursery. Ten years later the same book, a charming little primer measuring only three by two inches, was reissued by the firms of Kneeland and Adams, and of John Boyle. *The Life of Tom Thumb* is one of the most famous of all nursery classics in the English language. In addition to owning what is probably a unique copy of the first American edition, printed by Thomas and John Fleet about 1780, I am also fortunate in having been able to acquire the solitary copy extant of the first English edition printed in London in 1621, at one time in the library of that famous collector Bishop Heber. In this edition the story is signed R. I., the initials probably standing for Richard Johnson, the author of an almost equally well-known romance, *The Seven Champions of Christendom.*

It is worth noticing that already in 1767 John Fleming, a bookseller, was advertising on the title-page of *The Adventures of Urad,* published by Mein and Fleeming, *a great variety of Entertaining and Instructive Books for Children.*

The first really important name in the history of American children's literature is that of the famous English publisher, John Newbery, who has been so well described by Goldsmith in *The Vicar of Wakefield* (quoted in the note to no. 419), for it was his children's books which were imitated and pirated in this country, and which gave the first genuine impetus to the development of books written for the young as distinct from books written for grownups and considered suitable for children. Newbery realized the importance of training and educating the childish taste from every point of view, and pressed into his service men of genius in all branches of book production, notably Oliver Goldsmith for the stories, and the Bewicks for the illustrations. The books were all

Introduction

small in size and attractively bound in Dutch flowered boards, details which were faithfully reproduced in America. Hugh Gaine of New York was one of the early American printers to realize the charm of the Newbery publications, and the copy of an abridged Robinson Crusoe, the first American edition of this classic, published by Gaine in 1774, is a beautiful example of a Newbery imitation.

The outstanding name in America to be linked with John Newbery is that of Isaiah Thomas, one of America's greatest printers, and the founder of the American Antiquarian Society in Worcester. Thomas deliberately set himself to imitate the Lilliputian library of Newbery, and succeeded admirably, copying the binding and the illustrations as well as the text of the books. His press at Worcester, which later was carried on by his son, Isaiah Thomas junior, issued first editions of many important nursery books. These include *Little Goody Two Shoes*, the authorship of which is sometimes ascribed to Oliver Goldsmith, though, in the opinion of such a competent judge as Mr. E. V. Lucas, wrongly so; *Mother Goose's Melodies*, the first edition of which is now extant in only one or two imperfect copies, and in addition to my own, the only known remaining example of the second, is in the library of the Antiquarian Society at Worcester; *Pilgrim's Progress*, and numerous other favorites. Very popular, too, were the abridgments intended for children of all the outstanding novels of the day, such as Tom Jones, Pamela, and Clarissa. These abridgments have also been fathered on Oliver Goldsmith; they were considered most proper for the children of the late eighteenth and early nineteenth centuries and were read aloud in the evenings to all members of the family.

Introduction

Thomas was no slavish imitator of the publications of New-bery, and he sensibly endeavored to acclimatize his books as much as possible. The dedications are addressed to the Little Masters and Misses, or to the Parents and Guardians *of America*; the reward for the good little girl on the title-page of *Nurse Truelove's New-Year's Gift* is to ride in the *Governour's* gilt coach, not in the *Lord Mayor's* coach as in the English edition; *London* town in *Mother Goose's Melodies* becomes *Boston* town, and so forth.

John Newbery's methods of self advertisement in the text of his books were faithfully copied by Thomas, his own name replacing that of Newbery in all such cases. These advertising methods were approved and adopted by printers and publishers for many years to come. One of the most notable exponents in later years was Mahlon Day of New York, still printing in 1836, when this catalogue closes. Like Thomas, Day lost no opportunity of introducing a list of his books for sale into the body of the story, usually enhanced by a picture of his store, whilst his title-pages and covers were almost always enriched with persuasive rhymes.

> I had three cents to spend
> I ran to DAY's with glee
> To get a picture book;
> And here I've got it—see!

and

> In New-York, that famous city,
> Many books like this are sold
> And for such 'twould be a pity
> One cent only to withold.

The ideas of Isaiah Thomas were soon copied by printers in New England and in other parts of America, and attractive chil-

Introduction

dren's books were issued from innumerable presses, not only from Boston, New York, Philadelphia, New Haven, Hartford and other large cities, but from smaller towns such as Wilmington, where Peter Brynberg and James Adams became famous for the pleasing wallpaper bindings in which they issued their books, Norristown, where the very first book printed was an abridgment for children of *The History of Pamela*, Salem, Dedham, Fairhaven, Windsor, Stoningtonport, Newmarket (Virginia) and numerous others.

In the early nineteenth century, Philadelphia, always interested in the production of children's books, now took its place as the leading city for their publication. The imprints of important firms such as Mathew Carey and John Adams will be found on the title-pages of many juveniles, and, as we have already seen Benjamin and Jacob Johnson, later Johnson and Warner, confined themselves almost exclusively to the production of this class of literature. To these names must be added that of William Charles, an engraver and publisher who came to the city about 1808, and who had a far-reaching influence on the art of book production for children, due to the fact that he was one of the earliest American publishers to produce juvenile books with colored plates.

By this time the fashion for the Newbery publications had died, and Charles took as his model the square duodecimo or octavo books published in London by Mary Jane Godwin, the second wife of the famous William Godwin, himself the author of children's books under the name of Edward Baldwin. William Charles, followed by Morgan & Yeager and Morgan and Sons copied the productions of M. J. Godwin as faithfully as Thomas had done those of Newbery. From about 1814 Charles issued all

Introduction

his juveniles in two styles, with plain and colored plates, the latter variety being slightly more expensive than the former.

Meanwhile the Hell and Damnation school of the Puritans was not dead, but had developed with the times into the Sunday school type of literature, as exemplified in the works of Mrs. Barbauld, Hannah More, Elizabeth Turner, Maria Edgeworth, Jane and Ann Taylor and many others. It may be mentioned here that Mrs. Barbauld has an additional typographical interest for the American reader, for her books were selected by Benjamin Franklin Bache in 1788 to be printed by him under the tutelage of his grandfather, Benjamin Franklin. The Sunday school style of literature, which embraced the supporters of the realistic school, as opposed to the adherents of the fairy tale, had many violent opponents, and arguments on both sides of this vexed question will be found in many of the prefaces to the books in the catalogue.

In our own day Max Beerbohm has very adequately described the troubles of the children of the period, his object lesson being Elizabeth Turner, author of *The Daisy* (no. 382 in this catalogue).

Children were not then recognized as human creatures. They were a race apart; savages that must be driven from the gates; beasts to be kept in cages; devils to whose voices one must not listen. Indeed, the very nature of children was held to be sinful. Lies and sloth, untidiness and irreverence, and a tendency to steal black currant jam, were taken to be its chief constituents. And so all nurseries, as one may learn from old books or from the oral tradition, were the darkened scene of temporal oppression, fitfully lighted with the gaunt reflections of hell-fire. How strange a picture is to be found in those books of "cautionary verses for children," irrelevantly entitled The Daisy *and* The Cowslip. *Anything less flower-like* than their tone could not be easily conceived. The good children who move through their pages are the merest puppets, worked by the monstrous autocrat, Mamma, whilst the bad children, placed there as foils, are the most mechanical of drones and dunces. Never once does the authoress betray the briefest wish to treat children objectively. Yet, curious though it seem to modern ideas, she typifies the parents of her period.

This opinion agrees with that of Charles Lamb, a real lover of children, who, on October 23, 1802, wrote to Samuel Taylor Coleridge:

Goody Two Shoes is almost out of print. Mrs. Barbauld's stuff has banished all the old classics of the nursery; and the shopman at Newbery's hardly deigned to reach them off an old exploded corner of a shelf, when Mary asked for them. Mrs. B.'s and Mrs. Trimmer's nonsense lay in piles about. Knowledge insignificant and vapid as Mrs. B.'s books convey, it seems, must come to a child in the shape of knowledge and his empty noddle must be turned with conceit of his own powers when he has learnt that a Horse is an animal, and Billy is better than a Horse, and such like; instead of that beautiful Interest in wild tales which made the child a man, while all the time he suspected himself to be no bigger than a child. Science has succeeded to Poetry no less in the little walks of children than with men. Is there no possibility of averting this sore evil? Think what you would have been now, if instead of being fed with Tales and old wives' fables in childhood, you had been crammed with geography and natural history?

Damn them!—I mean the cursed Barbauld Crew, those Blights and Blasts of all that is Human in man and child.

Leigh Hunt has well depicted the detrimental effect the Sunday

Introduction

school hero might have on any small boy who tried to imitate him. *The good little boy, the hero of the infant literature of those days, stood, it must be acknowledged, the chance of being a very selfish man. His virtue consisted in being different from some other little boy, perhaps his brother, and his reward was having a fine coach to ride in, and being a King Pepin . . . One of the most pernicious mistakes of the old children's books, was the inculcation of a spirit of revenge and cruelty, in the tragic examples which were intended to deter their readers from idleness and disobedience . . . contrary to the real spirit of Christianity.*

The great Dr. Johnson was a firm upholder of fairy tales for children. He relates how he *withdrew his attention* from the celebrity who was boring him, and *thought about Tom Thumb* and believed that *babies do not want to hear about babies, they like to be told of giants and castles, and of somewhat which can stretch and stimulate their little minds.*

By far the most important exponent of the Sunday school stories in this country was Hannah More, the famous originator of the *Cheap Repository Tracts.* Her fame in America does not depend entirely on the popularity of her own tracts, which were, however, prolifically reprinted, but on her influence over Samuel Griswold Goodrich, the original Peter Parley. In spite of George Fox, the founder of the Society of Friends, who desired to suppress among *other sins of children* the *telling of Tales, Stories, Jests, Rhimes, Fables, which feeds the nature that is out of the Fear of God,* fairy tales had flourished in this country, and were imported from all over the world, chiefly from France through Charles Perrault, Madame Le Prince de Beaumont, and others, and from the East, through the Arabian Nights and other sources.

Introduction

As Michael Angelo Titmarsh, better known possibly as William Makepeace Thackeray, has so well pointed out, *there is no calculating the distance through which the stories come to us, the number of languages through which they have been filtered, or the centuries during which they have been told. Many of them have been narrated, almost in their present shape, for thousands of years since, to little copper-colored Sanscrit children, listening to their mother, under the palm trees by the banks of the yellow Jumna—their Brahmin mother, who softly narrated them through the ring in her nose.*

In spite of their antiquity, however, Samuel Griswold Goodrich was a most active opponent of fairy tales, and considered that the stories of *Little Red Riding Hood, Puss in Boots, Blue Beard,* and other old nursery favorites were tales of horror, calculated to do untold damage to the infant mind. He could not consider as an extenuating circumstance in their favor Mr. Titmarsh's argument that *Ogres have been much maligned. They eat children, it is true, but only occasionally.* Hannah More's *The Shepherd of Salisbury Plain,* irreverently referred to by Mr. Titmarsh as the Washerwoman of Finchley Common, became his inspiration. It was in talking over this tract with Hannah More that Goodrich first conceived the idea of the Parley tales, one of the most momentous and influential events in the history of American children's literature of the nineteenth century.

The story of children's books in America is naturally more bound up with the history of English juvenile literature than with that of any other country. After the Declaration of Independence, the gradual development of patriotism and the elimination of the English and European element from American juveniles forms a most interesting study. Even before that date we have seen how

Introduction

Cotton Mather added his *Token for the Children of New England* to Janeway's *Token*, but that was rather due to puritanical zeal in improving the shining hour than to any attempt at localization for its own sake.

The efforts of Isaiah Thomas to make such changes in the English books as would render them more interesting to American readers have been mentioned, and were usually sensible and discreet. The zeal of other printers and publishers, however, frequently outran discretion and resulted in absurdities. It is remarkable how many times the names of Newbery or his successors and their London addresses are allowed to remain in the body of the story, of which the locale has been changed to America, usually Philadelphia, for the Philadelphia publishers seem to have had more local pride combined with less discretion than those of any other city.

Dame Partlet's Farm is a case in point. The English edition was printed by Harris, successor to Newbery, whose advertising rhyme began:

> At Harris's, St. Paul's Church-yard,
> Good children meet a sure reward.

appropriately changed in Johnson and Warner's Philadelphia edition to

> At Johnson's store in Market Street
> A sure reward good children meet

and yet it is not at Johnson's in Market Street that the good rector bought his books in the course of the story, but from the corner of St. Paul's Church-yard. Again the same publishers in reprinting Darton's *Chapter of Accidents*, headed one of the chapters *Cautions to Walkers in the City of Philadelphia*, whilst leaving the word *London* in the text of the chapter.

Introduction

Even less discreet were the publishers who from anti-British feeling changed the words of well known poems. William Charles, a Scot by birth, substituted the *President* for the *King* in the last verse of Cowper's ballad of *John Gilpin*. As everybody knows, the action of this famous poem takes place on the road to the Bell at Edmonton, near London, and yet in William Charles's version the last stanza reads:

> Let's sing—"Long live our President;
> And Gilpin long live he;
> And when he next doth ride abroad,
> May I be there to see!"

John Taylor, the Water Poet, is made by his American publishers to dedicate at least one edition of *Verbum Sempiternum* to George Washington and others to the Clergy of the United States.

The dedication of the edition of 1765 is as in the English edition: *To His Illustrious Highness William Duke of Gloucester, Knight of the Most Noble Order of the Garter*, and the accompanying *Epistle*, with the verses to the Reader, are both signed *J. Taylor*. The Epistle opens:

> Most Hopeful Prince, into Your hands I give
> The sum of that which makes us ever live.

After the Declaration of Independence, The Duke of Gloucester was ousted in favor of George Washington in the dedication, which was now addressed to *Most Hopeful George* and signed *The Editors*, Taylor's name being retained as the signature of the verses to the Reader. The edition of 1798 is addressed to Washington as President, although his term of office had expired in 1797. Later presidents were ignored, and from the edition of

Introduction

1800 the dedication is to the Rev. Clergy of the United States, who are addressed as *Most Hopeful Sires*.

On the other hand the text of the books was sometimes changed to such an extent that without a knowledge of the original English edition it would be almost impossible to be aware that the books were not native to America. A noteworthy example of this is to be found in Hannah More's poetical tract *The Shopkeeper turned Sailor*. In Johnson's Philadelphia edition of 1806, this is reprinted exactly from the English edition, and the long sermon at the end addressed to *Britons wearied with their lot*, and full of references to life in England, is as its author wrote it. In reprinting this work in 1814, the same publisher revised this sermon without acknowledgement or apology, and taking out all the English references has so changed the text as to make the interest generally applicable to the *Freemen wearied with their lot* in America or any other country. The same publisher performed a similar operation in his second edition of *A Mother's Remarks on a Set of Cuts*. The first edition of that work, printed with that title in 1803, is a reprint of the English edition. The edition of 1804, however, in which the title has been changed to *A Father's Gift*, has been rewritten and made to read as though it were indigenous to this side of the Atlantic.

From an early date Philadelphia publishers had exhibited more civic pride than those in any other city, and the changes, alterations and interpolations made by them in the text, and even in the titles of the books they reprinted, are numerous and interesting. No respect for the exact words of an author was ever allowed to stand in the way of extolling the glories of their city, and we are sometimes apt to be startled at reading in humdrum

Introduction

treatises on geography hailing from England that the women of Philadelphia are more beautiful than those of any other city in the world, and other equally surprising statements. Some books naturally gave greater scope for civic pride than others, and the Cries of New York and Philadelphia, though founded on the Cries of London, are full of most interesting local material.

It must not be supposed that all American juveniles were imported from abroad, and that there was no indigenous children's literature. In the early days of the development of this country, however, as was natural, the children's books were chiefly of an instructive and educational nature, and catechisms, primers, spellers, Latin grammars, geography books and other school books were the most usual form of native literature provided.

Even the few books which did not come into this class were hardly of a nature to interest a child. The poem of John Hubbard, for example, New-London, 1727, *A Monumental Gratitude Attempted, in a Poetical Relation of the Danger and Deliverance of Several of the Members of Yale-College, in Passing the Sound, from South-hold to New-Haven,* is of the greatest interest to the modern adult, as being one of the earliest compositions ever written by a young American student, but might not have been particularly interesting to his youthful contemporaries.

After 1776 a spirit of patriotism led to the desire to teach this virtue to children, and many lives of heroes such as George Washington and Benjamin Franklin were issued. The idea of native born fiction did not really take hold until well into the nineteenth century, in spite of a few sporadic examples of earlier dates. Of these, a noteworthy book is John Davis's *Captain Smith and Princess Pocahontas,* first issued in Philadelphia in 1805,

Introduction

and now excessively rare. Even more remarkable, as being the only work of fiction by its famous author, is *The Pirates*, by Noah Webster, 1813.

After about 1825 American names as authors of fiction for children became more common, though even then the idea of instruction still to a great extent persisted, and the titles all had a somewhat patriotic flavor. The genuine native children were not forgotten, and several extremely interesting books for youthful Indians will be found scattered throughout the catalogue. The unfortunate little papooses seem not to have fared any better than their white brothers, if anything can be judged from the fact that these titles include *Triumphant Deaths of Pious Children* in the Choctaw Language.

Much could be written about the illustrations of the early American children's books, and in them the history of the development of the art of woodcutting can be clearly followed. With few exceptions the earliest children's books, those of the puritanical era, were unillustrated. The exceptions, however, are noteworthy. Some extremely crude cuts are to be found in many of the chapbooks and ballads sold by the peddlers. Thomas and John Fleet of Boston employed a negro to make the woodcut illustrations for their publications, and he was probably responsible for the very unfinished cut at the head of the broadside editions of *The Babes in the Wood*, printed about 1770 and 1785.

The illustrations signed I. T. and possibly by James Turner, in some of the early editions of that frequently reprinted poem, *The History of the Holy Jesus*, must rank as the most anachronistically naive examples of eighteenth century work. In these illustrations the costumes of the biblical figures are those of eight-

Introduction

eenth century America. Even in such a well-known subject as Christ delivering the Sermon on the Mount to the multitude, the principal figure is represented as a New England preacher clad in gown and bands, addressing from a Church pulpit a multitude consisting of three Puritan men and three Puritan maidens. Similar anachronisms can be noticed in the illustrations of other books as, for example, in the *History of America*, printed in Philadelphia by Wrigley & Berriman for John Curtis in 1795, where one cut is made to do not only for several eighteenth century heroes, but also for that most famous fifteenth century explorer, the great Christopher Columbus himself. In this case it is probable that the motive was economy rather than ignorance. The early editors of the *New England Primer* tried to make that little book more attractive to children by providing it with illustrations, and the idea developed so that in time all primers were illustrated, the alphabets, and the fables at the end giving the most scope to the artists.

With the Worcester editions of Isaiah Thomas of the John Newbery publications, the art of woodcutting in this country received a real impetus, for they introduced the charming cuts of Thomas and John Bewick and their pupils and followers. The illustrations of these artists are not only important in themselves but doubly so in America, for they were the inspiration which caused Alexander Anderson, the father of woodcutting in the United States, to forsake copperplate engraving and to devote himself to the art of woodcutting. Anderson, whom I consider as great an artist as Bewick, made the woodcut illustrations for many of the children's books published in various cities. He illustrated extensively for William Durell and Samuel Wood of New York, for Sidney Babcock of New Haven, for Munroe and

Introduction

Francis of Boston and for other equally prominent printers and publishers. He was followed by Nathaniel Dearborn, Abel Bowen, Gilbert and many other noted craftsmen, all of whom made cuts for toy books as a means of practising their art.

Many of the early nursery books were illustrated by engravings on copper, and illustrations by important artists are to be found in books intended for the pleasure and amusement of children. Among these may be mentioned James Poupard of Philadelphia, responsible for a Metamorphosis, and W. Ralph of the same city, whose frontispieces decorate a number of volumes. By far the most outstanding of the later copperplate engravers was William Charles, also of Philadelphia, who was responsible for a long series of toy books, and, as we have seen already, was one of the earliest American publishers to issue toy books with colored plates, thus enhancing both their charm and their value.

A number of interesting "firsts" are to be found amongst these children's books, and many books important to collectors in other fields than juvenilia. Among these may be mentioned the first American edition of the *Poetry for Children* by Charles and Mary Lamb, and the *Tales from Shakspeare* by the same authors; the first miniature book printed in America; the first purely arithmetical work printed in America; the first edition of the Andover Catechism, of the catechism of the Moravian brethren and of other religious bodies; the first children's Bible; the first hieroglyphical Bible; the earliest history of America edited especially for American children; the first Metamorphosis; the first book printed in Reading, Pennsylvania; the first Norristown imprint; books from the first German printing office south of the Mason & Dixon line; the first edition of Noah Webster's only piece of fiction for the young; the first book printed by the House of Appleton and many others of equal interest.

My collection of children's books is contained in two miniature bookcases in my private library in Philadelphia, and as I glance at them I sometimes think that my favorite of all is that immortal tongue-twister, *Peter Piper's Practical Principles of Perfect Pronunciation*, with its brilliantly colored illustrations, published by Willard Johnson in Philadelphia in 1836:

> Peter Piper pick'd a Peck of Pickled Peppers:
> Did Peter Piper pick a Peck of Pickled Peppers?
> If Peter Piper pick'd a Peck of Pickled Peppers,
> Where's the Peck of Pickled Peppers Peter Piper pick'd?

or again:

> Billy Button bought a Butter'd Biscuit:
> Did Billy Button buy a Butter'd Biscuit?
> If Billy Button bought a Butter'd Biscuit,
> Where's the Butter'd Biscuit Billy Button bought?

Billy Button's greed brings me quite naturally to the end of my discourse, for Peter Piper was published in 1836, the year I have chosen to close this volume. The new era of children's books was just beginning with the graceful efforts of Nathaniel Hawthorne, and later of Louisa M. Alcott. This is another chapter in the history of American children's books, which I leave for other more capable but not more loving hands.

Billy Button was breaking all the rules; the children of his day were expected to buy their own books out of their own pocket money, and to leave the purchase of butter'd biscuits to their mothers. It seems to me a pity that the publishers of children's books today have lost the art of advertising their wares by amusing

Introduction

rhymes, enticing their Saturday pennies from the pockets of the children. I cannot refrain from quoting in full the siren rhyme used by the founder of my Uncle's ancient firm, Jacob Johnson, as in his little juvenile publications:

> At Johnson's store, in Market-street,
> A sure reward, good children meet.
> In coming home the other day
> I heard a little master say
> For ev'ry three-pence there he took
> He had receiv'd a little book,
> With covers neat, and cuts so pretty,
> There's not its like in all the City;
> And that for three-pence he could buy
> A story-book would make one cry;
> For little more a book of riddles:
> Then let us not buy drums or fiddles,
> Nor yet be stopt at pastry-cooks,
> But spend our money all in books;
> For when we've learnt each book by heart
> Mamma will treat us with a tart.

The greatest children's book, at least in my opinion, *Alice's Adventures in Wonderland*, I regret can find no place here. The only connection with the United States, apart from the many editions published in this country, is the fact that thousands of American children came in droves to see the original manuscript when it was exhibited in Philadelphia, Boston, Washington and New York, through the courtesy and real kindness of its generous owner, Mr. Eldridge R. Johnson.

It is to be hoped that this volume will encourage others to collect early American children's books. I thank my lucky stars

Introduction

that there were few competitors when I first stalked the booksellers' shelves! My uncle Moses Polock had no rivals when he started the collection almost a century ago. Today there are a few collectors with unbounding enthusiasm. The chase has just begun and there will be many more. I wish the new gatherers of juvenile books good hunting! My dear friend, A. Edward Newton, has a number; Barton W. Currie has written charmingly about them; Gumuchian of Paris has issued a noteworthy catalogue describing some of his treasures; F. J. Harvey Darton has just published a history of Children's Books in England. The first really good account of the early juvenile literature of America was Miss Rosalie V. Halsey's *Forgotten Books of the American Nursery*, issued more than twenty years ago, and I need not say how much I am indebted to this interesting volume.

This catalogue is in no sense a bibliography. It contains descriptions of the books in my own collection. A complete list of all juvenile publications from the American press would be most welcome at the present day, and anyone who would undertake this pleasant task would receive the grateful thanks of all students and scholars. The great storehouse of the American Antiquarian Society with its rich treasures would be available, and I am sure its distinguished director, Clarence S. Brigham, who has always been so kind to me, would be of assistance to a project that must be dear to his heart.

All my friends have been most generous, and many instead of selling them, have presented to me some of the rarest books in this collection. In this connection I cannot but mention Wilberforce Eames, Lathrop C. Harper, Thomas W. Streeter, William M. Elkins, M. Harzof, and Charles F. Heartman. Alas, my

Introduction

dear sister, Rebecca Rosenbach, who helped me to form this collection and was even more interested in it than I was myself, is no more. How pleased she would have been to have seen this beautifully printed volume.

This catalogue owes much to my friend Miss E. Millicent Sowerby, who has done so much to make the catalogue attractive. From her rich store of knowledge I am indebted for a great portion of the notes concerning both authors and publishers. It is a real pleasure to acknowledge the great assistance she has rendered to me, not only in the compilation, but in seeing the volume through the press.

There are many other friends who have been of real service to me, among them Clarence S. Brigham, Lawrence C. Wroth, Randolph G. Adams, Robert W. G. Vail, Wilbur Macey Stone, Charles E. Goodspeed, Christopher Morley, Walter Hart Blumenthal, Frank B. Bemis, Harry M. Lydenberg, Victor Hugo Paltsits, Albert Carlos Bates, P. K. Foley, George Parker Winship, Harry B. Weiss, James F. Drake, Ernest Spofford, and Franklin H. Price.

To Wilberforce Eames, who read this book in proof, I cannot express in words my indebtedness. Throughout my whole life he has been an inspiration and the inexhaustible treasury of his keen and brilliant mind has always been open to me.

To my faithful staff, Percy E. Lawler, Harry H. Hymes, John Fleming, Ann M. Brennan and Edwin Wolf I wish to express my appreciation of their unfaltering assistance.

A. S. W. R.

EARLY
AMERICAN CHILDREN'S BOOKS

Early American Children's Books

1682

THE RULE of the New-Creature To be Practised every Day, in all the Particulars of it which are ten. Printed at Boston in New-England, for Mary Avery, near the Blue Anchor, 1682. [1]

Octavo, 8 leaves, with signature A.

This is the second American edition of this extremely popular Puritan book, and probably the only copy which has survived.

Evans 333 does not locate a copy; it is not mentioned by Littlefield in *The Early Massachusetts Press*, and Sabin has only a much later edition.

The work was first published anonymously in London in 1644, and was reprinted in Cambridge, Massachusetts, by Samuel Green in 1668. Of this first American edition no copy was known to exist until recently when a copy was discovered by Mr. Clarence S. Brigham in the Library of the American Antiquarian Society at Worcester.

The author opens his work with the following cheerless admonition: *Be sensible of thy Original Corruption daily, how it inclines thee to evil, and indisposeth thee to good; groan under it, & bewail it as Paul did, Rom. 7, 24. Also take special notice of your actual sins, or daily infirmities in Thought, Word, Deed. Endeavour to make your peace with God for them before you go to bed.* Then follow the rules how this may be accomplished.

1684

COTTON, JOHN. Spiritual Milk for Boston Babes. In either England: Drawn out of the breasts of both Testaments for their Souls nourishment. But may be of like use to any Children. By John Cotton, B.D. Late Teacher to the Church of Boston in New England. Printed at Boston: 1684. [2]

Octavo, 8 leaves, A⁸.

Unbound.

Not in Evans. Not in Sabin. Not in Eames, *Early New England Catechisms*. Not mentioned by Littlefield in *The Early Massachusetts Press*.

This copy is the only one known of this date. It was first published in England in 1646, and was written by John Cotton in order to settle a growing dissension among the Puritans, who could not decide which catechism of the several then in use was the best for their children.

John Cotton (1584-1652), famous nonconformist divine, was at one time vicar of Boston, in Lincolnshire, England. According to some authorities it was in his honor that the city of Boston, Massachusetts, received its name, which was changed from Trimountain on the arrival of Cotton as an emigrant from England on September 3 or 4, 1633.

1699

MATHER, COTTON. A Family Well-Ordered. Or An Essay to render Parents and Children Happy in one another. Handling two very Important cases. I. What are the Duties to be done by Pious Parents, for the promoting of Piety in their Children. II. What are the Duties that must be paid by Children to their Parents, that they may obtain the Blessings of the Dutiful. Boston: B[artholomew] Green and J[ohn] Allen, for Michael Perry & Benjamin Eliot, 1699.   [3]

Duodecimo, 42 leaves, A-G⁶. On G₄ verso is the caption: *An Address*, *Ad Fratres in Eremo*, pages 1-5.

Original sheep.
Evans 875. Sabin 46324.
First edition of a most interesting work by this celebrated New England divine. The first part is devoted to the duties of parents to their children, who as *the Children of Death, and the Children of Hell, and the Children of Wrath, by Nature*, need much parental guidance in overcoming these handicaps. The second part, beginning at page 38, is addressed to the children and deals with their duties to their parents. On page 41 there stands out in heavy black letter type the awful sentence *The Heavy Curse of God, will fall upon those Children, that make Light of their Parents*. A perusal of this book makes it easy to understand why so many children have an instinctive fear of the dark. Darkness was used as the final horror for undutiful children: *Children, If by Undutifulness to your Parents, you incur the Curse of God, it won't be long before you go down into Obscure Darkness, even, into Utter Darkness: God has Reserv'd for you the Blackness of Darkness forever*.
Cotton Mather (1663-1728) was the son of Increase Mather. He was born in Boston and was a graduate of Harvard College.

1702

CULMANN, LEONHART. Sententiæ Pueriles Anglo-Latinæ. Quas e diversis Authoribus olim collegerat, Leonardus Culman; Et in Vernaculum Sermonem nuperrime transtulit, Carolus Hoole: Pro primis Latinæ Linguæ Tyronibus . . . Sentences for Children, English and Latin. Collected out of sundry Authors long since, by Leonard Culman; and now Translated into English by Charles Hoole: For the first Entrers into Latin . . . Boston in N. E.: B. Green & J. Allen for Samuel Phillips, 1702.   [4]

16mo, 37 leaves, A-H⁴, I⁵, Latin and English on opposite pages, the English in italic, the Latin in roman type, contemporary and later signatures on the flyleaves.

Original sheep over wooden boards.
Evans 1045.
This is the first American edition of an extremely popular European textbook. It was intended for beginners in Latin and consists simply of sentences in English and Latin graduating from two (Latin) words to long sentences. The last chapter contains *Holy Sentences to be taught Scholars upon Holy-Days*. The characteristic binding of all colonial school books was full leather, either sheep or calf.
Leonhart Culmann, a German theologian and preacher was born in 1498 and died in 1562. Charles Hoole (1610-1667) was a native of Yorkshire, England, and became famous as an educational writer. The first edition of his translation of Culmann was published in England in 1658.

THE
RULE

OF THE
NEW·CREATURE

To be Practifed every Day, in all the
Particulars of it which are Tea.

Gal. 6. 16. *And as many as walk according to this Rule, peace be on them, and mercy,
and upon the Ifrael of God.*

Printed at *Bofton* in *New England*, for
Mary Avery, near the *Blue Anchor*,
1 6 8 2.

Title-page from "The Rule of the New-Creature"

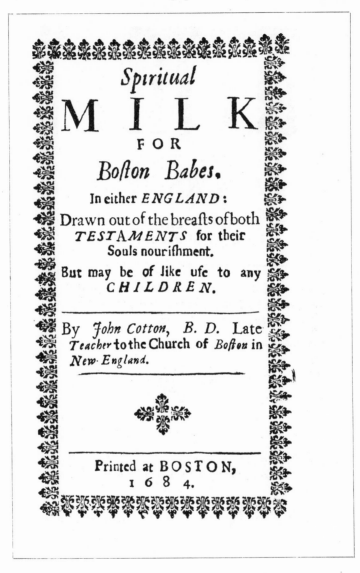

Spiritual

M I L K

F O R

Boſton Babes.

In either *ENGLAND*:

Drawn out of the breaſts of both *TESTAMENTS* for their Souls nouriſhment.

But may be of like uſe to any *CHILDREN.*

By *John Cotton*, *B. D.* Late *Teacher* to the Church of *Boſton* in *New-England.*

Printed at BOSTON, 1 6 8 4.

Title-page from "Spiritual Milk for Boston Babes"

Fox, George. Instructions for Right-Spelling and Plain Directions for Reading and Writing True English. With several delightful things very Useful and Necessary, both for Young and Old, to Read and Learn. Re-printed at Philadelphia by Reynier Jansen, 1702. [5]

Octavo, 52 leaves, A⁸, B-M⁴, title within an ornamental border.

Original sheep.
Evans 1049. Hildeburn 89.

The first American edition of this little known work by the English founder of the Society of Friends.

The *several delightful things very useful and necessary* include: The Marks of a true Christian; the Catechism; the Names which the children of God are call'd by; Proverbs, tables of Numeration, Multiplication, etc.; A ready Way to reckon what one's daily Expenditure comes unto in a whole year; Proper Names in Scripture, with their signification in English, and much other equally interesting information.

The earliest primer in this collection. All primers, including ABC books (known to Shakespeare as *absey books*), syllabaries, spellers, and elementary readers are developments of the hornbook, and we know from Florio's *World of Wordes* that the ABC book (referred to by him as *teacher of ABC*) and the *horne booke* were used as synonymous terms. The present work contains the alphabet in hornbook form, a syllabary (not in columns, the usual arrangement, but running across the page), and a Reading made easy, known to the trade as a *Reading Easy*, and to the common people as a *Readamadeasy*.

1705

Secker, William. A Wedding Ring fit for the Finger. Or, the Salve of Divinity on the Sore of Humanity . . . laid open in a Sermon, at a Wedding in Edmonton, by William Secker, Preacher of the Gospel. Boston in N. E.: Printed by T[imothy] G[reen] for N[icholas] Buttolph, 1705. [6]

16mo, 47 leaves, A-E⁸, F⁷, including the first blank, 3 pp. advertisements at the end.

Original sheep over wooden boards.
Not in Evans; only a much later edition in Sabin.
Measures 3¼ x 1⅛ inches. This is the only perfect copy known of the first miniature book published in America.
William Secker was a celebrated English divine. His dates are unknown but he is presumed to have died in 1681.

1707

K[each], B[enjamin]. War with the Devil, or, The Young Man's Conflict with the Powers of Darkness, in a Dialogue Discovering the Corruption and Vanity of Youth, the horrible Nature of Sin, and Deplorable Condition of Fallen Man, Also, A Description of the Power and Rule of Conscience, and the nature of True Conversion. To which is added, An Appendix, containing a Dialogue between an Old Apostate and a Young Professor, Worthy the Perusal of all, but chiefly intended for the Instruction of the Younger sort. [New York: William Bradford, 1707].   [7]

Duodecimo, 92 leaves, A-L⁸, M⁴.

Original sheep over wooden boards, some edges uncut.
Evans 1682.
In verse.
A fine copy, in a Bradford binding, with waste sheet of Leed's Almanack for 1708 in the lining of the back cover. At the beginning are commendatory verses by William and Elizabeth Bradford, signed W. B. and E. B.

This is the first American edition, from the twelfth English edition. It was probably printed in 1707 during the progress of the Almanac of 1708 through the press. The Brinley-HSP copy was dated about 1714, as, quoting from the Brinley Catalogue, *the inside of the cover is lined with parts of a Proclamation for Thanksgiving Day, by Gov. Hunter, dated in August, the 12th year of Queen Anne* [1713], *which indicates, nearly, the date of publication.* The only other known copy has in the binding waste leaves of Cotton Mather's *A Man of his Word*, Boston, 1713. According to Mr. Wilberforce Eames these facts would indicate that a remainder of the edition of [1707] was being bound in 1713.

This book appears to be the same as Evans 1207 under date 1705. Hildeburn: *Sketches of Printers and Printing in Colonial New York, page* 12, assigns the book to 1714: *a small duodecimo volume whose chief interest now lies in the doggerel recommendatory verses prefixed to it by the printer and his wife.*

Sabin 37125: *Printed in New York by William Bradford, not earlier than* 1715. *A poem in 'Commemoration of these Poems,' is signed 'W. B.,' and is bad enough poetry to be the work of Bradford himself.*

Benjamin Keach (1640-1704) was an English Baptist divine, who suffered imprisonment, fines, and the pillory for his teaching and books. The first English edition of his work appeared in 1676.

1708

[BURTON, RICHARD, i. e., CROUCH, NATHANIEL.] Some Excellent Verses For the Education of Youth, Taken from Eccles. 12, 1. Remember thy Creator in the Dayes of thy Youth, &c. To which are added Verses for Little Children. By a Friend. Boston: Bartholomew Green, 1708. [8]

Duodecimo, 6 leaves, without signatures.

Unbound.
Not in Evans. Not mentioned by Littlefield.
This is apparently the only copy of this book which has survived.
On the verso of the first leaf is a rhymed version of the Ten Commandments. Then follow the Excellent Verses, consisting of fourteen stanzas of eight lines each, the last two lines of every verse being with slight variations the same:

> Oh! therefore in your Youthful Dayes
> your great Creator mind.

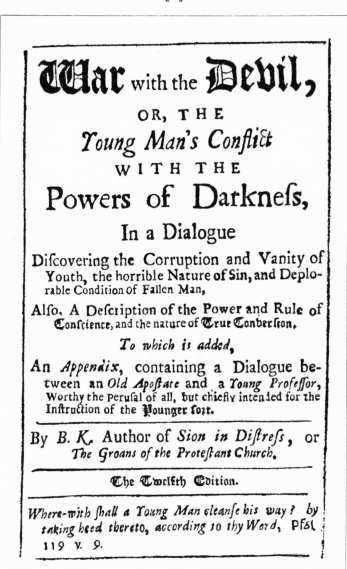

War with the Devil,

OR, THE
Young Man's Conflict
WITH THE
Powers of Darkness,

In a Dialogue

Difcovering the Corruption and Vanity of Youth, the horrible Nature of Sin, and Deplorable Condition of Fallen Man,

Alfo, A Defcription of the Power and Rule of Confcience, and the nature of True Converfion.

To which is added,

An *Appendix*, containing a Dialogue between an *Old Apoftate* and a *Young Profeffor*, Worthy the Perufal of all, but chiefly intended for the Inftruction of the Younger fort.

By *B. K.* Author of *Sion in Diftrefs*, or *The Groans of the Proteftant Church.*

The Twelfth Edition.

Where-with fhall a Young Man cleanfe his way? by taking heed thereto, according to thy Word, Pfal. 119 v. 9.

Title page from "War with the Devil"

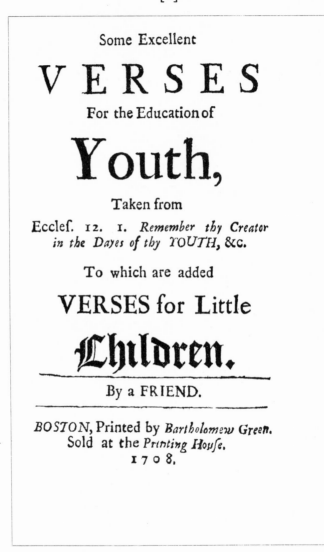

Some Excellent

VERSES

For the Education of

Youth,

Taken from

Ecclef. 12. 1. *Remember thy Creator*
in the Dayes of thy YOUTH, &c.

To which are added

VERSES for Little

𝕮𝖍𝖎𝖑𝖉𝖗𝖊𝖓.

By a FRIEND.

BOSTON, Printed by *Bartholomew Green.*
Sold at the *Printing Houfe.*
1 7 0 8,

Title-page from "Some Excellent Verses
for the Education of Youth"

Early American Children's Books

The children are warned that

> Upon a World, Vain, Toylsom, Foul,
> a Journey now ye enter,
> The welfare of your living Soul
> you dangerously adventure.

This poem, with the title *Epistle to Youth*, is prefixed to *Youth's Divine Pastime*, by Richard Burton (i. e. Nathaniel Crouch), third edition, 1691.

The Verses for Little Children begin on page 8. These verses were used later in many of the editions of the *New England Primer*.

> Though I am Young, a Little one,
> If I can speak, and go alone
> Then I must learn to know the Lord,
> And learn to read his holy Word. . .
>
> Though I am Young, yet I may Die,
> and hasten to Eternity,
> There is a dreadful fiery Hell,
> Where Wicked ones must always dwell. . .

and examples are given of the dreadful fate that overcomes wicked children, those for instance who *mocking said, to a good man 'Go up Bald-head.' God was displeas'd with them and sent Two Bears which them in pieces rent.*

On the title-page and at the end is the contemporary childish signature of *Judith Sewall, her Book*. The original small owner was the daughter of Samuel Sewall, the famous author and the Chief Justice of the Superior Court of Massachusetts from 1718 to 1728.

Richard Burton (1632?-1725?), whose real name was Nathaniel Crouch, was a London publisher and miscellaneous writer.

A USEFUL and Necessary Companion in two parts . . . To which is Added, An Appendix, Containing Useful Forms of Letters, &c. Boston: Printed for, and Sold by Nicholas Boone, 1708.   [9]

Duodecimo, 44 leaves, A^2, B-H^6, the first leaf is blank on the recto, and has advertisements on the verso.

Original sheep over wooden boards, several uncut edges, linings from sheets of *Milk and Honey*.

Not in Evans. This appears to be the only known copy.

This is not strictly speaking a child's book but has been included on account of the appendix with its *several useful forms of letters*. This contains two letters from scholars to their parents and we quote the last paragraph of one of them. The letter is addressed by the young writer to his *Ever Honoured Father and Mother*, and closes thus, *I beg your earnest Prayers to God for His Blessing on my weak endeavours, that you may at length reap the Harvest of your Expectation with Joy, and God have all the Glory. To whose Protection I commit you, and remain Your Dutiful Son*.

This can be compared with *The American Letter-Writer*, 1793.

1714

COLMAN, BENJAMIN. A Devout Contemplation On the Meaning of Divine Providence, in the Early Death of Pious and Lovely Children.

Preached upon the Sudden and Lamented Death of Mrs. Elizabeth Wainwright. Who Departed this Life, April the 8th. 1714. Having just compleated the Fourteenth Year of Her Age. By Benjamin Colman, Pastor to a church in Boston. Boston: Printed by John Allen, for Joanna Perry, 1714. [10]

Octavo, 18 leaves, A-D⁴, E².

Unbound.

Evans 1671.

First edition. Contains an Address to the Mournful Relatives of the deceased Mrs. Elizabeth Wainwright, an Address to the Children of the Town, and the Sermon itself, each with a caption title. On the title are the initials J. S., and on page iv the signature of *Judith Sewall, April* 30, 1714 (see no. 8).

An early example of the juvenile funeral elegy, one of the most popular manifestations of the Puritan spirit, and of which several examples will be found in this collection.

Benjamin Colman was born in 1673 at Boston. He was educated at Harvard College and was the first minister of the Brattle Street Church, Boston.

MOODEY, SAMUEL. Judas the Traitor Hung up in Chains, To Give Warning to Professors, That they Beware of Worldlymindedness, and Hypocrisy: A Discourse concluding with a Dialogue; Preach'd at York in New-England. Boston: B. Green, 1714. [11]

Duodecimo, 48 leaves, A-H⁶.

Original sheep over wooden boards, lined with leaves from an almanack.

First edition.

Evans 1704. Sabin 50301.

The dedication to the reader is dated from York, December 30, 1713. It is written for the most part to *Little Children, Unconverted Ones especially*, and the author cleverly adapts the Bible to their understanding and his own purpose. He begins with *the Word of the Lord that came to Ezekiel, Chap. xxxiii.* 11. (*with some Variation*) *Turn ye, turn ye from your Evil ways; for why will ye die, O Children of New England? Poor Hearts; You are going to Hell indeed: but will it not be a dreadful thing to go to Hell from New-England, from this Land of Light to that Dungeon of Eternal Darkness?*

Samuel Moodey (1676-1747) was a minister of the Congregational Church at York, Maine, and was instrumental in founding a Congregational Church in Providence, R. I.

NOYES, JAMES. A Short Catechism Composed by Mr. James Noyes, Late Teacher of the Church of Christ in Newbury, in New-England. For the use of the Children there. Boston: Printed by Bartholomew Green, 1714. [12]

Octavo, 8 leaves, A⁸.

Straight-grain olive morocco, gilt, g. e., by F. Bedford.

Evans 1708 (does not locate a copy). Sabin 56219.

This edition of the Newbury Catechism is the fourth in the list given by Mr. Wilber-force Eames in *Early New England Catechisms*.

The first edition, of which no copy has been found, was probably printed ln 1642. Of this edition of 1714 only one or two copies are known to exist, of which the present was the Brinley copy.

Mr. Eames, in the above mentioned work, explains that the Newbury Catechism, ac-cording to tradition, was published in compliance with the recommendation of the General Court in 1641. It was composed by James Noyes (1608-1656), one of the first ministers of Newbury (Massachusetts), and a teacher of the church there from 1635 until his death. He was a native of Wiltshire, England, and emigrated to New England in 1634.

1717

A LEGACY for Children, being Some of the Last Expressions, and Dying Sayings, of Hannah Hill, Junr. Of the City of Philadelphia, in the Prov-ince of Pennsilvania, in America, Aged Eleven Years and near Three Months. The Third Eddition (*sic*). Philadelphia: Andrew Bradford, 1717. [13]

16mo, 18 leaves, A²⁻⁸, B⁸, C³.

Wrappers. Only one other copy of this edition is known.

Evans 1884. Sabin 31826. Hildeburn 141.

Both the earlier editions of this morbid account of the death of this little Quakeress were undated, the first appeared in 1714 and the second in 1715.

The preface to the *Tender Reader* explains that the book is published at the *Ardent Desire of the Deceased*. The account of her death occupies pages 5 to 22; on page 23 begins the Postscript; page 25, The Substance of a Letter from H. H. junior, to her cousin E. Norris; page 26, Griffith Owen, His Testimony; page 30, Thomas Chalkley, His Testimony, end-ing on page 35 with an Acrostic poem, by Chalkley.

Hannah took several days to die, and occupied the time by giving moral advice to her family and friends, *the Council which she gave to her Dear and only Sister and Cousin* Loyd Zachary, *whom she dearly loved, was very grave and Pithy*.

For an interesting account of Thomas Chalkley, the celebrated Quaker, see the Diction-ary of National Biography, where he is described as *probably the most influential Quaker minister in America during the eighteenth century*.

1719

HODDER, JAMES. Hodder's Arithmetick: or, that Necessary Art Made most Easy. Being explained in a way familiar to the Capacity of any that desire to learn it in a little Time. By James Hodder, Writing-Master. The Five and Twentieth Edition, Revised, Augmented, and above a Thousand Faults Amended, by Henry Mose, late Servant and Succes-sor to the Author. Boston: Printed by J. Franklin, for S. Phillips, N. Buttolph [and others], 1719. [14]

Octavo, 114 leaves, (A)-O⁸, P², a curious woodcut portrait as frontispiece.

Original calf.

Evans 2026.

The first American edition. Apart from the arithmetical section in Bradford's *Young Man's Companion*, this was the first purely arithmetical work published in Colonial America, arithmetic having been taught previously without printed textbooks but with manuscript *sumbooks* which the teachers had made when they themselves were in *statu pupilarii*.

James Hodder (fl. 1661) was an English schoolmaster, writing master, and arithmetician. His *Arithmetick*, first published in London in 1661, was the popular manual upon which Cocker based his better known work.

MATHER, INCREASE. The Duty of Parents to Pray For their Children, Opened & Applyed in a Sermon, preached May 19. 1703. Which Day was set apart by One of the Churches in Boston, New-England, humbly to Seek unto God by Prayer with Fasting for the Rising Generation . . . The second impression. Boston: John Allen for Benjamin Gray, 1719.   [15]

Duodecimo, 2 parts in 1, 53 leaves, A-H⁶, I⁵.

Original sheep over wooden boards.

At page 41, sig. D₆, the title: *The Duty of Children, whose Parents have pray'd for them. Or, early and real godliness urged; especially upon such as are descended from godly ancestors. In a sermon preached . . . By Cotton Mather. The second impression. Boston: for J. Edwards and B. Gray*, 1719.

Evans 2052. Sabin 46673.

Second edition.

Increase Mather (1639-1723) was born in New England where his father had emigrated in 1635. He was minister of the New North Church, Boston, from 1664 until his death, and for a time was President of Harvard College. Cotton Mather was his eldest son.

1720

BAILEY, NATHAN. English and Latine Exercises for School-Boys, Comprising all the Rules of Syntaxis, with Explanations, and other necessary Observations on each Rule. And shewing, The Genitive Case, and Gender of Nouns and Pronouns; as also the Preterperfect Tense, Supine and Conjugation of Verbs. Answering Perfectly to the Design of Mr. Garretson, and Hermes Romanus, in bringing on Learners most gradually and expeditiously to the Translating of English into Latine. By N. Bayley, School-master. The Fifth Edition, newly Improv'd and Revis'd by several Hands. Boston: T. Fleet for Samuel Phillips, 1720. [16]

Octavo, 108 leaves, A-N⁸, O⁴.

Original sheep over wooden boards.
Evans 2092.

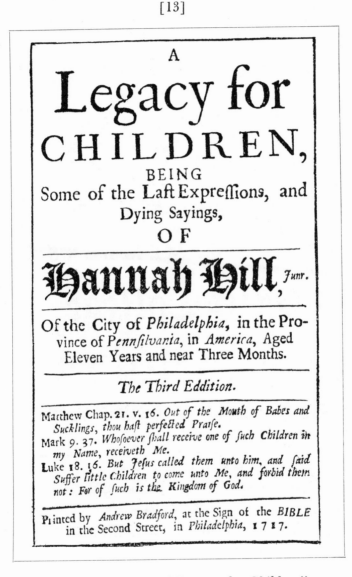

A

Legacy for
CHILDREN,

BEING
Some of the Laſt Expreſſions, and
Dying Sayings,
OF

Hannah Hill, *Junr.*

Of the City of *Philadelphia*, in the Province of *Pennſilvania*, in *America*, Aged
Eleven Years and near Three Months.

The Third Eddition.

Matthew Chap. 21. v. 16. *Out of the Mouth of Babes and Sucklings, thou haſt perfected Praiſe.*
Mark 9. 37. *Whoſoever ſhall receive one of ſuch Children in my Name, receiveth Me.*
Luke 18. 16. *But Jeſus called them unto him, and ſaid Suffer little Children to come unto Me, and forbid them not: For of ſuch is the Kingdom of God.*

Printed by *Andrew Bradford*, at the Sign of the *BIBLE* in the Second Street, in *Philadelphia*, 1717.

Title-page from "A Legacy for Children"

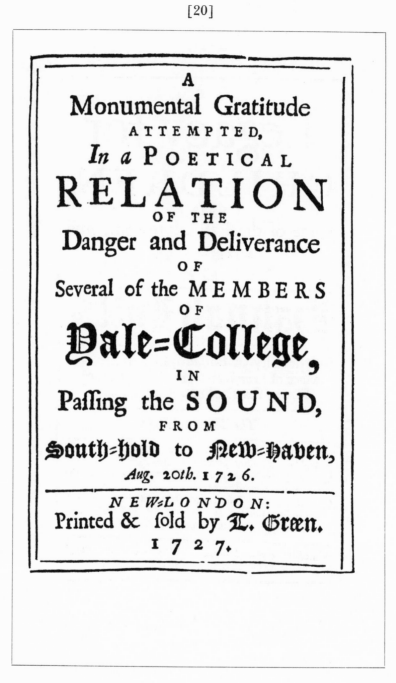

A
Monumental Gratitude
ATTEMPTED,
In a POETICAL
RELATION
OF THE
Danger and Deliverance
OF
Several of the MEMBERS
OF
𝕭𝖆𝖑𝖊=𝕮𝖔𝖑𝖑𝖊𝖌𝖊,
IN
Paffing the SOUND,
FROM
𝕾𝖔𝖚𝖙𝖍=𝖍𝖔𝖑𝖉 to 𝕹𝖊𝖜=𝕳𝖆𝖛𝖊𝖓,
Aug. 20*th.* 1 7 2 6.

NEW=LONDON:
Printed & fold by 𝕿. 𝕲𝖗𝖊𝖊𝖓.
1 7 2 7.

Title-page from "*A Monumental Gratitude*"

Early American Children's Books

The dedication *To all the worthy and ingenious Teachers of the Latine-Tongue* is signed by James Holland.

This *English and Latine Exercises* was an extremely popular textbook in colonial schools. It contains grammatical rules followed by illustrative sentences in Latin and English. Some of these sentences are a little unexpected. To illustrate the use of the verb *sum* we have *Jane is a nasty girl; Joanna sum puella spurcus* followed a few sentences lower by *God is an Infinite Spirit; Deus sum spiritus infinitus.* One of the illustrations for the dative case is *Greedy Gluttons buy many dainty bits for their ungodly Guts,* and amongst the prepositional sentences are included *The Maid eats lice for the Jaundice,* and *Children drink Brimestone and Milk for the itch.*

Nathan Bailey (d. 1742) was an English schoolmaster and lexicographer. He belonged to the seventh-day baptists, and kept a boarding school at Stepney. He is chiefly famous for the compilation of a dictionary which was the foundation for Johnson's still more celebrated work.

THE TESTAMENT of the Twelve Patriarchs, the Sons of Jacob Translated out of Greek into Latin, by Robert Grosthead, sometime Bishop of Lincoln; and out of his Copy into French and Dutch by others, and now Englished. To the Truth whereof, an Ancient Greek Copy, written on Parchment, is kept in the University Library of Cambridge. Boston: Re-printed by T. Fleet, for S. Phillips, N. Buttolph, B. Eliot, & D. Henchman, and E. Phillips in Charleston, 1720.   [17]

Duodecimo, 60 leaves, A-K⁶.

Original sheep over wooden boards. Contemporary signatures on the end leaves.
Not in Evans.
Edited with a preface, by Richard Day, English printer, translator, and divine (1552-1607?). The work was *Englished* by Antony Gilby.

1723

COLMAN, BENJAMIN and Cooper, William. Two Sermons Preached in Boston, March 5, 1723. On a Day of Prayer, Had by the Church and Congregation usually meeting in Brattle-Street, to ask the Effusion of the Spirit of Grace on their Children, and on the Children of the Town. By Benjamin Colman and William Cooper. Boston: S. Kneeland for J. Edwards, 1723.   [18]

Duodecimo, 42 leaves, (A)³, B-K⁴, L³.

Red half morocco.
This issue not in Evans. Sabin 16641.
At sig. F₄ is the half title: *The Duty of Parents to pray for their Children, and especially to ask of God for them the Spiritual Blessing, By Benjamin Colman;* with continuous signatures and separate pagination. The dedication *To my Honoured Father, Mr. Thomas Clark* is dated from Boston, March, 1723.

Benjamin Colman was the minister of the Church in Brattle Street. William Cooper was also a minister of Boston. In 1737, he was elected President of Harvard College, but declined the trust. He died in 1743, at the age of 49.

1724

CORDIER, MATHURIN. Corderii Colloquiorum Centuria Selecta; or, A Select Century of Cordery's Colloquies: with an English Translation as Literal as possible, design'd for the Use of Beginners in the Latin Tongue. By John Clarke, Master of the Publick Grammar School in Hull, and Author of the Introduction to the making of Latin. The Third Edition. Boston: for Benjamin Eliot and Daniel Henchman, 1724. [19]

Duodecimo, 88 leaves, A-Y⁴, Latin and English in opposite columns.

Original sheep.
Evans 2517.
Mathurin Cordier (1479-1564) was a French schoolmaster. He taught in Paris, where John Calvin was one of his pupils, and later in Geneva. His *Colloquiorum Centuria Selecta* was one of the chief Latin books in common use amongst the more youthful scholars of the New England schools. The book has additional interest as a study of scholarly life in the time of the author. The form is question and answer.

1727

[HUBBARD, JOHN.] A Monumental Gratitude Attempted, In a Poetical Relation of the Danger and Deliverance of Several of the Members of Yale-College, in Passing the Sound, from South-hold to New-Haven, Aug. 20th, 1726. New-London: Printed & sold by T.Green, 1727. [20]

Octavo, 7 leaves including half title, A⁴, B³.

Half morocco.
Evans 2882. Wegelin 216. No copy in the Fiske Harris Collection. Trumbull 1113.
An excessively rare volume of American poetry, and one of the earliest compositions written by an American child and published in America. Only two other copies are known. On the half title of this copy is the signature of J. Trumble 1727.
A Latin poem, on pages 9 and 10, with this caption, *Nomine quaerenti* Juvenum *indigenum quasi Carmen indicare non recusat*, gives the initials of the names of the ten students who composed the party, arranged as an acrostic, in the following order: D. H., E. S., G. B., G. Vu., E. L., J. L., J. H., J. P., J. C., and E. K. [for Daniel Hubbard, Ebenezer Silliman, of the class of 1727; George Beckwith, 1728; George Wyllys, Epaphres Lord, Ichabod Lord, Joseph Hunt, Jona. Parsons, Jacob Cadwell and Elisha Kent, 1729.] — *Trumbull*.

PENN, WILLIAM. Fruits of a Father's Love. Being the Advice of William Penn to His Children, Relating to Their Civil and Religious Conduct. Written Occasionally many Years ago, and now made Pub-

lick for a General Good. By A Lover of His Memory. London: Printed, Philadelphia: Reprinted and Sold by Andrew Bradford, 1727. [21]

Octavo, 48 leaves, A-F⁸.

Original wrappers.
Evans 2941. Hildeburn 312. Sabin 59698.
The first American edition. Advertised in Leeds's Almanac for 1728; Hildeburn can
only quote the title from this source. This appears to be the only copy known.
William Penn (1644-1718) was the celebrated Quaker and founder of Pennsylvania.
Fruits of a Father's Love was first published posthumously in London in 1726. The *Lover of
his Memory* who edited the work was Sir John Rhodes.

PRINCE, THOMAS. Morning Health no Security Against the Sudden Ar-
rest of Death before Night. A Sermon Occasioned by the very sudden
Death of Two young Gentlemen in Boston, on Saturday, January 14,
1726, 7. Dedicated to the Youth of the Town. Boston: Printed for Daniel Henchman, 1727. [22]

Quarto, 13 leaves, A², B-D⁴ (lacks Aᵢ, a blank), partly uncut.

Green cloth.
Evans 2947. Sabin 65605.
First edition.
The two young gentlemen were Samuel Hirst and Thomas Lewis.
Thomas Prince (1687-1771) was co-pastor with Dr. Joseph Sewall of the Old South
Church, Boston.

1729

VINCENT, THOMAS. An Explicatory Catechism: or, an Explanation of
the Assemblies Shorter Catechism. Wherein all the Answers in the
Assemblies Catechism are taken abroad in Under-Questions and Answers, the Truth explain'd, and proved by Reason and Scripture; several Cases of Conscience resolv'd, some chief Controversies in Religion
stated, with Arguments against divers Errors. Useful to be read in
private Families, after Examination in the Catechism it self, for the
more clear and thorough understanding of what is therein Learn'd.
Boston: for D. Henchman, John Phillips, and T. Hancock, 1729. [23]

Octavo, 164 leaves, A-V⁸, X⁴, including last blank.

Original sheep over wooden boards.
Evans 3229. Eames: *Early New England Catechisms*, p. 92.
The Epistle to the Reader has forty signatures, including those of Edm. Calamy, Jam.
Janeway and Hen. Vaughan. There are two dedications by the author, one *To the Masters
and Governours of Families belonging to my Congregation*, the other *To the Young Ones of*

Early American Children's Books

my Congregation, especially Those that answer this Explicatory Catechism in our Publick Assembly.

Thomas Vincent (1634-1678) was an English nonconformist divine. On the title-page he is described as, *sometimes Minister of Maudlin Milk-street in London.* The *Explicatory Catechism* was first published in England in 1673.

The Westminster Assembly's Shorter Catechism was the backbone of the New England Primer. It was the work of the great Westminster Assembly, which was called together by Parliament in 1643 and which lasted six years. All children were expected to memorize the catechism, which contained 107 questions with long and heavy answers. Several editions of it will be found in this collection.

1736

MARTYROLOGY, or, A brief Account of the Lives, Sufferings and Deaths of those two holy Martyrs, viz. Mr. John Rogers, and Mr. John Bradford, Who suffered for the Gospel, by the bloody Tyranny, Rage and Persecution of the Church of Rome, in the Kingdom of England, under the Reign of Queen Mary, and were burnt at Smithfield, the former on the 14th of February, 1554, the latter July 1st, 1555. Boston: S. Kneeland and T. Green, 1736. [24]

Duodecimo, 12 leaves, A-B⁶, the first and last blanks serve as wrappers, original stitching, as issued.

Evans 4032.

First American edition. John Bradford and John Rogers were both Protestant martyrs burnt by the orders of Bloody Mary. Rogers was the first victim of the Marian persecution and a woodcut depicting his martyrdom, accompanied by the verses of Advice to his Children, is to be found in most of the editions of the New England Primer.

1737

FOX, GEORGE. Instructions for Right Spelling, and Plain Directions for Reading and Writing True English. With several delightful Things, very useful and necessary, both for Young and Old, to read and learn. Re-printed at Philadelphia by B. Franklin, 1737. [25]

Duodecimo, 60 leaves, A-K⁶.

Original calf.

Not in Evans. Not in Hildeburn. Campbell (Curtis Collection) page 57.

This is the only perfect copy known. The copy in the Curtis Collection is the only other known copy. The catalogue of that collection erroneously states that it was first published in 1706. A copy of the first edition, dated 1702, is in the present collection, no. 5 *supra.*

In this edition, the black letter alphabets are placed at the end, instead of at the beginning, as in the former edition, of the page devoted to alphabets. Contemporary signatures on the flyleaves.

Early American Children's Books

1738

PHILLIPS, SAMUEL. The History of our Lord and Saviour Jesus Christ Epitomiz'd: In a Catechetical Way. For the Use of the Children in the South Parish in Andover: To whom it is Dedicated. Boston: S. Kneeland and T. Green for D. Henchman, 1738. [26]

Duodecimo, 36 leaves, including the half title, A-F^6.

Original marble wrappers.
Evans 4301. Sabin 62517^n.
First edition. Only one other copy of this little book is known, and is to be found in the Boston Public Library.
At the end are two leaves of Hymns with the explanation *To supply a few vacant Pages, the following Hymns from Dr. Watts, are here inserted.*
Samuel Phillips (1690-1771) was a native of Salem, Massachusetts, and a graduate of Harvard College. He was a minister at Andover from 1711 until his death.

PHILLIPS, SAMUEL. The Orthodox Christian: or, A Child well instructed in the Principles of the Christian Religion: Exhibited in a Discourse by Way of Catechizing. Design'd for the Use and Benefit of the Children, in the South Parish in Andover: To whom it is Dedicated. Boston: S. Kneeland and T. Green for D. Henchman, 1738. [27]

Duodecimo, 77 leaves, including the half title, A-M^6, N^5.

Original sheep over thin wooden boards.
Evans 4302. Sabin 62517^n. Eames: *Early New England Catechisms*, p. 49.
First edition of the Andover Catechism. On page 136, is the Errata, following which are six pages of Hymns from Dr. Watts, *To supply a few vacant Pages.*
The half title reads: *Mr. Phillips's Well instructed Child;* and the dedication *To The Children under my Pastoral Care,* is dated from Andover, March 30, 1738. Contemporary signatures on the flyleaves.

1742

BECHTEL, JOHN. Kurzer Catechismus Vor etliche Gemeinen Jesu Aus der Reformirten Religion in Pennsylvania, Die sich zum alten Berner Synodo halten: Herausgegeben von Johannes Bechteln, Diener des Worts Gottes. Philadelphia: Benjamin Franklin, 1742. [28]

Duodecimo, 22 leaves, A-C^6, D^4.

Original wrappers.
Evans 4889. Sabin 4223. Hildeburn 750. Campbell, page 73: *One of the few books with the imprint Benjamin Franklin. It is usually B. Franklin.*
First edition of the Catechism of the Moravian Brethren in America. The honour of printing it was originally intended for Christopher Sower, but was refused by him on account of his dislike for several members of the Synod. It was then offered to Benjamin Franklin.

Early American Children's Books

John Bechtel was born in 1690, at Weinheim in the Palatinate. He emigrated to Pennsylvania in 1726, and lived in Germantown for twenty years, later settling in Bethlehem. He was an active member of the Moravian Brotherhood, of which body he was for two years a pastor (1742-1744). He died in Bethlehem in 1758. The borough of Bechtelsville in Berks County, Pennsylvania, was named in honour of him and his family.

The Catechism was compiled by Bechtel in conjunction with Count Zinzendorf; an account of it is given in *John Bechtel, his Contributions to Literature*, by J. W. Jordan.

1743

SERGEANT, JOHN. A Letter From the Rev^d Mr. Sergeant of Stockbridge, to Dr. Colman of Boston; Containing Mr. Sergeant's Proposal of a more effectual Method for the Education of Indian Children; to raise 'em if possible into a civil and industrious People; by introducing the English Language among them; and thereby instilling into their Minds and Hearts, with a more lasting Impression, the Principles of Virtue and Piety. Made publick by Dr. Colman at the Desire of Mr. Sergeant, with some general Account of what the Rev. Mr. Isaac Hollis of——— has already done for the Sons of this Indian Tribe of Houssatannoc, now erected into a Township by the General Court, and called Stockbridge. Boston: Rogers and Fowle, for D. Henchman, 1743.   [29]

Octavo, 8 leaves, A-B^4.

Half red morocco.
Evans 5288. Sabin 79194.
Pages 10-16 contain *Dr. Colman's Return in Compliance with Mr. Sergeant's Request*, dated August 22, 1743, signed *Benjamin Colman*.
John Sergeant (d. 1749) was a missionary to the Houssatannoc Indians. Benjamin Colman was the first minister of the Brattle Street Church, Boston.

1744

[TERSTEEGEN, GERHARD.] Der Frommen Lotterie, oder Geistliches Schatz-Kästlein. [Germantown: Christoph Saur, 1744.]   [30]

381 tickets on pasteboard measuring $3\frac{15}{16}$ x $2\frac{1}{16}$ inches, enclosed in the original leather case.

Evans 5501. Hildeburn 905. Neither is able to locate a copy.
The tickets are numbered like lottery tickets, and each contains a poetic gem composed by Gerhard Tersteegen, and a verse or passage from the Scriptures. Hildeburn thus describes this extremely interesting production: *These tickets were enclosed in neat cases, some made of leather, and others of wood nicely dove-tailed. The good people in olden time enjoyed themselves, generally on Sunday afternoons, by drawing prizes out of this sacred or spiritual treasury, and often when they felt gloomy or despondent they would resort to it in the hope of drawing some promise or consolation to cheer their drooping spirits.*
Gerhard Tersteegen (1697-1769) was a German ascetic and poet.

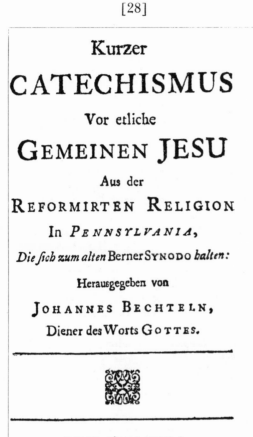

Kurzer

CATECHISMUS

Vor etliche

GEMEINEN JESU

Aus der

REFORMIRTEN RELIGION

In PENNSYLVANIA,

Die sich zum alten Berner SYNODO *halten:*

Herausgegeben von

JOHANNES BECHTELN,

Diener des Worts GOTTES.

PHILADELPHIA,
Gedruckt bey BENJAMIN FRANKLIN, 1742.

Title-page from "Kurzer Catechismus"

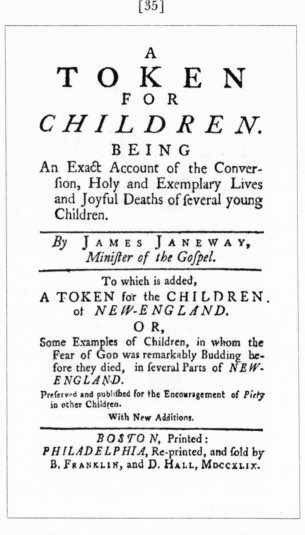

A

T O K E N

FOR

CHILDREN.

BEING

An Exact Account of the Converfion, Holy and Exemplary Lives
and Joyful Deaths of feveral young
Children.

By JAMES JANEWAY,
Minifter of the Gofpel.

To which is added,
A TOKEN for the CHILDREN.
of *NEW-ENGLAND.*
OR,
Some Examples of Children, in whom the
Fear of GOD was remarkably Budding be-
fore they died, in feveral Parts of *NEW-
ENGLAND.*
Preferved and publifhed for the Encouragement of *Piety*
in other Children.
With New Additions.

BOSTON, Printed:
PHILADELPHIA, Re-printed, and fold by
B. FRANKLIN, and D. HALL, MDCCXLIX.

Title-page from "A Token for Children"

Early American Children's Books

1748

FISHER, GEORGE. The American Instructor: or, Young Man's Best Companion. Containing, Spelling, Reading, Writing and Arithmetick, in an easier Way than any yet published . . . The whole better adapted to these American Colonies, than any other Book of the like Kind. By George Fisher, Accomptant. The Ninth edition Revised and Corrected. Philadelphia: B. Franklin and D. Hall, 1748. [31]

Duodecimo, 193 leaves, A³, A-X⁶, Bb-Ii⁶, Kk⁴, the last a blank. Five plates of examples of calligraphy, woodcuts in the text.

Original calf.
Evans 6238. Sabin 24459. Hildeburn 1062. Campbell page 96.
The first American edition. The author's name is probably a pseudonym. The British Museum catalogue attributes the authorship to Mrs. Slack.
The last paragraph of the preface reads as follows: *In the British Edition of this Book, there were many Things of little or no Use in these Parts of the World: In this Edition those Things are omitted, and in their Room Many other Matters inserted, more immediately useful to us Americans . . .*

1749

[FRANKLIN, BENJAMIN.] Proposals Relating to the Education of Youth in Pensilvania. Philadelphia: [Franklin & Hall] 1749. [32]

Octavo, 16 leaves, A-D⁴. Ornament on title.

Blue wrappers, uncut.
Evans 6321. Sabin 25575. Hildeburn 1129. Campbell page 103.
First edition. The publication of this pamphlet by Franklin led to the establishment of the University of Pennsylvania.

HEYWOOD, HENRY. Two Catechisms by Way of Question and Answer: Each divided into Two Parts. Designed for the Instruction of the Children of the Christian Brethren Owning One God, One Lord Jesus Christ, And One Holy Spirit. Who are commonly known and distinguished by the Name of General Baptists. Together with References to the Texts of Scripture and Testimonies of other Writers, which may be alledged in Proof or Confirmation of the several Answers. Charles-Town, South Carolina: P. Timothy, 1749. [33]

Quarto, 52 leaves, with irregular signatures: A, C, C, D-I, H, I, H, L, in fours, errata at the end.

Original condition, unbound, sewed, uncut edges.
Not in Evans. Not in Sabin.

Early American Children's Books

The book is dedicated to Mrs. Amarantha Farr, Mrs. Frances Elliott, Mrs. Elizabeth Elliott, and Mrs. Elizabeth Williamson, in the hope that for their own children they *will make a diligent use thereof, that so your Houses may be little Schools of Christianity, and your Families Nurseries for Christ's Church, and the Kingdom of the great God.*

THE HISTORY of the Holy Jesus. Containing a brief and plain Account of his Birth, Life, Death, Resurrection and Ascension into Heaven; and his coming again at the great and last Day of Judgment. Being a pleasant and profitable Companion for Children; compos'd on Purpose for their Use. By a Lover of their precious Souls. The Sixth Edition. Boston: Printed by J. Bushell and J. Green, 1749. [34]

Sm. octavo, 24 leaves, (A) B (C⁸), first and last leaves pasted down to covers.

Original wrappers.

Evans 6331 (no copy located). Bates: *History of the Holy Jesus*, page 6. Sabin XXI, p. 98. Church Catalogue 967.

In verse, with six pages of hymns at the end, including the Child's Body of Divinity, the lines of which are in alphabetical order.

There are sixteen woodcut illustrations in this edition, one of which is signed I. T. on the block. Some of these blocks had been previously used in the fourth edition, and a number, considerably worked over, were used again in Boyle's edition of 1774 (no. 79), five of the cuts in that edition having the signature I. T.

The portrait frontispiece is unsigned and unlettered; in the edition of 1774 it is signed, and lettered *The Author.*

On A₅ recto is a cut lettered *Wise Men come from the East, &c.* consisting of a group of Puritan men gazing through telescopes at a shooting star, the moon and many stationary stars filling the rest of the sky. On the verso of the same leaf is *Herod slaying the innocent Children,* signed I. T. It represents Herod, fully armed and with sword in hand, on a charger between two armies, each carrying their banners, one of which is the British flag; a few corpses are on the ground. A cut on B₁ verso in two compartments represents the *Rich and Great Ones here below* and poor Lazarus at their Gates, all in eighteenth-century costume. On B₅ is an extraordinary cut of Christ teaching the multitude, unlettered in this edition, but so named in the edition of 1774. Christ, in the gown and bands of a New England preacher, is in a pulpit, the multitude consisting of three Puritan men on one side and three Puritan women on the other. The remaining cuts are equally naive and medieval in spirit.

The History of the Holy Jesus was one of the most popular children's books of the period, and appeared in numerous editions, a list of which is given in Sabin: *Bibliotheca Americana,* vol. XXI, pp. 97-100. The initials I.T. are supposed to be those of James Turner, famous as the engraver of Scull's map of the Province of Pennsylvania. He died in Philadelphia in 1759.

JANEWAY, JAMES. A Token for Children. Being An Exact Account of the Conversion, Holy and Exemplary Lives, and Joyful Deaths of several young Children. By James Janeway, Minister of the Gospel. To which is added, A Token for the Children of New-England. Or, Some Examples of Children, in whom the Fear of God was remarkably Bud-

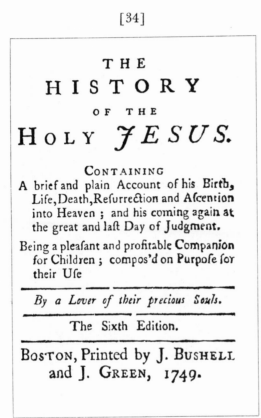

THE
HISTORY
OF THE
HOLY *JESUS*.

CONTAINING
A brief and plain Account of his Birth,
Life, Death, Refurrection and Afcention
into Heaven ; and his coming again at
the great and laft Day of Judgment.

Being a pleafant and profitable Companion
for Children ; compos'd on Purpofe for
their Ufe

By a Lover of their precious Souls.

The Sixth Edition.

BOSTON, Printed by J. BUSHELL
and J. GREEN, 1749.

Title-page from "History of the Holy Jesus"

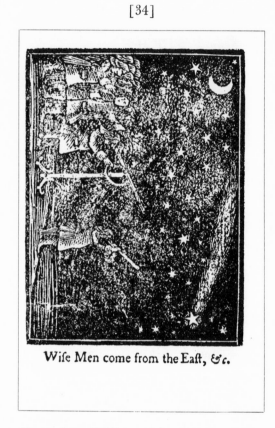

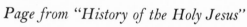
Wise Men come from the East, &c.

Page from "History of the Holy Jesus"

Early American Children's Books

ding before they died, in several Parts of New-England. Preserved and published for the Encouragement of Piety in other Children. With New Additions. Boston, Printed: Philadelphia, Re-printed, and sold by B. Franklin, and D. Hall, 1749. [35]

Duodecimo, 60 leaves, A-K⁶.

Original calf.
Evans 6339. Hildeburn 1133. Campbell 420. This edition not in Sabin.
The work opens with a letter addressed to all Parents, School-Masters and School-Mistresses, or any that have any hand in the Education of Children. This is followed by A Preface, Containing Directions to Children, which opens: *You may now hear (my dear Lambs) what other good Children have done, and remember how they wept and prayed by themselves; how earnestly they cried out for an Interest in the Lord Jesus Christ*, and goes on to enquire, *Do you do as these Children did? Did you ever see your miserable state by Nature? Did you ever get by yourself and weep for sin?* and other searching questions.
The author, James Janeway (1636?-1674) was a celebrated English nonconformist divine. His famous Token was first published in England in two parts, 1671 and 1672.
The first American edition was published in Boston in 1700, and to this edition was added the Token for the Children of New England, by Cotton Mather. The work was extremely popular in England and her colonies, and not only passed through many editions, but gave rise to numerous imitations.
Of the present edition from the press of Benjamin Franklin, only one other copy seems to have survived, and is in the Boston Public Library.

THE NEW-ENGLAND PRIMER Further improved with various Additions. For the more easy attaining the true Reading of English. To which is added, The Assembly of Divines Catechism. Boston: Rogers and Fowle, for the Booksellers, 1749. [36]

16mo, 38 leaves (should be 40), A²⁻⁸, B-D⁸, E⁷ (lacks A¹ and E⁸), alphabet woodcuts, and cut of the burning of John Rogers.

Original calf over wooden boards.
Not in Heartman. This is probably the only known copy of this edition.
The first edition in this collection of the most popular schoolbook for children in New England. Numerous editions were issued, and although the subject matter varied to some extent, all editions had certain features in common. Alphabets in hornbook form were followed by a syllabary, and the alphabet in couplets illustrated with woodcuts, the couplets varying with time from the secular to the religious. The alphabet also appeared in a series of admonitory sentences, and occasionally a rhymed alphabet was inserted. The Catechism of the Assembly of Divines at Westminster; Dr. Watts's Cradle Hymn; the Verses for Little Children (see no. 8); various hymns and prayers, including Agur's prayer, are to be found in most editions of the Primer. A woodcut of the burning of John Rogers, retained from the Protestant Tutor, the violently anti-Catholic forerunner of the New England Primer, was rarely omitted, and was usually accompanied by the verses of Advice to his Children.
The method of using the table of syllables was doubtless the same in Colonial as in English schools, and we learn from Brinley, *Ludus Literarius*, 1612, that the child was expected to learn it up and down, backwards and forwards and across, until he knew it by heart.

Early American Children's Books

1751

PETERS, RICHARD. A Sermon on Education. Wherein Some Account is given of the Academy, Established in the City of Philadelphia. Preach'd at the Opening thereof, on the Seventh Day of January, 1750-1. By the Reverend Mr. Richard Peters. Philadelphia: B. Franklin and D. Hall, 1751. [37]

Octavo, 32 leaves, A⁴, B-D⁸, A⁴. Woodcut vignette at head of A₂ recto.

Blue wrappers, original front grey wrapper preserved.
First edition. Campbell, page 112. Evans 6754. Hildeburn 1234.

The four leaves at the end, signature A, with separate pagination, contain *Idea of the English School, Sketch'd out for the Consideration of the Trustees of the Philadelphia Academy*. Signed B. F. [Benjamin Franklin.]

This *Idea* was eventually responsible for the development of the Academy into the College of Philadelphia and subsequently into the University of Pennsylvania.

Richard Peters (1704-1776) came to Philadelphia as a clergyman of the Church of England about 1735, and remained in that city, holding many important posts, until his death.

1752

[GREGORY, FRANCIS.] Nomenclatura brevis Anglo-Latino in usum Scholarum. Together with Examples of the Five Declensions of Nouns: With the Words in *Propria quæ Maribus* and *Quæ Genus* reduced to each Declension. Per F. G. Boston: Z. Fowle for J. Edwards, 1752. [38]

Sm. octavo, 46 leaves, A-E⁸, F⁶.

Original sheep over wooden boards, some uncut edges.
Evans 6850.
English and Latin in parallel columns.

The first edition of this classified vocabulary was published in England in 1675 for the use of Westminster School, where Gregory was at one time a scholar, and where he returned as an usher after graduating from Trinity College, Cambridge. The first American edition was published in 1735.

1753

FULLER, SAMUEL. Some Principles and Precepts of the Christian Religion. By Way of Question and Answer. Recommended to Parents and Tutors for the Use of Children. By Samuel Fuller, one of the People called Quakers, the same read and approved of by their national Meeting held at Dublin in the 9th Month, 1733. Dublin printed. Philadelphia: reprinted by James Chattin, 1753. [39]

16mo, 64 leaves, A-H⁸, last page with advertisements.

Original sheep, a blind-stamped lozenge-shaped ornament, containing a crown on sides.

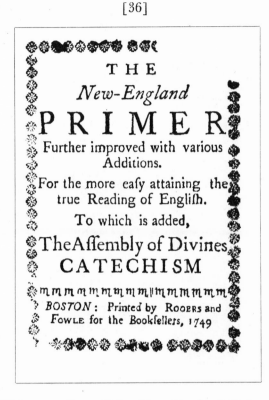

Title-page from "The New-England Primer"

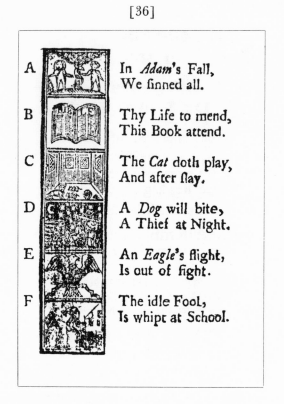

A	In *Adam*'s Fall, We finned all.
B	Thy Life to mend, This Book attend.
C	The *Cat* doth play, And after flay.
D	A *Dog* will bite, A Thief at Night.
E	An *Eagle*'s flight, Is out of fight.
F	The idle Fool, Is whipt at School.

Page from "The New-England Primer"

Early American Children's Books

Evans 7005. Hildeburn 1300. Smith, page 826.

The first American edition. The first edition appeared in Dublin in 1733. Smith had apparently not seen a copy for he queries the date. He describes the author as a schoolmaster of Dublin. In his P. S. to the Dedication, the author states that the book is intended principally for the use of children. The Catechism gives information on such points as the reasons why the Quakers do not uncover their heads; why they do not baptize their children, why they use the second person singular, and other interesting matter.

THE ROYAL PRIMER Improved: Being an easy and pleasant Guide to the Art of Reading. Philadelphia: James Chattin, 1753. [40]

Sm. octavo, 48 leaves, A-F⁸, title with woodcut Royal arms, within an ornamental border, woodcut illustrations, advertisement on the last page.

Original sheep, partly uncut.

First American edition of *The Royal Primer* and the only copy known. On the flyleaf is the autograph signature of the original owner, *Thos. Pearsall D. D. his book* 1754. For an account of this book, see Percival Merritt: *The Royal Primer* in *Bibliographical Essays, A Tribute to Wilberforce Eames*, 1924, who says in part: *Of this edition only one copy is known to exist, in the private collection of Dr. A. S. W. Rosenbach of Philadelphia. Sabin, Evans, and Hildeburn cite a 'Royal Primer improved' as 'The Second Edition, Philadelphia: James Chattin, 1753, 18mo.' No copy is located or collation given, and it would seem as if the entry might have been derived from some catalogue or advertisement, that none of the bibliographers had had the opportunity of examining it, and that one had followed the other in recording it.*

The Royal Primer was first published in London for John Newbery, the famous publisher of children's books. As Mr. Merritt points out, this first American reprint differs more widely from the Newbery publication than any of the other eighteenth century American editions. This edition contains alphabets, a syllabary, and easy lessons consisting of extracts from the Bible, proverbs and other didactic matter, together with the creed, prayers, the ten commandments, etc., various poetical items including a Divine Poem *wrote by the excellent Addison* and hymns by Dr. Watts; a few lessons on natural history and Biblical subjects, each accompanied by a woodcut, and a series of five woodcut illustrations of sailing vessels.

The cuts in the American edition are copied from those in the English edition with the exception of the cuts of sailing vessels, which, according to Mr. Merritt, are not to be found in any other primer.

1754

THE SCHOOL of Good Manners, containing I. Twenty Mixt Precepts. II. One Hundred and Sixty Three Rules for Childrens Behaviour. III. Good Advice for the Ordering of their Lives; With a Baptismal Covenant. IV. Eight wholesome Cautions. V. A short, plain, & Scriptural Catechism. VI. Principles of the Christian Religion. VII. Eleven short Exhortations. VIII. Good Thoughts for Children, A compendious Body of Divinity; An Alphabet of useful Copies; and Cyprian's Twelve Absurdities, &c. The Fifth Edition. New-London: T. & J. Green, 1754. [41]

Duodecimo, 42 leaves, A-G⁶ (lacks 2 leaves in signature C), the alphabet on the verso of the title-page.

Original sheep.

Not in Evans. This edition not in Trumbull.

Treatises on manners and courtesy were popular in Europe since the beginning of western civilization, and were circulated in manuscript long before the discovery of printing.

Separate treatises were compiled for the use of boys and of girls.

The immediate source of the *School of Good Manners*, which is for boys, is English, being derived from a work with the same title *by the author of English Exercises* [J. Garretson], first published in London in 1685, and frequently reprinted. Extracts from it will be found in several of the reading and spelling books by English authors in the present collection. The preface to this American edition, signed by T. Green, contains the statement that it was *compiled (chiefly) by Eleazer Moodey, late a famous School-Master in Boston, etc.*

The One Hundred and Sixty Three Rules for Childrens Behaviour relate to manners at the Meeting House; at Home; at the Table; in Company; in Discourse; at the School; when Abroad; and when among other Children.

The code of manners is excellent, and very thorough, due allowance being made for human weakness. When in Company, *If thou canst not avoid Yawning, shut thy mouth with thine hand or handkerchief before it, turning thy face aside . . . Spit not in the Room, but in the Corner, and rub it with thy Foot, or rather go out and do it abroad . . .* Politeness to superiors is insisted on with great firmness. *If thy Superior be relating a Story, say not I have heard it before, but attend to it as if it were to thee altogether new: Seem not to question the Truth of it; If he tell it not right, snigger not, nor endeavor to help him out or add to his Relation.*

1757

[CHURCH, BENJAMIN.] The Choice: A Poem, After the Manner of Mr. Promfret. By a young Gentleman. Boston: Edes and Gill, 1757. [42]

Quarto, 8 leaves, A-B⁴.

Red morocco, gilt.

Evans 7872. Sabin 12985. Wegelin 67.

First edition. At the foot of the last page: *In the Title-Page for Promfret, read Pomfret.*

Although this is the first edition, the poem was evidently written some years before publication, as a later edition states on the title-page *while at college at the age of* 18. The author was graduated from Harvard in 1754.

Benjamin Church led a colorful life, and was one of the leaders in the Boston Tea Party. In 1775, he was found guilty of treason and sentenced to imprisonment for life. On account of his ill health his sentence was mitigated, and he was allowed to leave the country. He embarked for the West Indies, and the ship in which he sailed was never heard of again.

1758

GORDON, JOHN. John Gordon's mathematical Traverse Table &c. Philadelphia: W. Dunlap; New York: G. Noel; Boston: B. Mecom, 1758. [43]

Duodecimo, 34 leaves, including the last blank without signature, 2 leaves with copper-plate diagrams (colored).

Original Dutch flowered wrappers.

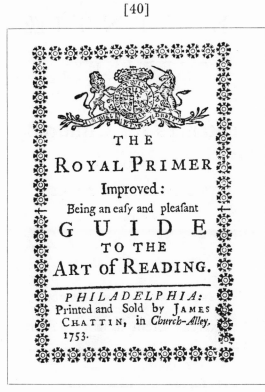

Title-page from "The Royal Primer"

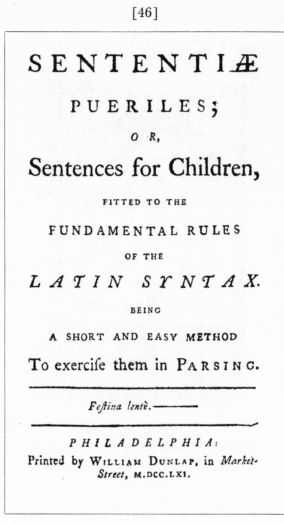

SENTENTIÆ

PUERILES;

O R,

Sentences for Children,

FITTED TO THE

FUNDAMENTAL RULES

OF THE

LATIN SYNTAX.

BEING

A SHORT AND EASY METHOD

To exercise them in PARSING.

Festina lentè.————

PHILADELPHIA:
Printed by WILLIAM DUNLAP, in *Market-Street*, M.DCC.LXI.

Title-page from "Sententiæ Pueriles"

Evans 8140. Hildeburn 1586.

First edition. The author gives a brief account of his life, at the end of the Preface. He was born in Pembrokeshire in the year 1700, and at the age of fourteen, came to Philadelphia. He eventually settled in *Sommerset County, near Prince Town, in New Jersey*, where he taught mathematics.

1760

THE SHORTER CATECHISM. Presented by the Assembly of Divines at Westminster, to both Houses of Parliament, and by them approved. Containing The Principles of the Christian Religion. With Scripture Proofs. Philadelphia: William Bradford, 1760. [44]

Octavo, 24 leaves, A-F⁴, unbound, uncut and unopened, stitched as issued.

Evans 8767. Hildeburn 1663. Not in Eames: *Early New England Catechisms*. On the verso of the first leaf are *Plain Directions for the more profitable Use of this Book*. See note to Thomas Vincent's *Explicatory Catechism*, 1729, no. 23.

1761

DAVIES, SAMUEL. Little Children Invited to Jesus Christ. A Sermon preached in Hanover County Virginia, May 8, 1758. With An Account of the late remarkable Religious Impressions among the Students in the College of New Jersey. By Samuel Davies, A. M. The Third Edition. Boston: Printed and sold by Fowle & Draper in Marlborough-Street, 1761. [45]

Duodecimo, 12 leaves, A-B⁶.

Wrappers.
Not in Evans. Not in Sabin.
The Rev. Samuel Davies (1724-1761) was a native of Newcastle, Delaware. In 1759 he succeeded Jonathan Edwards in the Presidency of the College of New Jersey at Princeton.

SENTENTIAE PUERILES; or, Sentences for Children, fitted to the Fundamental Rules of the Latin Syntax. Being A short and easy method To exercise them in Parsing. Philadelphia: William Dunlap, 1761. [46]

Duodecimo, 36 leaves, A-D⁶, a-b⁶, English and Latin on opposite pages.

Original sheep.
Not in Evans. Not in Hildeburn.
This is apparently the only known copy. It is not the work of Leonhart Culmann with a similar title, no. 4 *supra*. The text begins on the verso of the first leaf without any preliminary matter. At the end is an Index (i. e. Vocabulary) on twenty-four pages.

Early American Children's Books

1762

AN ACCOUNT of the Remarkable Conversion of a Little Boy and Girl. Boston: Printed and sold by Fowle and Draper, 1762. [47]

Duodecimo, 12 leaves, A-B⁶, woodcut on the title-page and a woodcut in the text.

Unbound and stitched.

Not in Evans. Probably the only copy known.

A chapbook. The account of the Conversion of a little Girl, a native of Guernsey, pages 15-22, is in verse, and contains the woodcut. The little boy lived in Newington-Butts (London). At the end is *A remarkable Story of a Father's extraordinary Care and Contrivance to reclaim an extravagant Son* (in prose).

THE NEW-ENGLAND PRIMER Improved. For the more easy attaining the true Reading of English. To which is added, The Assembly of Divines, and Mr. Cotton's Catechism. Boston: Printed and sold by S. Kneeland, in Queen-Street, 1762. [48]

16mo, 40 leaves, A-E⁸, woodcut portrait of King George the Third as frontispiece, alphabet and John Rogers woodcuts.

Original boards, covered with flowered paper, leather back.

Heartman 16 (with the imprint of S. Adams in place of S. Kneeland). On the back of the frontispiece is *A Divine Song of Praise for a Child* by Dr. Watts, and on the back of the title two prayers for a child, also by Dr. Watts. In addition to the Shorter Catechism this edition contains *Spiritual Milk for American Babes. Drawn out of the Breasts of both Testaments, for their Souls Nourishment. By John Cotton.* At the end is *A Dialogue between Christ, Youth and the Devil.*

The alphabet couplets in this edition differ from those of the Rogers and Fowle edition of 1749, the change being from the secular to the biblical. A few, though not all, of the couplets which were already of a biblical nature are allowed to stand. The couplet for the letter U in the earlier edition

Uriah's beauteous wife
made David seek his life

was disapproved, and replaced by

Vashti for Pride
Was set aside.

Some of the new verses do not add dignity to the Primer alphabet. The early quatrain for the letter O read:

The Royal Oak
It was the Tree
That sav'd his
Royal Majesty.

The biblical triplet which replaces this reads:

Young Obadias,
David, Josias
All were pious.

THE

New-England

P R I M E R

Improved.

For the more eafy attaining the true
Reading of Englifh.

To which is added,

The Affembly of Divines,

and Mr. COTTON'S

Catechifm.

B O S T O N :

Printed and Sold by S. KNEELAND,
in Queen-ftreet. 1762.

Title-page from "The New-England Primer"

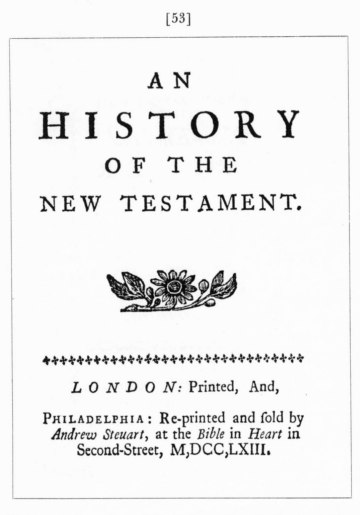

Title-page from Part III of the earliest Bible for children printed in America "The Children's Bible"

Early American Children's Books

THE SHORTER CATECHISM, Composed by the Reverend Assembly of Divines. With the Proofs thereof out of the Scriptures, in Words at length. Which are either some of the formerly quoted Places, or others gathered from their other Writings: All fitted, both for Brevity and Clearness, to this Form of Sound Words. For the Benefit of Christians in general, and of Youth and Children in Understanding in particular; that they may with more Ease acquaint themselves with the Truth according to the Scriptures, and with the Scriptures themselves. Boston: D. and J. Kneeland and Sold by the Booksellers, 1762.   [49]

Duodecimo, 26 leaves, A-D⁶, E².

Wrappers, stitched as issued.
Evans 9306. Eames: *Early New England Catechisms;* p. 73 : *Title from Haven's list. There was a copy in the Brinley collection, No. 5872.*
On the recto of the last leaf are verses with the following explanation: *In order to fill up a vacant Page, as well as further the Instruction of Youth, we have thought proper to add Dr. Watt's* (sic) *Paraphrase on the Repenting Prodigal.*

WHITTENHALL, EDWARD. A Short Introduction to Grammar. For the Use of the College and Academy in Philadelphia. Being a New Edition of Whittenhall's Latin Grammar, with many Alterations, Additions and Amendments From antient and late Grammarians. Philadelphia: Printed by Andrew Steuart, for the College and Academy of Philadelphia, 1762.   [50]

Octavo, 73 leaves, 2 leaves without signature marks, A-R⁴, S³, with a leaf of errata after the 3 pages of catalogue at the end.

Original calf.
Evans 9309. Hildeburn 1852.
Evans and Hildeburn cite the HSP copy only. On the inside of the front cover of the present copy is pasted the engraved advertisement of Samuel Taylor Book-Binder *at the Book & Hand the Corner of Market & Water-Street Philadelphia.*

1763

CATECHISMUS, Oder Anfänglicher Unterricht Christlicher Glaubens-Lehre; Allen Christlichen Glaubens-Schülern, Jung oder Alt, Nöthig und Nützlich sich drin zu üben. Philadelphia: Henrich Miller, 1763.   [51]

Duodecimo, 75 leaves, (-)², A-L⁶, M⁷. M₂ is a large folded table. (The table is really inserted between M and M₂, but it is included in the pagination and M₂ is marked M₃.)

Original calf, stamped borders and corners, upper with A. K. and the date, 1772.
Evans 9512. Hildeburn 1882. Not in Sabin.

Early American Children's Books

The first American edition of the Catechismus of the Schwenkfeldians, the followers of Kaspar Schwenkfeld, a number of whom had fled to Philadelphia about 1734, and had established a small community in the neighborhood of what is now known as Schwenksville.

CATECHISMUS, oder Kurtzer Unterricht Christlicher Lehre: Für die angehende Jugend in der Churfürstlichen Pfaltz und andern Reformirten Orten zu gebrauchen; Samt der Haus-Tafel, mit und ohne Biblischen Sprüch-Büchlein. Alles zur Ehre und Lob Gottes. Heydelberg: gedruck im Jahr 1751. Und nun auf Schesnot-Hill, 1763. [Chestnut-Hill: ? Nicolaus Hasselbach, 1763.] [52]

Duodecimo, 48 leaves, A-H⁶.

Original half calf.
Not in Evans. Not in Hildeburn. Not in Sabin.
Second American edition of the Heidelberg Catechism, the first being printed by Peter Miller at Philadelphia in the previous year. The Catechism was prepared by Z. Ursinus and C. Olevianus under the direction of the Elector Friedrich III, and accepted by a Synod of the Palatinate.

[THE CHILDREN'S BIBLE, or an History of the Holy Scriptures.] London printed: Philadelphia: re-printed and sold by Andrew Steuart, 1763. [53]

16mo, 3 parts in 1, 96 leaves, (should be 112, lacks sig. A). (A)-G¹⁶, woodcut frontispiece to each part (that to Part 1 lacking).

Original sheep, gilt.
Printed in double columns. Each part has a separate title-page, that to Part I is missing; that to Part II reads: *The Principles of the Christian Religion, Adapted to the Minds of Children: With a small Manual of Devotions Fitted for their Use*, and that to Part III: *An History of the New Testament*.
Not in Evans. Not in Hildeburn.
This is the earliest Bible for children printed in America. It was first printed in London in 1759, and an edition was printed in Dublin in 1763, the same year as the present publication. Very few copies of any edition have survived, and this appears to be the only known copy of this American edition, and unknown to bibliographers.
The first title, missing in this copy, reads: *The Children's Bible or History of the Holy Scriptures. In which, the several Passages of the Old and New Testament are laid down in a Method never before attempted; being reduced to the tender Capacities of little Readers, by a lively and striking Abstract, so as, under God, to make those excellent Books take such a firm Hold of their young Minds and Memories, and leave such Impressions there, both of Moral and Religious Vertue, as no Accidents of their future Lives will ever be able to blot out* . . . The preface is signed N. H.

A HYMN-BOOK for the Children belonging to the Brethren's Congregations. Taken chiefly out of the German Little Book. In Three Books. Philadelphia: [Henry Miller] 1763. [54]

Duodecimo, 46 leaves, A-B⁶, C⁴, D-H⁶.

Original half sheep and marbled boards.
English and German. Only two copies known.
Evans 9527. Hildeburn 4649.
At the end is *End of the First Book*, though no more was published.
The preface is the preface of the German Children's Book, and is in the form of a dedication, beginning *My dear children;* the last leaf is cancelled by having a leaf pasted over it.
The first hymn begins:

> Were I requir'd to shew
> My Life's Work hitherto,
> I've the Lamb been loving.
> . . .
>
> Orig'nally by Nature I
> No Angel am of God;
> Yet does like Office on me lie,
> With Aids to make it good.

1765

THE SHORTER CATECHISM, Agreed upon by the Reverend Assembly of Divines at Westminster. Boston: Thomas and John Fleet, 1765. [55]

Duodecimo, 12 leaves, uncut and almost entirely unopened; sewed as issued.

Evans 10206. Eames: *Early New England Catechisms*, p. 72.

VERBUM SEMPITERNUM. The Third Edition with Amendments. Boston: Printed for and sold by N. Proctor, 1765.   [56]

142 leaves, including the last blank, A-R⁸, S⁶. A miniature book measuring 1¾ x 2 inches.

Original calf, gilt.
The second American edition of the famous Thumb Bible of John Taylor, the Water-poet.
The book is dedicated by J. Taylor to William, Duke of Gloucester. Signatures A₁ and L₁ are half titles, the first reading *The Bible*, and the second *The New Testament*. Signature K₂ has the title *Salvator Mundi. The Third Edition with Amendments*, with the imprint.
Evans 10179 believes this to be the first American edition, and says: *An epitome of the Bible in verse, by the Water-poet, reprinted from the London edition of* 1693. *It is commonly called 'The Thumb Bible' from its diminutive size, which is less than two inches square. This is the earliest known American edition, and the copy in the Lenox Collection of the New York Public Library is believed to be unique.*
According to Wilbur Macey Stone in *The Thumb Bible of John Taylor*, the first American edition was published in New York in 1760, a copy of which is in the Harvard Library. Only three other copies of this second edition are known.

1766

THE NEW-ENGLAND PRIMER Improved. For the more easy attaining the true reading of English. To which is added, The Assembly of

Divines, and Mr. Cotton's Catechism. Boston: for Timothy White, 1766. [57]

16mo, 40 leaves, A-E⁸.

Original thin wooden boards and paper, leather back.
Heartman 22 copies the entry from Evans, but does not locate a copy. This edition is page for page the same as that of S. Kneeland, 1762, no. 48, with the exception of the alphabet couplets, and their accompanying woodcuts, which in this edition are the same as those in the edition of Rogers and Fowle, no. 36.

1767

THE ADVENTURES OF URAD; or, the Fair Wanderer. Boston: Mein & Fleeming, 1767. [58]

16mo, 32 leaves, A-D⁸. A₁ with an admonition *To guard the Soft Female Heart from the delusions of the faithless sex*, pasted down inside front cover. Woodcut frontispiece and one other full-page woodcut.

Original boards covered with Dutch flowered paper.
Not in Evans. Not in Sabin.
This is described as *A very interesting tale in which the protection of the Almighty is proved to be the first and chief support of the Female Sex.*
Beneath the imprint: *At which Place may be had, a great variety of Entertaining and Instructive Books for Children.*
The fore-edge of the title is shaved and it is possible that the last figure of the date in the imprint, which is in roman numerals, may have been shaved off, in which case the date would be 1768.

THE FRIAR AND BOY: or, the young Piper's pleasant Pastime. Containing the witty Adventures betwixt the Friar and Boy, in relation to his Step Mother, whom he fairly fitted for her unmerciful cruelty. Boston: Printed, and sold by A. Barclay, 1767. [59]

Duodecimo, 12 leaves, (A)-B⁶, 2 woodcut illustrations, publisher's advertisements on the verso of the first leaf.

Full green morocco, gilt.
Not in Evans.
First American edition. In verse.
This American chapbook appears to be unknown to bibliographers. It is taken from an extremely popular English chapbook first printed without a date in Aldermary Church Yard, London, a famous chapbook printing house.
The two woodcuts in the American version are quite different from those in the English editions.
The first English version of the romance was printed by Wynkyn de Worde without date. Ritson says of it: *From the mention made in v.* 429 *of the city of 'Orlyance,' and the character of the 'Offycial,' it may be conjectured that the poem is of French extraction; and, indeed, it is not at all improbable that the original is extant in some collection of old Fabliaux.*

1768

JOHNSON, SAMUEL. The History of Rasselas, Prince of Abissinia. An Asiatic Tale. The two volumes complete in one. Volume the first [second]. America: Printed for every Purchaser [Philadelphia: Robert Bell] 1768. [60]

Duodecimo, 96 leaves, A-Q⁶, engraved frontispiece.

Half calf.
Evans 10939. Hildeburn 2368.
The first volume ends on H₅, page 94, and is followed by the title to the second volume. *Rasselas* ends on page 188, signature Q₄, and is followed by *The Voyage of Life. By Samuel Johnson, L. L. D. Author of the Rambler, Rasselas, &c.*
The frontispiece is an etching with the title *A Perspective View of Grand Cairo*. Hildeburn suggests that it is the work of some local engraver, probably Dawkins or Claypoole.
This is the first American edition of *Rasselas*, and is extremely rare.
It is included in this collection as it was considered a suitable book for the young at that time, and editions of it will be found in many of the publisher's lists of books suitable for young people. It is to be found in the reading list supplied to Lady Pennington's young daughters in 1792. See no. 163.

THE ROYAL PRIMER: Or, an easy and pleasant Guide to the Art of Reading. Authorized by His Majesty King George II. To be used throughout His Majesty's Dominions. Adorned with Cuts. Boston: Printed and sold By W. M'Alpine, between the Governor's and Dr. Gardinar's, Marlborough-Street, 1768. [61]

Duodecimo, 21 leaves, including leaf of title, A⁷, B⁸, C⁶ (lacks one or two leaves), woodcuts.

Unbound, stitched as issued.
The first Boston edition. Apparently the only copy known.
Not in Evans. See Percival Merritt: *The Royal Primer* in *Bibliographical Essays, A Tribute to Wilberforce Eames*, 1924, where an account of this edition is given.
This edition follows the Newbery Royal Primer much more closely than Chattin did in his Philadelphia edition, 1753, no. 40.
The woodcuts are as in the Newbery edition, and include a set of alphabet cuts not used in the Philadelphia edition.

1769

FOX, GEORGE. Instructions for Right Spelling, and Plain Directions for Reading and Writing True English. With several of other Things, very useful and necessary, both for Young and Old, to read and learn. Newport: S. Southwick, 1769. [62]

Duodecimo, 48 leaves, A-H⁶.

Original sheep over wooden boards.
Evans 11258 locates only one copy. Rhode Island Imprints, page 24.
For the first edition see no. 5.

THE NEW-ENGLAND PRIMER Enlarged. For the more easy attaining the true Reading of English. To which is added, The Assembly's Catechism. Philadelphia: D. Hall and W. Sellers, 1769.   [63]

16mo, 39 leaves, A-E⁸ (lacks A₈). Woodcut portrait of George III on verso of half title, full-page royal arms on verso of last leaf, alphabet and John Rogers woodcuts.

Original binding (defective).
Heartman 31 cites this copy only, which appears to be the only one known.
This edition ends with the Shorter Catechism, and is without the Dialogue. The portrait of George III differs from that in the Boston editions. The alphabet couplets are the same as those in the Boston editions of 1749 and 1762, nos. 36 and 48. The alphabets at the beginning include a set in black letter type.
At the end is written *Eden Merseilles his book November* 1771.

1770

THE CHILDREN in the Woods. Being A true Relation of the inhuman Murder of two Children of a deceased Gentleman in *Norfolk*, whom he left to the Care of his Brother; but this wicked Uncle, in order to get the Childrens Estate, contrived to have them destroyed by two Ruffians, whom he had hired for that Purpose; with an Account of the heavy Judgments of God which befel him for this inhuman Deed, and the untimely End of the two bloody Ruffians. To which is added, A Word of Advice to Executors, &c. [Boston: Printed by Thomas and John Fleet] Sold at the Heart & Crown in Cornhill, n. d. [c. 1770]   [64]

Broadside, folio, 1 leaf, woodcut illustration, in verse, printed in three columns.

Not in Evans. This is apparently the only copy extant of this broadside.
Thomas and John Fleet printed at the Heart & Crown from 1731 to 1776.
This is the famous ballad beginning *Now pondĕr well you parents dear*. It is of English origin, and was first licensed at Stationers' Hall on October 15, 1595, though the earliest printed edition now known is that of 1670, entitled *The Cruel Uncle*. It has been supposed by some that there may be some connection with the murder of the Princes in the Tower.
The woodcut at the head of this edition represents the strife between the *Ruffians rude*. For another broadside edition see no. 101.

DILWORTH, THOMAS. A New Guide to the English Tongue: In Five Parts ... The Whole, being recommended by several Clergymen and eminent Schoolmasters, as the most useful Performance for the Instruc-

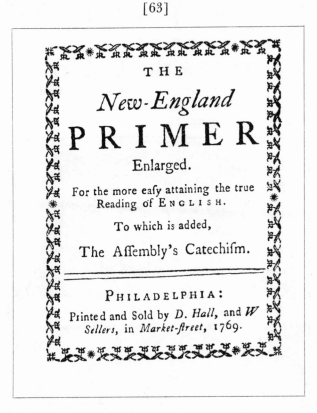

THE

New-England

PRIMER

Enlarged.

For the more eafy attaining the true
Reading of ENGLISH.

To which is added,

The Affembly's Catechifm.

PHILADELPHIA:

Printed and Sold by *D. Hall*, and *W*
Sellers, in *Market-ftreet*, 1769.

Title-page from "The New-England Primer"

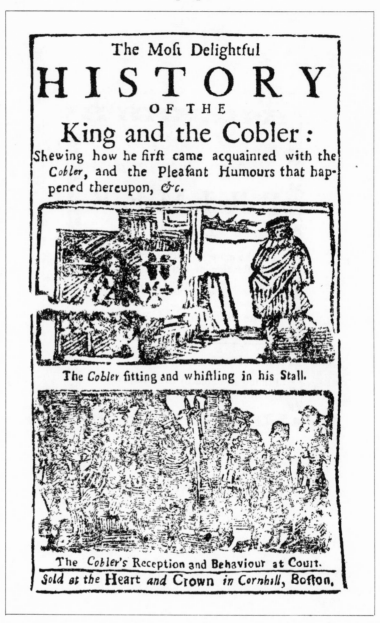

The Moſt Delightful

HISTORY

OF THE

King and the Cobler :

Shewing how he firſt came acquainted with the
Cobler, and the Pleaſant Humours that happened thereupon, *&c.*

The *Cobler* ſitting and whiſtling in his Stall.

The *Cobler's* Reception and Behaviour at Court.

Sold at the Heart and Crown in *Cornhill*, Boſton.

Title-page from "History of the King and the Cobler"

tion of Youth, is designed for the Use of Schools in Great Britain, Ireland, and America. Philadelphia: Thomas & William Bradford, n. d. [c. 1770]

Duodecimo, 80 leaves, (-)², A⁶, B-G¹². [65]

Original half binding of boards and leather with paper label on the back, uncut and partly unopened.

Evans 11634. Hildeburn 2520.

Dilworth's Guide was the most popular speller of the eighteenth century. The two leaves before the title contain a woodcut portrait of the author, and the alphabet with woodcut illustrations. The work consists of alphabets, syllabaries, a grammar, sentences, and a number of *Select Fables*, each with a large woodcut at the head. Part V, on two leaves at the end, contains Forms of Prayer.

THE MOST DELIGHTFUL HISTORY of the King and the Cobler: Shewing how he first came acquainted with the Cobler, and the Pleasant Humours that happened thereupon, &c. Boston: [Printed by Thomas and John Fleet] sold at the Heart and Crown in Cornhill, n. d. [c. 1770] [66]

Octavo, 8 leaves, A-B⁴, two curious woodcuts on the title-page, and one on the last page.

Unbound.

Not in Evans.

Probably the only known copy of this chapbook, containing a story of Henry VIII, King of England, and his incognito visit to one of his more lowly subjects.

The story was very popular in England, and numerous chapbook editions were printed. The earliest known printed version appeared in 1680 with the title: *Cobler turned Courtier, being a Pleasant Humour between K. Henry 8th and a Cobler.*

1771

JANEWAY, JAMES. A Token for Children, being An Exact Account of the Conversion, Holy and Exemplary Lives and Joyful Deaths of several Young Children. By James Janeway, Minister of the Gospel. To which is added, A Token for the Children of New-England, or, Some Examples of Children, in whom the Fear of God was remarkably Budding before they died; in several Parts of New-England. Preserved and Published for the Encouragement of Piety in other Children. With New Additions. Boston: Z. Fowle, 1771. [67]

Duodecimo, 78 leaves, A-N⁶, uncut and unopened.

Half brown morocco, gilt.

Evans 12085. Sabin 35754.

This edition contains the address to Parents and Schoolmasters, but is without the Directions to Children to be found in the edition of 1749, no. 35. The *Token for the Children of New England* by Cotton Mather, begins on signature I₆, page 107.

Early American Children's Books

LATHROP, JOHN. The Importance of Early Piety: Illustrated in a Discourse, Preached at the Desire of a Religious Society of Young Men, in Medford, New-England, March 20th, 1771. By John Lathrop, M. A. Pastor of the second Church in Boston. Published at the Request and Expence of those who heard it. Boston: Printed by Isaiah Thomas, 1771. [68]

Duodecimo, 12 leaves including a half title, A-C⁴.

Half green morocco.
Evans 12093.
First edition.
John Lathrop (1740-1816) was a native of England and a descendant of the Rev. John Lathrop, first minister of Scituate and Barnstable, Mass.

THE NEW-ENGLAND PRIMER Enlarged: For the more easy attaining the true Reading of English. To which is added, several Chapters and Sentences of the Holy Scriptures. Also Mr. Roger's *(sic.)* Verses, &c. Germantown: Printed and sold by Christopher Sower, 1771. [69]

16mo, 40 leaves, A-E⁸, frontispiece portrait of George III, ornamental border around title, alphabet and John Rogers woodcuts.

Original half binding.
This appears to be the only known copy of this edition.
Not in Heartman. Not in Hildeburn.
J. P. Wickersham, in his *History of Education in Pennsylvania* mentions this edition in a passage referred to by both Hildeburn and Heartman who are, however, unable to cite a copy.
This edition differs considerably from the earlier editions. It is without the catechism, and contains the Sermon on the Mount, and chapters from the Psalms and Proverbs. The alphabet couplets are as in the Boston edition, no. 36.
The lettering on the frontispiece referring to King George III has been crossed out in ink, and a capital W (for Washington) substituted for *The Third* after the word *George*.

THE PRODIGAL DAUGHTER; Or a strange and wonderful relation, shewing, how a Gentleman of a vast Estate in Bristol, had a proud and disobedient Daughter, who because her parents would not support her in all her extravagance, bargained with the Devil to poison them. How an Angel informed her parents of her design. How she lay in a trance four days; and when she was put in the grave, she came to life again, &c. &c. Boston: Printed and sold at I. Thomas's Printing-Office near the Mill Bridge [1771]. [70]

Octavo, 8 leaves, in verse, A-B⁴, 6 woodcuts, including one repeat, the one on title signed I.T. (Isaiah Thomas).

Half red morocco, lower edges uncut.

THE
PRODIGAL DAUGHTER;

Or a ſtrange and wonderful relation, ſhewing, how a
Gentleman of a vaſt Eſtate in BRISTOL, had a proud
and diſobedient Daughter, who becauſe her parents
would not ſupport her in all her extravagance, bargained
with the Devil to poiſon them. How an Angel informed her parents of her deſign. How ſhe lay in a trance
four days ; and when ſhe was put in the grave, ſhe
came to life again, &c. &c.

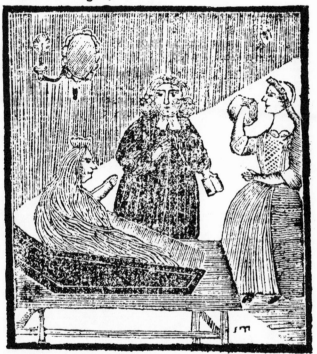

BOSTON, printed and ſold at I. THOMAS's Printing-Office near the MILL BRIDGE.

Title-page from "The Prodigal Daughter"

THE

WONDERFUL LIFE.

AND

SURPRIZING ADVENTURES

OF THE RENOWNED HERO,

ROBINSON CRUSOE:

Who lived TWENTY-EIGHT YEARS

ON AN

UNINHABITED ISLAND,

Which he afterwards colonifed.

N E W - Y O R K :

Printed by H U G H G A I N E, at his Book-Store in
Hanover-Square, where may be had a great Variety
of Little Books for *Young Mafters* and *Miffes*.
M,DCC,LXXIV.

Title-page from "Robinson Crusoe"

Early American Children's Books

Evans 12532 has an entry, under date 1772, which possibly refers to this book, but he is unable to quote the title-page or locate a copy. Sabin 65952 has only an undated Greenfield edition.

This chapbook is the earliest complete copy recorded of any American edition of this extraordinary work, and appears to be the only copy known. A fragment of an earlier edition, printed in Boston by B. Mecom about 1760, exists in the Library of the American Antiquarian Society at Worcester. The present edition was printed by Isaiah Thomas in Boston before he became famous as the publisher of children's books in Worcester, and the woodcuts are by him.

At the end is *The Substance of a Sermon preached on the occasion.*

No edition of this work is mentioned in Ashton's *Chapbooks of the Eighteenth Century.*

TOM THUMB'S PLAY-BOOK; To teach Children their Letters as soon as they can speak. Being A New and pleasant Method to allure Little Ones in the first Principles of learning. Boston: Kneeland and Adams, 1771.

Sm. 16 mo, 16 leaves, numerous woodcut ornaments. [71]

Wall paper wrappers.

Not in Evans.

This appears to be the only known copy of this edition of this delightful primer.

The recto of the first leaf is blank, the verso having alphabets. The recto of the second leaf has the title, and on the verso begins the famous rhyme *A Apple Pye.* On page 6 begins the equally famous rhyme, *A was an Archer who shot at a Frog,* each page containing the rhymes for two letters which are within ornaments at the head, otherwise the series is unillustrated; following this is a syllabary, a scripture catechism, and several prayers, including graces to be used before and after meals.

The origin of *A Apple Pye* is lost in antiquity. *A was an Archer* first appeared in Thomas White's *Little Book for Little Children* (12th edition 1702) and has been described as the sole redeeming feature of that otherwise forgotten work.

The book is a toy book known as the *snuff-box* or *waistcoat pocket size,* and measures 3 by 2 inches.

An edition of *Tom Thumb's Play-Book,* issued by A. Barclay in Boston, 1761, was the *Prentice's Token* (specimen of work as a printer's apprentice) of Isaiah Thomas, a significant fact in the light of his subsequent interest in the production of books for children.

TOM THUMB'S PLAY-BOOK, To teach Children their Letters as soon as they can speak. Being A New and pleasant Method to allure Little Ones in the first Principles of Learning. Boston: for J. Boyle, 1771. [72]

16 mo, 16 leaves, type ornamental borders.

Old wall paper covers.

Evans 12250.

Measures 3 by 1⅞ inches. A similar production to the previous number, arranged slightly differently. The title is on the recto of the first leaf, the verso being blank. An alphabet of large roman capitals is on the last page.

Early American Children's Books

FRENEAU, PHILIP, and Brackenridge, Hugh Henry. A Poem, on the Rising Glory of America; being an Exercise Delivered at the Public Commencement at Nassau-Hall, September 25, 1771. Philadelphia: Joseph Crukshank, for R. Aitken, 1772. [73]

Octavo, 14 leaves, A-C⁴, D², Aitken's advertisement on last page.

Unbound.

Evans 12398. Hildeburn 2776. Sabin 25904.

The first edition.

In the edition of Freneau's poems printed at his own press and under his supervision at Monmouth in 1809, this poem is given a prominent place without any reference being made to Brackenridge's share in it. Brackenridge is usually considered to be the joint author, and the poem was recited by him at his and Freneau's graduation from the College of New Jersey.

[GOLDSMITH, OLIVER.] The Vicar of Wakefield: A Tale. Supposed to be written by Himself. Vol. I [II]. Philadelphia: Printed for William Mentz, and sold by most of the Booksellers in America, 1772. [74]

Duodecimo, 90 leaves, (A)-P⁶.

Half green morocco.

Evans 12405. Hildeburn 2780.

This is the first American edition of this famous book, and is an exact reprint of the edition printed in Salisbury in 1766.

This book was considered extremely suitable for the young at the time it was written.

In the *Young Lady's Parental Monitor* (no. 163), Lady Pennington severely condemns all novel reading, but makes one exception in favour of this work: *In justice however to a late ingenious author, this Letter must not be reprinted, without my acknowledging that, since the last edition was published, I have accidentally met with one exception to my general rule, namely,* The Vicar of Wakefield. *That novel is equally entertaining and instructive without being liable to any of the objections that occasioned the above restriction.*

THE SCHOOL OF GOOD MANNERS. Composed for the Help of Parents in Teaching their Children how to carry it in their Places during their Minority. Boston: Re-Printed and Sold by T. & J. Fleet, 1772. [75]

Sm. octavo, 40 leaves, A-E⁸.

Original wall paper covers.

Evans 12553 gives no collation, and does not locate a copy.

This edition varies slightly from the New London edition of 1754. The preface is the same as in that edition, and contains the name of Eleazer Moodey, but is unsigned. *The Alphabet of Useful Copies* is quite different. In the New London edition it begins, *At Table guard thy Tongue, a civil Guest*; in this edition the first line is, *Attend the Advice of the Old and the Wise.* This is followed by prayers, and *The Child's Complaint* from Dr. Watts's *Divine*

Early American Children's Books

Songs, not included in the earlier edition. *Cyprian's Twelve Absurdities*, which occupies the last page of the former edition, in which it is mentioned on the title-page, is omitted from this edition.

1774

A COMPENDIOUS HISTORY of the World, from the Creation to the Dissolution of the Roman Republic. Compiled for the use of young Gentlemen and Ladies. Embellished with Variety of Copperplates. Vol. II. Philadelphia: Printed and sold by R. Aitken, 1774. [76]

16mo, 88 leaves, (A)-L⁸, 6 plates, printed in sanguine, including the frontispiece which is pasted down to the front cover.

Original half binding.
Evans 13205. Hildeburn 2996.
An edition was published by John Newbery in 1763.

[DEFOE, DANIEL.] The Wonderful Life, and surprizing adventures of the renowned hero, Robinson Crusoe: Who lived Twenty-eight Years on an Uninhabited Island, Which he afterwards colonised. New York: Hugh Gaine, 1774. [77]

16mo, 72 leaves, including the last blank, A-I⁸, the first and last pasted down to the cover, woodcut frontispiece, full-page woodcuts in the text.

Original fancy wrappers.
Ford, *The Journals of Hugh Gaine, Printer*, page 138. Evans 14004.
This abridgement is the first American edition of this famous romance. In format and binding it resembles the publications for children of John Newbery, the famous London publisher of children's books, and it is possible that it was copied from a Newbery edition now lost. The text is the same as that of the edition printed in London in 1789 and *sold by F. Power and Co. (Grandson of the late Mr. John Newbery)*. The woodcut illustrations in these two editions show very slight variations, and are obviously copied from the same originals. In the list of Newbery's publications in the Appendix of Charles Welsh's *A Bookseller of the last Century* the only edition of *Robinson Crusoe* is quoted as *From Carnan's List*, 1787.
This is the only known copy of this edition.
In the Bibliography of the issues of Gaine's press in his *The Journals of Hugh Gaine, Printer*, Ford tentatively places the entry under the date 1775, having quoted the title from the advertisement at the end of Gaine's edition of the *Young Clerks' Vade Mecum* (1776) and in *The Mercury* no. 1377.
Hugh Gaine, who resembled John Newbery in several ways, including the fact that he sold patent medicines as well as printed books, was one of the pioneer printers of children's books in Colonial America, some of his attractive toy books antedating the famous Worcester editions of Isaiah Thomas. At the end of the present volume are four pages of advertisement, announcing as just published *The History of Little Goody Two-Shoes; The New Year's Gift; Grammatical Institutes;* and *A Pretty Play-Thing for Children of all Denominations*.

Early American Children's Books

The imprint on the title is also used as a means of advertising: *Printed by Hugh Gaine, at his Book Store in Hanover Square, where may be had a great Variety of Little Books for* Young Masters *and* Misses.

THE HAPPY CHILD. Or, A remarkable and surprizing Relation of a Little Girl, Who dwelt at Barnart. Boston: Sold at the Heart & Crown in Cornhill, n. d. [Thomas and John Fleet, 1774.] [78]

32 mo, 4 leaves, in verse, small woodcut on the first page.

Original wrappers composed of a portion of a newspaper, in which one of the advertisements is dated Nov. 26, 1774.

Not in Evans. Apparently the only known copy of this edition of an English juvenile chapbook.

There is no title-page, the first page having a caption title; the imprint is at the end.

This is a rhymed version of an old story, the life and death of a pious child. The opening line *You Parents that have Children Dear* is also the first line of the last verse of the celebrated Doleful Ditty in *Mother Goose's Melodies*. The last four lines contain the moral:

> You children who live piously
> Like her, you'll also like her die;
> God will you bless while here on Earth,
> And make you happy after Death.

Amongst the advertisements on the newspaper cover is one of a public auction to be held by Benjamin Church.

THE HISTORY OF THE HOLY JESUS. Containing A brief and plain Account of his Birth, Life, Death, Resurrection and Ascension into Heaven; and his coming again at the great and last Day of Judgment. Being a pleasant and profitable Companion for Children; composed on Purpose for their Use. By a Lover of their precious Souls. The Twenty-Fifth Edition. Boston: John Boyle, 1774. [79]

16 mo, 24 leaves, including the last blank, A-C⁸, woodcut portrait frontispiece of the author, with the initials I. T. on the block, woodcuts in this text.

Wrappers.

Not in Evans. Bates, page 9.

There are nineteen woodcut illustrations in this edition, of which five (including one repeat) are signed I. T. A number of them are re-engraved from the same blocks as were used in the edition of 1749.

The portrait frontispiece of *The Author* is signed, and is so lettered, the figure faces to the left. The back of the title is blank, the large cut of Adam and Eve on that page in the former edition being reduced to a small cut at the head of the Introduction. The cut of *The Wise Men* is replaced by *The Star*, showing three stars. The cut of *Herod slaying the Innocent Children* in the former edition is omitted, and is replaced by *Herod slaying the Innocent*, the singular number being necessary as the cut is that for Abraham sacrificing Isaac in a later part of the book. The picture of *Christ teaching the Multitude* is so lettered, and is similar to the one in

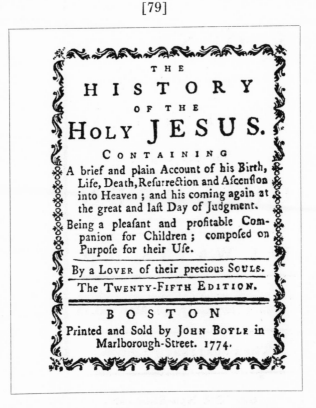

THE
HISTORY
OF THE
HOLY JESUS.

CONTAINING

A brief and plain Account of his Birth, Life, Death, Resurrection and Ascension into Heaven ; and his coming again at the great and last Day of Judgment.

Being a pleasant and profitable Companion for Children ; composed on Purpose for their Use.

By a LOVER of their precious SOULS.

The TWENTY-FIFTH EDITION.

BOSTON

Printed and Sold by JOHN BOYLE in Marlborough-Street. 1774.

Title-page from "The History of the Holy Jesus"

DIVINE SONGS,

ATTEMPTED

In Easy LANGUAGE,

For the Use of

CHILDREN.

By I. WATTS, D.D.

Out of the mouths of babes and suckling thou hast perfected praise. **Mat. xxi.** 16

The FOURTEENTH Edition.

BOSTON, New-England .
Printed and Sold at Greenleaf's
Printing-Office, Hanover-
Street, 1774.

Title-page from "Divine Songs"

the 1749 edition, but re-engraved, and the position of the men and women of the multitude reversed.

This edition has *The Child's Body of Divinity* at the end, the two hymns in the 1749 edition are replaced by *Upon the Day of Judgment*, and *St. Paul's Shipwreck*, the latter with a cut, signed.

WATTS, ISAAC. Divine Songs, attempted In Easy Language, For the Use of Children. The Fourteenth Edition. Boston, New-England: Green-leaf's Printing-Office, 1774. [80]

Duodecimo 22 leaves, A-E⁴, F², uncut.

Wrappers.
Not in Evans. Not in Stone: *The Divine and Moral Songs of Isaac Watts.*

The Divine Songs occupy pages 5 to 34. On page 35 begins A Slight Specimen of Moral Songs, and is followed on page 38 by Prayers. The Preface at the beginning is addressed To all who are Concerned in the Education of Children, and contains the author's reasons for writing in verse, which *was at first design'd for the service of God, tho' it hath been wretchedly abused since,* rather than in prose.

Watts's *Divine Songs* was the first hymn book composed for children and was one of the most popular books of the period. It was originally printed in England in 1715, and ran through a hundred editions before the middle of the century. It was equally popular in America, and was frequently reprinted.

The present copy seems to be the only one extant of this edition. The author, the son of a nonconformist schoolmaster, was born in 1674 and died in 1748.

1775

GREGORY, JOHN. A Father's Legacy to his Daughters. By the late Dr. Gregory, of Edinburgh. New-York: Shober and Loudon, for Samuel Loudon, 1775. [81]

Duodecimo, 23 leaves, A-E⁴, F³.

Unbound, uncut, original stitching, as issued.
Not in Evans.
This edition has the editor's preface.

The author of this popular work was an eminent physician, and professor of medicine at Edinburgh University. He was born in Aberdeen in 1724, and died in 1773.

POUPARD, JAMES. [Metamorphosis, The Stage of Life.] [Philadelphia: 1775.] [82]

4 folding plates, three of which are signed by J. Poupard, 21 verses of text.

Marbled wrappers.
Not in Evans. Not in Hildeburn. Not in Stauffer.

Each leaf is extended at the top and bottom, the extensions folding on to the leaf as flaps, and, meeting in the middle, form an additional leaf completely covering the original one. By folding each flap separately over half the original leaf, two new pictures can be thus formed, so that in all each leaf has four combinations. This arrangement is known as a *Metamorphosis*.

Verses 1, 4, 7 and 10 of the text, each within an ornamental frame, are so printed that they form the headpieces to the four folded plates of the Metamorphosis. The remaining verses, with the exception of the last one, which occupies the last page, are printed on the inner sides of the flaps, where they do not interfere with the illustrations. The verses give instructions as to how to proceed with the foldings:

> Adam came first upon the Stage
> And Eve from out his side
> Who was given to him in Marriage
> Turn up and see his Bride.

> Here Eve in shape you may behold,
> One body sheweth Twain;
> Once more do but the leaf downfold,
> And it's as strange again.

The ornamental design composing the head- and tailpieces of the inner plates consists of the letters of the alphabet, numerals, etc. arranged in imitation of musical signs on series of eight parallel lines resembling staves.

This edition has no title. The edition of 1811 in this collection (no. 448) has the title: *Metamorphosis; or, a Transformation of Pictures, with Poetical Explanations, for the Amusement of Young Persons.*

James Poupard, the engraver, is supposed to have come to America from the Island of Martinique, where he is said to have been an actor. In his advertisement in the *Pennsylvania Gazette*, Philadelphia, December 9, 1772, he describes himself as *Engraver, Jeweller and Goldsmith. From London.* The earliest engraving by him of which we have any note is mentioned in the *Gazette* of June 29, 1774. In 1788 and 1789 he was engraving diagrams for the *Transactions of the American Philosophical Society*, and his name constantly appears as an engraver in the Philadelphia directories from 1793 to 1807. He eventually moved to New York, and is known to have been engraving for publishers in that city in 1814.

1776

ASTLEY, PHILIP. The Modern Riding-Master: or, A Key to the Knowledge of the Horse, and Horsemanship; with several Necessary Rules for Young Horsemen. By Philip Astley, Riding-Master, Late of His Majesty's Royal Light Dragoons. Adorned with various Engravings. Philadelphia: Printed and sold by Robert Aitken, 1776. [83]

Duodecimo, 20 leaves, A-C⁶, D², numerous illustrations.

Crushed red morocco, original wrappers bound in.
Evans 14653. Hildeburn 3328.
Dedicated *To the King's most Excellent Majesty.*
The author, Philip Astley, led a most colorful life, as a cabinetmaker, equestrian performer, theatrical manager and soldier, and was the best horse tamer of his time. He was born at Newcastle-under-Lyne in 1742, and died in Paris in 1814. This book is not mentioned in the account of Astley in the *Dictionary of National Biography*.

The MODERN

RIDING - MASTER:

OR, A

Key to the Knowledge of the Horfe,

AND

HORSEMANSHIP;

WITH SEVERAL

Neceffary RULES for YOUNG HORSEMEN.

By *PHILIP ASTLEY*,

RIDING - MASTER,

Late of His MAJESTY's Royal Light Dragoons.

ADORNED WITH VARIOUS ENGRAVINGS.

PHILADELPHIA:
Printed and fold by ROBERT AITKEN, Printer
and Bookfeller in Front-Street.
MDCCLXXVI.
[Price EIGHTEEN PENCE.]

Title-page from "The Modern Riding-Master"

A VALEDICTORY

ADDRESS

TO THE

YOUNG GENTLEMEN,

WHO COMMENCED

BACHELORS OF ARTS,

AT YALE-COLLEGE,

JULY 25th. 1776.

NEW-HAVEN;

Printed by THOMAS and SAMUEL GREEN.

Title-page from "A Valedictory Address"

Early American Children's Books

[DWIGHT, TIMOTHY.] A valedictory Address to the Young Gentlemen, who commenced Bachelors of Arts, at Yale-College, July 25th, 1776. New-Haven: Thomas and Samuel Green [1776].   [84]

Octavo, 11 leaves, A-B⁴, C³.

Half red morocco.
Evans 14747. Sabin 21562. Trumbull 628.
On the title-page is written *By Timothy Dwight Tutor.* The signature *H. P. Dering*, 1785, occurs in several places.
In a note at the beginning the author explains how it is that there are *scarce any allusions to those great and important events, which have rendered the present year so distinguished an Æra in the history of mankind.*
Timothy Dwight (1752-1817) was a native of Northampton, Massachusetts. He entered Yale College at the age of thirteen, and on his graduation in 1769 became a tutor of his college. This valedictory address was probably written on his resignation from that post.

ZEISBERGER, DAVID. Essay of a Delaware-Indian and English Spelling-Book, for the Use of the Schools of the Christian Indians on Muskingum River. By David Zeisberger, Missionary among the Western Indians. Philadelphia: Henry Miller, 1776.   [85]

Duodecimo, 58 leaves, 1 leaf without signature (half title), A-N⁴, O⁵.

Old half calf.
Evans 15228. Hildeburn 3499. Pilling, page 544.
First edition.
David Zeisberger was born in Moravia, Germany, in 1721, emigrated to Georgia in 1738, and, removing to Pennsylvania, was one of the founders of the Moravian settlements of Bethlehem and Nazareth. He subsequently went to Ohio, and was a Moravian preacher among the Indians from 1746 until his death in 1808. The original manuscript of the present work is preserved in the Archives of the Moravian Church in Bethlehem, Pennsylvania.

1779

BENEZET, ANTHONY. The Pennsylvania Spelling-Book, or Youth's friendly Instructor and Monitor: On an easy Plan, for exciting the Attention, and facilitating the Instruction of Children and others, in Spelling and Reading; and acquainting them with the essential Parts of Orthography, Pointing, &c. As also, training their Minds to early Sentiments of Piety and Virtue. More particularly calculated for the use of Parents, Guardians and others, remote from Schools; in the private Tuition of their Children, and illiterate Domesticks, &c. The Second edition, Improved and enlarged. Compiled by Anthony Benezet. Philadelphia: Printed by Joseph Crukshank, 1779.   [86]

Duodecimo, 84 leaves, A-O⁶.

Original half sheep.

Evans 16204. Hildeburn 3855. Each locate only one copy, that in the Pennsylvania Historical Society.

Contains the alphabets in hornbook form, a syllabary, a reading-easy, and other matter.

The passages for reading include extracts from the Bible; hymns from Dr. Watts; Select Reflections and Maxims by William Penn; Wise Precepts from *The Oeconomy of Human Life;* an account of the Plague, etc. There is also a Useful Instruction by way of Question and Answer, a portion of which is used to express the author's views on the harmfulness of drinking *spirituous liquors.*

Anthony Benezet (1713-1784) was a native of St. Quentin, France. His father became a Protestant refugee and fled to London where he joined the Society of Friends. In 1731 the family emigrated to America and settled in Philadelphia. In 1742 Anthony became English master in the Friends' School founded by William Penn, and in 1755 he established a school of his own *for the instruction of females.* He also interested himself in the negro slaves of America, and established an evening school for them in Philadelphia.

FRANKLIN, BENJAMIN. [The Story of the Whistle.] Passy [privately printed by Benjamin Franklin] 1779. [87]

Octavo, 4 leaves without signatures, French and English on opposite pages, the French text in italic letter, the English text in roman.

This is the only non-American imprint included in this catalogue. It was one of the few pieces composed and printed by Benjamin Franklin on the private printing press set up by him in his house at Passy during his residence there as minister to France, a ministry which began in December 1776, when Franklin was in his seventy-first year. Like all the Passy imprints, this *bagatelle* is excessively rare and only one other copy is known. The original manuscript in Franklin's own handwriting, which is also in this collection, was contained in a letter from him to Madame Brillon.

The Story of the Whistle appears in the edition of Franklin's works published in London in 1793, where it is headed *The Whistle: A True Story. Written to his Nephew.*

For an account of this interesting pamphlet see Livingston: *Franklin and his Press at Passy.*

THE HISTORY OF THE HOLY JESUS. Containing a brief and plain Account of his Birth, Life, Death, Resurrection and Ascension into Heaven; and his coming again at the great and last Day of Judgment. Being a pleasant and profitable Companion for children; composed on Purpose for their Use. By a Lover of their precious Souls. The Twenty-Sixth Edition. Boston: for John Boyle, 1779. [88]

16 mo, 23 leaves, A-B⁸, C⁷.

Wrappers.

Not in Evans. Bates page 10.

Woodcut, *The Man of Sin*, on recto of the first leaf, with the portrait, *The Author*, on verso; on the verso of the title, a woodcut *The Angel Gabriel;* otherwise this edition is a reprint of Boyle's edition of 1774, no. 79. The cut of the Angel Gabriel was later used by Isaiah Thomas at Worcester (see no. 103).

1780

MUCKARSIE, JOHN. The Children's Catechism: or, an Help to the more easy Understanding of the Doctrine Taught in our Confession of Faith, and Catechisms, Larger and Shorter. Humbly offered for instructing the Young and Ignorant. Philadelphia: R. Aitken, 1780. [89]

Duodecimo, 12 leaves, A-B⁶, double columns.

Unbound.
Not in Evans.
John Muckarsie is described on the title as *Minister of the Gospel at Kinkell.*
At the end is an appendix containing Advices to Parents and Children.
A Presbyterian Catechism for the use of the Scotch Presbyterians.

THE NEW-ENGLAND PRIMER. For the more easy attaining the true Reading of English. Philadelphia: Printed by R. Aitken, 1780. [90]

16mo, 24 leaves, A⁴, B-C⁸, D⁴ woodcuts (alphabet and John Rogers).

Original half binding, the boards covered with a map of Gloucester County.
Not listed by Heartman.
This is apparently the only copy known.
In addition to the usual alphabets, syllabaries and the Shorter Catechism, this edition has the Exhortation of John Rogers to his Children, and some verses entitled Praise to God for learning to read. It is without the Verses for Little Children, the Hymns of Dr. Watts, and other supplementary material to be found in many of the editions of the New England Primer. The alphabet couplets are the same as in the edition of Rogers and Fowle, 1749, no. 36, with the exception of the couplet for the letter K.
In the editions before the Declaration of Independence this couplet reads:

Our King the good
No man of Blood.

In the present edition the statement is to a certain extent generalized:

The king should be good
No man of blood.

In later editions the generalization is made absolute by the use of the plural number. The use of the singular in this case may be intended as a personal reproach to King George III.

TOM THUMB'S FOLIO, For Little Giants. To which is prefixed, An Abstract of the Life of Mr. Thumb. And an Historical Account of The wonderful Deeds he performed. Together with Some Anecdotes respecting Grumbo, the great Giant. Boston: Sold at the Bible and Heart [by T. & J. Fleet, c. 1780]. [91]

Early American Children's Books

16mo, 16 leaves, A-B⁸, woodcut vignette on title and numeₚous woodcuts in text.

Original marbled wrappers.

Not in Evans.

This appears to be the first American edition of this famous children's classic, and its publication places the printers, Thomas and John Fleet, amongst the pioneers in the production of purely amusing books for children. It is copied from the English edition printed for Newbery and Carnan in 1768; the illustrations are after Newbery originals.

The story of Tom Thumb is one of the national tales of England, and as Sir Walter Scott says *Thomas Thumb landed in England from the very same keels and warships which conveyed Hengist and Horsa, and Ebba the Saxon.*

1782

THE HOLY BIBLE Abridged: or, the History of the Old and New Testament illustrated With Notes, and adorned with Cuts. For the Use of Children. Boston: Robert Hodge for Nathaniel Coverly [1782].   [92]

54 leaves, A-C¹⁸; numerous half-page woodcut illustrations.

Original half leather over wooden boards.

Evans 17474. Sabin 5167.

The leaf of dedication reads: *To the Parents, Guardians, and Governesses, of America, this History of the Old and New Testament, is humbly inscribed, By their most obedient Humble Servant, The Editor.*

The author states in his preface that his design is *to give children such a taste of the writings of the holy penmen, as may engage them earnestly and seriously in the study of the Sacred Books,* and he also explains that *to render this little Book the more pleasing to children, it is embellished with a great number of cuts.*

This work was on John Newbery's list, 1758, though no copy of that edition seems to be known. Editions were also issued by T. Carnan in 1782 and 1786.

This is the first American edition of this book, and is extremely rare. O'Callaghan, p. 31, cites two copies only, the Brinley and Livermore. He places the item under the date 1782. The printer, Robert Hodge, printed in Boston from about 1778 to 1782.

This edition is apparently copied directly from the English edition. The cuts are numerous, and somewhat unsophisticated, that of Solomon's Temple is the same as the one used in the Royal Primer.

On the last leaf is written: *Abigail Wilson Her Book 1734. Price One Shilling.*

THE NEW-ENGLAND PRIMER. Philadelphia: Charles Cist, 1782.   [93]

Duodecimo, 40 leaves, (-), A-F⁴,⁸, woodcut vignette and ornamental border on title, woodcuts in the text (alphabet and John Rogers).

Original grey covers, old leather back, some uncut edges.

Heartman 71 with no collation, and the note: *Offered to the compiler, no details procurable.*

This edition has no frontispiece. The alphabet couplets are the same as those in the edition of Rogers and Fowle, 1749, with the exception of that for the letter K, which here reads:

> Kings should be good
> Not men of Blood.

Dr. Watts's Cradle Hymn is omitted from this edition. On the last page is a rhymed alphabet beginning:

A was an Admiral over the Main
B was a Bomb, by which Thousands were slain.

1783

A PRESENT TO CHILDREN. Consisting of several new Divine Hymns and Moral Songs. New-London: T. Green [not after 1783]. [94]

Octavo, 8 leaves without signatures, type ornaments on title, and in text.

Old brown paper wrappers.
Not in Evans. Not in Trumbull.
The dedication to children begins: *Children. You must die in a short Time. You have Souls in you that must go to a Heaven of Joy, or a burning Hell when you die.*
The following verses include amongst others An Hymn for the Gift of Food; A Morning Hymn; An Evening Hymn; and A Song for little Miss, in which she expresses shame at her liking for dolls and resolves that

No more shall Baubles be my Choice,
Nor Play, nor Idleness.

On the title is the signature of Eber Chapman dated 1783.

SPRING, SAMUEL. Three Sermons to Little Children; on the Nature and Beauty of the Dutiful Temper. (Published by Desire.) Newbury-port: John Mycall, 1783. [95]

Duodecimo, 42 leaves, A-G⁶, partly uncut.

Original sheep.
Not in Evans, who has a Boston edition of the same year without locating a copy.
On the back of the title: *The Author's Love waits on the Little Children of his Charge, in the following Discourses, which contain an enlargement of the Thoughts lately delivered to them from the Pulpit; and hopes they will be acceptable and useful to his young Readers. January* 1, 1783.
Samuel Spring (1746-1819) was minister of a congregation at Newburyport, Massachusetts. He is described on the title as *Pastor of the North Church, in Newbury-Port.*

1784

[DAVIDSON, ROBERT.] Geography Epitomized; or, a Tour round the World: being A short but comprehensive Description of the Terraqueous Globe; Attempted in Verse, (for the sake of the memory;) And principally designed for the Use of Schools. By an American. Philadelphia: Joseph Crukshank, 1784. [96]

Duodecimo, 30 leaves, A-E⁶.

Original wrappers.
First edition.

Early American Children's Books

Evans 18435. Sabin 18736. Hildeburn 4465. This edition not in Wegelin. Only a copy of the Morristown reprint of 1803 in the Fiske Harris Collection.

The portion relating to America is on pages 49-60, and begins:

> Having cross'd the *Pacific*, we'll now take our stand,
> On this happy, prolific, and wide-spreading land,
> Where nature has wrought with a far bolder hand.
> No more let the *Old World* be proud of her *Mountains*,
> Her *Rivers*, her *Mines*, and her *Lakes*, and her *Fountains*,—
> Tho' great in themselves—they no longer appear
> To be great—when compar'd to the great that are here.

There are numerous explanatory footnotes in prose.

Robert Davidson (1750-1812) was a celebrated Philadelphia educator. He graduated from the University of Pennsylvania in 1771, was appointed instructor there in 1773, and in 1774 was given the chair of history and belle-lettres. In 1777 the occupation of Philadelphia by the British compelled him to retire to Delaware, and in 1784 he was appointed vice-president of the newly organized Dickinson College in Carlisle, Pennsylvania, of which institution he became president in 1804.

THE NEW-ENGLAND PRIMER Improved. For the more easy attaining the true reading of English to which is added, The Assembly of Divines Catechism. Boston: Printed and Sold by the Book-sellers, 1784. [97]

Octavo, 32 leaves, A-D⁸. Fine portrait of Washington on the recto of the first leaf. Woodcuts in the text.

Original half sheep over wooden boards, uncut.

Heartman 76 (with a slight variation in the form of the date) locates only one copy.

Contains the Shorter Catechism, and the Dialogue between Christ, Youth and the Devil, with Watts's Cradle Hymn and John Rogers' Advice to his Children, but is without the Verses for Little Children and other hymns.

The alphabet couplets do not conform to those as in the edition of Rogers and Fowle, 1749, some few, though not all, of the biblical couplets as in the edition of S. Kneeland, 1762 being used.

Many of the cuts are the same as in the Philadelphia edition of Charles Cist, 1782. It is noticeable that although the triplet for the letter O is the one concerning Young Obadias, David, Josias, the cut for the Royal Oak, the tree that saved his Royal Majesty, has been retained. This edition contains several woodcuts in addition to those in illustration of the alphabet couplets and the burning of John Rogers.

THE NEW-ENGLAND PSALTER: or Psalms of David: with the Proverbs of Solomon, and Christ's Sermon on the Mount. Being an Introduction for the training up Children in the Reading of the Holy Scriptures. Boston: Benjamin Edes & Sons, 1784. [98]

Duodecimo, 86 leaves, A-W⁴, X² (wants Q₂,₃).

Original sheep.
Evans 18358.

The title is on the recto of the first leaf, the verso is blank. The text is printed in double columns and begins on the second leaf without any prefatory matter.

The Psalms end on the recto of sig. Q$_i$, p. 121, and on the verso of the same leaf begins the Proverbs of Solomon. On W$_3$ recto, p. 165, begins Christ's Sermon on the Mount, and on the last page is the Nicene Creed.

Evans quotes this title entry without citing a copy. O'Callaghan, p. 32, has not this title, but has two separate entries, one for *The Proverbs of Solomon. (With The Psalter.)* and one for *Christ's Sermon on the Mount . . . (With The Psalter.)*, citing the George Livermore copy in each case.

1785

THE A, B, C. with the Church of England Catechism. To which is annexed, Prayers used in the Academy of the Protestant Episcopal Church, in Philadelphia. Also, A Hymn on the Nativity of our Saviour; and another for Easter-Day. Philadelphia: Printed by Young, Stewart, and M'Culloch, 1785. [99]

Duodecimo, 6 leaves, A$^{(1)\text{-}6}$, uncut and unopened, stitched.

Evans 19208.

On the verso of the first leaf are alphabets and a syllabary and at the foot is the following note: *The Blanks left in Page 6, were formerly filled with the Words* (King), *and* (him); *but as that Form of Expression does not suit our Republican Governments, the Teacher will be pleased to fill up the Blanks with what Words he may deem Expedient.*

CHESTERFIELD, PHILIP DORMER STANHOPE, Earl of: Principles of Politeness, and of Knowing the World; By the late Lord Chesterfield. Methodised and digested under distinct Heads. With Additions, By the Rev. Dr. John Trusler: containing: Every Instruction necessary to complete the Gentleman and Man of Fashion, to teach him a knowledge of Life, and make him well received in all Companies. For the Improvement of Youth; Yet not beneath the Attention of any. Norwich: John Trumbull, 1785. [100]

Duodecimo, 72 leaves, A-M^6.

Original sheep.
Evans 19258. Trumbull 1276.

The editor in his Advertisement *humbly apprehends, he could not do the rising generation a greater service, than by collecting those valuable precepts that are contained in his* (Lord Chesterfield's) *letters to his son . . .*

John Trusler, described as an *eccentric divine, literary compiler, and medical emperic* was born in 1735, and died in 1820. *The Principles of Politeness*, a compilation from Lord Chesterfield's Letters, was first published in England in 1775.

Early American Children's Books

THE CHILDREN IN THE WOODS. Being a true Relation of the inhuman Murder of two Children of a deceased Gentleman in Norfolk ... [Boston:] Sold at the Bible and Heart in Cornhill [c. 1785]. [101]

Broadside, folio, 1 leaf, woodcut illustration. In verse, printed in 3 columns.

Evans 19401 cites one copy only, that in Harvard College.
Thomas and John Fleet printed at the Bible and Heart from 1780 to 1795.
This broadside is set up slightly differently from the broadside edition printed at the Heart and Crown, c. 1770, no. 64. In the present edition the verses are divided into stanzas of four lines each; in the former edition there is no division. The short bar which marks the end in the former edition is replaced in this edition by the word *Finis*. The woodcut is the same in both editions.

GENLIS, STÉPHANIE-FÉLICITÉ DE. The Beauty and the Monster. A Comedy. From the French of the Countess de Genlis. Extracted from The Theatre of Education. Worcester, Massachusetts: Isaiah Thomas, sold at his Bookstore, sold also by E. Battelle, Boston, 1785. [102]

Duodecimo, 18 leaves, A-C⁶.

Original marbled wrappers, several edges uncut.
Evans 19021. Nichols 57.
A play for children, based on the fairy story by Madame Leprince de Beaumont.
Stéphanie-Félicité du Crest de Saint-Aubin, Comtesse de Genlis (1746-1830) was a famous French writer and educator. As *gouverneur* of the sons of the Duc de Chartres, she wrote several books for the use of her pupils, amongst the best known being the *Théâtre d'Education*, a collection of short comedies, first published in French in 1779.

[GENLIS, STÉPHANIE FÉLICITÉ DE.] Hagar in the Desert. Translated from the French, for the use of Children. The Fourth edition. Worcester, Massachusetts: Isaiah Thomas, 1785. [103]

16mo, 16 leaves, without signatures, woodcut frontispiece.

Paper wrappers consisting of the wrapper of an Almanac for the Year 1783, with the imprint of E. Russell in Boston.
Evans 19032. Nichols 59.
The woodcut frontispiece represents Wisdom in the form of an angel, the sword blossoming into an olive branch in her right hand, scales in her left. This cut is the one previously used by John Boyle for the Angel Gabriel in his edition of *The History of the Holy Jesus*, 1779, no. 88, with the difference that the sword of the Angel Gabriel is not blossoming. On the blank recto of this leaf is written *Calvin Hays given him by Rev. L. Sanger Feby. 6th, 1792 for reading his lesson best at the Visitation of the Town-School.*

GREGORY, JOHN. A Father's Legacy to his Daughters. By the late Dr. Gregory of Edinburgh. A New Edition, under the following Heads,

Early American Children's Books

Introduction, Religion, Conduct, Behaviour, Amusements, Friendship, Love and Marriage. Norwich: Printed by John Trumbull, 1785.

Duodecimo, 42 leaves A-G⁶. [104]

Original sheepskin over wooden boards.
Evans 19030. Trumbull 780: *Advertised in the Norwich Packet, Dec.* 15, 1785.
A few lines of printer's advertisement of books for the young at the foot of the last page. This edition is without the preface.

OSBORNE, HENRY. An English Grammar, adapted to the capacities of children. Charleston: Burd and Boden for the author, n. d. [1785.]

16 mo, 33 leaves (-)ⁱ, A-H⁴. [105]

Original yellow wrappers.
Not in Evans.
Printed at Charleston in South Carolina.
Founded on the famous English Grammar of Robert Lowth. At the beginning is a list of subscribers. The author is described on the title-page as *B. A. and formerly of University College, Oxford.*

1786

BE MERRY AND WISE; or, the Cream of the Jests, and the Marrow of Maxims, For the Conduct of Life. Published for the Use of all good Little Boys and Girls. By Tommy Trapwit, Esq. Adorned with Cuts. The First Worcester Edition. Worcester (Massachusetts): Isaiah Thomas, Sold also by E. Battelle, Boston, 1786. [106]

16 mo, 64 leaves, A-H⁸, woodcut frontispiece, woodcut illustrations.

Dark blue morocco, gilt, t. e. g., original front wrapper bound in.
Evans 20028. Nichols 75.
In two parts. The first part contains Jests for the Entertainment of Youth, and is illustrated with woodcuts, which are probably copied from the English edition. The frontispiece represents a boy reading the book at a table, and his enjoyment is expressed by the legend beneath: *He! He! He!* The second part begins on page 52, and contains Maxims and Cautions for the Instruction of Youth. This part is unillustrated.
The original English edition from which this is copied was published by John Newbery in London, though no copies of the first English edition seem to have survived.
In the Appendix of his *A Bookseller of the Last Century* in which he gives a list of the Newbery publications, Charles Welsh cites the second edition *From J. Newbery's List,* 1758. The fifth edition was printed in 1761.
Isaiah Thomas (1749-1831), a native of Boston, was the first American printer who seriously undertook to provide American children with a homemade library, and to this end he reprinted and pirated with complete success the charming juvenile books of John Newbery, and Newbery and Carnan, the famous London publishers of books for children.

Early American Children's Books

[BUCKLAND, JAMES.] A Wonderful Discovery of a Hermit, Who lived upwards of two hundred years. Worcester: Printed and Sold at the Printing-Office, 1786. [107]

Duodecimo, 6 leaves, no signatures, woodcut portrait on the title-page.

Unbound, stitched.
Unknown to Evans, Nichols and Sabin. Evans cites six editions for this year.
This story was one of the best sellers of the year 1786. It concerns the discovery of a Hermit by Captain James Buckland and Mr. John Fielding, described as two gentlemen of undoubted veracity, living in some part of Virginia, who agreed to make a voyage of discovery into the western parts of this vast country.

The Hermit, who was discovered in an otherwise uninhabited district, told them his mournful story. He was born in London (*as I have been very exact to keep my age*) *two hundred and twenty-seven years ago*. He then describes how at the age of nineteen he fell in love with a Nobleman's daughter, and his suit being frowned upon, *the lady was taken sick and died, at whose remembrance I cannot refrain from tears*, and he himself left home on the voyage which ended in shipwreck, and his solitary condition as a Hermit. Captain Buckland then tells him of the present state of the nation, *how some of them had left their native country, and come to this, which is now called America*.

The woodcut portrait on the title-page is also used by Thomas in his toy editions of *Robinson Crusoe*.

THE NEW-ENGLAND PRIMER, Improved, For the more easy attaining the true Reading of English. To which is added, The Assembly of Divines Catechism. Middletown: Woodward & Green, 1786. [108]

16mo, 40 leaves, A-E⁸, woodcuts (alphabet and Rogers).

Original limp leather.
Heartman 82.
The first leaf has the half title on the recto and Watts's Divine Song on the verso.
In addition to the Shorter Catechism this edition has at the end a set of questions and answers out of the Holy Scripture. The alphabet couplets are a curious mixture of the secular and the religious.
The King is omitted from this edition, and is replaced by *proud Korah's troop*.

NURSE TRUELOVE'S NEW-YEAR'S GIFT: or, the Book of Books for Children, adorned with Cuts. And designed for a present to every little Boy who would become a great Man, and ride upon a fine Horse; and to every little Girl, who would become a fine Woman, and ride in a Governour's gilt Coach. But let us turn over the leaf and see more of the matter. The First Worcester Edition. Worcester (Massachusetts): Printed by Isaiah Thomas, 1786. [109]

24mo, 32 leaves, A-D⁸ (A₁ and D₈, probably blank, are missing). 4 pages of advertisements at the end, numerous woodcuts.

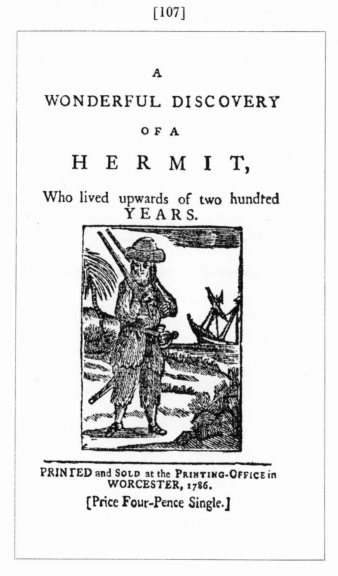

A

WONDERFUL DISCOVERY

OF A

H E R M I T,

Who lived upwards of two hundred
Y E A R S.

PRINTED and SOLD at the PRINTING-OFFICE in
WORCESTER, 1786.
[Price Four-Pence Single.]

Title-page from "A Wonderful Discovery of a Hermit"

THE

SCHOOL

OF

Good Manners.

compofed for the help of Parents—
teaching Children how to behave
during their minority.

PORTLAND:
Printed and fold, by Thomas B. Wait.
1786.

Title-page from "The School of Good Manners"

Early American Children's Books

Wrappers gone, original stitching.

Evans 20033. Nichols 81.

This work contains a number of stories and rhymes, the House that Jack Built, and a Catechism. It is one of Isaiah Thomas's imitations of a John Newbery book.

The original edition was advertised as *just published* in the (London) Public Ledger, February 12, 1760.

It is to be noticed that in transplanting the book Thomas not only adapts to his own use Newbery's methods of advertising, but makes certain other changes in order to fit it to its new environment.

The child is to be bribed to learn the New Testament by the gift of *one of the little Spelling-Books, and some of the other pretty Books which are to be sold by I. Thomas, in Worcester, near the Court House;* and The History of Mrs. Williams and her Plumb Cake contains a list of books used by Mrs. Williams for her pupils, also *sold by I. Thomas,* at the same address.

In the English edition the little girl on the title-page is to ride in a Lord Mayor's gilt coach. In this edition this becomes a Governour's gilt coach. This change is not carried, however, into the story itself, the little girl (Miss Polly Friendly) becomes a *great Lady Mayoress* and rides in a *grand gilt coach.*

One of the stories, *The Merry Haymakers,* includes the rhyme used at the end of some editions of the New England Primer, with the same woodcut.

A Pack of Cards Changed into a compleat Almanac and Prayer-Book. Adapted to the Entertainment of the Humorous, as well as to the Satisfaction of the Grave, Learned and Ingenious. Boston: Printed and Sold [by John Boyle] at the Printing-Office in Marlborough-Street n. d. [c. 1786.]   [110]

Octavo, 4 leaves, woodcut on title, uncut.

Original wrappers.
Not in Evans.
A chapbook edition, *Price 3 Coppers.* Relates in the form of a dialogue how a man accused by a fellow servant of gambling with cards, cleared himself by explaining how he used the cards as an almanack and prayer book.

A Pretty New-Year's Gift; or, Entertaining Histories, for the Amusement and Instruction of Young Ladies and Gentlemen in Winter Evenings. By Solomon Sobersides ... The First Worcester edition. Worcester (Massachusetts): Isaiah Thomas, 1786.   [111]

Octavo, 78 leaves, A-I⁸, K⁶, including 2 leaves of advertisements at the end, woodcut frontispiece, woodcut illustrations.

Original boards with wood engravings on each cover.
Evans 19995: *Originally published as 'Christmas tales for the amusement and instruction of young ladies and gentlemen' in Glasgow in* 1782. Nichols 82.
Contains xxi short stories (wrongly numbered xx) from various sources, including the Oriental and the Chinese, fully illustrated, the woodcuts showing Bewick influence.

The engravings on the cover vary in different copies. The copy described has the frontispiece repeated on the upper cover and, on the lower, an engraving not used in the text.

THE SCHOOL OF GOOD MANNERS, Composed for the help of Parents— teaching Children how to behave during their minority. Portland: Printed and sold, by Thomas B. Wait, 1786. [112]

Duodecimo, 29 leaves, (A)-C⁶, D¹¹.

Original calf.
Evans 19807.
In this edition the name of Eleazer Moodey is omitted from the preface, which is unsigned, and which, omitting the qualifying word *chiefly* to be found in the former editions, states that *the following instructions were compiled by a late famous schoolmaster in Boston.*
This edition does not contain the Alphabet of Useful Copies, or Cyprian's Twelve Absurdities.

THE WISDOM of Crop the Conjurer. Exemplified In Several Characters of Good and Bad Boys, with an Impartial Account of the celebrated Tom Trot, who rode before all the Boys in the Kingdom till he arrived at the Top of the Hill, called Learning. Written for the Imitation of those who love themselves. The First Worcester Edition. Worcester [Massachusetts]: Printed by Isaiah Thomas, 1786. [113]

Duodecimo, 24 leaves, A-C⁸, first and last leaves pasted down to covers. Woodcut frontispiece and numerous woodcuts in text.

Original Dutch flowered wrappers.
Evans 20153. Nichols 1263 and 121.
Internal evidence proves this book to be of English origin. It does not appear in the Newbery or Carnan lists, though the references to Giles Gingerbread which it contains make it seem possible that it was originally a Newbery publication. The mention of *Machusett mountain* may be an attempt at Americanization, though it has not been possible to verify this by comparison with an English edition.
The book contains an extremely interesting preface condoning the promises of *coaches*, *horses*, &c. as rewards for children, and the representing of *hobgoblins*, *monsters*, &c. as punishments, in direct opposition to the realistic school of thought supported later by Samuel Goodrich and others. At the end are four pages of advertisements of children's books.

1787

ADGATE, ANDREW. Select Psalms and Hymns for the Use of Mr. Adgate's Pupils: and proper for all Singing-Schools. Philadelphia: At the Uranian Press by Young and M'Culloch, 1787. [114]

Duodecimo, 36 leaves, A-F⁶ (A₁ and D₆ missing).

Original sheep.

Early American Children's Books

Evans 20181. Not in Sabin.
Contains an introduction on Church music, with a long quotation of the sentiments of *the ingenious and philosophic Mr. Harrison of London.*

CORDIER, MATHURIN. Corderii Colloquiorum Centuria selecta. Or, a select century, of the Colloquies of Corderius, with an English Translation, as literal as possible. Designed for the use of Beginners in the Latin Tongue. By John Clarke, late master of the grammar school in Hull. The twenty-third edition. Philadelphia: Printed by Joseph James, 1787. [115]

Duodecimo, 89 leaves. A-J⁹, K⁸.

Original calf.
Evans 20301.
English and Latin text in parallel columns.
For an earlier edition see no. 19.

THE EXHIBITION of TOM THUMB; being an Account of many valuable and surprising Curiosities Which he has collected In the Course of his Travels, for the Instruction and Amusement of the American Youth. The First Worcester Edition. Worcester, Mass.: Isaiah Thomas, 1787. [116]

24 mo, 32 leaves, A-D⁸, including wrappers, numerous woodcuts throughout text, 3 pages advertisements at the end.

Original wrappers (included in quires) with woodcuts in two compartments on back and front.
Evans 20749 Nichols 106.
Text and illustrations copied from the English edition of John Newbery.
Contains much moral precept *for all the pretty masters and misses in America* in an allegorical form. The exhibition was held at *Mr. Lovegood's, No.* 3 *Wiseman's buildings in Education-Road* and contained VIII Curiosities. Curiosity VII was a mahogany conjuring box. *The first thing I put under it was one of Mr. Thomas's little books, which, the moment I lifted up the box, I found to be changed into a swinging folio, very magnificently gilt and lettered* . . . The persons concerned bear such names as *Jack Idle, Anthony Greedy-guts, Mr. Sober-man, Mr. Thirsty-man, Jack Never-spell,* etc. At the end is a poem entitled *The Wonderful Old Man.*

GREENWOOD, JAMES. The Philadelphia Vocabulary, English and Latin: Put into a New Method, proper to acquaint the Learner with Things as well as pure Latin words. Adorned with twenty-six pictures. For the use of Schools. By James Greenwood, Author of the *English Grammar,* and late Sur-Master of St. Paul's School. Philadelphia: Carey and Co., 1787. [117]

Duodecimo, 66 leaves, A⁴, B-L⁶, M².

Woodcut on title representing Philadelphia and London, with Britannia greeting Philadelphia; numerous woodcut illustrations in the text.

Original sheep; front cover missing.

Evans 20398. Sabin 28690.

The first American edition of this popular textbook. The work is an abridgement of Jan Amos Komensky's *Orbis Pictura*, one of the earliest children's books to be illustrated.

The present edition is copied from the English version, first published in London about 1710, with the title *The London Vocabulary*. Many editions have been published both in America and in England.

James Greenwood, an English grammarian and schoolmaster, was, according to the Dictionary of National Biography, a master at St. Paul's School, London, at the time of his death in 1737. He was the author of several grammatical works.

THE HISTORY of Little Goody Twoshoes; otherwise called Mrs. Margery Twoshoes. With The Means by which she acquired her Learning and Wisdom, and in Consequence thereof her Estate. Set forth at large for the Benefit of those,

> Who from a State of Rags and Care,
> And having Shoes but half a Pair,
> Their Fortune and their Fame would fix,
> And gallop in their Coach and Six.

See the original Manuscript in the Vatican at Rome, and the Cuts by Michael Angelo; illustrated with the Comments of our great modern Criticks. The First Worcester Edition. Worcester, Massachusetts: Isaiah Thomas, 1787. [118]

Sm. octavo, 80 leaves, A-K⁸, woodcut frontispiece and numerous woodcut illustrations, 2 pages advertisements at the end.

Original Dutch flowered boards.

Evans 20412. Nichols 108.

The History of Goody Two shoes ends on page 142, sig. I₇. On page 143, sig. I₈, with caption title, begins the *Appendix. The Golden Dream; or the Ingenuous Confession.* The running title of Part I, which ends on page 66, is *The Renowned History of Goody Two shoes*, and of Part II, pages 67-142, *The Renowned History of Mrs. Margery Twoshoes*.

The dedication makes the necessary changes from the English edition and reads: *To all Young Gentlemen and Ladies, who are good, or intend to be good, This American Edition, is inscribed by their old friend in Worcester.*

The first American edition of this famous nursery classic, the most celebrated of all the books in John Newbery's Lilliputian library, and first issued in April, 1765. E. Pearson, in *Banbury Chapbooks*, comments on this edition: *There was an American edition of Goody Two Shoes, and is very interesting, having a woodcut frontispiece engraved by Thomas Bewick, and was printed at Worcester, Mass. U. S. A., by Isaiah Thomas, and sold wholesale and retail at his bookstore, 1787.* Miss Halsey in *Forgotten Books of the American Nursery* discusses the

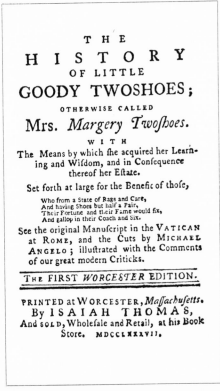

THE
HISTORY
OF LITTLE
GOODY TWOSHOES;
OTHERWISE CALLED
Mrs. *Margery Twoshoes.*

WITH

The Means by which she acquired her Learning and Wisdom, and in Consequence thereof her Estate.

Set forth at large for the Benefit of those,

Who from a State of Rags and Care,
And having Shoes but half a Pair,
Their Fortune and their Fame would fix,
And gallop in their Coach and Six.

See the original Manuscript in the VATICAN at ROME, and the Cuts by MICHAEL ANGELO; illustrated with the Comments of our great modern Criticks.

THE FIRST *WORCESTER* EDITION.

PRINTED at WORCESTER, *Massachusetts.*
By ISAIAH THOMAS,
And SOLD, Wholesale and Retail, at his Book Store. MDCCLXXXVII.

Title-page from "The History of Little Goody Twoshoes"

THE
ADVENTURES
OF
CAPTAIN GULLIVER,
IN A
VOYAGE

To the ISLANDS of

LILLIPUT and BROBDINGNAG.

Abridged from the WORKS of

The Celebrated DEAN SWIFT.

ADORNED WITH CUTS.

PHILADELPHIA:

Printed by YOUNG and M'CULLOCH, the
corner of *Chefnut* and *Second-ftreets*
1787.

Title-page from "The Adventures of
Captain Gulliver"

frontispiece at some length, and is of the opinion that the drawing was made after, and not by, Bewick.

The remaining cuts in the American edition are not by Bewick, but are from cuts in earlier English editions, some being the same as those reproduced by Mr. Pearson, from early York editions.

Much has been written as to the authorship of Little Goody Two Shoes, and it is now usually attributed to Oliver Goldsmith.

Many authors contributed to the Lilliputian Library of John Newbery, including that famous publisher himself, Oliver Goldsmith, the brothers Giles and Griffith Jones, and others less well known, and it is not always possible to assign correctly the authorship of the various books. According to Pearson in *Banbury Chapbooks*, quoted above, Goldsmith admitted the authorship: *No wonder when Goldsmith the poet had an interview with Bewick that, delighted with his cuts, he confessed to writing Goody Two Shoes, Tommy Trip, etc. Bewick's daughter supplied this information.* This statement cannot be taken too seriously, however, for the *History of Mr. Thomas Trip* first came out in the Lilliputian Magazine before Goldsmith had come to London. The reference to *Dr. James's Powder* (p.15), for lack of which the father of Goody Two Shoes died, might mean possibly that Newbery himself had something to do with it, the sale of that patent medicine forming an important part of his trade and livelihood.

Isaiah Thomas has edited Part I, the Introduction for the benefit of his American readers, and has introduced his own name in the places where that of John Newbery appears in the English edition.

THE JUVENILE BIOGRAPHER; Containing the Lives of little Masters and Misses; including a Variety of Good and Bad Characters. By a Little Biographer. The First Worcester Edition. Worcester [Massachusetts]: Printed by Isaiah Thomas and sold at his Book-Store. Sold also by E. Battelle, Boston: 1787. [119]

Octavo, 62 leaves, A-G⁸, H⁶. Woodcut frontispiece, *The Bust of the Little Author*, woodcut illustrations in the text, 4 pages advertisements at the end.

Original silver wrappers.
Evans 20440. Nichols 110.
First American edition.
Originally published by John Newbery in London, although the title cited by Welsh (unseen) is from E. Newbery's list, 1789, two years later than this Worcester edition. The woodcuts as well as the text of this edition appear to be copied from the English edition.

The book contains notices of the *Conduct and Behaviour of such young Gentlemen and Ladies, whose good Sense and Prudence render them highly worthy of Imitation*, and also of some bad characters to serve as a *Caution to all good Children*. These include Miss Betsey Allgood, Master Billy Bad-enough, Miss Nancy Careful, and young gentlemen alternating with young ladies. Pages 110 to 119 contain *Some Account of the little Author written by himself*.

A LITTLE PRETTY POCKET-BOOK, Intended for the Instruction and Amusement of Little Master Tommy, and Pretty Miss Polly. With Two Letters from Jack the Giant-Killer; as also A Ball and Pincushion; The Use of which will infallibly make Tommy a good Boy, and Polly a good Girl. To which is added, A Little Song-Book, Being A New Attempt to teach Children the Use of the English Alphabet, by Way of Diversion. The First Worcester Edition. Worcester: Isaiah Thomas, 1787. [120]

Octavo, 64 leaves, A-H⁸, the last 2 being blanks, the first and last leaves pasted down to covers; many lower edges uncut; woodcut frontispiece and numerous woodcuts in the text in rectangular and oval compartments, 2 pages of advertisement at the end.

Original gilt and green stamped wrappers.

Evans 20459. Nichols 113.

One of the most influential and important books in the history of juvenile literature.

Text and woodcuts from the English edition of John Newbery. The woodcuts are probably by Bewick. *The Little Pretty Pocket Book* was first published by Newbery in 1744, and was his first juvenile publication. This edition had no mention of the Little Song-Book on the title. The first edition with the title as in this Worcester edition was published by Newbery & Carnan in 1770.

The author's theories on the education of children, based on the principles of John Locke, are explained in the preface. The contents of the book are an attempt to put these theories into practice.

Following the letters from Jack the Giant-Killer are rhymed descriptions of games, each with a woodcut, and each accompanied by a Moral or Rule of Life alternately. Base-Ball for example is thus described:

> The Ball once struck off,
> Away flies the Boy
> To the next destin'd Post
> And then Home with Joy.

> Moral

> Thus Seamen, for Lucre
> Fly over the Main
> But, with Pleasure transported
> Return back again.

Each of the games has an alphabetical headline, *The great A Play*, *The little a Play* etc. which have no connection with the game they accompany.

Following the games are a rhymed alphabet; fables; a poetical description of the seasons; proverbs; rules for behaviour in children (as in *The School of Good Manners*, see note to no. 41); and other matters, all fully illustrated, and some of the woodcuts being in oval compartments.

In preparing this book for American use Isaiah Thomas has made a slight attempt at naturalization. The dedication is to the parents, guardians, and nurses, *in the United States of America*, and the postscripts of Jack the Giant-Killer's letters refer to the gentlemen and ladies *of America*.

MISCELLANIES, Moral and Instructive, in Prose and Verse; collected from Various Authors, for the Use of Schools, and Improvement of Young Persons of Both Sexes. Philadelphia: Joseph James, 1787.   [121]

Duodecimo, 102 leaves, A-R⁶, the last a leaf of advertisement.

Original half morocco.
Evans 20526.
First edition. Contains a letter of commendation from Benjamin Franklin to the anonymous editor, who may have been Mrs. Martha Moore, or John Ralling.
Wegelin has not this edition but catalogues the London reprint of 1790 under John Ralling.
On the flyleaf of this copy is the MS. note: *The following Extracts were collected by Mrs. Martha Moore, wife of Dr. Charles Moore of Montgomery County—Jos Cooper. Jun.* Jos. Cooper, Jun. was evidently the original owner of the book, for his signature appears on the title-page with the date May 20th, 1787.

THE NEW-ENGLAND PRIMER Improved, For the more easy attaining the true reading of English. To which is added, The Assembly of Divine's Catechism. Boston: Printed and Sold by the Book-Sellers, 1787. [122]

16mo, 32 leaves, A-D⁸, woodcut frontispiece portrait of General Washington on recto of the first leaf, woodcuts in the text.

Original wooden boards, covered with paper, leather back.
Heartman 84 (one copy only).
A reprint of the edition of 1784, no. 97.

THE SUGAR PLUMB; or Sweet Amusement for Leisure Hours: being an Entertaining and Instructive Collection of Stories. Embellished with curious cuts. The First Worcester Edition. Worcester, Massachusetts: Isaiah Thomas, 1787. [123]

16mo, 62 leaves, A-G⁸, H⁶, advertisements at the end. Woodcut frontispiece. Numerous woodcut illustrations in oval compartments.

Original Dutch flowered boards.
Evans 20735. Nichols 118.
Contains twelve stories in prose, preceded by an item in verse entitled The Castle Builder. The stories include King Lear, and his three daughters, Florio and Florella, Damon and Dorcas, and The American Merchant.
The dedication reads: *To all Good Little Masters and Misses, who have a true relish for the sweet meats of Learning, this Sugar Plumb, is Most humbly inscribed, by their obedient servant, the Author.*
This was originally a Newbery publication. The title in Welsh's list is quoted only from E. Newbery's list, 1789, the year of the present edition. It has not been possible to refer to a copy of the English edition, but it is probable that the title of the story *The American Merchant* is an attempt at naturalization, for the tale concerns an English merchant who was on the point of leaving the West Indies with his family at the time the story opens.

SWIFT, JONATHAN: The Adventures of Captain Gulliver, in a Voyage to the Islands of Lilliput and Brobdingnag. Abridged from the Works of The Celebrated Dean Swift. Adorned with cuts. Philadelphia: Young and M'Culloch, 1787.   [124]

16 mo, 64 leaves, A-D¹⁶, woodcut illustrations.

Original Dutch flowered boards, leather back.
Not in Evans.

This abridgement for children appears to be the first edition of this famous work published in America. It is the same as the edition published in London by P. Osborne & T. Griffin, and J. Mozley, Gainsborough, 1785. Both probably go back to a Newbery original, though the only edition quoted in Welsh's list is from E. Newbery's list, about 1789.

In this copy, 1 leaf (sig. B₁₆) has been torn out and repaired, and sig. D is misbound, 7 leaves being repeated in the place of 7 leaves which are missing.

1788

[BARBAULD, ANNA LETITIA.] Lessons for Children, from two to four years old. Philadelphia: B. F. Bache, 1788.   [125]

16mo, 56 leaves, the last a blank, printed throughout on one side of leaf only.

Original blue wrappers.
Evans 20946.

This, with the two following numbers, was printed by Benjamin Franklin Bache under the tutelage of his grandfather, Benjamin Franklin.

The first American edition of the most famous *Reading Easy* of its day, written originally for the instruction of Mrs. Barbauld's nephew Charles. In his preface to this edition, Benjamin Franklin Bache explains that *some alterations were thought necessary to be made in this American Edition, to make it agree with the original design of rendring instruction easy and useful, by calling the attention of the child to the surrounding objects. The climate and familiar objects of this country suggested these alterations.*

These alterations are so trifling as to be almost negligible, although any effort to Americanize the English books reprinted in America for American children has a certain importance.

Mrs. Barbauld (1743-1825) was a celebrated English poet and miscellaneous writer. She and her husband established a boys' school at Palgrave in Suffolk. The nephew, Charles Rochemont Aikin, seems to have justified the *Lessons* for he became a famous scientist and doctor.

[BARBAULD, ANNA LETITIA.] Lessons for Children of Four Years Old. Part II. Philadelphia, B. F. Bache, 1788.   [126]

16mo, 48 leaves, A-C¹⁶, partly unopened.

Original blue paper wrappers.
Evans 20947.

[BARBAULD, ANNA LETITIA.] Lessons for Children from four to five years old. Philadelphia: B. F. Bache, 1788.   [127]

16mo, 54 leaves, A⁶, B-D¹⁶.

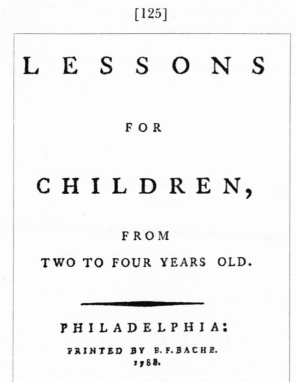

Title-page from "Lessons for Children"

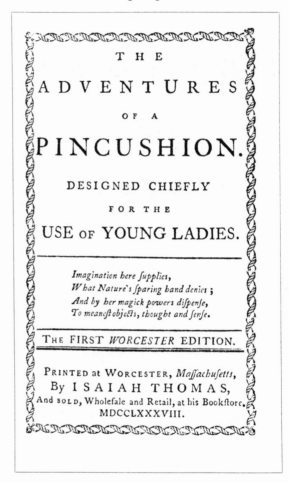

THE

ADVENTURES

OF A

PINCUSHION.

DESIGNED CHIEFLY

FOR THE

USE OF YOUNG LADIES.

Imagination here supplies,
What Nature's sparing hand denies ;
And by her magick powers dispense,
To meanest objects, thought and sense.

THE FIRST *WORCESTER* EDITION.

PRINTED at WORCESTER, *Massachusetts,*
By ISAIAH THOMAS,
And SOLD, Wholesale and Retail, at his Bookstore.
MDCCLXXXVIII.

Title-page from "The Adventures of a Pincushion"

Original blue wrappers.

Evans 20948.

A continuation of the lessons for Mrs. Barbauld's nephew Charles, designed to be more suitable to his increasing years.

This copy at one time belonged to F. M. Etting, and has his autograph signature on the title, and a note on the wrapper.

A CURIOUS HIEROGLYPHICK BIBLE; or, Select Passages in the Old and New Testaments, represented with Emblematical Figures, for the Amusement of Youth: designed chiefly to familiarize tender Age, in a pleasing and diverting Manner, with early Ideas of the Holy Scriptures. To which are subjoined, A short Account of the Lives of the Evangelists, and other Pieces. Illustrated with nearly Five Hundred Cuts. The First Worcester Edition. Worcester, Massachusetts: Isaiah Thomas: 1788.   [128]

Duodecimo, 72 leaves, A-M⁶; (A₁ with woodcut frontispiece missing). Numerous woodcut illustrations; text within ornamental borders.

Olive morocco.

Evans 20961. Nichols 128. Sabin 17990: *The first work of its kind printed in the United States.*

First American edition.

The work ends on page 134; page 135 (wrongly marked 235) contains a poem *On the Incomparable Treasure of the Holy Scriptures;* pages 136-139 contain an account of each Evangelist with woodcut portrait, followed by a hymn, prayer, and Catechism.

The Preface begins *Among the Variety of small Books published for the Instruction of Youth, there appears not to have been any of this Kind yet offered for their Amusement; and as this pleasing Method of teaching Children has been found, by Experience, to be an easy Way of leading them on in Reading, the Author has been induced . . . to publish this small Hieroglyphick Bible . . .*

Hieroglyphical Bibles became very popular in the late eighteenth century as an easy means of teaching the Scriptures to the young.

A GENERAL DESCRIPTION of the Thirteen United States of America. Containing, Their Situation, Boundaries, Soil and Produce, Rivers, Capitals, Constitution, Religious Test and Number of Inhabitants. Reading: B. Johnson and T. Barton, 1788.   [129]

Duodecimo, 12 leaves, A-C⁴.

Half olive morocco with the original wrappers bound in.

The first book printed in Reading, Pennsylvania.

Not in Evans. Not in Sabin.

Nolan: *Bibliography of the First Decade of Printing in Reading, Pennsylvania,* locates only one other copy.

JACKY DANDY's Delight: or the History of Birds and Beasts; in Verse and Prose. Adorned with a variety of cuts.

> These are my theme, am I to blame
> If men in morals are the same?
> I no man call an Ape or Ass,
> 'Tis his own conscience holds the glass.

The First Worcester Edition. Worcester, Massachusetts: Isaiah Thomas, 1788. [130]

24mo, 14 leaves, numerous woodcuts of birds and beasts in the text.

Unbound.

Evans 21174. Nichols 135.

A nature story book in prose and verse.

The verse passages which accompany the prose descriptions are printed in italic letter. They usually contain a moral:

> The Bear in coldest climate lives,
>   Screen'd by his shaggy hair;
> But boys may cold and hunger dread,
>   Who naught for learning care.

This is a copy of the original edition, published by Newbery in London, though no edition appears in Welsh's list. The authorship has been attributed to Oliver Goldsmith.

[KILNER, MARY JANE.] The Adventures of a Pincushion. Designed chiefly For the Use of Young Ladies.

> Imagination here supplies
> What Nature's sparing hand denies;
> And by her magick powers dispense
> To meanest objects, thought and sense.

The First Worcester Edition. Worcester, Massachusetts: Isaiah Thomas, 1788. [131]

Duodecimo, 52 leaves, A-H⁶, I⁴. Woodcut frontispiece, numerous woodcut illustrations.

Original flowered boards.

Evans 21187. Nichols 133.

The author explains in the preface her motive in writing this work: *That of presenting the juvenile reader with a few pages which should be innocent of corrupting, if they did not amuse.* First published in London earlier in the same year.

The stories of Mary Jane and Dorothy Kilner were amongst the most popular of the later Newbery books. These two women were sisters-in-law and lived at Maryland Point in Essex. They wrote originally for their nephews, publishing their stories anonymously or over pseudonyms. The present edition of this work is anonymous, but the English edition bore the initials S. S., a pseudonym usually considered to belong to Mary Jane Kilner, whilst stories signed M. P. (for Maryland Point) are assigned to Dorothy.

The woodcuts in this American edition are from those in the English edition, which were by John Bewick. That on page 57 is reproduced by E. Pearson in *Banbury Chapbooks* and described as *early John Bewick.*

[KILNER, MARY JANE.] Memoirs of a Pegtop. By the Author of Adventures of a Pincushion.

> Those *Trifles* that amuse in life
> Promote a higher end,
> Since *Reason* in this lighter dress
> With Pleasure we attend.

The first Worcester edition. Worcester, Massachusetts: Isaiah Thomas, 1788. [132]

Duodecimo, 54 leaves, A-I^6 (lacks G$_1$). Woodcut frontispiece and numerous woodcuts throughout the text, after the originals by John Bewick.

Original Dutch flowered boards.
Evans 21188. Nichols 137.
The original English edition was probably published in the same year.

THE NEW-ENGLAND PRIMER Improved, For the more easy attaining the true Reading of English. To which is added, The Assembly's Shorter Catechism; Also, Some Short and Easy Questions for Children. New York: S. Loudon: 1788. [133]

Duodecimo, 36 leaves, A-C^{12}, woodcuts.

Original limp leather with flap and tie.
Not in Heartman. This is apparently the only copy known.
This edition has no frontispiece; the only illustrations are the woodcuts accompanying the alphabet couplets, and the cut of the martyrdom of John Rogers.
The alphabet couplets are the same as those in the edition of Rogers and Fowle, 1749, with the exception of that for the letter K, which in this edition reads:

> The British King
> Lost States Thirteen.

THE PICTURE EXHIBITION; containing the original Drawings of Eighteen Disciples. To which are added, Moral and Historical Explanations. Published under the Inspection of Mr. Peter Paul Rubens, Professor of Polite Arts. Worcester, Massachusetts: Isaiah Thomas, 1788. [134]

Duodecimo, 63 leaves, A-G^8, H^7, including 2 blanks and 4 leaves of advertisements at the end, woodcuts in the text.

Calf.

Evans 21392. Nichols 138.

Amongst the eighteen items on exhibition, each of which has a woodcut illustration and an explanation, are: The Taking of the Bird's Nest, by Master Avis; The Idler, by Master Johnson; The Creation of the World, by Master Adam; The Hunting of the Cat, by Master Nimrod, etc.

The work was originally published in London by T. Carnan in 1783.

Welsh suggests that *the reference to the great artist might suggest the same hand as wrote 'Goody Two Shoes' and 'Fables in Verse'* [i. e. Oliver Goldsmith].

THE PROVERBS OF SOLOMON; and Ecclesiastes: Newly translated out of the Original Tongues. Very necessary for the Instruction of Youth. Philadelphia: Peter Stewart, 1788. [135]

Duodecimo, 30 leaves, A-E⁶, printed in double columns.

Half red morocco, partly uncut.

Evans 20965.

At the beginning is a short introduction by the Rev. John Brown, late Minister of the Gospel at Haddington. Certain passages thought unsuitable for the young are omitted, the omissions being indicated by dots.

THOMAS A KEMPIS. Der kleine Kempis, oder kurze Sprüche und Gebätlein, aus dem meistens unbekannten Wercklein des Thomae á Kempis. zusammen getragen, zur Erbauuing der Kleinen. Sechste und verbesserte Auflage. Germantown: Peter Leibert, 1788. [136]

Duodecimo, 84 leaves, A-G¹², the last a blank.

Original sheep.

Evans 21183.

At the beginning is *Das Kleine A, B, C, in der Schule Christi* and on ten pages at the end a poem *Ermunterungs-Lied für die Pilger*.

The second leaf contains the *Erlauterung des Kupfer-Blätgens*, in three stanzas of verse, but no plate seems to have been issued with the book. The Vorbericht is signed G. T. St.

WATTS, ISAAC. Divine and Moral Songs for Children; revised and altered so as to render them of General Use. To which are added, a short Catechism and Prayers. Worcester, Massachusetts: Isaiah Thomas, 1788. [137]

Duodecimo, 60 leaves, A-K⁸,⁴ (the blank first leaf is missing). Woodcut frontispiece and numerous woodcuts in the text.

Purple morocco, gilt.

Evans 21576. Nichols 151. Not in Stone.

The frontispiece represents the author, seated at a table in his library. The charming woodcuts throughout are after John Bewick.

Early American Children's Books

In addition to the author's preface, addressed to *all that are concerned in the education of children*, this edition contains an *Advertisement to this Edition*.

1789

[DEFOE, DANIEL.] Die Wunderbare Lebensbeschreibung, und Erstaunliche Begebenheiten des berühmten Helden Robinson Crusoe, Welcher 28 Jahr auf einer Unbewohnten Insel wohnete, die er nachderhand Bevölkert hat. Philadelphia: Carl Cist, 1789.   [138]

Duodecimo, 80 leaves, (-)², A-N⁶, including the last blank; woodcut portrait frontispiece of Robinson Crusoe, 5 other full-page woodcuts, all within borders.

Unbound.
Not in Evans, who has an edition by the same printer, and with the same collation for the previous year (NYPL).
This is a translation of the same version of the story as that printed by Hugh Gaine in 1774 (see no. 77), with the same woodcuts.

THE NEW-ENGLAND PRIMER, Or, an easy and pleasant Guide to the Art of Reading. Adorn'd with cutts. To which are added, The Assembly of Divines Catechism. Boston: J. White, n. d. [1789.]   [139]

16 mo., 30 leaves, (A)⁶, B-D⁸, several uncut lower edges. On the recto of the first leaf is a woodcut portrait of *The President of the United States*, woodcuts in the text

Boards.
Differs from Heartman, 314, 315 and 316 which are all undated editions by the same printer. It is probable that sig. A in this edition lacks two leaves, with words in syllables.
The frontispiece is on the recto of the first leaf, and Watts's Divine Song on the verso.
On the verso of the title is a woodcut and three quotations from the Scriptures.
The alphabet couplets do not conform exactly to the arrangement in any of the preceding editions in this collection, though no new couplets are introduced.
Following these couplets are two pages with the alphabet and illustrations in 24 compartments, 12 to a page, copied from the Royal Primer (*see the second edition, no*. 62). On the last page is a woodcut and verse from The Merry Haymakers, see *Nurse Truelove's New Year's Gift*, no. 109.

A PACK OF CARDS Changed into a Complete Almanack, and Prayer-Book. Adopted to the Entertainment of the Humourous, as well as the Satisfaction of the Grave, Learned and Ingenious. The eleventh edition. Norwich: [without name of printer] 1789.   [140]

Duodecimo, 6 leaves, A⁴, B².

Original wrappers.
Not in Evans. Not in Trumbull.
Another edition of no. 110.

[ROBERTSON, JOSEPH.] An Essay on Punctuation. Philadelphia: Joseph James, 1789. [141]

Duodecimo, 72 leaves, A-H¹², ⁶.

Original sheep.
Evans 22119.
At the end is an Appendix which contains a short chapter dealing with technical terms relative to books.
Originally published in England in 1785. The author was a clergyman, author and literary critic. He was born in Westmoreland in 1726, and died in 1802, whilst vicar of Horncastle, Lincolnshire.

VICE IN ITS PROPER SHAPE; or, the Wonderful and Melancholy Transformation of several Naughty Masters and Misses into those Contemptible Animals which they most Resemble in Disposition. Printed for the Benefit of all Good Boys and Girls. The First Worcester Edition. Worcester, Massachusetts: Isaiah Thomas, 1789. [142]

16mo, 64 leaves, A-H⁸, woodcut frontispiece pasted down inside cover, numerous woodcut illustrations.

Original Dutch flowered boards.
Evans 22221. Nichols 161.
Tells *Of the wonderful Transmigration of Jack Idle into the body of an ass; of the surprizing Transmigration of Master Anthony Greedyguts, into the Body of a Pig; of the Transmigration of Miss Dorothy Chatterfast into the Body of a Magpie*, and others.
A Newbery publication. Evidently no copy of the original English edition was seen by Welsh, whose only entry of this title is *from E. Newbery's List*, 1789.

WITHERSPOON, JOHN. A Sermon on the religious education of Children. Preached, in the Old Presbyterian Church in New-York, to a very numerous Audience, on the Evening of the second Sabbath in May. By the Rev. John Witherspoon, D. D. President of Princeton College. Elizabeth-Town: Printed by Shepard Kollock, 1789. [143]

Duodecimo, 12 leaves, A-C⁴.

Unbound and uncut, stitched as issued.
Evans 22284.
John Witherspoon (1723 to 1794), a Signer of the Declaration of Independence, was a native of Scotland, who first came to America at the invitation of Princeton College, New Jersey, to become the President of that foundation.

Early American Children's Books

THE BERKSHIRE LADY. [? Philadelphia] Printed in the year 1790. [144]

Duodecimo, 4 leaves. Woodcut of a ship on the title.

Unbound.
Not in Evans.
In verse.
This chapbook is apparently of great rarity. No edition of it is included in Ashton: *Chapbooks of the Eighteenth Century*.

THE BIBLE in Miniature or a Concise History of the Old & New Testaments. New York: A. Brower, Jun'. n. d. [not after 1790.] [145]

16 mo, 128 leaves, A-H¹⁶, engraved title and illustrations.

Original sheep.
Not in Evans.
A *Thumb Bible* measuring 1⅞ by 1⅜ inches, containing an abridgement in prose of the Scriptures. On the flyleaf is written *H. Fortin her Book* 1790 *Born*, 1782.
The original English edition was published by E. Newbery, 1780.

DEATH AND THE LADY. To which is added The Bride's Burial. Philadelphia; for Henry Green [not after 1790]. [146]

Duodecimo, 4 leaves.

Unbound.
Not in Evans.
In verse. The Bride's Burial begins on page five. On the title-page is the autograph signature of Adam Boyd, 1790.
The former piece is one of the numerous colloquies to which the Dance of Death gave rise. The ballad of the Bride's Burial was originally licensed by William White, London, June 11, 1603. No edition of this chapbook is included in Ashton's *Chapbooks of the Eighteenth Century*.

POTTER, JOHN. The Words of the Wise. Designed for the Entertainment and instruction of younger minds. Philadelphia: Printed by Joseph Crukshank, 1790. [147]

Duodecimo, 38 leaves, A-F⁶, G².

Original Dutch flowered wrappers.
Not in Evans.
In his dedication to Lady Mawbey (dated from Vaux-Hall Jan. 1768) the author explains that *the following Sheets contain the Sentiments of most of our Moral Writers of Eminence on the cardinal Virtues, blended with my own, and digested in a familiar manner, so as to render them entertaining as well as instructive to Young Minds, for whom this Work is principally intended.*

First published in England in 1768. The author was a well-known dramatic critic and miscellaneous writer. The dates of his birth and death are not known; he was born in London somewhere about 1735 and he published a two-volume novel in 1813.

This copy has the autograph signature of J. Comly, 1796, on the flyleaf.

RICHARDSON, SAMUEL. The History of Sir Charles Grandison, abridged from the works of Samuel Richardson, Esq. Author of Pamela and Clarissa. The Tenth Edition. Philadelphia: Carey, Stewart and Co. [1790.]   [148]

16 mo, 80 leaves, A-K⁸.

Original boards.

Evans 22852 has an edition *printed by M. Carey*, 1790, of which he gives no collation, and cites no copy.

Abridgements of adult novels were considered highly suitable reading for children in the eighteenth century. Abridged editions of the works of Richardson, Fielding and others were issued by John Newbery, for whom Oliver Goldsmith did much of the work of rewriting the novels in suitable form for children. Newbery's first edition of the present work is not recorded by Welsh. The third edition was on E. Newbery's list for 1789.

THE SCHOOL OF GOOD MANNERS. Composed for the Help of Parents, in teaching their Children how to behave during their Minority. Boston: S. Hall, 1790.   [149]

Sm. sq. octavo, 27 leaves, A⁷, B-C⁸, D⁴, the last pasted down to wrapper, woodcut on title.

Original wrappers (upper missing).
Not in Evans.

The Preface is unsigned; it contains the name of Eleazer Moodey as being (*chiefly*) responsible for the compilation. This edition contains the Alphabet of Useful Copies beginning *Attend the advice of the old and the wise*, but Cyprian's Twelve Absurdities are replaced by The Child's Complaint, from Dr. Watts's Divine Songs.

The woodcut on the title representing the author in his library was one of the illustrations in the *New House that Jack Built*, printed by Rusher in his *Banbury Penny Books*. It is reproduced by Pearson in *Banbury Chapbooks*. A similar idea is seen in the cut used by Thomas at Worcester in his edition of Watts, *Divine and Moral Songs*, 1788, no. 137.

TOM THUMB'S FOLIO: or, a new Threepenny Play Thing for Little Giants. To which is prefixed, An abstrbct [*sic*] of The Life of Mr. Thumb, and An Historical Account of the Wonderful Deeds he performed Together with Some Annecdotes respecting Grumbo the Great Giant. Boston: John Norman, n. d. [c. 1790.]   [150]

16 mo, 14 leaves, without signatures, woodcut illustrations.

Half red morocco.

Not in Evans.

John Norman evidently copied directly from the original English edition, for he failed to remove Mr. Newbery's self-advertising name in the second chapter: *Tom's father bought for his son all the little books published by Mr. Newbery.* In the Boston edition of 1780 (no. 91) the name is omitted entirely. Samuel Hall, in his edition of 1794 (no. 185) introduced his own name in the place of that of Newbery. The woodcuts in this edition are not after the Newbery cuts.

1791

THE BABES IN THE WOOD. Their Death and Burial. Philadelphia: Printed in the Year, 1791. [151]

Duodecimo, 4 leaves.

Unbound.

Not in Evans. Apparently unrecorded.

A chapbook containing simply the ballad: *Now ponder well, ye parents dear.* There are no illustrations.

The caption title on the second page is *The Babes Dying in The Wood.* This version shows several variations from that printed by Thomas and John Fleet, nos. 64 and 101, one of the chief being the size of the dowry, which in this edition is two thousand pounds, instead of two hundred as formerly.

[RICHARDSON, SAMUEL.] The Paths of Virtue Delineated; or The History in Miniature of the Celebrated Clarissa Harlowe, Familiarised and Adapted to the Capacities of Youth. Philadelphia: W. Woodhouse, 1791. [152]

135 pages, engraved frontispiece.

Original boards.

Evans 23740.

This abridgement of Clarissa was first published by John Newbery. It was reprinted in 1772 by his son Francis Newbery. The earliest edition mentioned in Welsh's list is from E. Newbery's list, 1789. According to Welsh *The Paths of Virtue Delineated* was the title of Pamela, and not of Clarissa. Referring to the abridged edition of the former work on Newbery's list, 1789, Welsh says: *Probably a reprint of an earlier book, The Paths of Virtue Delineated; or, Pamela, &c.,* of which Newbery sold Collins of Salisbury a half share for £6, 8s. 6d.

WATTS, ISAAC. Dr. Watts' Plain and Easy Catechisms for Children. The first Exeter edition. Exeter: Henry Ranlet, 1791. [153]

Duodecimo, 18 leaves, A-C⁶, woodcut vignette on title.

Original wrappers.

Evans 23961. Eames: *Early New England Catechisms*, p. 98.

One of the most popular catechisms for children, and a standard work in both America and England until past the middle of the nineteenth century.

On the flyleaf is the signature of Betsy Jenness, March 27, 1794.

1792

[DEFOE, DANIEL.] Travels of Robinson Crusoe. Written by Himself. Windham: Printed by John Byrne, 1792. [154]

16 mo, 16 leaves, without signatures, first and last leaf pasted down to covers; woodcut frontispiece, and woodcut illustrations in the text.

Original pictorial covers, with two of the woodcut illustrations on each side.
Not in Evans. Not in Trumbull.
A chapbook version.
This version was also used by Thomas in his Worcester editions (see no. 171). John Byrne's edition is a very inferior production to the editions of Thomas, the woodcuts in particular being extremely rough and crude.

[DEFOE, DANIEL.] The Wonderful Life and Surprising Adventures Of that Renowned Hero Robinson Crusoe, Who lived Twenty-eight Years on an Uninhabited Island, Which he afterwards colonised. Boston: J. White and C. Cambridge, 1792. [155]

Duodecimo, 36 leaves, A-F⁶; woodcut portrait frontispiece (pasted down to front cover), woodcut illustrations in the text

Original half-binding over wooden boards.
Evans 24253.
The portrait at the beginning represents Crusoe with his two guns and sword, and the explanation below: *Robinson Crusoe, when he had been 22 years on a desolate Island where he was shipwreck'd, went to see what he could discover;—armed himself with 2 guns, 2 pistols, and a sword.*
This abridgement is the same as that used by Hugh Gaine, 1774, no. 77. The first sentence, either by accident or design, omits the phrase *who was a native of Bremen*, in referring to Crusoe's father, otherwise the text is the same. The two three-quarter page woodcut illustrations in the text may have been copied from the same originals.
At the end is the autograph signature of Jacob Cram, Exeter, July 4, 1793.

A DESCRIPTION of the Geographical Clock: which contains the Names and Situations of the most remarkable Places In the World; and exhibits at one view the Time of Day or Night at all those places Round the Globe: with a Copious Index; intended for the Instruction and Amusement of Youth. Philadelphia: for Joseph Scott and sold by Francis Bailey and Peter Stewart, 1792. [156]

Duodecimo, 12 leaves, A-B⁶.

Original grey wrappers, uncut.
Not in Evans. Not in Sabin.
A description for adults of this clock was issued in the same year by Francis Bailey (Evans 24347).

A FATHER'S ADVICE TO HIS CHILD; or the Maiden's Best Adorning. Exeter: Henry Ranlet, 1792.   [157]

Quarto, 4 leaves.

Unbound, partly uncut.
Evans 24310.
In verse.
Begins:

> Dear Child, these words which briefly I declare,
> Let them not hang like Jewels in thine ear;
> But in the secret closet of thine heart,
> Safe lock them up, that they may ne'er depart.

The first printed version of this didactic poem seems to have been in broadside form in England, 1678.

THE HISTORY of George Barnwell, of London. Norwich: Printed by John Trumbull, 1792.   [158]

Duodecimo, 11 leaves, (A)⁴, B⁷.

Unbound, stitched.
Not in Evans. Not in Trumbull.
A chapbook.
The title is on the recto of the first leaf, the verso being blank; the text begins on the recto of (A)₂ without any preliminary matter.
The story is based on an old ballad (to be found in Percy's *Reliques*, 3rd series, Book iii, No. vi), and was frequently issued in chapbook form. It was the basis for George Lillo's celebrated play first acted at Drury Lane Theatre, London, in 1731.

THE HISTORY of Joseph and his Brethren: Wherein we may behold the wonderful Providence of God, in all their Troubles and Advancements. Philadelphia: Daniel Lawrence [?1792].   [159]

Octavo, 8 leaves, caption title, imprint at end.

Unbound, uncut and unopened.
Not in Evans.
In verse.
This metrical *History of Joseph and his Brethren* was extremely popular in England.
The first printed metrical version was entitled *Thystorie of Jacob and his twelue Sones*, and was published without date by Wynkyn de Worde. The first chapbook version was printed in Aldermary Church Yard, London, without date.

THE LIFE and Death of Robin Hood, complete in Twenty-four Songs. Philadelphia: Stewart & Cochran [c. 1792].   [160]

Duodecimo, 54 leaves, A-F¹²,⁶ (lacks 2 leaves in sig. E).

Modern grey boards, original wrappers bound in.
Not in Evans.

Early American Children's Books

The running title throughout is *Robin Hood's Garland*.

The earliest known printed version of the famous *Robin Hood's Garland* is a copy in the Bodleian Library, printed for W. Gilbertson in 1663, and containing seventeen ballads.

Garlands of the eighteenth century increased the number to twenty-seven; the present edition, as stated on the title-page, contains twenty-four songs.

Although Robin Hood is supposed to have been the Earl of Huntington and an authentic personage, the ballads were really founded on the French *trouvère* drama, *Le Jeu de Robin et Marion*, which is itself a dramatized version of the Nature myth, Robin and Maid Marian being directly descended from the King and Queen of the May-day ceremonies.

THE NEW-ENGLAND PRIMER, Improved, For the more easy attaining the true reading of English. To which is added, The Assembly of Divines Catechism. Hartford: Printed by Nath. Patten, 1792.   [161]

16mo., 32 leaves, A-D⁸, woodcuts (alphabet and John Rogers).

Original wrappers, leather back.
One of two copies known.
Heartman 108. This edition not in Trumbull.
The alphabet couplets are the religious set as in S. Kneeland's Boston edition, 1762, no. 48. Many of the accompanying woodcuts are the same as in that edition, including the one for the letter O, which really represents Young Obadias, David and Josias, unlike some of the editions which have used this rhyme, whilst retaining the cut for the Royal Oak. On the last page is *The late Reverend and Venerable Mr. Nathaniel Clap, of Newport, on Rhode-Island; his Advice to children.*

THE NEW-ENGLAND PRIMER; much improved. Contaning [*sic*], A Variety of easy Lessons, for Attaining the true reading of English. Philadelphia: Johnston and Justice for [Robert] Campbell [1792].   [162]

Duodecimo, 36 leaves, A-C¹², woodcuts (alphabet and John Rogers).

Original wrappers.
On the flyleaf is written: *Rebecca Carpenter her Book* 1792.
Heartman 322 locates this copy only, which would appear to be the only one known.
This edition has no frontispiece. It contains a set of Lessons in Reading after the manner of Mrs. Barbauld's *Easy Lessons*. The alphabet couplets are as in the New York edition of S. Loudon, 1788, no. 133. The accompanying woodcuts are extremely crude.

THE YOUNG LADY'S PARENTAL MONITOR: containing I. Dr. Gregory's "Father's Legacy to his Daughters." II. Lady Pennington's "Unfortunate Mother's Advice to her Absent Daughters." III. Marchioness de Lambert's "Advice of a Mother to her Daughter." London: Printed: Hartford: Re-printed, and Sold by Nathaniel Patten, 1792.   [163]

Octavo, 82 leaves, (A)⁴, B-U⁴, V², woodcut frontispiece.

Original calf.

Early American Children's Books

Evans 25067. Trumbull 1736: *Advertised in the American Mercury.*

Each part has a half title. Gregory's *Father's Legacy to his Daughters* contains the preface.

Lady Pennington's opinions on the education and upbringing of girls are extremely interesting. She is very scathing on the subject of novel reading: *Of Novels and Romances, very few are worth the trouble of reading: some of them perhaps do contain a few good morals, but they are not worth the finding where so much rubbish is intermixed.* This theme is considerably enlarged, but Lady Pennington does make one notable exception: *In justice however to a late ingenious author, this Letter must not be reprinted, without my acknowledging that, since the last edition was published, I have accidentally met with one exception to my general rule, namely* The Vicar of Wakefield. *This novel is equally entertaining and instructive, without being liable to any of the objections that occasioned the above restriction.*

Pages 80 and 81 contain a list of books considered by Lady Pennington to be suitable for the perusal of her daughters, and to these the editor adds a number which have *appeared since Lady P's Letter was first printed.* This supplementary list includes *Rasselas; Prince of Abyssinia,* and other equally unsuitable material.

1793

AN ABRIDGEMENT of the History of the Holy Bible. Adorned with cuts. Hudson (New York): Ashbel Stoddard, 1793.   [164]

16 mo., 16 leaves, A⁴, B¹², emblematic woodcut frontispiece (pasted down to upper cover) and numerous woodcuts in text.

Original marbled wrappers.
Not in Evans.
An entirely different work from *The Holy Bible Abridged,* printed in Boston in 1782.
The cuts are extremely naive.

THE AMERICAN LETTER-WRITER: Containing, a Variety of Letters on the most common Occasions in Life, viz. Friendship, Duty, Advice, Business, Amusement, Love, Marriage, Courtship, &c. with forms of message cards. To which are Prefixed, Directions for Writing Letters, and the proper Forms of Address. Philadelphia: Printed and sold by John M'Culloch, 1793.   [165]

Duodecimo, 54 leaves, 4 leaves without signatures, A-E¹², ⁶, F².

Boards.
Evans 25097. Not in Sabin.
The introduction of six pages contains general instructions. The body of the work contains examples of letters, and the last page *a few short and intelligible Forms of Messages for Cards or Billets.*

Letter I is a *Son's Letter at School to his Father;* Letter II is a *Letter of Excuse to Father or Mother,* and Letter III a *Letter from a Youth at school to his parents.* Letter II begins: *Honoured Sir, or Madam,*

I am informed, and it gives me a great concern, that you have heard an ill report of me, which, I suppose, was raised by some of my school-fellows, who either envy my happiness, or by aggravating my faults, would be thought to seem less criminal themselves; though I must own I have been a little too remiss in my school-business, and am now sensible I have lost, in some measure, my time and credit thereby . . .

This can be compared with the letter from the Scholar to his Parents in *A Useful and Necessary Companion*, 1708, no. 9.

[DEFOE, DANIEL.] The Wonderful Life and most Surprising Adventures of Robinson Crusoe of York, Mariner: Containing A full and particular Account how he lived eight and twenty years in an uninhabited Island on the Coast of America; how his ship was lost in a storm, and all his Companions drowned; and how he was cast upon the shore by the wreck. With a true Relation how he was at last miraculously preserved by Pirates. Faithfully Epitomized from the three Volumes, & adorned with Cuts suitable to the most remarkable Stories. New York: W. Durell [1793]. [166]

Duodecimo, 74 leaves, A-H$^{12, 6}$, I^2. Woodcut portrait frontispiece, 11 woodcut illustrations in text.

Original sheep.
Evans 25386.
This abridgement is quite different from that used by Hugh Gaine, 1774, no. 77. It closes with six lugubrious lines of verse beginning:

> Life's but a snare, a labyrinth of woe;
> Which wretched man is doom'd to struggle thro'. . .

An English edition of this abridgement with different woodcuts was published in London by C. Hitch and L. Hawes in 1759.

DODDRIDGE, PHILIP. Sermons to Young Persons, on the following Subjects, viz. I. The importance of the rising generation. II. Christ formed in the soul the foundation of hope. III. A dissuasive from keeping bad Company. IV. The young Christian invited to an early attendance on the Lord's table. V. The orphan's hope. VI. The reflection of a pious parent on the death of a wicked child. VII. Youth reminded of approaching judgment. Philadelphia: William Young, 1793. [167]

Duodecimo, 96 leaves, A^4, B-Q^6, R^2.

Original sheep.
Not in Evans.
The dedication is: *To the young persons belonging to the Dissenting Congregations at Hinckley, Harborough, and Kibworth in Leicestershire, and at Ashley, and Northampton*, dated from Northampton, Dec. 30, 1734.

The author, Philip Doddridge (1702-1751), was a nonconformist divine, and at different times ministered to congregations at all the places mentioned in the dedication.

Early American Children's Books

[ELY, JOHN.] The Child's Instructor: Consisting of Easy Lessons for Children; on Subjects which are Familiar to them, in language adapted to their capacities. By a Teacher of Little Children in Philadelphia. Volume I. The Second Edition. Philadelphia: Printed by John M'Culloch, 1793. [168]

Duodecimo, 54 leaves, A⁸, B-H⁶, I⁴.

Original boards (front cover missing).

This edition not in Evans, who cites an edition the same year, printed in New-London. Not in Sabin.

Although the title-page reads Volume I, no second volume appears to have been issued.

The book is an abecedarium, syllabary and reader. The passages for reading are in prose and verse, and include an extract from Goldsmith's Hermit; Description of a Good Boy; Description of a Bad Boy; The Advice of William Penn to his Children; proverbs, hymns from Dr. Watts; extracts from the works of Pope, and other items.

The list of words in chapter XXVII *which are somewhat similar in Sound, and which are vulgarly sounded alike, but should be pronounced distinctly different* is an even more interesting commentary on the pronunciation of the period than the preceding chapter of homonyms. Chapter XXIX contains a rhymed alphabet, *In this Chapter the Child may learn the Italian Alphabet.* The sentences are apt and pithy, but whether always inspiring to children is another matter. *C was a christian resigned to his fate* hardly accords with *R was religion which made sorrows cease*, and the propaganda spirit of *D was a drunkard and spent his estate* is not maintained in *V was a vineyard and cheered the whole town.*

John Ely was a schoolmaster who taught at the Adelphia School, Pegg's Street, between Front and Second Streets, Philadelphia.

THE FORTUNE-TELLER, by which Young Gentlemen and Ladies may foretell a variety of future events. By the renowned Dr. Hurlothrumbo, Chief Magician and Astrologer to the King of the Cuckows. Philadelphia: Francis Bailey, 1793. [169]

16mo., 28 leaves, A-B¹⁴ (last leaf pasted to back cover), woodcut illustrations.

Half blue morocco, original back cover bound in.

Not in Evans.

This book—an Alphabet without Tears—is copied from the English original. The woodcuts are after John Bewick. The preface explains the scheme of the book. This is followed by a rhymed alphabet, illustrated with fine woodcuts in oval compartments. *I is an Indian— how neat he appears,*—the second statement being necessary to explain the accompanying illustration, which represents a Georgian courtier taking snuff; *Z is a Zany without learning or parts* is illustrated by an unfortunate in the stocks. This is followed by the magical table, and the great and small alphabets with mottoes.

WEBSTER, NOAH. The American Spelling Book: Containing an easy standard of pronunciation. Being the first part of a Grammatical Institute of the English Language. By Noah Webster, Jun. Esquire . . .

Early American Children's Books

Thomas & Andrews's Fifth Edition. With many corrections and improvements, by the Author. Boston: Isaiah Thomas and Ebenezer T. Andrews, 1793. [170]

Duodecimo, 72 leaves, A-M⁶, woodcut portrait frontispiece, woodcut illustrations in the text in oval compartments.

Original half binding over wooden boards.
Not in Evans.
Dedicated to the Rev. Ezra Stiles, S. T. D., President of Yale College.
The American Spelling Book is the first part of the *Grammatical Institute of the English Language*.
The running title throughout is *An Easy Standard of Pronunciation*. The work contains an abecedarium, syllabary, reading easy, and other matter, including eight fables with woodcut illustrations.
It is interesting to compare the list of homonyms with that given by Dilworth (no. 65) and Ely (no. 168).
Webster expresses his scorn of Dilworth in this connection: *In this table I have omitted several words which are found in Dilworth and Fenning; either because the* English *differs from the* American *pronunciation, or because they have inserted words together as nearly the same in sound, which may lead into error. For instance the words* consort *and* concert *are placed together in Dilworth, and they are commonly pronounced alike; but it is an offence against propriety, and I choose to admit no words but such as sound exactly alike.* Webster, Ely and Dilworth all class together *Air*, an element, *Heir*, to an estate, and *are*, plural of is, and several other of the pronunciations conceded by the three grammarians would be equally an offence against propriety today.
It is noticeable that Webster is the only one of the three who classes *Bow*, to bend, *Bough*, a branch; *Bow*, to shoot with, and *Beau*, a gay fellow, in one group to be pronounced alike; both Dilworth and Ely place these in two groups as in the modern pronunciation.
The statistics given in the tables of countries are interesting: New York State had at that time 340,120 inhabitants and Pennsylvania 434,373; Virginia had the largest number with 747,610.
This spelling book almost entirely supplanted that of Dilworth, which, until the publication of Webster's, had been the standard speller.
The famous lexicographer was born in 1758 at Hartford, Connecticut, and died in 1843.

1794

[DEFOE, DANIEL.] Travels of Robinson Crusoe. Written by Himself. The third Worcester Edition. Worcester, Massachusetts: Isaiah Thomas, 1794. [171]

16 mo, 16 leaves including wrappers, no signatures, woodcut portrait frontispiece, woodcuts in the text.

Original blue pictorial wrappers with woodcuts in two compartments on both sides.
Not in Evans or Nichols.
The woodcut portrait was used by Thomas as the frontispiece to *A wonderful Discovery of a Hermit*, 1786, no. 107. The story ends on page 24, and at the foot of the same page is a *Note—If you learn this Book well, and are good, you can buy a larger and more com-*

Early American Children's Books

plete History of Mr. Crusoe, *at your friend the Bookseller's, in* Worcester, *near the* Court House. On page 25 begins *Of taking our Parents' Advice,* and on page 28 *A Dialogue between a little good Boy and Girl, which if rightly attended to, will shew them how they may be wiser than the rest of their school fellows,* a popular story for the end of books.

On the last page is a cut of a ship, and the lines:

> 'Twas in this ship, which sail'd from Hull,
> That Crusoe did embark;
> Which did him vex, and much perplex,
> And broke his parent's heart.

The woodcuts in this edition are infinitely superior to those in the edition of John Byrne, at Windham, 1792, no. 154, which were after the same originals.

This is the third Worcester edition. Thomas himself has stated that he printed three editions of this work. The only recorded edition earlier than the present one was printed in 1786 (Nichols 83), and was probably the first. A copy of each of these editions is in the Library of the American Antiquarian Society at Worcester.

EASY LESSONS for Young Children. Philadelphia: W. Young, 1794. [172]

16 mo, 56 leaves, A-C¹⁶, D⁸, including two leaves of advertisements at the end.

Fancy boards, back cover missing.
Not in Evans.

The anonymous author states in the Advertisement that the chief object of the book is to provide *lessons consisting of so great a variety of words as young children may be taught to read . . . In this respect it will be found to differ from the generality of books intended as first Lessons . . . Mrs. Barbauld's Lessons are exceptions to this remark, but I have already offered my opinion, that they are too difficult to begin with . . .*

The work contains stories of good and bad children, and is divided into three parts. Part I consists of XVI Lessons in words of one syllable. The XI Lessons contained in Parts II and III are numbered continuously, and contain polysyllabic words. Lesson II in Part II contains an account of the sights of Philadelphia: *I shall take you to Phi-la-del-phi-a, Wil-li-am, said Mr. Chand-ler to his son, on pur-pose to shew you some sights . . . First they went to see the ci-ty li-bra-ry, then the mu-se-um . . . Then . . . Mar-ket-street meet-ing-house, which is a ve-ry fine place in-deed, and mount-ed to the gal-le-ry's; af-ter-wards they went to the con-gress-hall and saw the Pre-si-dent de-li-ver an ad-dress to both hou-ses of con-gress . . .*

At the end are three pages of *Books for the Instruction and Amusement of Children. Printed by William Young . . .*

ENTERTAINING FABLES for the Instruction of Children. Embellished with Cuts. The Second Worcester edition. Worcester, Massachusetts: Isaiah Thomas, 1794. [173]

16 mo, 16 leaves, without signatures, first and last pasted down to covers, woodcut frontispiece with 12 lines of verse, a woodcut on each page of text.

Dark blue morocco, gilt, original green wrappers bound in.
Evans 26947. Not in Nichols.
Contains XVII fables in verse, each accompanied by a woodcut.

Early American Children's Books

At the end are four pages of Advertisements of Books for the Instruction and Amusement of Children printed and sold by I. Thomas.

From the original Newbery edition. The only edition in Welsh's list (unseen) is from Carnan's list, 1789.

GESSNER, SOLOMON. The Death of Abel. In Five Books. Attempted from the German of Mr. Gessner. By Mary Collyer. New York: Printed and sold by S[amuel] Campbell, 1794. [174]

Duodecimo, 120 leaves, A-U⁶, woodcut frontispiece, one leaf of advertisements at the end.

Original wooden boards and half binding.
Evans 27049.
Mary Collyer, formerly Mitchell, was the wife of Joseph Collyer, famous as a compiler and translator. The translation of *The Death of Abel* was Mrs. Collyer's most famous work; it was originally published in 1761, and passed through many editions. Mrs. Collyer died in 1763.

THE HISTORY OF THE HOLY JESUS. Containing A brief and plain Account of his Birth, Life, Death, Resurrection and Ascension into Heaven; and his coming again at the great and last Day of Judgment. Being a pleasant and profitable Companion for Children; composed on purpose for their Use. Together with a Number of Innocent Songs. By a Lover of their precious Souls. The Second Worcester Edition. Worcester, Massachusetts: Isaiah Thomas, 1794. [175]

Sm. octavo, 32 leaves, (A)-D⁸, first and last leaves pasted down to covers, woodcut frontispiece, woodcuts in the text.

Original Dutch flowered wrappers.
Evans 27122. Nichols 248. Bates p. 11.
Of the thirty illustrations in this edition, eighteen are printed from blocks used in the first Worcester edition, 1786, and twelve are new to this work. The frontispiece in an oval compartment represents *The Rev. Mr. Instructwell, teaching the Principles of the Christian Religion to Master Learnwell*. At the end is *The Child's Body of Divinity; St. Paul's Shipwreck; The Cradle Hymn* by Dr. Watts and nine *Songs for Children*, each of the songs being accompanied by a woodcut in an oval compartment probably after Bewick.

[LANE, JEREMIAH.] A Few Drops of Choice Honey, extracted from the Old Comb of a very ancient Hive; or, Some Pious and very instructive Sentiments taken from an old book which was printed in 1640, entituled, A Son's Patrimony, and a Daughter's Portion; Payable to them at all times, but best received in their first times, when they are young and tender: Laid out without expence of money, only by teaching them to

improve their time, and attend to the words of wisdom. Exeter: Henry
Ranlet, 1794. [176]

Duodecimo, 24 leaves, A-D⁶.

Original marbled wrappers.
Evans 26970. Not in Sabin.
A notice on the back of the title reads: *To the Public. The following Miscellaneous Extracts were collected by Deac. Jeremiah Lane, of Hamptonfalls, for his own perusal and
amusement; but now published by the advice of friends, in hopes that many christians may
receive spiritual benefit from them.*
Pages 41 to the end contain Extracts from Mr. Henry's Exposition of the Bible.

THE LIFE OF GEN. WASHINGTON, Commander in Chief of the American
Army during the late War, and present President of the United States.
Also, of the brave General Montgomery. Embellished with Cuts. Phil-
adelphia: Jones, Hoff & Derrick, 1794. [177]

Duodecimo, 2 parts in 1, 18 leaves, sig. A¹⁸. Woodcut frontispiece portrait to each
part, half title to the Life of General Montgomery.

Original wrappers.
Evans 27221.
The block for the woodcut portrait of General Montgomery is used for several of the
portraits in the *History of America* printed for John Curtis by Wrigley & Berriman in the
following year (no. 192). The blurred condition of the name at the foot would seem to
indicate that it had already done much service and undergone several alterations.
This account of General Montgomery, which is also to be found in the above mentioned
History of America, contains a tribute to Benjamin Franklin, who, in Paris at the time, was
commissioned to procure a monument to the memory of the General. The monument was
duly obtained, and the inscription on it, *worthy of the modest, but great mind of Franklin,*
is quoted at length.
Following the lives is an appendix of five pages containing four poems: *On Washington,
Montgomery, etc.; On the Vanity of Youthful Hopes; On General Washington; An Epitaph
on a poor, but honest man;* and a *Federal Prayer,* in prose.

MARTINET, JOHANNES FLORENTIUS. The Catechism of Nature; for the use
of Children. By Doctor Martinet, Professor of Philosophy at Zutphen.
Translated from the Dutch. Philadelphia: Printed by Hoff & Derrick,
1794. [178]

Duodecimo, 54 leaves, A-C¹⁸.

Original grey wrappers.
This edition not in Evans.
Contains an Introductory Dialogue and XIII numbered dialogues between Tutor and Pupil.
Johannes Florentius Martinet was born in 1729 in Holland. He became pastor of the
Mennonites at Zutphen, and died there in 1796. His *Catechism of Nature* did much to

arouse interest in the study of natural history in his native land, and it was quickly translated into other languages. The present edition was translated by John Hall.

MOTHER GOOSE'S MELODY: or Sonnets for the Cradle. In Two Parts. Part I. Contains the most celebrated Songs and Lullabies of the good old Nurses, calculated to amuse Children and to excite them to sleep. Part II. Those of that sweet Songster and Nurse of Wit and Humour, Master William Shakespeare. Embellished with Cuts, And illustrated with Notes and Maxims, Historical, Philosophical, and Critical. The Second Worcester Edition. Worcester (Massachusetts): Isaiah Thomas, 1794. [179]

16 mo, 48 leaves, A-F⁸, woodcut frontispiece pasted down inside cover. Woodcut illustrations to each song; on page vi printed musical notation; half title to Part II containing the Lullabies of Shakespeare; advertisements on last leaf.

Original blue wrappers with woodcuts.
Not in Evans. Not in Nichols.
This is one of the most famous of the reproductions of Isaiah Thomas of the children's books of John Newbery. It is Thomas's second edition, his first, of which no perfect copy is known, having been published about 1785. Of the present edition the one other copy known is in the library of the American Antiquarian Society at Worcester
The name Mother Goose derives from Charles Perrault's *Contes de ma Mère L'Oye*, and most of the songs belong to the region of folklore. The collection was first made for and by John Newbery and published by him about 1760, internal and external evidence pointing to Oliver Goldsmith as editor for Newbery. The internal evidence is contained in the wit and humour of the Maxims and Notes, written in burlesque imitation of the styles of Dr. Johnson and his school, which accompany each Song; the principal piece of external evidence is the fact that the rhyme in the preface, *There was an old Woman toss'd in a Blanket* which is introduced there without much reason, was Goldsmith's favorite song, and was sung by him to his friends on the night of the production of *The Good Natur'd Man*.
The adaptation of the famous Doleful Ditty, *Three children sliding on the ice*, from the old ballad *The Lamentation of a Bad Market; or, The Drownding of Three Children in the Thames*, has been sometimes attributed to John Gay.
The text and illustrations of the American edition follow the English edition very closely, but Isaiah Thomas has made a few alterations. The order of the songs is changed in one or two places, and a more important innovation, *Se saw, sacaradown, Which is the way to London town*, becomes *Se saw sacaradown, Which is the way to Boston town*.

THE NATURAL HISTORY of Beasts, Which are to be met with In the four Quarters of the Globe. By Charley Columbus. Embellished with pictures. The first Worcester Edition. Worcester, Massachusetts: Isaiah Thomas, 1794. [180]

24 mo, 80 leaves, A⁴, B-K⁸, L⁴, woodcut frontispiece and numerous woodcuts in text.

THE

L I F E

O F

GEN. WASHINGTON,

Commander in Chief of the American Army
during the late War, and prefent Prefident
of the United States.

A L S O,

OF THE BRAVE

GENERAL MONTGOMERY.

Embellifhed with Cuts.

PHILADELPHIA:

PRINTED BY *JONES, HOFF & DERRICK,*

No. 8, NORTH FIFTH-STREET.

M, D CC, X C I V.

Title-page from "The Life of Gen. Washington"

Page from "The Life of Gen. Washington"

Red morocco, gilt, t. e. g. The American Antiquarian Society stamp on title.
Evans 26797. Nichols 251.

The dedication *To all Good Little Masters and Misses in the United States of America* is signed by Charley Columbus, and dated from Worcester, July, 1794.

This book contains prose descriptions, each accompanied by a woodcut, of sixty-two animals. The cuts are probably copied from Bewick originals. Some few were used by Thomas in *Jacky Dandy's Delight*, a slighter work on natural history, no. 130.

See also *The Natural History of Four Footed Beasts*. By Tommy Trip, 1795, no. 196, which is another edition of the same work.

A NEW HIEROGLYPHICAL BIBLE For the Amusement & Instruction of Children; Being A Selection of the most useful Lessons; and most interesting Narratives; (Scripturally Arranged) From Genesis to the Revelations. Embellished with Familiar Figures and Striking Emblems Neatly Engraved To the whole is Added a Sketch of the life of Our Blessed Saviour, The Holy Apostles &c. Recommended by the Rev^d. Rowland Hill M. A. Boston: for W. Norman, n. d. [c. 1794]   [181]

Duodecimo, 72 leaves, A-M⁶, engraved title-page, folded engraved frontispiece in two compartments, emblematic woodcuts throughout the *Hieroglyphical Bible*, ornamental borders on each page; woodcut portraits and other subjects in the life of Christ, the text of this portion being without borders.

Original wooden boards covered with Dutch flowered paper.
Evans 26651. Sabin 53019. O'Callaghan, p. 47.

First American edition. A different work from the *Curious Hieroglyphick Bible* printed by Thomas at Worcester in 1788, no. 128.

The commendation to *Mr. Thompson* is signed *R. Hill*, and dated from Surry Chapel, May 12, 1794. Following this is a preface, and verses by Theodosius Beza *On the Incomparable Treasure of the Holy Scriptures*. The woodcuts of the original English edition (London, 1794) from which these were copied, were attributed to Bewick.

Rowland Hill (1744-1833) was a famous irregular preacher; Surrey Chapel was built for him in 1783. He was the first chairman of the committee of the Religious Tract Society, and an active worker in the interests of the British and Foreign Bible Society and the London Missionary Society.

RICHARDSON, SAMUEL. The History of Pamela; or, Virtue Rewarded. Abridged from the Works of Samuel Richardson, Esq; Adorned with copperplates. The First Worcester Edition. Worcester: Isaiah Thomas, Sold at his Bookstore and by Thomas and Andrews in Boston and Thomas and Carlisle in Walpole, 1794.   [182]

Duodecimo, 90 leaves, including three blanks at the end, A-P⁶, last leaf pasted down to the back cover, six engraved plates at the beginning after those in the English edition by John Lodge.

Original half binding.

Evans 27622. Nichols 258.

Originally a Newbery publication, and possibly abridged for the use of children by Oliver Goldsmith.

The note to the English edition in Welsh's list is *From E. Newbery's List*, 1789. *Probably a reprint of an earlier book, The Paths of Virtue Delineated; or, Pamela, &c., of which Newbery sold Collins of Salisbury a half share for £6. 8s. 6d.* In the American editions *The Paths of Virtue Delineated* is the title of Clarissa, see no. 152.

THE SCHOOL OF GOOD MANNERS. Composed for the Help of Parents in teaching their Children how to carry it in their Places during their Minority. Boston: B. Edes & Son, 1794. [183]

Duodecimo, 48 leaves, A-F⁸ (first and last blanks pasted down to cover), partly uncut, woodcut on title.

Original blue wrappers.

Evans 27337.

The cut on the title is in Bewick style, and represents a woman teaching a boy and girl.

The preface is unsigned, and omits the name of Eleazer Moody—*The following instructions were compiled by a late famous School-Master in Boston.*

The Alphabet of Useful Copies and Cyprian's Twelve Absurdities are omitted.

THE SEVEN VOYAGES OF SINBAD THE SAILOR. And the Story of Aladdin; or, The Wonderful Lamp. Philadelphia; H. and P. Rice, 1794. [184]

Octavo, 48 leaves; B¹², C⁸, D-E¹², F⁴, woodcut on title.

Original half binding.

Not in Evans.

Contains also the Story of the little Hunchback.

These stories from the Arabian Nights came to America via England from the French of M. Galland.

TOM THUMB's FOLIO: or, A new Threepenny Plaything for Little Giants. To which is prefixed, an Abstract of the Life of Mr. Thumb, and an Historical Account of the Wonderful Deeds he performed. Together with some Anecdotes respecting Grumbo, the great Giant. Boston: Samuel Hall, 1794. [185]

16mo, 16 leaves, without signatures, woodcuts, 3 pp. advertisements at the end.

Original flowered wrappers (front wrapper missing).

This edition not in Evans.

On the recto of the first leaf are two large capital M's, probably intended to be pasted down. On the verso is Tom Thumb's Maxim in Trade and Politicks, accompanied by a woodcut. The alphabet is on the back of the title. The contents of the book are practically the same as in the Boston edition of (1780), with different illustrations.

MOTHER GOOSE's
M E L O D Y:
O R
SONNETS for the CRADLE.
IN TWO PARTS.

PART I. Contains the moft celebrated SONGS and LULLABIES of the good old Nurfes, calculated to amufe Children and to excite them to fleep.

PART II. Thofe of that fweet Songfter and Nurfe of Wit and Humour, Mafter William· Shakefpeare.

EMBELLISHED WITH CUTS,

And illuftrated with NOTES and MAXIMS, Hiftorical, Philofophical, and Critical.

THE SECOND *WORCESTER* EDITION.

WORCESTER, (MASSACHUSETTS)
PRINTED BY ISAIAH THOMAS,
AND SOLD AT HIS BOOKSTORE.
MDCCXCIV.

Title-page from "Mother Goose's Melody"

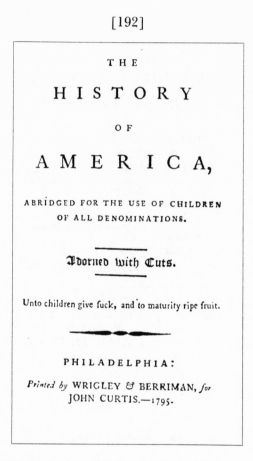

THE

HISTORY

O F

AMERICA,

ABRIDGED FOR THE USE OF CHILDREN
OF ALL DENOMINATIONS.

Adorned with Cuts.

Unto children give fuck, and to maturity ripe fruit.

PHILADELPHIA:

Printed by WRIGLEY & BERRIMAN, *for*
JOHN CURTIS.—1795.

Title-page from "The History of America"

Early American Children's Books

Some of the cuts in this book will be found in the books of Isaiah Thomas published in Worcester. The cuts for the Fables at the end occur also in Thomas's *Entertaining Fables*, published in the same year, no. 173.

This edition is without the poem at the end beginning: *On a pretty bay nag, Here comes Tommy Tag*, to be found in both the Boston editions, nos. 91 and 150.

Samuel Hall introduced his own name in the passage in the second chapter which originally contained Mr. Newbery's: *Tom's father . . . bought for his son all the little books, published by Mr. Hall . . .* see the note to no. 150. The advertisements at the end contain a list of twenty-two books *designed for Instruction and Amusement, and suited to Children of all Ages and Capacities.*

THE WISDOM OF CROP THE CONJURER. Exemplified In several Characters of Good and Bad Boys, with an impartial Account of the celebrated Tom Trot, who Rode Before all the Boys in the Kingdom till he arrived at the Top of the Hill, called Learning. Written For the Imitation of those who love themselves. To which are added, the Farmer, and his Two Daughters, and the Old Mouse. The second Worcester Edition. Worcester, Massachusetts: Isaiah Thomas, 1794.   [186]

16mo, 32 leaves, A-D⁸, first and last pasted down to wrappers, woodcuts in the text, advertisements at the end.

Original silver wrappers.
Evans 28117. Nichols 246.

This is a reprint of the first edition, no. 113, as far as the end of the story, page 43. In the first edition the lower blank half of this page has *The End* and this is followed by four pages of advertisements. In the present edition the lower half of page 43 has a small woodcut tree, and on page 44 begins The Farmer and his two Daughters, followed on page 53 by The Old Mouse. Both these stories, with the same woodcuts, are in *The Sugar Plumb*, no. 123.

1795

THE BROTHER'S GIFT: or, The Naughty Girl Reformed.

> Ye Misses shun the coxcomb of the Mall
> The Masquerade, the Rout, the midnight Ball;
> In lieu of these, more useful arts pursue,
> And, as you're Fair, be wise and virtuous too.

The Third Worcester Edition. Worcester, Massachusetts: Isaiah Thomas, jun. for Isaiah Thomas, 1795.   [187]

16mo, 16 leaves without signatures, woodcut frontispiece, first and last leaves pasted down inside wrappers, woodcut illustrations.

Blue and gold flowered wrappers.
Evans 28353. Nichols 284.

Relates the story of the reformation of Miss Kitty Bland, who was *apt, froward, and headstrong; and, had it not been for the care of her brother Billy, would probably have witnessed all the disadvantages of a modern education. She had been bred at boarding school, and returned home perfectly spoilt.*

The original woodcuts were probably by Bewick. The first and last are in oval compartments, the former with a quotation from Addison's *Cato*, and the latter with *The Naughty Girl becomes Good which makes her esteemed and beloved by everybody. The Brother's Gift* appears on F. Newbery's list 1776, and E. Newbery's list 1786.

COOPER, [W. D.] The History of North America. Containing, A Review of the Customs and Manners of the Original Inhabitants; The first Settlement of the British Colonies, their Rise and Progress, from The earliest Period to the Time of their becoming United, free and independent States. By the Rev. Mr. Cooper. Embellished with Copper Plate Cuts. [Second American Edition.] Lansingburgh: Silvester Tiffany for Thomas Spencer, Albany, 1795. [188]

Duodecimo, 78 leaves, A⁴, B-M⁶, N-O⁴, engraved frontispiece, 5 engraved illustrations.

Original calf.
Evans 28480. Not in Sabin.
The engraved frontispiece by Wightman represents *America trampling on Oppression* and has medallion portraits of Franklin and Washington.
Originally published by E. Newbery, 1789.
The identity of the author, an English clergyman, described on the title-pages of a number of his works as *The Rev. Mr. Cooper*, is somewhat obscure.
In Welsh's list of the books published by the Newberys, this author's works are variously placed under Cooper, Rev. Mr., and Cooper, Rev. W. *A New History of England* is placed under Cooper, Rev. Mr., though the title-page, according to Welsh, reads *By the Rev. Samuel Cooper*.
The catalogue of the Library of Congress lists all the Rev. Mr. Cooper's works under Cooper, W. D., without giving any further details concerning him. *Blossoms of Morality* (no. 412) was apparently translated and edited by the same Mr. Cooper. In Halkett & Laing *Dictionary of Anonymous and Pseudonymous English Literature*, this is ascribed, on the authority of the British Museum, to the *Rev. Charles Cooper*. Welsh says of it *it was issued under J. Cooper's editorship*, and in the bibliography at the end of his article on children's books in *The Cambridge History of English Literature*, Mr. Harvey Darton ascribes it to W. D. Cooper.

[DEFOE, DANIEL.] The Wonderful Life and most Surprising Adventures Of that Renowned Hero, Robinson Crusoe, Who lived Twenty-eight Years on an Uninhabited Island, Which he afterwards Colonised. New York: Hurtin & Commardinger, for E. Duyckinck, & Co., 1795. [189]

Duodecimo, 72 leaves, A-H¹²,⁶. Woodcut portrait of Crusoe as frontispiece, woodcut illustrations in the text.

Original half binding over wooden boards.

Evans 28555.

The text of this abridgement differs from any of the previously described editions, though a few passages are as in Hugh Gaine's edition, 1774, no. 77.

[DEFOE, DANIEL.] The Wonderful Life and most Surprising Adventures Of that Renowned Hero, Robinson Crusoe, Who lived Twenty-eight Years on an Uninhabited Island. Which he afterwards Colonised. New York: Printed by Hurtin & Commardinger, for Benjamin Gomez, 1795.   [190]

Duodecimo, 72 leaves, A-H$^{12, 6}$, portrait frontispiece, woodcuts in the text, as in the previous item. Sig. B in this copy lacks 2 leaves, and 4 leaves of sig. A (repeated) are inserted.

Original half binding over wooden boards (defective).

See Evans 28555 *supra*.

On the flyleaf is written: *David Glover's Book Bought of A Pedler price* 2/6 *January 3rd.* 1796.

FENNING, DANIEL. The American Youth's Instructor; or, a New and Easy guide to Practical Arithmetic . . . Recommended by several eminent Writing-Masters and Accomptants. Dover, New Hampshire: Samuel Bragg, jun., 1795.   [191]

Octavo, 128 leaves, A-Z, Aa-Ii^4.

Original sheep.

Evans 28665. Not in Sabin.

In the form of a series of dialogues between *Philo a Tutor, or Master; and Tyro, a young Scholar.*

David Fenning was a noted English eighteenth century mathematician.

THE HISTORY OF AMERICA, abridged for the use of children of all denominations. Adorned with Cuts. Philadelphia: Wrigley & Berriman for John Curtis, 1795.   [192]

16mo, 64 leaves, A-H^8. Woodcut frontispiece, numerous woodcut portraits.

Original Dutch flowered boards.

Evans 28831.

Possibly the earliest history of America edited especially for American children.

The general account of the discoveries of America, particularly those of Columbus and Vesputius, occupies pages 8 to 15. On page 17 begins the account of the various States, ending on page 78. On page 81 begins the Life of General Montgomery, and on page 103 A Sketch of the Life of Israel Putnam.

Early American Children's Books

The woodcuts for the most part consist of portraits of discoverers and heroes, and of the governors of the various states. In addition to these there is a frontispiece representing Columbus's first interview with the Natives of America, and a cut showing General Putnam captured by the Indians. The greatest economy was used in the portrait cuts. There is a strong family likeness between all the subjects, which divide naturally into two groups, a tricorn hat, with or without a cockade, being the distinguishing mark of the one, and a periwig of the other. In many cases one block is made quite frankly to do for two or more people. Christopher Columbus bears a striking resemblance to General Montgomery; one portrait represents Samuel Huntingdon and Joshua Clayton, another one Benjamin Franklin, Thomas S. Lee and Isaac Shelby; another one John Rutledge and General Greene. There is no life of General Washington, though his portrait is placed before the account of the State of Pennsylvania; the Life of General Montgomery is the same as in *The Life of Gen. Washington ... Also, of the brave General Montgomery*, 1794 (no. 177).

At the end is a list of *Books neatly bound and lettered by John Curtis, Book-Binder.*

THE HISTORY OF THE HOLY JESUS. Containing a brief and plain account of his birth, life, death, resurrection and ascension into Heaven; and his coming again at the great and last Day of Judgment. Being a pleasant and profitable Companion for Children; Composed on purpose for their use. By a Lover of their precious Souls. New York: John [? Bull] for Wm. Durell, n. d. [c. 1795.] [193]

24mo, no signatures, 16 leaves, woodcut frontispiece, 10 small woodcuts in the text.

Original wrappers.
Not in Evans. Not in Bates. This appears to be the only copy known.
The woodcuts are quite different from those of the editions of Boston, 1749 and 1774. The alphabet is on the back of the Bible, at the end is the Child's Body of Divinity, but the hymns to be found in the other edition are omitted. The title-page is slightly rubbed, partly obliterating the name of the printer.

JANEWAY, JAMES. A Token for Children being an exact Account of the Conversion, holy and exemplary Lives and joyful Deaths, of several Young Children. By James Janeway, Minister of the Gospel. To which is added, a Token for the Children of Newengland. Or, Some Examples of Children, in whom the fear of God was remarkably budding before they died; in several parts of Newengland. Preserved and published for the encouragement of Piety in other Children. Worcester, Massachusetts: James R. Hutchins for I. Thomas, 1795. [194]

Duodecimo, 94 leaves, A-M, L-N⁶, Q⁴.

Tree calf.
Evans 28895. Nichols 283. This edition not in Sabin.
The first Worcester edition.

This edition contains the letter addressed to all Parents, Schoolmasters, Schoolmistresses etc., but is without the preface containing Directions to Children. The Token for Children of New England by Cotton Mather begins on page 142.

THE LILLIPUTIAN MASQUERADE. Occasioned By the conclusion of Peace between those Potent Nations, the Lilliputians and the Tommythumbians . . . The Second Worcester edition. Worcester: Isaiah Thomas Jun. for Isaiah Thomas and Son, 1795. [195]

16mo, 32 leaves, A-D⁸, the first, with woodcut frontispiece, and last leaves pasted down inside covers, 2 pp. advertisements at the end.

Original pink and gold wrappers.
Evans 28908. Nichols 285.
The first Worcester edition was printed by Isaiah Thomas in 1787. The American editor made a new title for his editions, the original English edition containing the names of London places of amusement which might be unknown to his young American readers. Welsh mentions only an edition from Carnan's list, 1787.

THE NATURAL HISTORY of Four Footed Beasts. By Tommy Trip. Adorned with cuts. Hudson (New York): Ashbel Stoddard, 1795. [196]

32mo, 80 leaves, A-K⁸, numerous woodcut illustrations in the text, a leaf of advertisement at the end.

Original calf over wooden boards.
Evans 29656.
The descriptions of animals in this work are the same as those in *The Natural History of Beasts* by Charley Columbus, Worcester, 1794 (no. 180), though the present is a smaller work containing only forty-eight descriptions, whereas the Worcester volume has sixty-two. The text is for the most part the same in the two books, though a few passages have been revised or rewritten; a few only of the woodcuts are the same.

Tommy Trip's dedication *To all Pretty little Masters and Misses in America who love reading better than play*, dated from Hudson, January, 1795, is quite different from that of Charley Columbus.

DAS NEUE DEUTSCHE A B C- und Buchstabir—Büchlein, für Die Schulen aller Religionen in Nord-Amerika. Dem ist angehängt, in leichten Sprüchen verfasset, Eine allgemein verständliche Sittenlehre für Die Jugend. Copy-Right secured according to Law. Friederichstadt: Matthias Bärtgis, 1795. [197]

Sq. duodecimo, 20 leaves, A-B⁸, C⁴, first and last leaves pasted down to covers, woodcuts, 1 leaf of advertisement at the end.

Dark brown half morocco, original covers bound in.
Evans 29137 cites no copy. Not in Sabin.

Early American Children's Books

The *Anmerckung* of *Der Herausgeber* is dated from *Friederichstadt, im Jenner* 1795.

A German primer. The alphabet couplets which are accompanied by woodcuts, as in the New England Primer, are translations of the couplets in some of the editions of that work:

Nach Adams Falle
Wir sünd'gen alle . . .

Matthias Bärtgis settled in Frederickstown, Maryland, in 1779, and established the first printing press in that city.

[PINCHARD, MRS.] The Blind Child, or Anecdotes of the Wyndham Family. Written for the use of Young People. By a Lady. Boston: W. Spotswood, 1795. [198]

16mo, 96 leaves, A-M⁸, engraved frontispiece, 1 page advertisements at the end.

Original sheep.
Evans 29325.
The last eight leaves are occupied by an *Appendix. The story of Mr. Wentworth, from the Mirror, No. 27. [a periodical Paper, very deserving of attention.]*
Mrs. Pinchard was the wife of an attorney at Taunton, and her stories were very highly appreciated in her day. The preface to the present work states that the *principal aim, it will be seen, is to repress that excessive softness of heart, which too frequently involves its possessor in a train of evils, and which is by no means true* sensibility. The first edition was published by E. Newbery in London, 1791.

[RICHARDSON, SAMUEL.] The Paths of Virtue Delineated; or, the History in Miniature of the celebrated Clarissa Harlowe, Familiarised and Adapted To the Capacities of Youth. Cooperstown: E. Phinney, 1795. [199]

Duodecimo, 78 leaves, the first a blank, A-N⁶, advertisement on the last leaf.

Original half calf.
Evans 29414.
On the title-page is written in ink: *By Chester Clark Esq.*, and his signature in the same handwriting occurs on the flyleaf.
Another edition of no. 152.

ROWE, ELIZABETH. Devout Exercises of the Heart, By the Late Pious & Ingenious Mrs. Elizabeth Rowe. Abridged for the Use of The Pious. New York: Printed by Tiebout & O'Brien for E. Mitchell, n. d. [c. 1795.] [200]

24mo, 119 leaves, 3 leaves without signature marks, A-O⁸, P⁴, engraved portrait frontispiece, engraved title.

Red morocco, gilt, with the name *Hetty Edgar* in gilt on the front cover.
Not in Evans.
Originally published posthumously in 1737 by Isaac Watts, who is the author of the preface.

Early American Children's Books

Mrs. Elizabeth Rowe (1674-1737) was the daughter of Walter Singer, a nonconformist minister. She was a friend of Matthew Prior, Isaac Watts, Elizabeth Carter, and other literary people. Pope imitated some of her lines in his poems, and her personal character as well as her poetry was eulogized by Dr. Johnson.

WATTS, ISAAC. Divine Songs Attempted in easy Language for the use of Children. Hartford: J. Babcock, 1795.   [201]

16mo, 16 leaves, without signatures, full-page woodcut frontispiece, woodcut on back of title.

Wrappers.

Not in Evans. Not in Trumbull. Not in Stone.

The woodcut frontispiece is in Bewick style. It appears to be from the fairy tale Elmina, and has no apparent connection with the book. The cut of Time on the back of the title is used by Babcock as one of the alphabet cuts in his edition of the New England Primer, no. 261.

WISDOM IN MINIATURE; or the Young Gentleman and Lady's Pleasing Instructor, Being a Collection of Sentences, Divine, Moral and Historical, Selected from the writings of many ingenious and learned Authors, both ancient and modern. Intended not only for the use of Schools, but as a Pocket Companion for the Youth of both Sexes. First Worcester Edition. Worcester: Isaiah Thomas, jun., 1795.   [202]

16mo, 112 leaves, A-O⁸, woodcut frontispiece.

Original sheep.

Evans 29914 (cites AAS copy only). Not in Nichols.

Contains a number of quotations classified according to subject matter. At the end are short extracts from the works of Samuel Johnson and Laurence Sterne, and a selection of *Short Miscellaneous Sentences; alphabetically digested; which may be easily retained in the Memories of Youth.*

The frontispiece is the same as that used in Thomas's editions of *A pretty New-Year's Gift.*

The dedication is to Parents, Guardians, and to all who are concerned in the Education of Youth.

1796

ARABIAN NIGHTS ENTERTAINMENTS; Being a collection of Stories, told by the Sultaness of the Indies, To divert the Sultan from the Execution of a bloody Vow he had made to marry a Lady every Day, and have her head cut off next Morning, to avenge himself for the Disloyalty of the first Sultaness. Containing A better Account of the Customs, Manners, and Religion of the Eastern Nations, viz. Tartars, Persians, and Indians, than hitherto published. Translated into French from the Arabian MSS.

by M. Galland, of the Royal Academy; and now done in English from
the Paris Edition. Norwich: Re-printed by Thomas Hubbard, 1796.

Duodecimo, 54 leaves, A-C¹⁸. [203]

Original half-binding over wooden boards (defective).
Not in Trumbull.
This edition is not in Evans, who has (no. 29993) an edition, no copy located: *Norwich:
Printed? and sold by John Trumbull*, 1796.

THE BIBLE in Miniature or A Concise History of the Old & New Testaments. Philadelphia: for John Dickins [1796]. [204]

16mo, 96 leaves, A-F¹⁶, two engraved titles, engraved illustrations.

Original sheep, gilt.
Not in Evans. Not in Sabin.
A Thumb Bible measuring 2⅛ by 1½ inches. Another edition of no. 145, with differ-
ent engravings.

CHAMBAUD, LOUIS: Fables Choisies, À l'usage des Enfans, et Des autres
personnes qui commencent à apprendre La Langue Françoise, Avec un
Index alphabétique de tous les mots traduits en Anglois. Philadelphia:
Charles Cist, 1796. [205]

Duodecimo, 90 leaves, (-)⁶, A-O⁶, first 2 and last 2 leaves blank; the fore-margins
of the index, sig. H₅ to the end, have been cut for the alphabet by a contemporary
owner.

Original sheep.
Evans 30179.
Contains XCIX numbered fables from Aesop, Aviénus, Barlandus, Gabrias, Phaedrus,
*and other fable-writers of note. There is a moral added to every fable, to help the children's
understanding.*

A CHOICE COLLECTION of New and Approved Country Dances. Printed
at Northampton: 1796. [206]

Octavo, 8 leaves, without signatures, the last a blank.

Brown half morocco, original blue wrappers bound in.
Not in Evans. Not in Sabin.
The dances include Corn Planter, Sea Flower, Cream Pot, De La Bastille, New Jersey,
The President, Democratic Rage and others.

[DEFOE, DANIEL.] Travels of Robinson Crusoe. Written by himself.
Windham [Connecticut]: Printed by John Byrne, 1796. [207]

16 mo, 16 leaves, without signatures, the first and last pasted down to wrappers, woodcut portrait frontispiece, woodcuts in the text.

Original wrappers.
Not in Evans. Not in Trumbull.
The story of Robinson Crusoe ends on page 28. On pages 29-31, headed by a woodcut, is *A Dialogue between a little good Boy and Girl, which if rightly attended to, will shew them how they may be wiser than the rest of their schoolfellows*, also to be found in Thomas's Worcester edition of this work, 1794, and in other books. This reprint of Byrne's edition of 1792 is an infinitely superior piece of work to his former edition except in regard to the woodcut illustrations, which are as crudely printed as heretofore.

DEFOE, DANIEL. The Wonderful Life, and most Surprizing Adventures Of that renowned Seaman, Robinson Crusoe, Who lived Twenty-eight Years on an Uninhabited Island, And was afterwards relieved by Pirates. Together with some Account of his Man Friday. Fairhaven: Re-printed and sold by J. P. Spooner [c. 1796]. [208]

Duodecimo, 24 leaves, A-H⁴·², woodcut of a ship as frontispiece, repeated several times in text, one other woodcut in the text.

Wrappers.
Not in Evans.
On the recto of the last leaf (the verso is blank) beneath the cut of a ship are the lines beginning: *'Twas in this Ship which sail'd from Hull* followed by a list of books, *Printed, and for sale, very low, to Pedlars and others, at the Printing Office, Fairhaven*.
This version of the story follows the edition as printed by Hugh Gaine, 1774, for a few pages but later becomes an abridgement of that abridgement.

THE GRATEFUL RETURN; An Entertaining Story, for Children. Embelished (*sic*) with Cuts. The First Edition. Lansingsburgh: Luther Pratt, & Co., 1796. [209]

16 mo, 16 leaves, without signatures, first and last leaves pasted to covers, woodcut frontispiece, woodcut illustrations.

Original wall paper wrappers.
Evans 30507.
The grateful return is on the part of a poor boy, who returns to express his gratitude in the form of a nest of linnets to the little girl and her brother who had been kind to him, thus convincing the unkind brother who had despised his poor clothes, that to be a snob does not always pay: *Mary-Ann and Edward had another pleasure beside the approbation of their Mamma; for their brother George, reflecting on his conduct, and seeing how improper it was, became ever after very good-natured.*

GREGORY, JOHN. A Father's Legacy to his Daughters. By Dr. Gregory. To which is added a Collection of Thoughts on Civil Moral and Religious Subjects, Calculated to Improve the Minds of Both Sexes... Second Edition. Worcester, Massachusetts: Isaiah Thomas, Jun., April, 1796. [210]

> Sm. octavo, 60 leaves, A-P⁴.
>
> Original calf, several uncut lower edges.
> Evans 30515. Nichols 311.
> This edition has the preface.

[HELMUTH, JUSTUS HEINRICH CHRISTIAN.] Das Gute Kind vor, in und nach der Schule. Philadelphia: Steiner und Kämmerer, 1796. [211]

> Duodecimo, 12 leaves, A-B⁶, woodcut on title-page, woodcuts in the text, chiefly in oval compartments.
>
> Original wall paper covers.
> Evans 30525. Not in Sabin.
> First edition.
> A *School of Good Manners* in German in prose and verse, relating to the child's behaviour in school.
> The dedication is signed J. Heinrich C. Helmuth, and is dated from Philadelphia 12 May, 1796.
> The author was born in Helmstadt, Germany, in 1745. He was ordained to the ministry in 1769, and came to America in the same year in response to an urgent call from the Lutheran congregation in Pennsylvania, serving first in Lancaster and later in Philadelphia. He was interested in education and held important positions in the University of Pennsylvania, and, with Dr. Schmidtt, established a private seminary in Philadelphia. Helmuth wrote a number of books including several for children. He died in Philadelphia in 1825.

THE HISTORY OF LITTLE GOODY TWO-SHOES. Otherwise called Mrs. Margery Two-Shoes. With The means by which she acquired her learning and wisdom, and in consequence thereof her estate. Set forth at large for the benefit of all those pretty little Boys and Girls who wish to be good and happy. Wilmington: Printed by Peter Brynberg, 1796. [212]

> 16mo, 64 leaves, A-H⁸, woodcut frontispiece consisting of 2 cuts, woodcut illustrations in the text.
>
> Original half binding with wall paper boards.
> Not in Evans.
> The woodcuts are not copied from Thomas's edition, and are much cruder in type.
> The publisher of this edition has only revised the Introduction to the extent of omitting any name in such passages where John Newbery and Isaiah Thomas each introduced his

own. He has however inserted at the end the following note: [* ** *Such is the state of things in Britain.* Americans *prize your liberty, guard over your rights and be happy.*]

In this edition, the story closes before the *extempore lines* to be found in other editions. It has the first part of the Appendix, containing *The Golden Dream*, but is without the remainder of the Appendix containing *An Anecdote, of Tom Two-Shoes*, and is also without *A Letter From the Printer* at the end.

The book is in an attractive wall paper binding, a style for which Peter Brynberg became famous.

MACGOWAN, JOHN. The Life of Joseph, the Son of Israel. In eight books. Chiefly designed to allure Young Minds to a Love of the Sacred Scriptures. By John Maggowan (*sic*). The fifth edition. Wilmington: Joseph Johnson, 1796.   [213]

Duodecimo, 88 leaves, A-O⁶, P⁴.

Unbound.
Evans 30721.
Half title to each book.
Commendatory preface by William Rogers, D. D. Professor of English and Oratory in the College and Academy of Philadelphia, Jan. 1, 1791.

The *Life of Joseph* was first printed in England in 1771. It was very popular, and frequently reprinted. The author was born in Edinburgh in 1726, and after being a weaver, a baker, and a Wesleyan minister, eventually joined the particular baptists, and in 1766 became pastor of the old meeting-house in Devonshire Square, Bishopsgate, London, where he remained until his death in 1780.

THE NEW-ENGLAND PRIMER; much improved. Containing, a Variety of easy Lessons. For Attaining the true Reading of English. Germantown: Printed in the year 1796.   [214]

Octavo, 40 leaves, including the last blank, (A), B-E⁸, woodcut portrait of Washington as frontispiece, woodcuts (alphabet and John Rogers).

Original wrappers, uncut.
Probably printed by Michael Billmeyer, who succeeded Christopher Sower.

This appears to be the only copy known. It is not in Heartman, who (no. 126) has a differing Germantown edition of the same year, 75 pages, without signatures.

This edition is the same as the Philadelphia edition printed by Johnston and Justice for Robert Campbell in 1792 (no. 162), except that the latter has no frontispiece, and the order of the text is changed on two pages.

[PINCHARD, MRS.] The Blind Child, or Anecdotes of the Wyndham Family. Written for the use of Young People, By a Lady. Worcester: Printed by Isaiah Thomas, jun., 1796.   [215]

24mo, 96 leaves, A-M⁸ (A₁ blank lacking).

Half brown morocco.
Evans 31013 cites only one copy, that in the American Antiquarian Society at Worcester.
Nichols 314 locates no copy and says: *Title taken from sale catalogue.*
The Appendix is slightly shorter than in the edition of Boston, 1795, no. 198, lacking
the last two paragraphs. There are a few unimportant variations in the text.

A PRETTY NEW YEAR'S GIFT; or, Entertaining Histories, for the Amusement and Instruction of Young Ladies and Gentlemen, in Winter Evenings. By Solomon Sobersides . . . The Second Worcester Edition. Worcester (Massachusetts): Thomas, Son & Thomas, 1796. [216]

16mo, 68 leaves, A-H⁸, I⁴, woodcut frontispiece and numerous woodcut illustrations, advertisements on the last page.

Unbound as issued, stitched, lower edges uncut.
Evans 31218. Not in Nichols.
A reprint of no. 111; in this edition the error in numbering the stories has been corrected.

THE REMARKABLE HISTORY OF AUGI: or: A Picture of True Happiness.
Together with the Story of the Dreamer. First American Edition. Worcester: Printed by Isaiah Thomas, jun., 1796. [217]

24mo, 16 leaves, without signatures, first and last pasted down to covers, woodcut
frontispiece.

Original Dutch flowered wrappers.
Evans 31080 cites one copy only, that in the American Antiquarian Society. Nichols 317.
A truly remarkable history from the French. The moral is contained in the prefatory remarks: *True Happiness exists no where except in the representations of painters and poets, at
the Opera, or in certain dramas of the* Comedie Italienne.
The story closes on page 25 with the significant sentence: *O liberty! how dearly do thy
blessings cost a nation who purchases thee by* crimes. Pages 26-31 contain *The Dreamer*, a
short story representing *the situation of many idle boys, who instead of getting up early to
their study, lie in bed until the sun burns them out of it.*

RURAL FELICITY; or, the History of Tommy and Sally. Embellished with
cuts. New York: J. Oram for the Bookbinders Society, 1796. [218]

16mo, 16 leaves, A¹⁶, first and last leaf pasted down to covers, woodcut frontispiece
and illustrations, alphabets on the last leaf.

Original Dutch flowered wrappers.
Not in Evans.
Tommy and Sally, aged twelve and ten respectively, whose parents *cultivated a little farm,*
with which the children helped, *situated at no great distance from the splendid metropolis of*

England, amused themselves by telling each other stories illustrating the advantages of a simple life over one of pomp and ceremony. Tommy's last story ends as follows: *The toils of the day are succeeded by rural amusements, which consist of manly sports, and feats of activity. Away then with pomp and luxury, and leave me in the quiet possession of* Rural Felicity.

SALZMANN, CHRISTIAN GOTTHILF. Elements of Morality, for the Use of Children; with an Introductory Address to Parents. Translated from the German of the Rev. C. G. Salzmann. Illustrated with twenty copperplates. In two volumes. Vol. I. [II.] Philadelphia: Printed by F. Hoff & H. Kammerer, jun. 1796. [219]

Duodecimo, 2 volumes in 1: Vol. I, 124 leaves, A-U⁶, W⁴; Vol II, 132 leaves, 2 leaves without signatures, A-W⁶, X⁴. Eighteen plates by Weston.

Original calf.
Evans 31156.
Translated by Mary Wollstonecraft, with two leaves of advertisement written by her.
Christian Gotthilf Salzmann, the celebrated German educator, was born in 1744 and died in 1811. The *Moralisches Elementarbuch* was one of his most important publications for children. The translation by Mary Wollstonecraft (Godwin) first appeared in 1790 with illustrations by Blake.

THE SCHOOL OF GOOD MANNERS: Containing, I. Rules for children's behavior in every situation in life. II. A brief summary of the doctrines contained in the Holy Scriptures. III. An explanation of many terms used in moral philosophy and divinity. IV. Fourteen short forms of prayer composed for the use of children, particularly for such as attend schools, and academies, for every morning and evening, in the course of a week. By the Preceptor of the Ladies' Academy in New-London. New London: Samuel Green [c. 1796]. [220]

Duodecimo, 24 leaves, A-D⁶.

Dark blue half morocco.
Not in Evans. Not in Trumbull.
Parts I-III are in double columns, the fourteen prayers are in long lines.
This is not the same work as the *School of Good Manners* printed in New-London 1754, though the compiler of the present book was probably familiar with the other work. It opens with General Advice, which is followed by rules for children's behaviour at home, at table, at school, in the meeting house, in company, abroad, and more particular directions to young persons when journeying. The succeeding chapters are in the form of a catechism, and deal with politeness, a system of divinity, explanation of terms by which different sects and denominations of persons are called and questions in theology and metaphysics. Then follow the fourteen forms of prayer.

The rules for behaviour are thorough and succinct: *Wash your face and comb your head; Let your fore-fingers be upon the back of your knife, and towards the tines of your fork, hanging down; Put not a greasy knife into the salt; When helping your superior to an article he shall ask for, throw it not at him; Never tell a person that you have heard his story before,* etc.

SWIFT, JONATHAN. The Adventures of Capt. Gulliver, in a Voyage to the Islands of Lilliput. Abridged from the works of the celebrated Dean Swift. Printed at Fairhaven: and sold cheap by the gross, dozen, or single [c. 1796]. [221]

Duodecimo, 23 leaves, A$^{2-4}$, B-H$^{2, 4}$, woodcuts.

Unbound.
Not in Evans.
This edition is unillustrated save for a woodcut at the end and a small cut of a ship, both of which were used by the printer in his edition of *Robinson Crusoe*, no. 208.

THE TWO BABES IN THE WOOD: Together with Divine Songs for Children. Poughkeepsie: Nathan Douglas, 1796. [222]

Duodecimo, 6 leaves, (A)^4, B^2.

Dark blue half morocco.
Evans 31326.
A chapbook. *The Two Babes in the Wood* contains simply the ballad: *Now ponder well you parents dear*, the version used having slight textual differences from the earlier versions. The dowry of Jane is two hundred pounds in gold. The *Divine Songs* occupy pp. 9-12. The book is unillustrated.

WATTS, ISAAC. Divine Songs: in easy language, For the use of Children. By the late reverend and pious Doctor Watts. New London: James Springer, 1796. [223]

16mo, 16 leaves, without signatures, first and last (a blank) pasted down to cover, woodcut portrait frontispiece, woodcut at end of text.

Original Dutch flowered wrappers.
Not in Evans. Not in Trumbull. Not in Stone.
A charming little toy book, with a wonderful portrait as frontispiece, and the alphabets in hornbook form on the back of the title. The woodcut of a parrot at the end was probably copied from the parrot in the *Royal Primer*, and is of frequent occurrence.

WISDOM IN MINIATURE: or the Young Gentleman and Lady's Pleasing Instructor, being a Collection of Sentences, Divine, Moral and Historical, Selected from the writings of many ingenious and learned authors, both ancient and modern. Intended not only for the use of Schools, but as a Pocket Companion for the Youth of Both Sexes in America. Second Worcester Edition. Worcester (Massachusetts): Thomas, Son & Thomas, October, 1796.   [224]

16mo, 96 leaves, A-M⁸, frontispiece (lacking in this copy).

Original calf, paper label on back, many uncut lower edges.
Evans 31651. Nichols 318.
Another edition of no. 202.

WISDOM IN MINIATURE: or the Young Gentleman and Lady's Magazine—[No. I.] Being a collection of Sentences, Divine and Moral. Hartford: J. Babcock, 1796.   [225]

32mo, 14 leaves, without signatures, 13 woodcut illustrations in the text.

Unbound, sewed.
Evans 31650. Not in Trumbull.
This is a different publication from the preceding though on similar lines. It contains a number of moral sentences than which, according to the compiler in the preface *there is no kind of writing better calculated to form the minds of youth—to give them a just conception of things—to reform their loose and vicious habits—to improve their morals, and set vice and virtue in their proper colours.*

THE WONDERFUL ESCAPE, or Sagacity outwitted: A curious story. Boston: J. White, 1796.   [226]

Duodecimo, 11 leaves, A²⁻⁶, B⁶, many uncut edges, curious woodcut illustration.

Dark blue half morocco.
Not in Evans.

1797

THE HISTORY OF THOMAS THUMB, with His wonderful Adventures and Some Anecdotes respecting Grumbo the great Giant. Wilmington: Printed by James Adams, 1797.   [227]

Duodecimo, 16 leaves, including the wrappers, without signatures, woodcut frontispiece, woodcut of Tom Thumb's Monument at the end.

Original wrappers included in the pagination, a woodcut on each side.
Evans 32931 cites no copy.
On the verso of the first leaf (wrapper) is a woodcut representing Tom Thumb standing on the hand of a man; page three contains the title; pages four to six the alphabet in hornbook form and a syllabary. The story, an abridgement of that in the various editions of *Tom Thumb's Folio*, occupies pages 7 to 27, and is followed by Tom Thumb's frequently quoted Maxim in Trade and Politicks: *He who boys* (sic) *this book for Two-pence, and lays*

it up till it is woth (sic) *Three-pence, may get an hundred per cent. that is, one half by the bargain.* The penultimate leaf contains a list of Little Books, which may be had at James Adams's Bookstore, and the last leaf a notice that other little Books are shortly to be published. The book is a toy book, measuring 3⅛ by 2 inches, a form for which James Adams was famous. The woodcuts are copied from cuts originally used by Newbery.

THE HOLY BIBLE abridged; or, The History of the Old and New Testament. Illustrated With Notes, and adorned with Cuts, For the Use of Children. Wilmington: Peter Brynberg, 1797.   [228]

16 mo, 68 leaves, A-H⁸, I⁴, woodcut illustrations, partly unopened.

Original boards, covered with wall paper, leather back.
Evans 31809. Not in Sabin.
Another edition of no. 92 with different cuts and without the dedication. The woodcuts are taken from cuts in the books published by Newbery.

JUVENILE TRIALS for Robbing Orchards, telling Fibs, and other Heinous Offences. By Master Tommy Littleton, Secretary to the Court; with a Sequel by Dr. Aikin. Boston: for F. Nichols, 1797.   [229]

Duodecimo, 60 leaves, (Aⁱ), B-E¹², F⁸, G³.

Original boards, uncut.
Evans 31700.
An early exposition of self-government in the schoolroom, and an extremely popular work.
    On the verso of the title is the note: *This, says Dr. Aikin, is a very pleasing and ingenious little Work, in which a Court of Justice is supposed to be instituted in a School, composed of the Scholars themselves, for the purpose of trying offences committed at School.*
    The Introduction is in the form of a Dialogue between a Tutor and Governess.
    At the end is a poem entitled: *Phaeton Junior*, with the note: *The following humourous Poem is inserted here merely to fill a vacant space.*
    Dr. Aikin was the brother of Mrs. Barbauld, and her collaborator in *Evenings at Home* and other stories. *Juvenile Trials* was entered by T. Carnan at Stationers' Hall on Dec. 18, 1771. The work is probably of much earlier date.

WEED, ENOS. The American Orthographer, in three books. Book I. The Bibliographical-Spelling-Book. Book II. The Geographical-Spelling-Book. Book III. Part I. Amerrikan-Standard for Pronunsiashion. Part II. Ammerrikanz Jeograffikal Standard. Part III. Ammerikanz-Diksonarian Standard ... By Enos Weed, jun. Physician and Surgeon in Difficult Cases. Danbury: Douglas & Nichols for the author [1797].   [230]

Duodecimo, 30 leaves, A², B⁴, C⁷, D⁵, E-F⁶, uncut.

Grey boards, original wrappers bound in.

Trumbull 1604.

Contains alphabets, syllabaries, spelling columns of Scriptural names, Directions for Children's Behaviour (as in the *School of Good Manners*), Catechisms, Prayers, etc.

The title is written in phonetic symbols. The author's Address to the Public is dated from Stamford, in Connecticut, June 23d, A. D. 1797.

1798

A BAG OF NUTS ready cracked: or, instructive fables, ingenious riddles, and merry conundrums. By the Celebrated and Facetious Thomas Thumb, Esq. Published for the Benefit of all little Masters and Misses Who love Reading before Playing. Second Worcester Edition. Worcester, Massachusetts: I. Thomas, Jun., September, 1798.   [231]

Duodecimo, 46 leaves, A-E⁸, F⁶, (lacks A₁, possibly a blank) frontispiece consisting of two oval woodcuts, oval and rectangular woodcuts in the text.

Unbound, original stitching.

Not in Nichols.

Chapter I, pages 13-45, contains fables, each with a Moral appended, and illustrated with woodcuts. Chapter II, pages 46-69, contains XII Riddles, the riddle and its answer being on the recto of each leaf, the accompanying illustration being opposite on the verso of the previous page. Chapter III contains Conundrums, followed by Dialogues and Maxims.

This book was on E. Newbery's list, 1789. The woodcuts in the American edition are Newbery cuts and were probably in the English edition from which this is copied. Thomas Thumb's address to the reader has been revised for this American edition: *I, Thomas Thumb, Esq., having been informed that there are as many good little boys and girls in* America, *as in any part of the globe, have willingly put myself to the great trouble and hazard of taking a flight from the Land of Cuckows . . . that I might enquire into the truth of a report . . .* Thomas then proceeds to narrate how he fared in America, and describes the *Bag of Nuts, ready cracked—a collection of fables and conundrums; each of which, I hope, will be found to suggest and inculcate some useful lesson of morality.* The address closes as follows: *If, however, there are any persons so weak as to take pleasure in perusing romantic improbabilities, and trifling and impossible wonders, I shall refer them to the childish and contemptible histories of* Tom Hickathrift *and* Jack the Giant Killer, *or to the fabulous accounts which have been frequently published of, Your very obedient, humble Servant, and affectionate Well wisher, T. T.*

THE BIBLE. The Ninth Edition. Philadelphia: for W. Jones, 1798. [232]

144 leaves, including the last blank, A-I¹⁶, woodcut frontispiece, full-page woodcuts in the text, measures 2 by 1¾ inches.

Original sheep.

An edition of the Thumb Bible of John Taylor, the Water-Poet.

According to Stone, p. 67, this is one of two copies known, the other being in his own collection. In Mr. Stone's copy the title is followed by another title with the words *Eighth Edition*. In this copy the *Ninth Edition* title-page has been pasted down on to the next leaf, thus cancelling it.

Early American Children's Books

The Apocrypha is contained on two leaves, E_{16}, F_1. The New Testament begins on F_2 with the title *The New Testament* between type ornaments, and a woodcut on the verso; on F_3 *The History of the New Testament*, verso blank.

The dedication to *his Excellency G. Washington, President of the United States of America* is a paraphrase of the original dedication to Anne, the queen of James I, and retains the signature *J. Taylor*. The first line reads *Most worthy* George,* *into thy hands we give*, the asterisk pointing to an explanatory footnote, **G. Washington*, in order to avoid misunderstanding or confusion with King George III, who was still on the English throne.

[BUNYAN, JOHN.] The Christian Pilgrim: Containing an Account of the Wonderful Adventures and Miraculous Escapes of a Christian, in his Travels from the Land of Destruction to the New Jerusalem. First American Edition. Worcester: Isaiah Thomas, Jun. October 1798. [233]

Sm. octavo, 2 vol., together 113 leaves, A-G^8; $(G)^9$, H-N^8, the penultimate leaf with the advertisement of Isaiah Thomas, Jun., and the last a blank. Woodcut portrait frontispiece in each volume, that in Vol. II. forming the extra leaf in sig. (G.) Numerous woodcut illustrations.

Original wooden boards, covered with silver grey paper.

Nichols 369 can only quote the title from a newspaper advertisement.

The title of the second volume is the same as that of the first, except that the word *Adventure* is in the singular; *Vol. II.* is added after *First American Edition*, and the date is misprinted 1789.

The dedication reads: *To the Youth of America*: *The following pages calculated to inspire you with an early attachment to Religion & Virtue, is dedicated with every affectionate wish for your prosperity & happiness by your friend the Editor.*

An arrangement for children of *The Pilgrim's Progress*, a work which was not originally intended for the young, but which is one of the most popular and influential children's books ever written.

Although John Bunyan was the greatest Puritan of his day (1628 to 1668), he nevertheless in this work succeeded in reconciling religion and romance, so that a century later Richard Graves in the *Spiritual Quixote* compared the adventures of Christian with those of Jack the Giant Killer and Thomas Hickathrift the Conqueror. In this respect the work of Bunyan is in striking contrast to the Janeway school.

The original edition of this abridgement was probably a Newbery publication. An edition was on E. Newbery's list, 1789, which may possibly help to account for the misprinted date in the American edition.

CYNTHIA: with the Tragical account of The unfortunate loves of Almerin and Desdemoma (*sic*). A Novel. Illustrated with a variety of the chances of fortune; moralized with many useful observations, whereby the Reader may reap both pleasure and profit. New Haven: G. Bunce, 1798. [234]

Duodecimo, 66 leaves, A^{12}, B-$G^{12,6}$.

Original half binding.

Not in Trumbull.

Early American Children's Books

THE ENTERTAINING, Moral, and Religious Repository; Written in a simple yet pleasing Stile, Eminently Calculated for the Amusement and Instruction of the Youth of Both Sexes. Published by a Society in Great Britain, instituted for the beneficent purpose of aiding the intention of His Majesty, as expressed in his royal proclamation for the suppression of vice and immorality. Vol. I. Elizabeth-Town: Shepard Kollock for Cornelius Davis, 1798. [235]

Duodecimo, 48 leaves, A-H⁶.

Original half binding over wooden boards, wall paper sides, sheepskin back.

Contains The Shepherd of Salisbury Plain; The History of Tom White, the Postilion [both by Hannah More]; The Life of William Baker by the Rev. Mr. Gilpin; A Funeral Sermon; The Two Soldiers [by Hannah More].

These Sunday School Tracts were originally published by Hannah More in the series known as the Cheap Repository Tracts, for a note on which see *The Harvest Home*, 1800. William Baker was a parish impostor who completely deceived and imposed upon his vicar and biographer, the Rev. William Gilpin of Boldre in the New Forest (England).

THE HERMIT OF THE FOREST, and the Wandering Infants. A rural fragment. Embellished with cuts. Boston: S. Hall, 1798. [236]

16 mo., 16 leaves, without signatures, first and last leaves pasted down to covers, woodcut frontispiece, woodcut illustrations in the text, two leaves of advertisement at the end, alphabet on the back of the title.

Original marbled paper covers.

The scene of the story is laid in the forest of Englewood in Cumberland, England, and the motive is reminiscent of the *Babes in the Wood*.

The original edition was advertised in the *London Chronicle*, Dec. 27-29, 1787, to be published for E. Newbery in the Christmas Holidays.

THE HISTORY of the Holy Bible. Illustrated with Notes, And Adorned with Cuts. For the use of Children. Hartford: John Babcock, 1798. [237]

Duodecimo, 60 leaves, A-E¹². Frontispiece and numerous woodcut illustrations.

Original wooden boards and half binding.
Not in Trumbull.

John Babcock's advertisement on the back of the title. It ends: *Old Books rebound with care, and produce received in pay.*

This edition (another edition of no. 92 etc.) contains the Old Testament only.

A HISTORY of the Life of Aesop. According to Sir Roger L'Estrange. To which is added, A Choice Collection of Fables, with instructive morals.

Early American Children's Books

For the Benefit of Youth. Taken from the most eminent mythologists. Philadelphia: Printed at the Southwark office, 1798. [238]

16 mo., 69 leaves, A-G⁹, H⁶, a leaf of advertisement at the end, oval woodcuts in the text.

Half bound.
An abridgement of the chief literary work of Sir Roger L'Estrange (1616-1704), the celebrated Tory journalist and pamphleteer.

[PINCHARD, MRS.] Dramatic Dialogues, for the Use of Young Persons. By the author of The Blind Child, &c. Boston: for W. Spotswood, 1798. [239]

Sm. octavo, 170 leaves, a separate alphabet of signatures for each Dialogue, six separate title-pages, six engraved frontispieces, advertisement of New Publications for young people on the back of the general title.

Red morocco, gilt.
Contains:
1. The Misfortunes of Anger. A Drama. In two parts.
2. Sensibility. A Drama. In two parts.
3. The Little Trifler. A Drama. In three parts.
4. The Little Country Visitor. A Drama. In two parts.
5. The Distrest Family. A Drama. In two parts.
6. The Village Wedding. A Drama. In one part.
7. The Mocking Bird's Nest. A Dialogue.

The author explains in the preface that this work is not intended to fulfil the same purpose as the Theatre of Education of Madame de Genlis, that the Dialogues are not intended for performance, but are only thrown into this form in a *belief that young people are easily captivated and interested by this manner of writing, and the convenience of avoiding the* "said she," *and* "replied she," *which becomes so fatiguing in a narration of any length.*

The edition published by E. Newbery in 1792 contained the first five dialogues as in this edition, but the last two were replaced by two others.

THE REPROBATE'S REWARD, or, a Looking-Glass for Disobedient Children, being A full and true Account of the barbarous and bloody Murder of one Elizabeth Wood, living in the city of Cork, by her own Son, as she was riding, upon the 28th day of July, to Kingsale market. How he cut her throat from ear to ear; as also how the murder was found out by her apparition or ghost; the manner of his being taken; his dying words at the place of execution; with a true copy of verses written with his own hand in Cork jail, being a warning to all disobedient Children to repent, and obey their Parents. Philadelphia: Printed in the year 1798.

Duodecimo, 4 leaves, without signatures; in verse. [240]

Original grey wrappers.

A chapbook. An account in verse of the terrible deeds related on the title-page, and a call to children to repent and to obey their parents.

> Awake, awake, you graceless children all.
> And hear the Lord in time, while he does call.
> * * *
> For now to such a pass the world is come,
> The very babes do after vices run;
> As soon as they can speak, they curse and swear;
> Some parents take delight the same to hear.

The penultimate verse contains a popular threat:

> Just as the holy scriptures doth say,
> He that his parents dear doth disobey,
> A prey shall be to every bird that flies,
> The ravens likewise shall pick out his eyes.

Ross, James. A Practical, New Vocabulary Latin and English; consisting of more than two thousand Nouns Substantive, Appellative and Proper; serving to exemplify and illustrate the rules for the declensions and genders of nouns in the Latin Grammar: With an Appendix of Adjectives, Every one of which may be adapted to one or other of the foregoing substantives. By James Ross, A. M. Teacher of the Latin and Greek Languages; and Rector of the Franklin Academy in Chambersburg. Chambersburg: Snowden and M'Corkle, Nov. 10, 1798. [241]

Duodecimo, 36 leaves, (A)², B-E⁶, G⁶, H⁴ (the letter F was omitted from the signatures).

Original half binding, sheepskin back, sides covered with wall paper.
First edition.

James Ross was a schoolmaster at Chambersburg, Pennsylvania, from 1796 to 1801. Later he taught at Lancaster, Pennsylvania; and in Philadelphia. He was a professor of languages at Dickinson College.

Thomas a Kempis. An Extract of the Christian's Pattern; or, A Treatise of the Imitation of Christ. Written in Latin By Thomas à Kempis. Published by John Wesley, M. A. Philadelphia: Printed by Henry Tuckniss, sold by John Dickins, 1798. [242]

16 mo, 160 leaves, A-K¹⁶.

Original sheep.
Not in Sabin.

At the end are two leaves of publisher's advertisements, in which this book is included, priced at 2s., bound.

The reason given by John Wesley, the famous evangelist and leader of Methodism (1703-1791), for the publication of his revised edition of the *De Imitatione Christi*, which he had read in Stanhope's version, was that he was *very angry at Kempis for being too strict*. The first edition was published in 1753.

[WEBSTER, NOAH.] The Prompter; a commentary on common sayings and subjects, which are full of common sense, the best sense in the world. [Without name of place or printer.] Printed in the Year 1798.
[243]

Duodecimo, 44 leaves, A-F⁶, G⁸, the last a blank.

Original wooden boards covered with brown mottled paper.
Contains twenty-nine essays.

1799

[FIELDING, HENRY.] The Remarkable History of Tom Jones, a Foundling. Salem: N. & J. Coverly, 1799.
[244]

16 mo, 16 leaves, first and last (a blank) leaves pasted down to covers, woodcut frontispiece with four lines of verse below, alphabet on verso of title.

Original flowered wrappers.
Tapley; *Salem Imprints*, p. 368.
This abridgement is not mentioned in the Bibliography at the end of *The History of Henry Fielding*, by Wilbur L. Cross. An edition was on E. Newbery's list, 1789.
According to Miss Tapley *The Coverlys were a family of itinerant newspaper publishers, journeymen printers, publishers of ballads and other broadsides, who lived in more or less obscurity, but whose work today takes on an importance not really warranted by the quality of their output, but because of a certain historical value attached to them.*

[JOHNSON, RICHARD.] The Illustrious and Renowned History of the Seven Famous Champions of Christendom, In three parts. Containing their honorable Birth, Victories, and noble Atchievements, by Sea and Land, in diverse strange Countries; their Combats with Giants and Monsters; wonderful Adventures, Fortunes and Misfortunes, in Desarts, Wildernesses, inchanted Castles; their Conquests of Empires, Kingdoms; their relieving distressed Ladies, with their faithful Love to them; Honor they won in Tilts and Tournaments; and Success against the Enemies of Christendom. With the Manner of their untimely Deaths; and how they came to be styled Saints and Champions of Christendom. Also, The Heroic Adventures of St. Gforge's [*sic*] three Sons. Amherst, New-hampshire: Samuel Preston, 1799.
[245]

Duodecimo, 60 leaves, A-K⁶.

Original half binding and wooden boards.

A chapbook version based on Richard Johnson's celebrated romance.

The first known edition of *The Most famous History of the Seauen Champions of Christ-endome* was printed in London in 1596, and the first edition of the second part *shewing the Princely prowesse of Saint Georges three Sonnes, the liuely Sparke of Nobilitie* in 1597. The first edition of this abridgement appears to have been printed for T. Norris, A. Bettesworth, London 1719. A chapbook version was printed in London circa 1750, and was frequently reprinted. In the chapbook versions, St. George no longer comes from Cappadocia, but has become an Englishman born and bred. *St. George was born in the city of Coventry, and for his magnanimous deeds of arms in foreign adventures, had the title given him of the valiant knight of St. George of England.* His father, at the time of his birth, was lord steward of England.

Richard Johnson was born in London in 1573 and died about 1659.

LEDLY, EDWARD. The Foundling; or the History of Lucius Stanhope. By Edward Ledly, Gent. Printed at Rutland, 1799.   [246]

Sm. octavo, 16 leaves, A-B^8 (lacks B$_8$), uncut, partly unopened.

Old mottled calf.

Relates the history of Lucius Stanhope, *whose parents deserted him in his infancy, and left him in a basket, suspended to the knocker of the door of the good Sir John Honeycomb, who lived in a village in Yorkshire.*

First published as one of Newbery's Penny Books in 1787.

THE NEW-ENGLAND PRIMER, Or, an easy and pleasant Guide to the Art of Reading, Adorn'd with cutts. To which is added, The Assembly of Divines' Catechism. Albany: for Thomas, Andrews & Penniman, 1799.   [247]

Duodecimo, 35 leaves, A$^{2-6}$, B-F^6, woodcuts (alphabet, John Rogers and others).

Original wooden boards covered with paper leather back.

Not in Heartman. This is apparently the only copy known.

There is no frontispiece, which may have been on A$_1$, lacking in this copy. Except that it is without the alphabet in compartments from the Royal Primer, the contents of this edition are very much the same as in the undated Boston edition of J. White, no. 139. The alphabet couplets are the same as in that edition, the rhyme for Young Obadias being illustrated by the tree intended for the Royal Oak; it has the three texts from the Scriptures with the woodcut on the back of the title, and the Haymakers rhyme and woodcut at the end.

RICHARDSON, SAMUEL. The History of Pamela; or, Virtue Rewarded. Abridged from the Works of Samuel Richardson, Esq. Norristown: David Sower, 1799.   [248]

Duodecimo, 78 leaves, A-F^{12}, G^6.

Original half binding.

This is the first Norristown imprint.

The work is the same abridgement as that used by Thomas at Worcester, no.182. It does not contain the last few pages of that edition, with *the few brief observations which naturally result from this story*.

SONGS AND LULLABIES of the Good Old Nurses. Calculated to Amuse Children. Embellished with cuts; And illustrated with Notes and Maxims, Historical, Philosophical and Critical. First Worcester Edition. Worcester: Isaiah Thomas, Jun., 1799.   [249]

16 mo, 14 leaves without signatures; woodcut frontispiece (two woodcuts), a woodcut illustration to each song.

   Unbound, stitched.
   Not in Nichols.
   This work consists of twenty of the songs and lullabies from the first part of Mother Goose, with the same maxims and notes, and illustrations.
   The frontispiece and the woodcuts on the last page are not in Thomas's edition of Mother Goose, they each consist of two woodcuts, those on the last page representing a man in the pillory and a coffin. The *Songs and Lullabies* is without the preface to Mother Goose. The running title throughout is *Songs and Lullabies*, whereas in Mother Goose it is *Mother Goose's Melody*. The title-page states this to be the first Worcester edition, which must be taken to mean the first edition in this form, as Isaiah Thomas had previously published two complete editions of Mother Goose in which these songs and lullabies were included.

1800

THE AFFECTING HISTORY of the Children in the Wood. Embellished with Cuts.
            Peruse this little book, and you will find,
            How much the love of gold depraves mankind.
Stonington-port: Printed by S. Trumbull, 1800.   [250]

Duodecimo, 12 leaves, A-D$^{2,\,4}$, first and last pasted down on covers, woodcut frontispiece, woodcuts in the text.

   Original fancy wrappers.
   The alphabet in hornbook form on the back of the title.
   The History of the Children in the Wood ends on page 20; pages 21, 22 are occupied by the Story of Three Robbers, and page 23 by A Riddle. The story of *The Children in the Wood* is in prose, and the ballad, *Now ponder well you parents dear*, does not occur.

BARBAULD, ANNA LETITIA, and AIKIN, JOHN. Evening Tales; consisting of Miscellaneous Pieces for the Amusement and Instruction of Children, extracted from the works of Mrs. Barbauld and Mr. Aiken.

SONGS and LULLABIES

OF THE

GOOD OLD NURSES.

CALCULATED to AMUSE CHIL-
DREN.

EMBELLISHED WITH CUTS;

And illuftrated with NOTES and MAXIMS,
HISTORICAL, PHILOSOPHICAL
and CRITICAL.

FIRST *WORCESTER* EDITION.

Printed at WORCESTER: *Maffachnfetts,*
BY ISAIAH THOMAS, JUN.
Sold Wholefale and Retail by Him...1799.

*Title-page from "Songs and Lullabies
of the Good Old Nurses"*

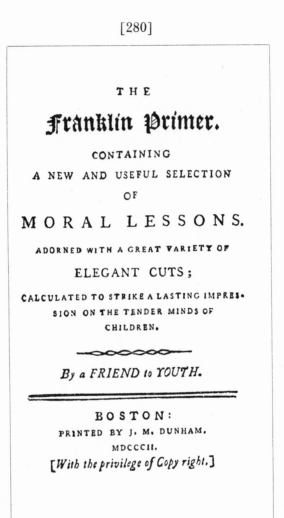

THE

Franklin Primer.

CONTAINING

A NEW AND USEFUL SELECTION

OF

MORAL LESSONS.

ADORNED WITH A GREAT VARIETY OF

ELEGANT CUTS;

CALCULATED TO STRIKE A LASTING IMPRES-
SION ON THE TENDER MINDS OF
CHILDREN.

By a FRIEND to YOUTH.

BOSTON:
PRINTED BY J. M. DUNHAM.
MDCCCII.
[*With the privilege of Copy right.*]

Title-page from "The Franklin Primer"

Early American Children's Books

Wilmington (Del.): Printed and sold by Peter Brynberg, n. d. [c. 1800.]

16mo, 54 leaves, A-C, E-G⁸, H⁶. [251]

Original half binding, with wall paper boards.

Alphabets on the back of the title. At the end is a list of *Books Printed and Sold by Peter Brynberg, Market Street, Wilmington, for the Entertainment and Instruction of the Little Masters and Misses in the United States.*

The tales cover a period of eight nights, and the chapter headings are *Night First, Night Second,* and so on. The story for Night Eighth is *The Farm-Yard Journal,* for a separate edition of which see no. 789.

John Aikin was the brother of Mrs. Barbauld.

THE BIBLE. The ninth Edition. New-England, Printed for the Purchaser [c. 1800]. [252]

138 leaves, measuring 1¾ by 1½ inches, woodcut frontispiece, many lower edges uncut.

Original calf.

Stone p. 67.

An edition of the *Thumb Bible* of John Taylor, the Water-poet, and apparently the only perfect copy known.

The woodcut frontispiece, which is the only illustration in the book, is different from that in the *Ninth Edition* printed for W. Jones in Philadelphia (no. 232). It is extremely crudely cut, and apparently is meant to represent a man holding up an open Bible. The dedication is to the Rev. Clergy of the United States of America, and the first line has again been paraphrased to read *Most hopeful Sires into thy hands we give.*

CHOICE TALES; consisting of an Elegant Collection of delightful Little Pieces for the Instruction & Amusement of Young Persons. Philadelphia: Joseph Charless, for Mathew Carey, 1800. [253]

Duodecimo, 86 leaves, A¹², C-H¹², I².

Original half binding of boards and leather.

Contains sixteen short stories, from various sources, one of which, *Phaeton Junior,* is in verse. The first story, *The Discontented Squirrel,* is from Mrs. Barbauld and John Aikin's *Evening Tales,* see no. 251 *supra.* A note prefixed to the *Migrations of Birds* reads: *When Children are reading this Essay, they ought to be informed that all the information it contains, applies to England.*

The story entitled *Half-a-Crown's Worth* contains some interesting comparative values. Speaking of the books half-a-crown a week would buy, the father instructing his son explains that this *sum laid out for old books would buy you more classics, and pretty editions too, in one year, than you could read in five.*

[DARTON, WILLIAM.] Little Truths Better Than Great Fables: Containing Information on divers Subjects, for the Instruction of Children ... Volume I. [II]. Illustrated with copper-plates. Philadelphia: J. & J. Crukshank, 1800. [254]

Duodecimo, 2 volumes, 28 and 32 leaves, A-B¹², C⁴; A⁸, B-C¹², engraved frontispiece and 3 engraved illustrations in each volume.

Original pictorial wrappers, a copper-plate illustration on each side, the first volume partly uncut.

This book, though written in England for English children, is of great importance in the history of American children's literature, as it contains an account of the discovery of America, and much interesting information concerning that continent and its people.

The first volume, which is in two parts, contains general information on matters connected with the farm, natural history, the making of wine, beer, cider and perry, paper making, silk manufacture etc. The second volume is largely devoted to America and its people; the frontispiece to this volume represents the well-known story, related in the body of the book, of Sir Walter Raleigh, his pipe, and his man. The book is written in dialogue form, the children's questions being printed in italics.

The same illustrations are not used on the covers of every copy of this book.

William Darton (1747-1819) was the founder of the famous Quaker publishing house in London. This book was originally published by his own firm. The engraved illustrations were by himself and his friend and partner, Joseph Harvey.

[DAVIDSON, ROBERT.] Geography Epitomized. A short but comprehensive Description of the Terraqueous Globe, in Verse, to assist the Memory. [Leominster, Mass.:] for Chapman Whitcomb [c. 1800].   [255]

Duodecimo, 30 leaves, A-E⁶.

Unbound and stitched as issued, uncut.

Wegelin 448. This edition not in Sabin.

For the first edition see no. 96.

Wegelin places this item under Whitcomb, although he correctly attributes the Stanford edition of 1805 (his no. 920) which has the author's name on the title-page.

Copyright was issued to Robert Davidson as author on February 24, 1794.

This item is placed in the year 1800 in accordance with the findings of Mr. J. C. L. Clark in his *Notes on Chapman Whitcomb*. Mr. Wegelin dates it *about* 1796, but according to Mr. Clark all the Chapman Whitcomb items from this Leominster press were printed about 1800 and 1801. It has not yet appeared in Mr. Evans's Bibliography, which has reached the year 1797.

Chapman Whitcomb was an eccentric New England peddler and schoolmaster, who travelled about Worcester County, Massachusetts, teaching English grammar. He was born in Hardwick in 1765, graduated from Dartmouth in 1785, and died at Hardwick in 1833. For an interesting account of him and the books printed for him at Leominster, see the pamphlet by Mr. Clark cited above.

[DEFOE, DANIEL.] Life and Surprising Adventures of the renowned Robinson Crusoe, Who lived Twenty-Eight Years on an Island Inhabited by no Human Creature but Himself, And which he afterwards Lived to Colonize. First American, from a much admired London Edition. Dedham: Herman Mann, 1800.   [256]

LITTLE TRUTHS

BETTER THAN GREAT FABLES:

Containing Information on divers Subjects, for the
Inſtruction of CHILDREN.

" *Children naturally love Truth, and when they read a Story, their*
" *firſt Queſtion is, whether it is true? If they find it true, they*
" *are pleaſed with it, if not they value it but little, and it ſoon*
" *becomes inſipid.*"

Winter Evenings.

———‹‹€€З З››·———

VOLUME II.

ILLUSTRATED WITH COPPER-PLATES.

———‹‹€€З З››·———

PHILADELPHIA:

PRINTED FOR, AND SOLD B", J. AND J. CRUKSHANK,
NO. 87, HIGH STREET.

1800.

*Title-page from "Little Truths Better
Than Great Fables"*

[254]

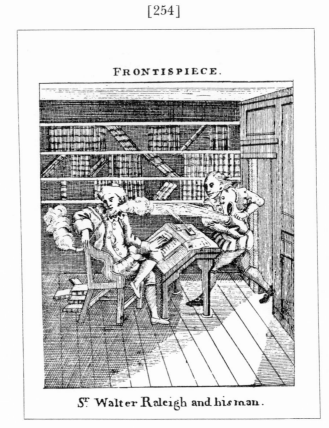

FRONTISPIECE.

S.ʳ Walter Raleigh and his man.

Page from "Little Truths Better
Than Great Fables"

Sq. duodecimo, 69 leaves, A-H⁸, I⁵, the last a blank, frontispiece portrait of Crusoe between two six-line stanzas, woodcuts in the text.

Original wooden boards and half binding.

This is a reprint of the Newbery edition of *Robinson Crusoe* with different woodcuts. From the statement on the title-page the printer was evidently unaware that the first American edition of this version had been printed by Hugh Gaine in New York in 1774 (no. 77).

The short last paragraph of this edition is not in Gaine's edition; it recounts that Mr. Crusoe settled *in a village near* London, *then called* Stoak Newton, *but now is pronounced* Stoke Newington; *and expired on the 27th of June*, 1721. This is followed by an *Account of the Island of Juan Fernandez, and of Alexander Selkirk*, from Morse's Geography, and Cowper's verses supposed to have been written by Alexander Selkirk beginning: *I am monarch of all I survey*.

The portrait frontispiece is very similar to that used by Isaiah Thomas. The woodcuts in the text consist chiefly of representations of birds and natural history subjects.

DWIGHT, NATHANIEL. A short but comprehensive System of the Geography of the World: By Way of Question and Answer. Principally designed for Children and Common Schools. By Nathaniel Dwight. The Fourth Connecticut Edition. Hartford: Hudson and Goodwin, 1800.

Duodecimo, 108 leaves, A-S⁶, last leaf pasted down on back cover. [257]

Original half sheep.

Trumbull 621. This edition not in Sabin. The first edition was published in Hartford in 1795.

Nathaniel Dwight (1770-1831), a famous surgeon and minister, was born in Northampton, Mass. He was the grandson of Jonathan Edwards, and the brother of Timothy Dwight, President of Yale College, and author of *A Valedictory Address*, no. 84 in this catalogue. That the author was also a schoolmaster, in addition to his activities as a surgeon and minister, we know from the preface to the first edition of the present work (dated from Hartford, May 12, 1795, and reprinted in this edition). His geography was extremely popular as being *better calculated to impress the facts which it contains on the minds of children than any heretofore published*, and went through numerous editions.

[MORE, HANNAH.] [Cheap Repository. Number 22.] Sunday Reading. The Harvest Home. Philadelphia: B. & J. Johnson, 1800. [258]

Sm. octavo, 18 leaves, sig. X¹⁸, woodcut on title, uncut, unbound.

At the end are four leaves of verse consisting of two hymns signed Z [i.e. Hannah More], followed by the announcement: *Next week will be publish'd The History of the Plague in London, in the year* 1665.

The Cheap Repository tracts were produced by Hannah More, with some help from her sisters and friends, at the rate of three tracts a month (a tale, a ballad, and a tract for Sunday reading) for three years. These were sold for a penny each, and afterwards collected into three volumes. Those signed Z were by Hannah More.

These tracts were extremely popular in England and the committee formed for their distribution eventually led to the formation of the Religious Tract Society. William Cobbett was largely responsible for their circulation in America.

This is the first item in this catalogue with the imprint of Benjamin and Jacob Johnson, the Quaker founders of the famous Philadelphia publishing house, which eventually passed, through Johnson and Warner and M'Carthy and Davis, into the hands of Moses Polock, the uncle of the present collector, whose juveniles formed the inspiration and the corner stone of this collection.

A short account of the history of these firms, and of Moses Polock, all of whom specialized in children's books, will be found in the introduction.

[MORE, HANNAH.] [Cheap Repository. Number 28.] The Fall of Adam. Philadelphia: B. & J. Johnson, 1800.   [259]

Sm. octavo, 18 leaves, sig. Dd¹⁸, woodcut on title, unbound, uncut.

At page 24 the caption title: *Book of Martyrs. An Account of Holy Men who died for the Christian Religion*, followed by accounts of Bishop Ridley, and Mr. George Wisheart.

On page 35 is the Martyr's Hymn, and at the end the announcement: *Next week will be publish'd The Life of William Baker*. (see no. 235.)

This number is unsigned.

[MORE, HANNAH.] [Cheap Repository. Number 40.] Onesimus; or, the Run-Away Servant Converted. A true story. Philadelphia: B. & J. Johnson, 1800.   [260]

Duodecimo, 17 leaves, Qq¹⁷, woodcut on title-page.

Unbound.

The story ends on page 18. On page 19 begins: *An Application of the above Story*, and on page 30: *The Old Man, his Children, and the Bundle of Sticks. A Fable*.

This fable is in verse, and although it is the usual Sunday school tale, the opening lines are distinctly more flippant than is customary in this class of story:

> A Good Old Man, no matter where,
> Whether in York or Lancashire,
> Or on a hill or in a dale,
> It cannot much concern the tale;
> Had children very much like others,
> Compos'd of sisters and of brothers . . .

This number is unsigned.

THE NEW ENGLAND PRIMER, improved, For the more easy attaining the true Reading of English. To which is added, The Assembly of Divines' Catechism. With other useful and pleasing Matter. Hartford: John Babcock, 1800.   [261]

16 mo, 32 leaves, A-B¹⁶, woodcuts (alphabet and John Rogers).

Original blue wrappers.

Early American Children's Books

Heartman 142 cites one copy only. Not in Trumbull.

The alphabet couplets are as in the very early editions of the primer with the exception of those for the letters K and W. The letter K has

> The British King
> Lost States thirteen.

which has already appeared in certain editions (see no. 133 etc.).

The couplet for the letter W
> By Washington,
> Great deeds were done.

has not appeared in any of the previous editions in this collection. It is accompanied by a portrait of the great general. All the woodcuts for the alphabet couplets are interesting, and that for

> The Cat doth play
> And after slay.

is a particularly happy one. One of the more usual illustrations for these lines represents a cat playing a fiddle to a dancing mouse, obviously reminiscent of *High, diddle diddle, the cat and the fiddle.* In this edition, however, the cat is playing to a group of mice dancing on their hind legs.

This alphabet is followed by a rhymed alphabet beginning:

> A Was an Angler, and fish'd with a hook,
> B Was a Blockhead, and ne'er learn'd his book.

WHALLEY, THOMAS SEDGWICK. Edwy and Edilda, A Tale, in five parts. By the Rev. Thomas Sedgwick Whalley, author of "A Poem on Mont Blanc," &c. &c. &c. Embellished with six fine engravings, from original designs, By A Young Lady. London Printed: Albany: Reprinted by Loring Andrews: 1800. [262]

Octavo, 88 leaves, A-L⁸, plates.

Original tree calf.

Thomas Sedgwick Whalley was born at Cambridge in 1746. He was educated at Cambridge, took Holy Orders, became famous as a poet and traveller, and was created D. D. of Edinburgh University in 1808. *Edwy and Edilda* was his first published work, and was issued anonymously in 1779. The first edition with the plates was published in 1794. The artist responsible for the designs for the engravings was a daughter of Lady Langham.

WISDOM IN MINIATURE: or the Young Gentleman and Lady's Pleasing Instructor, being a Collection of Sentences, Divine, Moral and Historical, Selected, from the writings of many ingenious and learned authors, both ancient and modern. Intended not only for the use of Schools, but as a Pocket Companion for the Youth of Both Sexes in America. Third Edition. Brooklyn: T. Kirk, 1800. [263]

16 mo, 104 leaves, A-F¹⁶, G-H⁴, (lacks G₄).

Original sheep (front cover loose).

T. Kirk was the first printer in Brooklyn. Another edition of nos. 202 and 224.

Early American Children's Books

[BARBAULD, ANNA LETITIA.] Lessons for Children from four to five years old. Wilmington (Del.): P. Brynberg, 1801. [264]

Sm. octavo, 34 leaves, A-D⁸, E².

Original wall paper wrappers, uncut and partly unopened.
Another edition of no. 127. The alphabet on the back of the title. At the end a list of *Chap-Books, Printed and Sold by Peter Brnberg,* (sic) *Market Street, Wilmington, for the Entertainment and Instruction of the Little Masters and Misses in the United States.*

BLOOMFIELD, ROBERT. The Farmer's Boy; A Rural Poem. Philadelphia: Printed from the London third edition by James Humphreys, 1801. [265]

Sq. octavo, 72 leaves, (A)-I⁸; two leaves of advertisement at the end.

Original wrappers, uncut and unopened.
The book is folded as an octavo, though the chain lines run across the paper.
This poem, written in a garret where five or six others were working, was first published in 1800, and had a remarkable success. This American edition is printed from the third London edition less than a year after its first publication.
The author, who lived and died in poverty, was born in 1766 and died in 1823.

THE BOOK OF BOOKS, for Children, To teach all good boys and Girls to be wiser than their school-fellows. Adorned with Cuts. Salem: N. Coverly, 1801. [266]

32 mo, 8 leaves, without signatures, woodcuts.

Original pink wrappers.
Tapley: *Salem Imprints* p. 376.
Contains Fables with morals, and the Dialogue between a little good Boy and Girl, *which if rightly attended to, will shew them how they might be wiser than the rest of their school fellows,* used in Thomas's Worcester edition of *Robinson Crusoe,* 1794, no. 171, John Byrne's Windham edition of the same work, no. 154, and others.

DILWORTH, W. H. The History of the Conquest of Mexico, By the Celebrated Hernan Cortes. Containing A faithful and entertaining Detail of all his Amazing Victories, in that vast Empire, its Laws, Customs, Religion, &c. A work abounding with Strokes of Generalship, and the most refined Maxims of Civil Policy. Philadelphia: H. Sweitzer, 1801. [267]

Duodecimo, 82 leaves, A-N⁶, O⁴, many lower edges uncut.
Original half binding.
Sabin 20184.
First American edition. Originally published in London in 1759.

Early American Children's Books

FÉNÉLON, FRANÇOIS DE SALIGNAC DE LA MOTHE. On Faithfulness in Little Things. By Fenelon, Archbishop of Cambray. Translated from the French into German, and thence into English. New York: Isaac Collins & Son, 1801. [268]

Duodecimo, 6 leaves, without signatures, title on recto of first leaf, verso blank, advertisement on verso of last leaf.

Unbound.
François de Salignac de la Mothe Fénélon (1651-1715) was a celebrated French writer, and the archbishop of Cambrai.

JUVENILE TRIALS for Robbing Orchards, Telling Fibs, and other Offences. With alterations and additions. Recommended by the Author of Evenings at Home. Philadelphia: B. & J. Johnson, 1801. [269]

Duodecimo, 76 leaves, A-I⁸, K⁴, engraved frontispiece, woodcut illustrations in the text.

Original dark grey paper covered boards.
For a former edition see no. 229.
The author of *Evenings at Home* who recommended the work was Dr. John Aikin. The former edition had Dr. Aikin's name on the title-page, together with that of Master Tommy Littleton, Secretary to the Court.

[KENDALL, EDWARD AUGUSTUS.] The Canary Bird: A moral story. Interspersed with Poetry. By the author of The Sparrow, Keeper's Travels, The Crested Wren, &c. Philadelphia: for Benjamin Johnson and Jacob Johnson, 1801. [270]

Sq. octavo, 40 leaves, A-E⁸, engraved frontispiece, by Tanner, some edges uncut.

Original boards.
The advertisement states: *The Subject of this Volume is the Escape of a Canary-Bird from his Cage:—the Design—to present to the young Readers a little Miscellany of Natural History, Moral Precept, Sentiment and Narrative.*
Edward Augustus Kendall (1776?-1842) was a famous English author of children's books.
The Canary Bird was first published by E. Newbery in London in 1799; it is not in Welsh's list.

THE LITTLE MASTERS AND MISSES DELIGHT: containing Polite Histories, Stories, Tales, Lives, & Adventures, For the early Improvement of Youth, in Virtue and good Manners. A new edition, improved by Young Slyboots. Published by Authority. Wilmington (Del.): Printed and sold by P. Brynberg, 1801. [271]

16 mo, 44 leaves, A-D⁸, E-G⁴, the last a blank, woodcut illustrations in the text, in rectangular and oval compartments, alphabets on the back of the title.

Original wall paper boards.

Contains fictional stories with morals, the biography of Cardinal Wolsey, stories of Scripture History, a few fairy tales, including Cinderella and Puss in Boots, etc.

The first tale in the book *The Story of Little Tom the Traveller and the Lion* is the story of Androcles, with Little Tom replacing Androcles as the hero. *The History of St. George and the Dragon* gives Coventry as the birthplace of the saint, *his father's name was Albert, high steward of England*.

One of the stories, *The Character of Prudiana*, is a portion of a tale to be found in *The Sugar Plumb*, no. 123. The book is evidently English, both with regard to text and illustrations. It is not in Welsh's edition of Newbery's list.

[MACGOWAN, JOHN.] The Life of Joseph, The Son of Israel. In eight books. Chiefly designed for the use of youth. Worcester: Isaiah Thomas, Jun., September, 1801. [272]

Duodecimo, 66 leaves, A-L⁶, woodcut ornament on title and at the head of each chapter, one leaf of advertisement at the end.

Original wooden boards, covered with dark blue paper, leather back.
Nichols 416.

This edition was published anonymously, although previous editions have the author's name on the title-page, see no. 213. It is without the commendatory preface to be found in the Wilmington edition.

WATTS, ISAAC. Divine Songs, attempted in Easy language for the use of Children. By I. Watts, D.D. Baltimore: Warner & Hanna, 1801. [273]

Duodecimo, 36 leaves, (A)⁴ B¹⁸ B (repeated)¹⁴, the last blank pasted down to cover.

Original wall paper covers.
Not in Stone.
With the exception of two tailpieces this edition is unillustrated.

1802

THE CHILD'S SPELLING BOOK: Calculated to render Reading Completely Easy to Little Children; To impress upon their minds the importance of Religion, and the advantages of Good Manners. Fourth Edition—By A Printer. Hartford: From Sidney's Press, for Increase Cooke & Co., 1802. [274]

Duodecimo, 56 leaves (A)-G⁸, frontispiece with four woodcuts, woodcut illustrations in the text, by A. Anderson.

Original half binding over wooden boards, with the Ellsworth and McKee bookplates.

Early American Children's Books

The first edition was published in Hartford in 1798.

Contains alphabets, a syllabary and a *Reading Easy* in prose and verse.

The passages for reading include extracts *altered from Mrs. Barbauld;* Dr. Watts's Cradle Hymn; part of the Sermon on the Mount; fables; hymns, etc. The instruction includes Dr. Watts's Catechism; Rules for the Behaviour of Children (from the *School of Good Manners*, New-London, 1754 etc.) and Instances of Ill-Manners, to be avoided by Children of every age. These last are very practical . . . *Asking unnecessary questions; enquiring the prices of, and inspecting articles at the stores, which you do not think of purchasing . . . standing between the light and any person wanting it . . . passing between the fire and persons sitting at it . . . Throwing things instead of handing them, or handing them awkwardly . . . Replying to a question put to another person . . .*

The woodcut illustrations are copies by Dr. Alexander Anderson of cuts by Bewick and others.

Alexander Anderson, known as *The Father of Wood-Engraving in the United States,* was born in New York in 1775. He early became interested in copper-plate engraving, but later his admiration for the work of the Bewicks and their followers influenced him to work in wood. A comparison between his woodcuts and those of the earlier American woodcutters in this collection will show to what extent he improved upon his predecessors, and how justly he deserves his title. He died in Jersey City in 1870.

HEMMENWAY, MOSES and FULLER, ANDREW. Discourse to Children. By the Reverend Moses Hemmenway, D.D. Also the Conversion and Death of Joseph: an affecting story, founded on fact. And A New Year's Gift for Youth. By the Rev. Andrew Fuller, D.D. Kettering. Charlestown: Samuel Etheridge, 1802. [275]

Duodecimo, 18 leaves, A-F⁴, ², sewed, uncut and unbound.

The Story of Joseph begins on page 22, and the New Year's Gift for Youth on page 25. Moses Hemmenway (1736?-1811) was a minister at Wells, Maine.

Andrew Fuller (1754-1815) was born in Cambridgeshire and, joining the Baptist church, eventually became the minister at Kettering, where he remained until his death. He was one of the founders of the Baptist Missionary Society, and its first Secretary. He received the degree of D.D. from the College of New Jersey (Princeton), and from Yale College.

On the back of the title is written: *Grace Howland's Book Given her by Master Jonathon H. Lyman,* 1803.

THE HERMIT OF THE FOREST, and the Wandering Infants, A Rural Fragment. Embellished with Cuts. Philadelphia: Published by Jacob Johnson, 1802. [276]

16mo, 16 leaves, A¹⁶, first and last pasted down to covers, woodcut frontispiece, woodcut illustrations in the text.

Original blue wrappers.

The woodcuts are from those in the edition of Boston, 1798, no. 236.

Early American Children's Books

THE HISTORY OF PRINCE LEE Boo a Native of the Pelew Islands brought to England by Capt.[n] Wilson a new Edition. Philadelphia: for B. Johnson and J. Johnson, 1802. [277]

Duodecimo, 72 leaves, A-M^6, engraved frontispiece, engraved title and five plates. Original sheep, gilt.

Not in Sabin who has only later Dublin and London editions of this work.

An extremely popular book, frequently reprinted. Prince Lee Boo was brought to England by Captain Wilson after the wreck of the *Antelope* and died there in 1784 from smallpox. References to him are frequently made in children's books of the period, as for example in *The Mother's Remarks on a Set of Cuts for Children*, no. 288 *infra*.

SAMPSON, EZRA. Beauties of the Bible: being a selection from the Old and New Testaments, with various Remarks and brief Dissertations, designed for the use of Christians in General, and particularly for the use of Schools, and for the Improvement of Youth. By Ezra Sampson of Hudson (New-York.) Second Hudson Edition. Hudson: Sampson, Chittenden & Croswell, 1802. [278]

Duodecimo, 170 leaves, A-Z, Aa-Dd^6, Ee^2.

Original calf, some edges uncut.
Sabin 75925.

Ezra Sampson (1749-1823) was a native of Middleborough, Massachusetts; graduated from Yale College in 1773, and in 1775 officiated as a chaplain in the Revolutionary army. He was at one time editor of the *Connecticut Courant* at Hartford, and was co-editor with Dr. H. Croswell of the *Balance* at Hudson.

WHITTINGTON, SIR RICHARD. The History of Whittington And his Cat. Shewing, How from a poor Country Boy, destitute of Parents or Relations, he attained great Riches, and was promoted to the high and honourable dignity of Lord Mayor of London. Embellished with Cuts. Philadelphia; Published by Jacob Johnson, 1802. [279]

16mo, 16 leaves, A^{16}, woodcut frontispiece portrait of Sir Richard as Lord Mayor, numerous illustrations in text, first and last leaves pasted down to covers.

Original green wrappers.

At the end is a *Reflection. This story of Whittington and his Cat, and all the misfortunes which happened to that poor boy, may be considered as a cure for despair, as it teaches us that God Almighty has always something good in store for those who endure the ills that befal them with patience and resignation.*

The first chapbook version of the story was printed and sold in Aldermary Church Yard, London.

Sir Richard Whittington, the famous hero of the tale, was an authentic personage, and was thrice Lord Mayor of London, serving in 1397, 1406 and 1419, in addition to a portion of the term of Adam Bamme in 1396. He died in 1423.

[WILLARD, SAMUEL.] The Franklin Primer. Containing a new and useful selection of Moral Lessons. Adorned with a great variety of Elegant Cuts; calculated to strike a lasting impression on the tender minds of children. By a Friend to Youth. Boston: J. M. Dunham, 1802. [280]

Duodecimo, 44 leaves, (A)-N⁴, ², O⁴, woodcut frontispiece portrait of Franklin, woodcuts in the text.

Wrappers.
Not in Sabin.
First edition.
The book is *dedicated to the Memory of Doct. Benjamin Franklin*. The woodcut portrait and the leaf of Dedication are placed before the title.

A development of the New England Primer, containing alphabets and syllabaries; lessons in verse, a concise history of the world, with scriptural lessons, *and a number of elegant cuts, representing some of the most striking passages in the course of the history;* hymns; Dr. Watts's catechism, and the catechism of the Assembly of Divines. In the Introduction the compiler gives the reasons that have induced him to issue this publication *as a substitute for the old Primer,* which *has of late become almost obsolete.* He explains that *he has introduced the* Bust of Doct. Franklin *for a frontispiece—a man whose manner of life from his youth up, is worthy the most minute observation, and imitation of the rising generation.*

Samuel Willard (1775-1859) was born at Petersham, Massachusetts. He graduated from Harvard College in 1803, the year following the publication of this book, which became very popular and ran into many editions. He was ordained over the church at Deerfield in 1807, but resigned from the pastorate on account of total loss of sight in 1829.

YOUTHFUL SPORTS. Philadelphia: Published by Jacob Johnson, 1802. [281]

Duodecimo, 18 leaves, A-C⁶, engraved title with vignette, 11 plates each in 2 compartments, placed before the text.

Original blue marbled wrappers.
The plates illustrate the twenty-three sports described in the text. These include: Shooting with Bow and Arrow; Bird-Nesting, *What a pity to call this a sport!* Thread the Needle; Dressing the Doll; Flydown; Playing at Horses; Hop, Stride and Jump; Whipping Top; Bathing; Battledore and Shuttlecock, *There is not much danger in this sport, but breaking of windows, which might be avoided with a little care;* Blindman's Buff; Flying the Kite; Peg Top; Trundling a Hoop; Cricket, *It must be allowed to be good diversion, and is of such note, that even men very frequently divert themselves with it;* Playing at Taw, *Marbles is a pretty diversion for little boys, but we would advise them not to play for money or one another's marbles;* Skating; Skipping, *a pretty play for active boys* and others. Most of the descriptions are accompanied by grave warnings of the dangers incurred in playing the game. No. 24, the last story in the book, is *The Young Mouse. A Fable.*

On the last page is Jacob Johnson's advertisement of *the greatest variety of useful and entertaining Books, ever offered for the instruction of the American Youth.*

Early American Children's Books

This work was originally published by Darton & Harvey in London, 1801. The plates of the present edition are printed the reverse way from those in the London edition.

1803

THE AMERICAN PRIMER, calculated for the instruction of Young Children. First edition. Norfolk: A. C. Jordan & Co. 1803.　　　[282]

36 mo, 36 leaves, with signature marks placed in haphazard fashion, a page of advertisements at the end, woodcuts.

Original wrappers.

This primer retains some of the features of the New England Primer, notably John Rodgers' (*sic*) Verses of Advice to his children, with the short account of him, and the woodcut of his martyrdom, and Dr. Watts's Cradle and other hymns. In addition, it contains passages for reading, including some as in the New England Primer of Johnston and Justice, no. 162, extracts from Mrs. Barbauld's *Easy Lessons*, etc. At the end are a few fables, and the fairy-tale: *Elmina: or, The Flower that never Fades*, a separate edition of which will be found elsewhere in this catalogue.

[BARBAULD, ANNA LETITIA.] Lessons for Children, Part II. From four to five years old. Adorned with Cuts Engraved by James Akin. Wilmington, Del.: James Wilson, 1803.　　　[283]

Duodecimo, 22 leaves, A-C⁶, D⁴, uncut, vignette woodcut on title, woodcuts in the text.

Original blue paper wrappers, two woodcuts on upper and two on the lower cover.
The words *Adorned with Cuts Engraved by James Akin* are cut in the wood block on the title. James Wilson's advertisements on the last two pages.
James Akin was born in 1773 in South Carolina and died in Philadelphia in 1846. He came to Philadelphia from Charleston, S.C., and was for a time a clerk in the State Department under Timothy Pickering. He was engraving book illustrations in Salem and Newburyport, Massachusetts from 1804 to 1808, when he returned to Philadelphia, and remained there until his death.

BINGHAM, CALEB. Juvenile Letters; being a Correspondence between Children, from eight to fifteen years of age. Boston: David Carlisle for Caleb Bingham, 1803.　　　[284]

Duodecimo, 54 leaves, A², B-I⁶, K⁴.

Original wooden boards covered with flowered paper.
Not in Sabin.
This book was written *to encourage children in their first attempts in this pleasing and important art*, and is of the greatest value for its pictures of the time.
The letters are written by young members of families and friends, separated by school and travel, and contain interesting commentaries on places visited and books read. The books read and recommended for reading give the author an opportunity of advertising his own

publications. Master Samuel Thoughtful, writing to his sister Lucy says: *You remember you told me, that when I had learned the 'Young Lady's Accidence' by heart, you would make me a present. I hope it will be a book. I like book presents the best of any. Simeon Sobriety tells me that the 'Token for Children' is a choice book, giving an account of good children.* The *Young Lady's Accidence* was Bingham's most popular book. For the *Token for Children*, a choice much approved by Lucy, see no. 35 etc.

Miss Sophronia Bellmont writes to Miss Caroline Courtland an account of every town visited by her in her travels. She is impressed by the Franklin Library in the city of Philadelphia, *it does honor to its founder, and the city,* which is described as being *larger and more regularly built than New-York.*

Other letters contain accounts of Bruce's *Travels*, of Phillis Wheatley's poems, etc. In copying Wordsworth's famous ballad, Maria Meanwell uses the original version of the first line which was suppressed after the first edition of the *Lyrical Ballads*: *A simple child, dear brother Jim.*

On the flyleaf the name of an early owner: *Clarissa Walker's Book. Presented to her by her affectionate Mother Susanna Walker, Concord, June* 2, 1806.

Caleb Bingham (1757-1817) was a native of Salisbury, Connecticut. He graduated from Dartmouth in 1782, and in 1784 went to Boston where he opened a school for girls. He became famous as a schoolmaster and writer of textbooks, and later set up as a bookseller, and occasional publisher.

BINGHAM, CALEB. Juvenile Letters; being a Correspondence between Children, from eight to fifteen years of age... Second edition. Boston: David Carlisle for Caleb Bingham, 1803. [285]

Duodecimo, 54 leaves, A-I⁶.

Original sheep.
A reprint of the previous item, with slight differences of arrangement.

A DESCRIPTION OF VARIOUS OBJECTS. Vol. I. [II.] Philadelphia: B. Graves for J. Johnson, 1803. [286]

2 volumes, 16 leaves each, without signatures.

Original marbled boards, partly unopened.
First edition.
Toy books measuring $1\frac{11}{16}$ by $1\frac{3}{8}$ inches. One of Jacob Johnson's contributions to children's book production was the presentation of knowledge in extremely small and attractive books. The two volumes here described both contain text. A different arrangement of type is used on the title-pages of the two volumes, one of which reads *Vol. I.* and the other *Vol. II.* The descriptions are evidently meant for illustrations, and according to Miss Halsey the *first volume contained the illustrations of the objects described in the other.* The first volume in the present copy opens with a description of The Country House. *The Lady has been to take a walk, and is now returning; she has just got over the stile, and will be soon at home.* The second volume opens with The Puppetshow. *Here are several little boys and girls looking at the puppetshow, I suppose you would like to make one among them.*

Early American Children's Books

JUVENILE MISCELLANY, including some Natural History, for the use of Children. Ornamented with Eighteen Engravings. Philadelphia: [J. W. Scott] for Jacob Johnson, 1803.   [287]

16 mo, 36 leaves, A-B⁴, C-D², E-F⁴, G-H², I-K⁴, L-M²; 18 pages with engraved half-page illustration and half-page of engraved text (6 lines of verse).

Original marbled boards.

The editor of the present little volume has been careful to select such matter for his young friends, as cannot fail to interest them, and at the same time, leave on their minds some useful impression. The volume contains a miscellaneous collection of material, in verse and prose.

THE MOTHER'S REMARKS on A Set of Cuts for Children. Part I [Part II.] Philadelphia: T. S. Manning for Jacob Johnson, 1803.   [288]

2 volumes, duodecimo, each vol. with 42 leaves. Vol. I. A¹⁸, B-I²,⁴. Vol. II. A-O²,⁴; accompanied by the cuts on 54 separate sheets of engraved plates, six pictures in compartments on each sheet.

Original marbled boards.

At the beginning is an *Address to Mothers*. The author of this work was an Englishwoman, possibly Lady Fenn, who is referred to on page 43 by her pseudonym of Mrs. Lovechild, or Mrs. Priscilla Wakefield, from whose works frequent quotations are made in the text.

This edition was printed from the English edition without any attempt at Americanization except in the engraving and description of the shop-window, plate XLVI, no. 272, the description being in part II, page 52. The shop-window in the engraving is lettered *Johnson's Book-Store*. The remarks read: *Of No. 147 Market-Street, Philadelphia. This house is well stored with books. Authors are our best friends, or worst enemies. Young persons should read no novels, no plays, nor any book but what is allowed by their parents.*

The engravings are evidently printed the reverse way from those in the English edition, and this would account for the *Map* (Plate III, no. 13), being a map of England printed in reverse.

In the edition of a portion of this work reprinted as *The Father's Gift*, see no. 294 *infra*, the text has been revised in several places with a view to Americanization.

For the Dictionary or Index, see no. 292.

THE PRIZE FOR YOUTHFUL OBEDIENCE. Part II. Philadelphia: T. L. Plowman for Jacob Johnson, 1803.   [289]

Duodecimo, 26 leaves, A-F⁴, G², woodcut vignette on title and other woodcut illustrations in the text by A. Anderson.

Original marbled paper boards with original paper label on upper cover lettered *The Prize. Part II.*

The work consists of a series of short stories, with connecting passages.

The woodcuts by A. Anderson are after those in the original edition published by Darton and Harvey, London, 1800.

A

DESCRIPTION

O F

VARIOUS OBJECTS

———•———

VOL. I.

PHILADELPHIA :
Published by J. JOHNSON.
....
1803.
(B. GRAVES, PRINTER.)

*Title-page from "A Description of
Various Objects," Vol. I*

A

DESCRIPTION

O F

Various Objects.

———•———

Vol. II.

*Philada. printed :
by* B. GRAVES, *for
J. Johnson...*1803.

*Title-page from "A Description of
Various Objects," Vol. II*

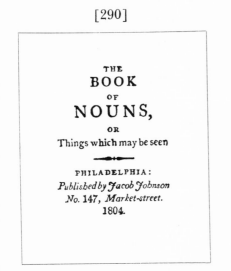

THE
BOOK
OF
NOUNS,
OR
Things which may be seen

———•———

PHILADELPHIA :
*Published by Jacob Johnson
No.* 147, *Market-street.*
1804.

Title-page from "The Book of Nouns"

BIRDS & BEASTS
——
Bit-tern
Black-bird
Bramb-ling
Bunt-ing
Buſ-tard
Buz-zard

Page from "The Book of Nouns"

CAPTAIN SMITH

AND

PRINCESS POCAHONTAS,

AN INDIAN TALE.

PHILADELPHIA:

PRINTED BY THOMAS L. PLOWMAN, FOR THE
AUTHOR, AT HIS BOOK STORE, NO. 86,
ARCH-STREET, OPPOSITE THE
PRESBYTERIAN CHURCH.

1805.

*Title-page from "Captain Smith and
Princess Pocahontas"*

Early American Children's Books

1804

THE BOOK OF NOUNS, or Things which may be seen. Philadelphia: Jacob Johnson, 1804. [290]

32mo, 32 leaves, A³².

Original paper covers.

A miniature book measuring 2⅜ by 2 inches.

Contains lists of words in single columns, six words to a page, the first 24 in alphabetical order. On page (57) is the half title: *Names of People, Trades, &c.*; the verso of the leaf is blank, and the list, in alphabetical order as far as the letter I, where it stops, follows on pages 59-64.

[DARTON, WILLIAM.] The First [Second] [Third] Chapter of Accidents, and Remarkable Events: Containing Caution and Instruction for Children. Philadelphia: Jacob Johnson, 1804, 1807. [291]

Duodecimo, 3 volumes, 24 leaves each, marked A-D³ as far as the strings, the second half unsigned, illustrated with copper-plate engravings.

Original marbled wrappers.

Not in Sabin.

This work was originally published in London by Darton and Harvey.

Of the present edition, the first volume was printed for J. Johnson by Dickinson & Heartt in 1804.

The second and third volumes were printed in 1807 by Robert Bailey, his imprint being at the end of the second volume, and the announcement *The third and last Chapter of Accidents, will be published in a few days, by J. Johnson.*

The greater number of the stories in the book end in disaster, as is implied in the title. One of the exceptions concerns a man falling from a balloon, which is accompanied by an interesting engraving illustrating the subject. The work contains much information on a remarkable variety of subjects. The chief interest for American readers, however, is an attempt on the part of the Philadelphia publisher to localize one of the stories in his own city. An item in the *Second Chapter* is headed *Cautions to Walkers in the Streets of Philadelphia*, and the street in the accompanying engraving is labelled *High-Street*, referring to what is now Market Street, Philadelphia. The text, however, has not been edited to meet the change in title, and the city is still London: *Endeavour to pass on the left hand of every person you meet, this practice renders walking in London more easy than heretofore . . .*

A DICTIONARY, or Index to a Set of Cuts for Children. Philadelphia: J. Rakestraw for Jacob Johnson, 1804. [292]

16mo, 18 leaves, sig. A, including the first and last blanks.

Original wrappers, partly unopened.

This is the Index to the *Mother's Remarks on a Set of Cuts for Children*, no.288.

The Dictionary is divided into five sections, each in alphabetical order, and consisting respectively of words of three letters; four letters; five or more letters; two syllables, and three or more syllables.

Some of the definitions are definition and erratum combined:

> *Gig, a toy that is whirled round: this was intended; but the engraver has done a little carriage so called*, 7.

Others include a moral lesson:

> *Rod, a bundle of pliant twigs, used for chastising naughty children; but not wanted where they are early trained to obedience*, 17.

The author's objection to horse racing is apparent in this Dictionary as well as in the book itself:

> *Jockey, a poor untaught being, little above the animals which he tends: kept to train race-horses*, 180.

The balloon is thus defined:

> *A ball filled with matter so much lighter than the air, as to float in it, and even keep up other things fastened to it*, 188.

The definition of the King, which is *The King*, not simply king, shows the English origin of the book:

> *The King, the supreme governor of our happy nation: Long may he reign*, 97.

[EDGEWORTH, MARIA.] Idleness and Industry exemplified, in the History of James Preston and Lazy Lawrence. Philadelphia: Archibald Bartram for J. Johnson, 1804. [293]

Duodecimo, 36 leaves, A-F⁶, engraved frontispiece, leaf of advertisement at the end.

Original half binding, partly unopened.

At the end are six pages of verse.

Maria Edgeworth (1767-1849) was a famous English novelist, and author of children's books of the moral and didactic school.

The present story was contained in the first volume of *The Parent's Assistant*, originally published in London by Joseph Johnson, 1796.

THE FATHER'S GIFT; containing an interesting description of one hundred and eight objects: With Plates. Philadelphia: J. Rakestraw for Jacob Johnson, 1804. [294]

Duodecimo, 36 leaves, A B⁴, C D², E F⁴, G H², I K⁴, L M² (B₂ and B₃ missing), 18 pages of engraved illustrations, each in six compartments. In this copy the plates have been colored, and plates II and III are lacking.

Original blue marbled paper boards.

This is a portion of the *Mother's Remarks on a Set of Cuts for Children* (no. 288). It consists, with slight variations in the order, of pages 33 to the end of the second part of that work, beginning with plate XXXVII, no. 217.

The Father's Gift has a new title-page, the plates and descriptions have been renumbered, and the plates form part of the book, and were not issued separately as in the *Mother's Remarks*.

In this edition an attempt is made to give the impression that the book was written in America, and the text is revised and edited in several places to produce that effect. The Mother's description of a Cucumber for example, is *The fruit of a plant which we cultivate chiefly in hot beds*, whereas in this book it is changed to *The fruit of a plant which we cul-*

THE

SECOND CHAPTER

OF

A C C I D E N T S

AND

REMARKABLE EVENTS:

CONTAINING,

CAUTION AND INSTRUCTION

FOR

C H I L D R E N.

PHILADELPHIA:
PUBLISHED BY JACOB JOHNSON,
MARKET-STREET.

1807.

Title-page from "The Second Chapter of
Accidents and Remarkable Events"

Never turn hastily round the corner of a street, by this some have been greatly hurt. One young woman in so doing, ran against a porter's load, and nearly lost one of her eyes by the blow she received: but this was partly owing to the porter not being in his proper place, for

CHAP. II.   D

Page from "The Second Chapter of Accidents and Remarkable Events"

Early American Children's Books

tivate in great abundance,—well known in this country. The Mother closes her remarks on the Tea-Kettle thus: *The comforts of life in a country cultivated and improved as Great-Britain is, cannot be prized too highly.* In the Father's book *Great-Britain* is replaced by the *United States.* The Father explains that a sedan chair is well known *in England*, whereas the location is taken for granted by the Mother, and these words omitted. The Rhinoceros, which in the Mother's book was preserved in the *Leverian* Museum, is in the Father's book preserved in the *Philadelphia* Museum. Numerous other instances could be cited. Johnson's Book-store is the same in both books. It is noticeable that the Father does not designate the source of the numerous quotations, which in the Mother's book are assigned to their several authors.

[JOHNSON, RICHARD.] The Most Illustrious and Renowned History of the Seven Champions of Christendom. In three parts. Containing their honourable Births, Victories and noble Atchievements, by Sea and Land, in divers strange countries; their combats with Giants, Monsters, &c. Wonderful Adventures in Desarts, Wildernesses, inchanted Castles; their Conquests of Empires, Kingdoms; relieving distressed Ladies, with their faithful Loves to them: The Honor they won in Tilts and Tournaments, and success against the Enemies of Christendom. Also, the Heroic Adventures of St. George's three Sons. Together—with the manner of their untimely Deaths; & how they came to be stiled Saints and Champions of Christendom. The eighteenth edition. Wilmington; Bonsal and Niles, also sold at their Bookstore, Baltimore, 1804.   [295]

Duodecimo, 72 leaves, A-M⁶.

Original boards.
Another edition of no. 245, with slight variations in the text.

A LIST OF NOUNS, or Things Which May Be Seen. Philadelphia: Published by Jacob Johnson, 1804.   [296]

Sm. octavo, 8 leaves, A⁸ including the last blank.

Original wrappers.
A syllabary arranged in columns varying from six to two on a page. The leaf before the blank at the end contains an advertisement.

THE NEW-ENGLAND PRIMER, enlarged and improved: Or, an easy and pleasant Guide to the Art of Reading. Adorn'd with cuts. To which is added, The Assembly of Divines Catechism. Boston: Thomas Fleet, 1804.   [297]

Octavo, 32 leaves, A-D⁸, woodcuts (alphabet and John Rogers).

Original wooden boards covered with blue paper, leather back.

Heartman 156.

This appears to be one of only two copies of this edition known.

The contents of this edition are much the same as in the early editions.

It contains the Verses for Little Children, the Alphabet of Lessons, the Cradle Hymn, John Roger's Advice, the Shorter Catechism; the Dialogue between Christ, Youth and the Devil, etc. The alphabet couplets are as in the early editions, except that for the letter K, which is the one relating to Proud Korah's troop.

[PERRAULT, CHARLES.] A New History of Blue Beard, written by Gaffer Black Beard, For the Amusement of Little Lack Beard and his Pretty Sisters. Adorned with cuts. Philadelphia: John Adams, 1804. [298]

Duodecimo, 16 leaves, A⁴-B¹², the first and last pasted down to covers, woodcut frontispiece, woodcut illustrations, alphabets in hornbook form on the back of the title.

Calf, original blue wrappers bound in.

The story of Bluebeard, which belongs to the common stock of folk-lore, came to England in this form, and thence to America, from the famous French fairy story of Charles Perrault (1628-1703), first printed in 1697 in his *Histoires et contes du tems passé*. French tradition attaches the Bluebeard legend to Gilles de Rais, a Breton chief of the 6th century, who dabbled in magic, slew children, and committed other atrocious crimes.

The editor of this present version of the story has seized any opportunity to point a moral. As soon as Fatima knew she would be forced to go with Bluebeard she wrote immediately to Selim. *Now only think what a fine thing it is to be a scholar, for if Fatima could not have wrote to her lover, nobody else would have done it for her . . . so above all things learn to read your book.*

The sister's name is Irene in this story, not the usual Anne.

TAKE YOUR CHOICE: or The Difference between Virtue and Vice, shown in Opposite Characters. Philadelphia: Jacob Johnson, 1804. [299]

Duodecimo, 29 leaves, A-D⁶, E⁵. First leaf has half title on the recto, woodcut of *The Balance of Worth* on the verso; numerous woodcuts in the text.

Original boards.

Contains sixteen stories, illustrative of eight virtues and their corresponding vices, arranged on alternate leaves, the stories of the virtues distinguished by being enclosed within borders. Each story is headed by a woodcut.

At the end are two pages of advertisements of children's books.

TRIFLES FOR CHILDREN; Part. II. Philadelphia: Published by J. Johnson, 1804. [300]

24mo, 24 leaves, with sig. B, engraved title-page with vignette, plates and woodcut illustrations in the text.

Original green wrappers.

Early American Children's Books

Contains extracts, in prose and verse, from the works of various children's authors.

Originally published by Darton and Harvey in London, 1801. The illustrations for this edition are by A. Anderson. Some of the engravings are to be found in others of Johnson's publications, as for example *The Prize for Youthful Obedience*, no. 289.

Parts I and II were published separately.

1805

BUNYAN, JOHN. Grace Abounding to the Chief of Sinners: or, a brief and faithful relation of the exceeding mercy of God in Christ, to his poor servant John Bunyan: Wherein is particularly shewn, the manner of his conversion, his fight and trouble for sin, his dreadful temptations; also, how he despaired of God's Mercy and how the Lord at length, through Christ, did deliver him from all the guilt and terror that lay upon him. All which was written by his own hand, and now published for the support of the weak and tempted people of God ... First Hudson Edition. Hudson: A[shbel] Stoddard, 1805.   [301]

Duodecimo, 60 leaves, A-K$^{8, 4}$, many uncut edges.

Original wooden boards and paper, covered with woodcuts in compartments.

The first English edition of this work was published in 1666, and the first American edition in Boston, 1717.

DAVIS, JOHN. Captain Smith and Princess Pocahontas, An Indian Tale. Philadelphia: Printed by Thomas L. Plowman, for the Author, 1805. [302]

Sm. octavo, 88 leaves, (A)-L^8, engraved frontispiece by Tanner after F. James.

Tree calf, gilt, by Sangorski & Sutcliffe.

Sabin 18848.

First edition. First issue.

The Appendix, containing a Memoir of the early life of Captain Smith and other matter, begins on page (117) and is followed by a leaf of advertisement. The list of Subscribers' Names begins on page (159), after which is a leaf of explanation addressed to the Inhabitants of the United States. The Subscribers' List is headed by Thomas Jefferson, President of the United States, and amongst the other names are Robert Aitken, William Mackenzie, Mordecai Noah, Isaac W. Norris, and other prominent men.

The dedication to *Edward Jenner, M. D. Discoverer of the Vaccine Inoculation, of Berkeley, in Gloucestershire, in England*, is dated from *Philadelphia, March* 12, 1805.

This issue has *Copy Right Secured* on the back of the title; the later issue, with varying imprint, has the copyright notice, dated April 29, 1805.

[DODDRIDGE, PHILIP.] The Principles of the Christian Religion: divided into lessons, And adapted to the Capacities of Children. Worcester: I. Thomas, Jun., 1805.   [303]

16 mo, 16 leaves, without signatures, first and last leaf pasted down to covers, two woodcut frontispieces, each in two compartments, emblematic woodcut on title and 24 woodcuts in the text.

Original wrappers.
Not in Nichols.
A series of hymns in verse. The greater number of the woodcuts were used by Thomas in his edition of *The Christian Pilgrim*, no. 233.

[EDGEWORTH, MARIA.] Harry and Lucy, Part I [Part II]. Being the first part of Early Lessons, by the author of The Parent's Assistant, six volumes. Philadelphia: Jacob Johnson, 1805. [304]

Two volumes, duodecimo, 48 leaves each, A-D¹². The half titles read: Early Lessons. Part I. and Early Lessons. Part II.

Original wrappers.
First American edition.
In Part I the text ends on page 59, page (60) is blank and on page 61 begins the Glossary. Part II has no glossary.
One of the most influential of the early nineteenth century children's books, containing moral precept combined with education and amusement. It was begun by Maria Edgeworth's father, Richard Lovell Edgeworth, and his wife, Honora (Sneyd), and was based on the principles of Rousseau.

AN ELEGY on the Death and Burial of Cock Robin. With the story of The Farmer's Daughters. To which is added, The Tragical Death of an Apple-Pye . . . Embellished with Elegant Cuts. Philadelphia: John Adams, 1805. [305]

16 mo, 16 leaves, A⁴-B¹², first and last leaves pasted down to cover, woodcut frontispiece and illustrations, advertisements on two pages at the end.

Original wrappers.
No other copy of this edition has been traced.
Alphabets on the back of the title. The Death of Cock Robin (*Who kill'd Cock Robin*), fully illustrated, occupies pages 5-17; page 18 is blank; on page 19 begins The Farmer's Daughters, and on page 27 The tragical death of an Apple-Pye.

> The letters on a time agreed,
> Upon an Apple-Pye to feed;
>
> * * *
>
> They all agree to stand in order,
> Around the *Apple-Pye's* fine border:
> Take turns as they in *horn-book* stand
> From great A, down to &;
> So being at their dinner sat,
> Some eat while others thus chit-chat.

AN ELEGY

ON the DEATH and BURIAL

OF

COCK ROBIN.

WITH THE STORY OF

The Farmer's Daughters.

To which is added,

THE TRAGICAL DEATH OF AN

APPLE-PYE.

Oft when the ground, all clad in snow,
   Denies the birds their food,
Poor ROBIN seeks the homely cot,
   And flies the leafless wood.

Embellished with Elegant Cuts.

PHILADELPHIA:
PRINTED BY JOHN ADAMS—1805

*Title-page from "An Elegy on the Death
and Burial of Cock Robin"*

THE
PHILADELPHIA VOCABULARY,
ENGLISH AND LATIN:

PUT INTO A NEW METHOD, PROPER TO ACQUAINT
THE LEARNER WITH THINGS AS WELL AS PURE
LATIN WORDS.

Adorned with Twenty-six Pictures.

FOR THE USE OF SCHOOLS.

By JAMES GREENWOOD,
*Author of the English Grammar, and late Sur-Master
of St. Paul's School.*

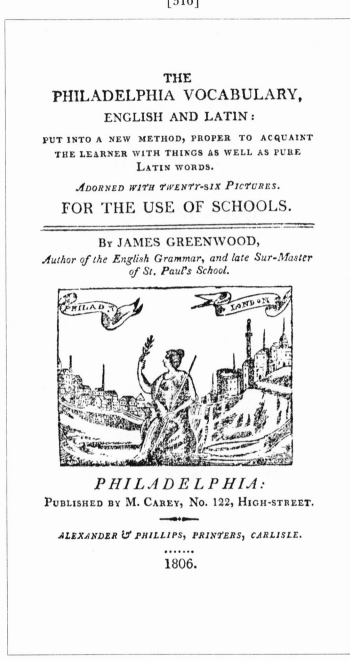

PHILADELPHIA:
PUBLISHED BY M. CAREY, No. 122, HIGH-STREET.

ALEXANDER & PHILLIPS, PRINTERS, CARLISLE.

. . . .

1806.

Title-page from "The Philadelphia Vocabulary"

The next page contains the chit-chat in the form of a rhymed alphabet:

Says A, give me a good large slice,
Says B, a little bit but nice.

* * *

Z sat as mute as any fish,
While & he lick'd the dish.

The story entitled *The Farmer's Daughters*, who in this version are named Fanny and Sally, is to be found also in *The Sugar Plumb*, no. 123, and *The Wisdom of Crop the Conjurer*, no. 186, with the title *The Farmer and his Two Daughters*, the daughters in those editions being named Betsey and Laura.

THE HISTORY OF THE HOLY JESUS, containing A brief and plain Account of his Birth, Life, Death, Resurrection, and Assention into Heaven; and his Coming again at the great and last Day of Judgment. Being a pleasant and profitable Companion for Children; Composed on Purpose for their Use. By a Lover of their precious Souls. Providence: Heaton & Williams [c. 1805]. [306]

Duodecimo, 12 leaves, without signatures, two woodcuts on verso of title, otherwise unillustrated.

Original wrappers.
Not in Bates. Sabin XXI, p. 99. The woodcuts are probably after Bewick.
This chapbook edition contains *The History of the Holy Jesus* only, and has none of the additional poems at the end.
The partnership of Heaton & Williams lasted during four years, from 1803-1806.

MACGOWAN, JOHN. The Life of Joseph, the Son of Israel. In eight books. Chiefly designed to allure young minds to a love of The Sacred Scriptures. By John Macgowan, Minister of the Gospel. A New Edition. Trenton: Printed by James Oram, 1805. [307]

Duodecimo, 86 leaves, A-O^6, P^2, engraved frontispiece, woodcut tailpiece.

Half morocco.
The frontispiece and tailpiece are by Alexander Anderson.

A PRETTY RIDDLE BOOK, for Little Children. By Christopher Conundrum. Newburyport: Printed for the purchasers, 1805. [308]

Sm. octavo, 8 leaves, without signatures, woodcut illustrations.

Dark green morocco, original wall paper covers bound in, padded with blanks.
The thirteen riddles are numbered and in rhyme; they are printed on the rectos of the leaves, with the corresponding answers on the versos, and hence not opposite their respective riddles.

The English origin of the work is apparent in some of the riddles:

> In England 'tis certain I ever shall be,
> Yet in no part of London you'll ever see me.
> In houses and churches I always am seen
> Yet in no kind of building have I ever been.

Riddle VII is to be found also in *The Puzzling-Cap*, following this item.
On the back of the title is written: *Elviva Harlow's Book, price 3 cents, bought at Hallowell.*

THE PUZZLING-CAP: a choice Collection of Riddles, in familiar verse, With a curious Cut to each. Philadelphia: John Adams, 1805. [309]

16mo, 16 leaves, A-B⁴, unsigned after the strings, woodcut frontispiece, woodcut on title, and woodcut illustration on the verso of each leaf.

Wrappers.
The fourteen numbered riddles contained in this collection are printed on the right hand pages of the book, with their answers, each with a woodcut illustration, on the opposite pages.
The Puzzling-Cap was printed in London by E. Newbery in 1789. Many of the illustrations have already appeared in other books. The frontispiece was used by Adams in his edition of *Blue Beard*, 1804, no. 298. The Pair of Stays (Riddle V.) is the same pair as was presented by Master Billy Bland to his sister Kitty, as a reward for her improved behaviour (*The Brother's Gift*, Worcester, 1795, no. 187). Riddle II. (*a cork-screw*) will be found also in the previous number, without the illustration.

A SKETCH, of the Geography and present state of the United Territories of North America; To which is added, A List of the several Nations and Tribes of Indians in Canada and the United States, &c. &c. Philadelphia: Printed by A. Bartram, 1805. [310]

16mo, 29 leaves, (A)¹, B-C⁶, D¹⁶, folded plate as frontispiece.

Original sheep.
The plate represents the tree of the United States of America.

WAKEFIELD, PRISCILLA. Domestic Recreation; or Dialogues illustrative of Natural and Scientific Subjects. By Priscilla Wakefield, Author of Mental Improvement, &c. Philadelphia: Robert Carr for Jacob Johnson, 1805. [311]

Duodecimo, 96 leaves, A-Q⁶, engraved frontispiece by Ralph and numerous engraved illustrations.

Original half binding of marbled boards, green leather back.
This first American edition is not in Smith: *Catalogue of Friends' Books*. The first English edition had appeared in the same year. The work contains much educational information in the form of *miscellaneous conversations, between a well informed mother and her daughters.*

Early American Children's Books

Mrs. Priscilla Wakefield (1751-1832) was an extremely interesting personality, and a widely known author of children's books. She was a member of the Society of Friends, and one of a family well known in the history of that Society, being the great granddaughter of Robert Barclay, the author of the *Apology*, and the aunt of Elizabeth Fry. In addition to her fame as an author Mrs. Wakefield was noted for her philanthropic undertakings, and was one of the earliest promoters of savings banks. She lived at Tottenham (near London) and almost the first savings bank in existence was that founded by her in that town.

W. Ralph or Rafe was a line engraver working in Philadelphia from 1794 to 1808.

WISDOM IN MINIATURE: or the Young Gentleman and Lady's Magazine. Being a Collection of Sentences, Divine & Moral . . . Embellished with Cuts. Philadelphia: John Adams, 1805. [312]

16mo, 16 leaves, A⁴-B¹² (first and last pasted down to covers), woodcut frontispiece, woodcut illustrations in text.

Wrappers.
Another edition of no. 225 with the same woodcuts (reversed). This edition has a frontispiece; it is without the preface which is in the former edition, its place on the back of the title being occupied by the alphabet; advertisement on the last leaf. Some of the cuts appear in other works published by Adams (see *A New History of Bluebeard*, no. 298).

1806

ADVENTURES IN A CASTLE. An Original Story, Written by a Citizen of Philadelphia. Harrisburg: J. Elder, 1806. [313]

Duodecimo, 36 leaves, A-F⁶.

Unbound, stitched, as issued.
Not in Sabin.
The scene of the story is laid in France.

C., G. S. Amusement for Good Children, by G. S. C. or, an Exhibition of Comic Pictures, by Bob Sketch. Be Merry and Wise. Baltimore: By and for Warner and Hanna, 1806. [314]

Duodecimo, 22 leaves, A-C⁶, D⁴, woodcut vignette on title, woodcuts in the text.

Original wrappers.
Contains twelve short articles, each with a woodcut illustration.
On page 24 begins the chapter *The riding of Two Horses at a Time*, which opens: *Bob Sketch happened to be one night at the entertainment at Astley's at Westminster bridge . . .* This is a reference to the wooden theatre with unroofed circus at the foot of Westminster Bridge, opened in 1770 by Philip Astley, author of *The Modern Riding Master*, no. 83 in this catalogue. On the last page is a list of *youthful and entertaining Books* which may be had at the publishers.
The illustrations are from the original London edition.

GEOGRAPHICAL statistical and political Amusement; by which may be obtained a general and particular knowledge of the United States. In a series of interesting games on a map designed for the purpose. Philadelphia: A. Bartram for Jacob Johnson, 1806. [315]

Duodecimo, 24 leaves, A⁸, B-C⁶, D⁴, including a blank leaf and a leaf of advertisement at beginning, first and last leaves pasted down to covers.

Original marbled wrappers.
First edition.
In the table at the end of the Relative Importance of the different States, as regards their Area and Population in 1790, Pennsylvania ranks third in area and second in population, being preceded in the former class by Georgia and Virginia, and in the latter by Virginia. New York is sixth in area, and fourth in population.

GREENWOOD, JAMES. The Philadelphia Vocabulary, English and Latin: put into a new method, proper to acquaint the learner with things as well as pure Latin words. Adorned with twenty-six Pictures. For the Use of Schools. By James Greenwood, Author of the English Grammar, and late Sur-Master of St. Paul's School, Philadelphia: Published by M. Carey, 1806. [316]

Duodecimo, 66 leaves, (A)⁴, B-L⁶, M², English and Latin in opposite columns, woodcut on the title, woodcuts in the text.

Original sheep.
This edition not in Sabin.
See the note to the earlier edition, no. 117.
The imprint of Alexander & Phillips, Printers, Carlisle, is at the foot of the title-page.

HENDLEY, GEORGE. A Memorial for Children; being an authentic account of the Conversion, Experience and happy Deaths of Eighteen Children. Designed as a continuation of Janeway's Token. By George Hendley, Minister of the Gospel. New-Haven: From Sidney's Press, 1806. [317]

Duodecimo, 54 leaves, A-I⁶.

Original wooden boards and flowered paper.
The deaths of eighteen children are described, boys and girls, their ages ranging from three to fifteen years. In the Preface dated from Hanley, May 28th, 1805, the author pays a tribute to Janeway's *Token for Children*, and considers that his own work has three great advantages over earlier works of a similar kind, namely, the shortness of the accounts, the large number of examples, and the fact that most of them are of recent date, strengthening credibility.

Early American Children's Books

The *Conclusion*, pp. 65, 66, is addressed to living children, and might well have the effect of driving the young generation into paths of wickedness in order to avoid an untimely death: *You have here a little book put into your hands, that tells you how good and happy some have lived and died who were as young as yourselves . . . Don't you think they were very good children? and don't you wish to be like them, and to die as they did? That it may be so you must do as they did . . .*

Pages 67 to the end are occupied by Religious Anecdotes, a series of fourteen stories of a highly morbid nature.

On the flyleaf, in a neat copy-book hand: *Lucy Fay's 2d. The gift of her brother Warren*, 1809.

THE HISTORY of Jacky Idle and Dicky Diligent, exhibiting a striking contrast between the different consequences arising from indolent inatention (*sic*) and laudable perseverance. Embellished with cuts. Philadelphia: John Adams, 1806. [318]

16mo, 32 leaves, A-D^{4,12}, printed in italic letter throughout, first leaf with frontispiece and last leaf, a blank, pasted down to covers, woodcut illustrations.

Original covers, consisting of the printed leaf of a book, colored green.

Dedicated by the editor *to the Young Ladies and Gentlemen of America*. At the end are two pages of advertisement.

The scene of this story, illustrating the axiom that *the ways of Providence are impenetrable, and the gifts of fortune more upon a level than we are in general apt to imagine*, is laid in London and Hertfordshire. The American editor has not changed the locale, nor has he removed the name of the original English publisher where it occurs in the body of the story on page 26: *It was indeed new to him, but he had read so many of mr. Newbery's little gilt books, in which the luxuries and parade of life are so justly exposed, that the novel scene gave him rather pain than pleasure.* One attempt at Americanization has been made. Dicky Diligent meets a Mr. Freeport, *a wealthy and creditable merchant in London*, who eventually offers him a position in his office, whereupon the next morning *Young Diligent set out for Philadelphia*. This, however, may have been merely an oversight.

The book has many errors of spelling and capitalization.

THE HISTORY OF THE HOLY JESUS. Containing A brief and plain account of his Birth, Life, Death, Resurrection, and Ascension into Heaven; and his coming again at the great and last Day of Judgment. Being a pleasant and profitable Companion for Children; composed on purpose for their use. Together with a number of Innocent Songs. Second Worcester Edition. Worcester, Massachusetts: Printed by Thomas & Sturtevant, for Isaiah Thomas Jun., 1806. [319]

Duodecimo, 36 leaves, A-F^6, 2 pp. of advertisement. Woodcut frontispiece and last page pasted down to covers, numerous woodcuts in text.

Original pink wrappers.

Nichols 494. Bates p. 13.

This is the third Worcester edition and not the second as stated on the title-page; the second edition was published in 1794 (no. 175).

This edition has XX songs at the end, the edition of 1794 had only IX. The woodcuts after Bewick for the additional songs are in oval compartments and were all previously used by Thomas in other works, one of them being the frontispiece for the 1794 edition of this book. The frontispiece to this edition is also the frontispiece to the *Divine and Moral Songs* of Dr. Watts, 1788 (no. 137). The woodcuts to the *History of the Holy Jesus* are as in the 1794 edition with a few additions. The imprint reads in full: Worcester, *Massachusetts: Printed by Thomas & Sturtevant, For Isaiah Thomas, Jun. Sold Wholesale and Retail at his Bookstore; by* Thomas & Whipple, *Newburyport; and by* Thomas & Tappan, *Portsmouth*, 1806. The last two pages are occupied by Thomas & Whipple's advertisements of *Valuable Presents*.

THE HOUSE THAT JACK BUILT: To which is prefixed, The History of Jack Jingle, Shewing by what means he acquired his Learning, and in consequence thereof got Rich, and Built himself a House. Set forth for the benefit of those,

> Who from being quite destitute, friend-
> less and poor;
> Would have a fine House, and a Coach at
> the Door.

Ornamented with Cuts. Hartford: Lincoln & Gleason, 1806.   [320]

16 mo, 16 leaves without signatures, first and last pasted down to covers, woodcut frontispiece, woodcuts in text.

Original green fancy wrappers.

The frontispiece consists of a woodcut of a coach and six between two stanzas of verse; alphabets on the back of the title; *The History of Jack Jingle* begins on page 5; *The House that Jack Built* on page 15; *The Dutiful Child: A Story*, on page 25; advertisement of a variety of books designed for the instruction and amusement of children on the recto of the last leaf.

The House that Jack Built is one of the most famous accumulative pieces in the English language.

MORAL STORIES. Written for the Instruction of Young Minds. Dedham: H[erman] Mann, March — 1806.   [321]

Duodecimo, 18 leaves, A⁶, B⁸, C⁴; first and last pasted down on covers, woodcuts.

Original wrappers.

The first story is *The Hermit, or Peter Wronghead, Reformed*, the half title for which, with a cut (the portrait frontispiece of Robinson Crusoe, issued by the same printer in 1800, no. 256), is pasted on to the front wrapper. At page 23 *Tom Tipler, or The vices of intemperance;* on four pages at the end, *Moral Songs From the Writings of Dr. Watt's (sic.)* The woodcut of the ship on page 10 and of the bird on page 15 are also to be found in Mann's edition of Robinsoe Crusoe as above. The alphabet is on the back of the general title.

Early American Children's Books

The imprint contains Herman Mann's advertisement: *First published by and for H. Mann, who keeps constantly for sale a variety of Childrens' Books.*

SMITH, FREDERICK. A Letter to the Children and Youth, of the Society of Friends. Philadelphia: Kimber, Conrad, and Co., 1806.   [322]

Octavo, 8 leaves, Sig. A. The letter is signed *Frederick Smith*, and dated from *London*, 20th *of* 12th *Mo.* 1805.

Unbound, but joined with *A Letter to Parents* from the same author, 1807, q.v.
This edition not in Smith.
The first London edition appeared in the same year.

THE WAY TO GET MARRIED: and the Advantages and Disadvantages of the Marriage State; represented under the similitude of a Dream. To which is added, A Father's Legacy to his Daughters. Philadelphia: [by Dickinson] for Jacob Johnson, 1806.   [323]

Duodecimo, 54 leaves, A-I⁶, including the last blank. Separate title for Dr. Gregory's *A Father's Legacy to his Daughters*, signatures and pagination continuous.

Original boards.
The edition of Gregory's *A Father's Legacy to his Daughters* contains the preface. The work has been annotated by the American editor. To the statement that *without an unusual share of natural sensibility, and very peculiar good fortune, a woman in this country has very little probability of marrying for love*, a footnote has been added: **These observations are happily inapplicable in America, although perfectly just in Great Britain.* At the end are four leaves of verse containing *King Dionysius, and Squire Damocles* [by Hannah More], and *Turn the Carpet; or the Two Weavers*.
The printer's imprint is at the end.

[WILLARD, SAMUEL.] The Franklin Family Primer: containing A new and useful selection of Moral Lessons. Adorned with a great variety of Cuts: calculated to strike a lasting impression on the Tender Minds of Children. By a Friend to Youth. Sixth edition. Boston: B. True for J. M. Dunham, 1806.   [324]

Duodecimo, 42 leaves, A-G⁶, large woodcut frontispiece portrait of Benjamin Franklin, large woodcut illustrations in the text.

Original half binding and wooden boards.
A revised edition of *The Franklin Primer*, no. 280.
This edition contains Franklin's famous Epitaph, written by himself, appended to the dedication. The Introduction has been rewritten, the paragraph describing Franklin reading: *a man whose manner of life, from youth's first dawning morn to man's meridian day, is worthy the imitation of all who would wish to thrive upon this* World's *vast theatre.* There are certain variations also in the contents of the book.

Early American Children's Books

THE YOUNG CHILD'S ABC, or, First Book. New York: [J. C. Totten for] Samuel Wood, 1806.   [325]

16mo, 8 leaves, without signatures, woodcut vignette on title and two woodcuts at head of each page of text, some leaves unopened.

Original grey wrappers, two woodcuts on each side.
Contains alphabets in hornbook form, a syllabary, with woodcuts illustrating objects in alphabetical order.
The woodcuts are by Anderson. The same woodcuts were not used for the wrappers in every copy. The printer's imprint is at the end: *J. C. Totten, print. No.* 155 *Chatham-street.*
This book is the first of the many thousands of children's religious, instructive, and nursery books printed by Samuel Wood, the founder of the present publishing house of medical works.

1807

THE BOOK OF TRADES, or Library of the Useful Arts. Part III. Illustrated with twenty copper-plates. First American Edition. Whitehall: Dickinson for Jacob Johnson in Philadelphia, and in Richmond, Virginia. 1807.   [326]

Duodecimo, 71 leaves, A^2, $B-M^6$, N^3, copper-plate engravings, lacks three leaves and one plate (B_5, I_6, $K_{1, 2}$).

Original half binding.
The plates are by W. Ralph.
First published in London in 1807. This part contains 21 trades.

[BUNYAN, JOHN.] The Christian Pilgrim: containing an account of the Wonderful Adventures and Miraculous Escapes of a Christian, in his Travels from the Land of Destruction to the New Jerusalem. Second American Edition. Worcester: for Isaiah Thomas, Jun. 1807.   [327]

16mo, 108 leaves, $(A)-M^8$, N^{12}, woodcut portrait frontispiece, woodcuts in the text.

Original sheep over wooden boards.
Nichols 505.
A reprint of the first Worcester edition, no. 233.
In this edition the two volumes have been joined into one without a break, otherwise it is a page for page reprint of the first edition as far as page 192 in the second volume, which is a longer type page than the corresponding page in the first edition, and hence from that point to the end the text arrangement differs. Being in one volume this edition has only one frontispiece, otherwise the woodcuts are the same as in the former edition. The imprint reads in full: Printed at Worcester For Isaiah Thomas, Jun. Sold Wholesale and Retail at his Bookstore, and by *Thomas & Whipple*, Newburyport, and by *Thomas & Tappan*, Portsmouth, 1807.

Early American Children's Books

[COWPER, WILLIAM, *and others.*] The History of John Gilpin of Cheapside, A Droll Story. And The Historical Ballad, of the Children in the Wood. Philadelphia: Published by Jacob Johnson, 1807.   [328]

Duodecimo, 17 leaves, the first half with signatures A-C³, the second half unsigned, engraved frontispiece, title and six plates, four of which are included in the pagination, but not in the signatures. Two gaps in the pagination, one in the first piece, and one in The Children in the Wood, may signify that two plates are missing, or, on the other hand, it is possible that the original intention to insert plates at those places was abandoned, and that the two plates not included in the pagination were supplied in their stead.

Original wrappers.

The History of John Gilpin ends on page 25; pages 25-31 are filled with a miscellaneous collection of prose and verse including *True Story of a Mastiff* (from Bewick) and *True Story of an Elephant* in prose, and *Three Black Crows* and *The Coach and Cart* in verse. The ballad of *The Children in the Wood* begins on page (32), and amongst other changes to be noticed in this edition is the fact that the father (who dwelt in England, not specifically in Norfolk, as formerly) and the wicked uncle are named respectively Pisarius and Androgus, whereas in the earlier editions in this catalogue they were unnamed. The ballad is followed by the *Conclusion* in prose, pointing the moral to the story. Pages 47 and 48 are occupied by *Dishonesty Punished*, and *Wise Sayings for the Use of Children*.

Some of the plates have been touched with colour, possibly by William Sharpless, whose signature, with the dates 1811 and 1814, occurs in many places in the book.

THE CRIES OF LONDON. as they are daily exhibited in that City: Represented by Characteristic Engravings. "Let none despise The merry Cries Of famous London Town." Hartford: A. Reed, 1807.   [329]

16 leaves, without signatures, engraved throughout, vignette on title, illustration of a cry on each leaf, with the text below, printed on one side only.

Original flowered wrappers.
Contains fifteen cries. The vignette on the title-page is signed W. M. *sc.*, the plates of cries are unsigned.

The *Cries of London* are of great importance in the history of American children's books, as being the inspiration for the New York and Philadelphia Cries, examples of which will be found in this catalogue.

ENGLISH, CLARA. The Children in the Wood. An Instructive Tale by Clara English. Philadelphia: [Joseph Rakestraw for] J. Johnson, 1807. [330]

Duodecimo, 32 leaves, A-B¹², C⁶, D², uncut and partly unopened. Engraved title-page, with vignette, engraved illustrations in the text.

Original marbled boards.
A modernized version of *The Babes in the Wood*, combining instruction (a digression on weaving explains that the word *worsted* comes from a town in Norfolk, and that the art of

weaving was brought into England in the year 1331) with moral precept. The story is in prose, interspersed with verse, and at the end is the ballad: *Now, ponder well, you parents dear.*

[GODWIN, WILLIAM.] Fables Ancient and Modern. Adapted for the Use of Children. By Edward Baldwin, Esq. Adorned with cuts by Anderson. [New Haven, Connecticut:] From Sidney's Press, for Increase Cooke and Co., 1807. [331]

Duodecimo, 71 leaves, A-L⁶, M⁵, woodcut on title, woodcuts in the text.

Original half binding.

Contains thirty-eight fables in prose from various sources, edited for children by William Godwin, who explains his objects in an interesting preface. Each fable is headed by a woodcut.

On pages 70-72 is the story of *The Old Man and the Bundle of Sticks*, of which a version in doggerel is included in Hannah More's Cheap Repository Tract, no. 40 (no. 260 in this catalogue).

William Godwin (1756-1836), the famous author of *Political Justice* and other works, and the father-in-law of Shelley, wrote several children's books under the pseudonym of Edward Baldwin.

THE HISTORY OF LITTLE DICK, written by Little John. Philadelphia: Jacob Johnson, 1807. [332]

Duodecimo, 36 leaves, A-F⁶, 12 plates including the frontispiece, woodcut tail-pieces.

Original half binding.

The author explains in the preface that *It is not an easy task to make very new a path so well trod as that of the history of Children. The writer of this hopes, however, he has thought of, at least, a pleasing way for little Folks to see how much better Virtue is than Vice.* At the end of each chapter is a summing up in four lines of moral verse, as for example:

> Drinking—worst of ev'ry vice
> That disgraces mortal man—
> Leads to swearing, cards, and dice:
> Nothing worse—nor nothing can!

At the end a Juvenile Catalogue of Books for Sale by Jacob Johnson, 10 pages, containing interesting publisher's *blurbs* on the Canary Bird, the Cheap Repository, and other works, copies of which are to be found in this collection.

THE HISTORY OF MARY WOOD. Philadelphia: B. Johnson, n.d. [c. 1807.]

Duodecimo, 18 leaves, A-C⁶; engraved title, with vignette. [333]

Half bound.

Probably originally issued as one of the Cheap Repository Tracts.

Early American Children's Books

HOCH-DEUTSCHES LUTHERISCHES ABC-und Namen-Büchlein für Kinder welche anfangen zu lernen. Verbesserte Ausgabe. Philadelphia: Conrad Zentler for Georg W. Mentz, 1807. [334]

Octavo, 16 leaves, A-B⁸, the first and last pasted down; alphabet woodcuts on the first leaf.

Original half binding over thin wooden boards; on the front cover a full-length portrait of Martin Luther in his library, with a short life of him beneath; on the back a picture of a hen, with verses beneath.

An abecedarium, syllabarium and reading-easy in German; the alphabet woodcuts on the first leaf, which are in twenty-four compartments, all represent natural history subjects, and have the names printed beneath. This leaf bears the name of an original owner, Wm. McClellan, Novʳ· 1, 1808.

THE HUBBUB. Philadelphia: B. Johnson, n. d. [c. 1807.] [335]

Duodecimo, 18 leaves, A-C⁶, engraved title, with vignette.

Half bound.
At the end are nine pages of verse: *The Hampshire Tragedy; Patient Joe; or the Newcastle Collier* [by Hannah More]; and *An Hymn on the Second Coming of Christ* [*Lo! He comes with clouds descending*]. Probably issued originally as one of the Cheap Repository Tracts. The caption title to the story is *The Hubbub; or, The History of Farmer Russel, the Hard-Hearted Overseer.*

JANEWAY, JAMES. A Token for Children, being an Exact Account of the Conversion, Holy and Exemplary Lives, and Joyful Deaths of Several Young Children. In two parts. Philadelphia: J. Adams for Benjamin and Thomas Kite, 1807. [336]

Duodecimo, 54 leaves, A-I⁶, last 2 leaves blank.

Original half binding.
This edition contains the Preface addressed to the Children, but is without the letter to Parents, Schoolmasters, etc. It does not contain Cotton Mather's *The Token for the Children of New England.*

THE LOTTERY. Philadelphia: B. Johnson, n. d. [c. 1807.] [337]

Duodecimo, 18 leaves, A-C⁶, engraved title, with vignette.

Half bound.
At the end are three leaves of verse, containing *The Trials of Virtue*, and *The Martyr's Hymn.*
Probably issued originally as one of the Cheap Repository Tracts.

Early American Children's Books

[MORE, HANNAH.] The Beggarly Boy. Philadelphia: Published by B. Johnson, n. d. [c. 1807.] [338]

> Duodecimo, 18 leaves, A-C⁶, engraved title-page with vignette.
>
> Unbound.
>
> Originally issued as one of the Cheap Repository Tracts. At the end are *The Old Man, His Children, and The Bundle of Sticks*, and *The Lady and the Pye*, both in verse by Hannah More. The former of these pieces occurs also in *Onesimus* by the same author, no. 260, and a version in prose in *Fables Ancient and Modern* by Edward Baldwin (i. e. William Godwin), no. 331.

[MORE, HANNAH.] Betty Brown, the St. Giles's Orange Girl: with an account of Mrs. Sponge, the Money Lender. Philadelphia: Benjamin Johnson, 1807. [339]

> Duodecimo, 18 leaves, engraved frontispiece.
>
> Half bound.
>
> At the end a poem entitled *The Horse-Race; or The Pleasures of the Course.*
>
> Originally issued as one of the Cheap Repository Tracts.

[MORE, HANNAH.] The Cheapside Apprentice. Philadelphia: B. Johnson, n. d. [c. 1807.] [340]

> Duodecimo, 18 leaves, A-C⁶, engraved title-page with vignette.
>
> Half bound.
>
> At the end are verses: *The Hymn*, and *Dan and Jane.*
>
> Originally issued as one of the Cheap Repository Tracts.

[MORE, HANNAH.] The Fortune Teller. Philadelphia: B. Johnson, n.d. [c. 1807.] [341]

> Duodecimo, 18 leaves, A-C⁶, engraved title-page with vignette.
>
> Half bound.
>
> The caption title on the first page of text is: *Tawney Rachel; or, the Fortune Teller: with some Account of Dreams, Omens, and Conjurers.* At the end is *The Gin Shop*, a poem by Hannah More.
>
> Tawney Rachel was the wife of Giles the Poacher, see no. 343.
>
> Originally issued as one of the Cheap Repository Tracts.

[MORE, HANNAH.] The Happy Waterman. Philadelphia: Published by B. Johnson, n.d. [c.1807.] [342]

> Duodecimo, 18 leaves, A-C⁶, engraved title-page with vignette.
>
> Unbound.

Originally issued as one of the Cheap Repository Tracts.

At page 17 begins *The Shopkeeper turned Sailor*, a poem by Hannah More. This version of the poem, which is in its original state, should be compared with the edition issued by the same publisher in 1814, in which the whole of the last part, beginning from the line *When Britons, wearied with their lot*, has been revised, and the interest made more general for the benefit of American readers.

The Happy Waterman, which is in prose, is not signed, and may have been written by Hannah More herself or by one of her friends.

[MORE, HANNAH.] The History of Black Giles. Philadelphia: Published by B. Johnson, n.d. [c. 1807.]   [343]

Duodecimo, 36 leaves, A-F⁶, engraved title-page with vignette, one engraved illustration.

Original marbled boards.

The caption on page 1 reads: *Black Giles the Poacher, with some account of a family who had rather live By Their Wits Than Their Work*. This story includes *The History of Widow Brown's Apple Tree*. Black Giles was the husband of Tawney Rachel, the Fortune Teller, who has a separate history, no. 341.

At the end are three poems by Hannah More: *King Dionysius and Squire Damocles; Turn the Carpet; or The Two Weavers* and *The Plow-Boy's Dream*.

Originally issued as one of the Cheap Repository Tracts.

[MORE, HANNAH.] Read and Reflect. The Pilgrims, an Allegory. Philadelphia: Kimber, Conrad, and Co., 1807.   [344]

Duodecimo, 18 leaves, without signatures, including half title, title, and the last blank.

Unbound, as issued.

[MORE, HANNAH.] The Shepherd of Salisbury Plain. Philadelphia: Published by B. Johnson, n.d. [c. 1807.]   [345]

Duodecimo, 36 leaves, A-D⁶, E¹², engraved title-page with vignette, one engraved illustration.

Unbound.

This is the most famous of Hannah More's Sunday School Tracts, and was originally issued as one of the Cheap Repository Tracts. The story is supposed to be founded on fact, and the exemplary shepherd to have been one Saunders of Cherrill Down. At the end are poems: *The Shepherd's Hymn* and *The History of Richard, A Ballad*.

The Shepherd of Salisbury Plain is doubly important in the history of American children's literature for it was in discussing this story with its author, that Samuel Griswold Goodrich, the original Peter Parley, *first formed the conception of the Parley Tales*.

An interesting contemporary American publisher's *blurb* of this work is to be found at the end of *The History of Little Dick*, no. 332 above.

Early American Children's Books

THE NEW-ENGLAND PRIMER, Improved For the more easy attaining the true Reading of English. To which is added, The Assembly of Divines' Catechism. Greenfield: J. Denio for Bryant & Denio, 1807.   [346]

Duodecimo, 36 leaves (misbound), (A)-C¹², (A)ᵢ serves as title-page and cover, woodcuts (alphabet and John Rogers).

Heartman 170 (one copy).
There is no frontispiece, the back of the title is occupied by texts.
This edition is without the Dialogue between Christ, Youth and the Devil, otherwise the contents are very much the same as the Middletown edition of 1786, no. 108. The alphabet couplets are the same as in that edition, with some of the same woodcuts; the cat is playing the fiddle to four dancing mice.

PEOPLE OF ALL NATIONS; an Useful Toy for Girl Or Boy. Philadelphia: for Jacob Johnson, 1807.   [347]

32 mo, 64 leaves, A-H⁸, 63 engraved illustrations of the costumes of the people.

Original marbled half binding, many lower edges uncut.
First edition.
A toy book, measuring 2 by 2¼ inches.
At the end is the printer's imprint: *Whitehall: printed by A. Dickinson.*
The first part of the book is an alphabet, though the order is not strictly preserved, probably due simply to an error in binding. Each illustration is accompanied by a description; the information is at times more interesting than accurate, and the phraseology is marked occasionally by the greatest tact.
In the account of the Egyptian, for example, we are told that *the French have lately paid a visit to Egypt with a large army*, the reference being probably to Napoleon's activities in that country . . . *G a German, appears to be a water doctor of Germany, which is a fruitful and pleasant country; the invention of printing is said to have arisen there. Vienna is the capital . . . A Highlander, of Scotland, is a very hardy man; he is fond of the music of the bagpipes, and takes snuff in great plenty. They are very civil to strangers . . . the Jews were a very respectable people . . . A Norwegian is a subject of the King of Denmark. They are a frank, openhearted people, yet not insolent . . . An Orang-Outang is a wild man of the woods, in the East Indies. He sleeps under trees, and builds himself a hut; he cannot speak, but when the natives make a fire in the woods, he will come to warm himself . . . V A Virginian is generally dressed after the manner of the English; but this is a poor African, and made a slave of to cultivate the earth for growing tobacco, rice, sugar, &c. . . . Y A Yeoman, or guard to the king's person; they are clad after the manner of Henry the Eighth's time; there are one hundred in constant waiting on the king at his palace . . . An Englishman is accused by foreigners with eating too much . . . A Venetian, from a republic in Italy, the poorer people of which display some qualities rarely to be found, being sober, obliging to strangers, and gentle to each other . . . A Friar, one of some religious order among the Roman Catholics;—they were generally learned men, and lived recluse.*
The book is copied from an English publication. The sixty-three plates give full-length portraits of the people described in the text.

[347]

[347]

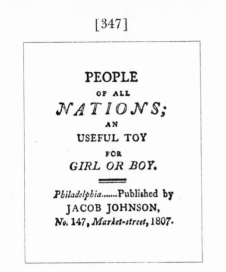

PEOPLE
OF ALL
NATIONS;
AN
USEFUL TOY
FOR
GIRL OR BOY.

*Philadelphia.......*Published by
JACOB JOHNSON,
No. 147, *Market-street,* 1807.

a Virginian

Title-page from "People of All Nations"   *Page from "People of All Nations"*

[56]

[56]

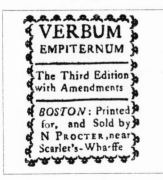

{ **VERBUM** }
EMPITERNUM

The Third Edition
with Amendments

BOSTON: Printed
for, and Sold by
N PROCTER, near
Scarlet's-Wha·ffe

TO HIS
Illuſtrious Highneſs
WILLIAM
Duke of *Gloucefter,*
KNIGHT of the
Moſt Noble Order
Of the GARTER.

Title-page from "Verbum Sempiternum"   *Page from "Verbum Sempiternum"*

THE

SILVER PENNY;

OR

NEW LOTTERY-BOOK

FOR CHILDREN,

By *J. HORNER, ESQ. fellow of the Royal Society of A, B, C, &c.*

EMBELLISHED WITH CUTS.

PHILADELPHIA:
PRINTED BY JOHN ADAMS.....1806.

Title-page from "The Silver Penny; or New Lottery-Book for Children"

Early American Children's Books

[PERRAULT, CHARLES.] Cinderella, or the Little Glass Slipper, a grand Allegorical Pantomimic Spectacle. As performed at the Philadelphia Theatre. New York: D. Longworth, 1807.   [348]

Duodecimo, 6 leaves, signature A⁶.

Half blue morocco, uncut.
Based on the famous fairy story by Charles Perrault.
In this piece the fairy gives place to Venus, and, by the direction of that goddess, the Graces entangle, Love conquers, and Hymen at length makes happy the hero of the piece.
At the end is a note containing the moral, in which the spectacle of Cinderella is described as *perhaps one of the happiest tales that possibly could be selected to instruct and amuse the rising generation.*

[PHILLIPS, SIR RICHARD.] Elements of Geography, compiled with a view to teach children at an early age, the Geography of the United States. Philadelphia: Kimber, Conrad & Co., 1807.   [349]

Duodecimo, 16 leaves, without signatures.

Unbound.
Not in Sabin.
Extracted from *Geography on a popular Plan for the Use of Schools and Young Persons* by the Rev. J. Goldsmith (i. e. Sir Richard Phillips).
Sir Richard Phillips (1767-1840) was an author, bookseller and publisher, who wrote under various pseudonyms, one of which was the Rev. J. Goldsmith, Vicar of Dunnington, and formerly of Trinity College, Cambridge.

[PHILLIPS, SIR RICHARD.] Elements of Geography, principally compiled with a view to teach children, at an early age, The Geography of The United States. Fourth Edition. Philadelphia: Kimber & Conrad [c. 1807].   [350]

Duodecimo, 18 leaves, A-C⁶.

Original grey wrappers, the upper with title, reading *Geography for Children*, and a woodcut of a globe, the lower with an advertisement.
This work, as the preceding number, is extracted from the *Geography on a popular Plan for the Use of Schools and Young Persons* by the Rev. J. Goldsmith (i. e. Sir Richard Phillips).

THE POST BOY.
Clear the road! Clear the Road! make room for me
That ev'ry little child may learn, its A. B. C.
Philadelphia: Published by Jacob Johnson, n. d. [c. 1807.]   [351]

Sm. octavo, 28 leaves, A-C⁸, D⁴ (lacks C₂), engraved title with vignette of a post-boy, plates, chiefly in two compartments, in the text.

Original marbled boards.

Contains the alphabet in hornbook form, the alphabet with illustrations, a syllabary, passages for reading headed *The Post Boy's Bag opened*, and other matter. At the end is a full-page plate of *Patrick Obrien the Irish Giant, and Peter Davis the welch Dwarf*. The book was originally published in England; the plates in this edition are probably by Anderson after English originals.

The illustrated alphabet is interesting, and the plates far superior to the illustrations usually to be found in this class of book. The letter X has proved too much for the artist however. It is illustrated by a fox lifting a dead bird from a box, and the accompanying note reads: X. *This Letter begins no word in the English tongue, but frequently ends them, as*, Fox. Box. Ox. &c.

THE PRIZE FOR YOUTHFUL OBEDIENCE. Part I. [Part II.] Philadelphia: John Bioren for Jacob Johnson, 1807. [352]

Octavo, two volumes, 28 and 26 leaves, (A)-C⁶, D¹⁰ (the last a blank and pasted down to the cover); (A)², B-E⁶, woodcut illustrations.

Original pink boards.

Contains short stories with connecting passages and is fully illustrated. For a previous edition of Part II, see no. 289. The woodcuts are by Anderson after those in the original English edition published by Darton and Harvey in 1800.

ROWSON, SUSANNA. A Spelling Dictionary, divided into Short Lessons, for the easier committing to memory by children and young persons; and calculated to assist youth in comprehending what they read: selected from Johnson's Dictionary, for the use of her pupils. By Susanna Rowson. Boston: David Carlisle for John West, 1807. [353]

Duodecimo, 68 leaves, A², B-M⁶, printed in double columns.

Original half binding, with a pigskin slip-cover.

At the end is *A Concise Account of the Heathen Deities, and other Fabulous Persons; with the Heroes and Heroines of Antiquity.*

Susanna Rowson (1762-1824) was born in England, but spent a large part of her life in America. She acted on the American stage for some years, and on giving up the theatre as a profession in 1797, opened a school for girls in Boston.

THE SILVER PENNY; or New Lottery-Book For Children, By J. Horner, Esq. fellow of the Royal Society of A, B, C, &c. Embellished with cuts. Philadelphia: John Adams, 1806. Philadelphia: James P. Parke, 1807. [354]

Early American Children's Books

16mo, 16 leaves, marked before the strings A-B⁴, unmarked after the strings, the first and last pasted down to covers, printed in italic letter throughout, woodcut frontispiece, woodcut at the head of each page, three leaves of advertisement at the end.

Original wrappers, front with *Toy-Book*, title, woodcut, and imprint of James P. Parke, dated 1807; back with woodcut and the alphabet; both woodcuts in oval compartments. The imprint on the title-page is that of John Adams, dated 1806 as above.

The work contains the alphabet, with an illustration for each letter and four lines of descriptive and instructive verse beneath. The rhymes appear to be all new to this work, and some of them show the English origin of the book; K for King for example:

> This is the man, who next to God
> Is plac'd to keep mankind in awe:
> Happy the people whose good KING,
> Is judg'd and judges by the law!

and Q for Queen:

> Some rais'd to majesty may shine
> With honours not their own;
> But all agree that Britain's QUEEN
> Adds lustre to the throne.

X for Xerxes, usually the *pons asinorum* for alphabet rhymesters, in this instance is treated with the greatest ingenuity:

> What Xerxes was 'tis hard to say
> And yet to say what's true;
> But what he is, 'tis past a doubt,
> That he is nothing now.

The letter Y, however, has completely defeated the poet, who has illustrated it by Young-Lamb, hyphenated thus in the heading, but separated in the verse:

> See here the young and tender LAMB,
> And take good note from thence,
> How sweet thro' ev'ry stage of life,
> How blest is innocence!

The woodcuts are probably by A. Anderson, but many are from English originals, and are to be found in other books and by other printers in this collection. The cut of Time on page 23 was a popular one with John Babcock at Hartford, and was used by him in several of his publications.

The advertisements at the end are of John Adams, and consist of two pages with lists of children's books, preceded by a note *New Books. A variety of New Books, for children, for sale by the Printer. They are offered ten per cent lower than they can be imported.*

SMITH, FREDERICK. A Letter to Parents and others who have the care of Youth in the Society of Friends. White-Hall: Dickinson, for Benjamin & Thomas Kite, 1807.   [355]

Duodecimo, 6 leaves, signature A⁶.

Unbound, but attached to *A Letter to the Children and Youth* by the same author, 1806, no. 322.

This edition not in Smith. Two editions were printed in London in 1806.

The letter is signed *Frederick Smith*, and dated from *London, 13th of 1st Mo.* 1805.

Early American Children's Books

SORROWFUL SAM The Black-Smith. Philadelphia: Published by B. Johnson, n. d. [c. 1807.]   [356]

Duodecimo, 18 leaves, A-C⁶, engraved title-page with vignette.

Unbound.

Probably originally issued as one of the Cheap Repository Tracts.

WATTS, ISAAC. Watts Divine Songs For the use of Children. With Plates. G. Love, sc. Philadelphia: [S. Probasco] for J. Johnson, 1807.   [357]

18 leaves, signature A, engraved frontispiece, title with vignette, and six plates by G. Love, the plates in two compartments.

Wrappers.

Stone: p. 84.

This edition has no preface.

Stauffer, *American Engravers on Copper and Steel* knows of G. Love, the engraver of the plates from this book only. He says somewhat inaccurately: *This name as engraver is appended to a very poor frontispiece to Watts' 'Divine Songs,' published in Philadelphia in 1807 by L. Johnson.* The frontispiece and plates are not signed, the name of the engraver being on the engraved title, as above.

WEBSTER, NOAH. A Dictionary of the English Language; Compiled for the Use of Common Schools in the United States. By Noah Webster, Esq. New Haven: Sidney's Press for John and David West, Boston; and others, 1807.   [358]

Duodecimo, 150 leaves, A-Z; Aa-Bb⁶.

Original calf.

At the end is a Chronological Table of Remarkable Events from the creation of the world and Adam and Eve, B. C. 4004, to the death of Lord Nelson, October, 1805.

The Table is of European interest, and neither the discovery of America by Columbus, nor the War of Independence is mentioned. There is no entry between the year 1773, *The society of Jesuits suppressed by the pope August 25th*, and the year 1782, *Balloons discovered by S. and J. Montgolfier in France*. The United States are mentioned in connection with treaties in 1783 and 1794. The signature of P. Battell, who bought the book at Wm. Brookfield's Seminary, No. 306 Market Street, Philadelphia, in 1812, occurs in many places.

WEBSTER, NOAH. Elements of Useful Knowledge. Volume I [Volume II.] Containing a Historical and Geographical account of the United States; For The Use Of Schools by Noah Webster, Esq. . . . Third Edition. New-London: Ebenezer P. Cady for O. D. Cooke, 1807, and [Vol. II] New-Haven: Sidney's Press for Increase Cooke & Co., 1808.   [359]

Two volumes in one, 108 and 114 leaves, sigs. A⁴, B-S⁶, T², and A-T⁶, three pages advertisements at the end.

Original half sheep.
Between Vol. I and II is *A Chronological Table of the most Remarkable Events, in or respecting America, intended as the outline of American History.*

1808

[BERQUIN, ARNAUD.] The Mountain Lute, or, The Happy Discovery. Ornamented with cuts. Litchfield: Hosmer & Goodwin, 1808.   [360]

16 mo, 16 leaves, without signatures, woodcut frontispiece and several woodcut illustrations, first and last leaves pasted down to covers, alphabets on the back of the title.

Original pink wrappers.
This story is an adaptation of one of the tales in *L'Ami des Enfants,* the famous collection of children's stories by Arnaud Berquin (1749-1791), a native of Bordeaux, France. These French stories were originally issued monthly during the years 1782 and 1783, and an English translation was issued in London in the latter year. In this adaptation of the present story the scene is laid in Breconshire, South Wales.

[BERQUIN, ARNAUD.] The Peasant's Repast: or, the Benevolent Physician. Embellished with three copper-plate engravings. Philadelphia: [Adams] for Jacob Johnson, 1808.   [361]

Duodecimo, 18 leaves, A-C⁶, frontispiece and two engraved plates.

Original paper wrappers, title on front cover, woodcut on the back.
From Johnson's *Juvenile Library.*
An adaptation of a story from *L'Ami des Enfants.*
The Peasant's Repast has been considerably changed; the locale is Radnorshire, Wales, and the appeal is for girls, for it is the eldest daughter Lucy who starves herself for her widowed mother and the three younger children, whereas in the original version it is a boy who thus strives to save food for his father and a larger family of little ones. For a version of the story more near the original French see *The History of Bertrand,* 1818. It is probable that *The Peasant's Repast* was adapted from Berquin, but it is possible that the plot was obtained independently from the same source as the French author drew his material.

A COMPEND OF RHETORIC in Question & Answer. Compiled for the use of the Young Ladies of the Schenectady Female Academy, principally from Blair's Lectures. Schenectady: Van Veghten & Son, 1808.   [362]

Duodecimo, 24 leaves, A-H⁴, ².

Half blue morocco, original fancy wrappers bound in.
Not in Sabin.
First edition.

Early American Children's Books

The compiler states in his *Advertisement* (dated from Schenectady, 1st June, 1808) that the whole, with the exception of two or three Questions, has been taken from Blair's Lectures and Lord Kaim's *Elements of Criticism*.

Hugh Blair (1718-1800), a Scottish divine, was professor of rhetoric at Edinburgh University.

COOPER, W. D. Cooper's Histories of Greece and Rome, of South and North America. [Boston:] Belcher and Armstrong for Joseph Avery, and for sale at his Bookstore in Plymouth, Massachusetts, 1808. [*363*]

Duodecimo, 150 leaves, A-Z⁶, Aa⁶, engraved frontispiece, 6 pages of advertisements at the end.

Original sheep.
Not in Sabin.
Engraved frontispiece by Wightman of *America trampling on Oppression* similar to that in the *History of North America*, 1795, no. 188.

The American editor in the preface, dated from Plymouth, April, 1808, explains that *The English edition, from which this work was copied, is embellished with copperplate cuts; it was thought best here to omit these, excepting the one used for the Frontispiece, to reduce the price of the volume which would otherwise have been considerably augmented. Cuts badly executed, as were those in the American editions of the histories of South and North America, were judged inexpedient.*

The author of the work, being an Englishman, will appear, perhaps to some not to have expressed himself, in certain instances, with sufficient respect for the American character and achievements in the late glorious revolution, which terminated in the independence of our country.

But it must be evident to every one, upon the bare inspection of the plate, which is here selected for a Frontispiece, that it would never have been admitted into Mr. Cooper's history of North America, had he entertained sentiments unfriendly to our cause.

The original English edition was a Newbery publication issued in 1789. In the preface to the History of South America, the author pays a tribute to Robertson's famous work, and explains that his own is based upon it. For a separate edition of The History of North America, and for a note on the author, see no. 188.

[EDGEWORTH, MARIA.] Frank, Part II. By the Author of The Parent's Assistant, Six Volumes. Philadelphia: [Adams] for Jacob Johnson, 1808. [*364*]

Duodecimo, 58 leaves, including the last blank, A-I⁶, K⁴.
Original half binding.

GAY, JOHN: Gay's Fables. In one volume complete. Veluti in Speculum. From the last London edition. Philadelphia: Mathew Carey, 1808. [*365*]

Duodecimo, 2 parts in 1, 62 leaves, A-I⁶, K⁸, engraved frontispiece and 5 engraved illustrations, some edges uncut.

Early American Children's Books

Original half binding.

The prefatory poem, entitled: *A Tale; written by a Lady, on reading Mr. Gay's Fables* earns for this work the right to be included in a collection of books for children:

> A Mother, who vast pleasure finds,
> In forming of her children's minds;
>
> * * *
>
> This happy Mother met, one day,
> A book of Fables, writ by Gay;
> And told her children, here's a treasure,
> A fund of wisdom and of pleasure.
> Such decency! such elegance!
> Such morals! such exalted sense!
>
> * * *

These verses were quoted by the Mother in her *Remarks on a set of Cuts for Children* (no. 288), and are ascribed by her to Parnell.

John Gay (1685-1732), the famous English poet and dramatist, originally wrote his Fables for William, Duke of Cumberland, to whom the book is dedicated.

GUPPY, MRS. Instructive and Entetaining [*sic*] Dialogues for Children. By Mrs. Guppy. First American Edition. Philadelphia: Dickinson for Jacob Johnson, 1808.   [366]

Duodecimo, 45 leaves, A-F⁶, G⁹; woodcut frontispiece, woodcut illustrations of various figures.

Half blue morocco.

The commendatory letter from Mr. Clarke, professor of mathematics and philosophy, late of Bristol, but now of Great-Marlow, is dated St. Michael's-Hall, Dec. 24, 1799.

The author states in her *Advertisement* that these dialogues were originally written *for the instruction of the children of the writer; who, after having read Mrs. Trimmer's and Mrs. Barbauld's Lessons, sought in vain for something to succeed them. Hearing of Practical Education, [by Edgeworth] she read it in the hope of finding what she so earnestly desired, but her disappointment was only confirmed, and her dissatisfaction increased, with respect to the generality of little Books that are put into the hands of children.* Acknowledgements are made to *Practical Education*, however, more than once in the body of the book.

AN INSTRUCTIVE and entertaining Medley: in eight lessons. Being A pleasant collection of tales, anecdotes, &c. Chiefly original. Philadelphia: [Adams] for Jacob Johnson, 1808.   [367]

Duodecimo, 18 leaves, sig. A, engraved frontispiece.

Original marbled wrappers.

The eight Lessons are followed by two short pieces in verse. The running title throughout is *The Medley*.

[143]

Early American Children's Books

JUVENAL POEMS, or the Alphabet in Verse. Designed for the Entertainment of all good Boys and Girls, and no others. Adorned with Cuts. New-Haven: Sidney's Press, 1808. [368]

16 mo, 16 leaves without signatures, large woodcut frontispiece, woodcut at head of each page, first and last leaves pasted down to covers, advertisement on the last leaf.

Original flowered wrappers.

Contains the alphabet, one letter to a page, and each with an illustration and four lines of descriptive verse. Some of the illustrations are the same as in *The Silver Penny*. The penultimate leaf contains alphabets on both sides.

On the back of the title are the Contents, in the form of an alphabet rhyme:

> Under A the Ant behold,
> B for Bible stands,
> C the Cat full plain declares,
> D the Dog commands . . .

The verses in the body of the book have not appeared previously in this collection with the exception of that for the letter X, which is a very popular one, and frequently used:

> Xerxes in all his pomp and state,
> Did like an infant cry,
> To think his host so vast, so great,
> In one poor age must die.

The penultimate leaf has advertisements on both sides. Several of the illustrations have been used in other books by various publishers. The advertisement at the end offers a variety of new children's books *to Booksellers, in boxes assorted, ten per cent lower than they can be imported. Cash paid for Rags.*

KEATINGE, HENRY S. Musical Preceptor; or a Key to Harmony. Baltimore: Henry S. Keatinge, 1808. [369]

Duodecimo, 42 leaves, (A)¹, (B)⁴, C-L⁴, M¹, woodcut vignette on title-page, musical notation, errata at the end.

Original half binding, wall paper sides, sheepskin back.
In the form of a catechism.

[KENDALL, EDWARD AUGUSTUS.] Keeper's Travels in search of His Master. Philadelphia: [Lydia R. Bailey] for Johnson & Warner, 1808. [370]

Duodecimo, 46 leaves, A-F⁶, G², H¹, I⁶, engraved frontispiece.

Original boards.
The first edition of this famous dog story was published by Newbery in 1798, and has been reprinted many times both in England and America; the dedication is dated April, 1798. The printer's imprint is on the last page.

LEIGH, EDWARD. The History of the Twelve Caesars, First Emperors of Rome; Namely, I. Julius Caesar, II. Augustus, III. Tiberius, IV. Caligula, V. Claudius, VI. Nero, VII. Galba, VIII. Otho, IX. Vitellius, X. Vespasian, XI. Titus, XII. Domitian, being an account of the most remarkable transactions revolutions and events, both in peace and war which happened during their reigns. Collected from the most authentic historians, both ancient and modern. By Edward Leigh, Esq. Carlisle: From the Press of A. Loudon (Whitehall), 1808. [371]

Duodecimo, 54 leaves, A-I⁶.

Original wrappers.
The first edition was published in Oxford in 1635. The author was an English miscellaneous writer and politician who lived from 1602 to 1671.

LITTLE PRATTLE OVER A BOOK OF PRINTS. With easy tales for children. Philadelphia: [Adams] for J. Johnson, 1808. [372]

16mo, 32 leaves, stitched in the middle, but with signatures A⁴, B-F²,³, before the stitches, first and last blanks pasted down to covers; engraved title-page, engraved illustrations and one or two woodcuts in the text.

Original marbled wrappers.
In verse and prose.
A copy of Darton and Harvey's edition, London, 1804, with the same illustrations (printed in reverse).
The scene of most of these stories is laid in London and the surrounding country, nevertheless a certain amount of local interest has been introduced. In the first story an asterisk in the text connects with a footnote: *See Anecdotes, of Dogs, just published by B. Johnson of Philadelphia.*
The story entitled *More Mischief. Playing with Gunpowder* has an interpolated sentence: *How many accidents have happened on rejoicing days, particularly on the 4th of July!*

THE LONDON CRIES, for the Amusement of all The Good Children Throughout the World. Embellished with Cuts taken from Life. Philadelphia: John Adams, 1808. [373]

16mo, 16 leaves, A⁴, B¹², first and last leaves pasted down, woodcut on the verso of the front wrapper, a woodcut for each Cry, 2 pages advertisement at the end.

Original wrappers, a woodcut in an oval compartment on each side, the upper cover with the title *Toy-Book*, and imprint dated 1808, the lower with two alphabets, one reading forwards, and the other backwards.
The imprint on the title-page is dated 1807.
There are twenty-four Cries in this set, each one, with its woodcut, occupying a page. The Cries are not amplified by descriptive verse or text as are the New York and Phila-

delphia Cries. The running title throughout is *The London Cries*. The woodcut illustrations are very charming. The complete set is reproduced by E. Pearson in *Banbury Chap-books* and described by him as York Cries, *early and prentice work of the Bewick School*. In style they are very similar to the *Newcastle Street Cries* of Thomas Bewick.

LUTHER, MARTIN. Der kleine Catechismus des sel. D. Martin Luthers. Nebst den gewöhnlichen Morgen-Tisch-und Abend-Gebeten Welchen die Ordnung des Heils, in einem Liede, in kurzen Sätzen, in Frag und Antwort, und in einer Tablle; Wie auch Eine Zergliederung des Catechismus Das Würtemburgische Kurze Kinder-Examen, Die Confirmation und Beichte, beygefüget; Und Etliche Lieder, Freylinghausens Ordnung des Heils, Das Güldene A, B, C, der Kinder, und die Sieben Buss-Psalmen, angehänget sind. Zum Gebrauch der Jungen und Alten. Carlisle: F. Sanno, 1808. [374]

    Sm. octavo, 68 leaves, (A)², B-J⁸, K².

    Original half binding.

[MORE, HANNAH.] Patient Joe; or the Newcastle Collier. Philadelphia: J. Rakestraw, 1808. [375]

    Two leaves, woodcut on title.

    Unbound.

    A chapbook edition of this ballad.

THE NEWTONIAN SYSTEM of Philosophy explained by familiar objects, in an entertaining manner, for the use of Young Ladies & Gentlemen, By Tom Telescope, A. M. Illustrated with Copperplates and Cuts. Second Philadelphia edition: with notes and alterations, By Robert Patterson. Professor of Mathematics, in the University of Pennsylvania. Philadelphia: Lydia R. Railey (*sic*) for Johnson & Warner, 1808. [376]

    Duodecimo, 72 leaves (-)², A-L⁶, M⁴, engraved frontispiece and 4 plates by W. Rafe, one engraving and numerous woodcut diagrams in text.

    Original sheep.

    This was originally a Newbery publication; John Newbery published a second edition in 1762. According to Mr. Welsh *it is not at all unlikely that this book was written by Oliver Goldsmith for John Newbery. Tom Telescope was published in a variety of forms and by a variety of publishers, but in many cases so altered that its author had he lived would have failed to recognize it.*

    This American edition was evidently copied from a later English edition. On page 110 *Walker's Pronouncing and Explanatory Dictionary* is recommended in the place of *New-*

bery's Pocket Dictionary in the Newbery editions. The first edition of John Walker's Dictionary was published in London in 1791. A minor change is to be noted in the title, for in the Newbery editions Young Gentlemen take precedence over Young Ladies.

On page 68, *the late ingenious Dr. Franklin of Philadelphia* is mentioned as the inventor of the lightning-rod. Page 78 shows the marks of the American editor; the explanatory word (*England*) is added to the mention of the town *Reading, in Berkshire,* and lower down there is a description of the bones of an enormous quadruped which have lately been found in the state of New York, with a footnote: *A complete skeleton of this animal is now to be seen at Peale's Museum, in Philadelphia.* The illustrations are interesting. The frontispiece representing *A Professor explaining the Polite Arts, to his Pupils* contains a representation of a balloon, and the woodcuts in the text include an orrery, a barometer, a balloon, a globe, a telescope, and other scientific objects.

Robert Patterson (1743-1824), the Philadelphia editor, was responsible for the several new footnotes inserted in this edition. He was a native of the north of Ireland, and emigrated to Philadelphia in 1768. He held several important posts including that of Professor of Mathematics in the University of Pennsylvania; Vice-Provost of the same University; Director of the United States Mint at Philadelphia and President of the American Philosophical Society.

THE ORPHANS, or, Honesty Rewarded. Ornamented with Copper-plate Engravings. Philadelphia: Bennett and Walton, 1808. [377]

Duodecimo, 18 leaves, A-C⁶, engraved frontispiece and 2 full-page engraved illustrations, advertisement on the last leaf.

Original marbled wrappers.

[PERRAULT, CHARLES.] An Accurate Descripion (*sic*) of the Grand Allegorical Pantomimic Spectacle of Cinderella; or, The Little Glass Slipper; as performed at the New Theatre, New-York. To which is added The Story of Cinderella. New York: W. Turner, 1808. [378]

Octavo, 12 leaves, A-C⁴.

Half blue morocco, uncut, partly unopened.
Another edition of no. 348, with the Story of Cinderella added (pages 15-24). It is practically the same version as that printed in Albany in 1810, no. 423.

PORTRAITS OF CURIOUS CHARACTERS in London, &c. &c. With Descriptive and Entertaining Anecdotes. Philadelphia: [Lydia R. Bailey] for Jacob Johnson, 1808. [379]

Duodecimo, 36 leaves, A-F⁶, woodcut portrait of each character.

Original half binding.
Contains the portraits of eighteen curious characters, some of which are partly in verse.
The book was probably published originally by W. and T. Darton, for at the end of the description of one of the characters there is a note: *N. B. There is a very good portrait of*

Daniel Lambert, published by W. and T. Darton, Holborn on a coloured sheet, with particulars concerning him, price One Shilling.

PRETTY POEMS, SONGS, &c. In Easy Language, for the Amusement of Little Boys and Girls. By Tommy Lovechild. Ornamented with cuts. Litchfield: Hosmer & Goodwin, 1808. [380]

16mo, 16 leaves, without signatures, first and last leaves pasted down to covers, woodcut illustration on each page.

Original green wall paper wrappers.

Contains twenty-six poems of one four-line stanza each, on twenty-six pages, each with a woodcut. The frontispiece represents Tommy Lovechild reading poetry; the alphabet on the back of the title, and the publisher's advertisement of children's books on the last leaf.

THE TAME GOLDFINCH: or, the Unfortunate Neglect. Embellished with three copper-plate engravings. Philadelphia: [Adams for] Jacob Johnson, 1808. [381]

Duodecimo, 18 leaves, A-C⁶, 3 engraved plates, including the frontispiece.

Original marbled boards.

The motive of this story, the starving of a goldfinch through neglect, was an extremely popular one amongst the writers of children's moralistic stories.

This book was evidently reprinted directly from the English edition, for the Philadelphia publisher has not changed the Newbery advertisement in the body of the story on page 32: *Mr. and Mrs. Manners came into the parlour, with a small trunk, full of elegant toys, and new books from the celebrated Juvenile Library at the Corner of St. Paul's Church-Yard* . . .

[TURNER, ELIZABETH.] The Daisy; or, Cautionary stories in verse. Adapted to the Ideas of Children from Four to Eight Years Old. Illustrated with sixteen engravings on copperplate. Part I. Philadelphia: J. Adams for Jacob Johnson, 1808. [382]

Duodecimo, 18 leaves, sig. A, half title with a poem entitled *Miss Peggy* engraved on the verso, 16 copper-plate engravings, some of which have been bound in upside down.

Original orange wrappers.

This copy is misbound, though otherwise perfect. Advertisement on the last page.

The plates are from the original English edition, printed for J. Harris successor to E. Newbery, 1807.

These stories are all of a moralistic nature, as the title implies.

> Miss Helen was always too giddy to heed
> What her mother had told her to shun;
> For frequently over the street, in full speed,
> She would cross where the carriages run.

And out she would go, to a very deep well,
To look at the water below;
How naughty! to run to a dangerous well,
Where her mother forbade her to go!

One morning, intending to take but one peep,
Her foot slipp'd away from the ground;
Unhappy misfortune! the water was deep,
And giddy Miss Helen was drown'd.

Mrs. Elizabeth Turner (1775?-1846) lived at Whitchurch, Shropshire, and was the author of a number of children's books.

1809

THE BAPTIST CATECHISM, or a Brief Instruction in the Principles of the Christian Religion, agreeably to the Confession of Faith Put forth by upwards of an Hundred Congregations in Great-Britain, July 3d, 1689; adopted by the General Association of Philadelphia September 22d, 1742, and now received by Churches of the same Denomination in the United States. To which are added Proofs from Scripture. Wilmington: P. Brynberg, 1809.   [383]

Duodecimo, 18 leaves, A-C⁶, some edges uncut.

Grey wrappers.
Pages 30 to 36 contain *Divine Songs for Children* [by Dr. Watts].

EIN CHRISTAGS-GESCHENK für kleine Knaben; oder eine Sammlung von verschiedenen Unterretungen. Das 3te Virginische Kinderbuch. Newmarket; Schenandoah County, Virg. [Andreas N. Henkel] for Salomon Henkel, 1809.   [384]

Duodecimo, 18 leaves, woodcut on the title, woodcuts in the text.

Original blue wrappers.
The preface is dated from Newmarket, 3 September 1809.
Printed at the first German printing office south of the Mason and Dixon line. The press was established in 1806 by the Rev. Ambrose Henkel, with the aid of his brother Dr. Solomon Henkel, owner of an apothecary shop, established in 1797.
The printer's imprint is at the end. The imprint on the title-page reads: *Neumarket: Schenandoah County, Virg. Gedruckt für Salomon Henkel*, 1809.
The cut on the title-page appears in various other books. In *Johnson's New Philadelphia Spelling-Book*, no. 393, it is engraved by Anderson.

Early American Children's Books

Ein Christags-Geschenk fur kleine Mägdlein; oder eine Sammlung von verschiedenen Unterredungen. Das 4te Virginische Kinderbuch. Newmarket; Schenandoah County, Virg. for Salomon Henkel, 1809. [385]

Duodecimo, 18 leaves, woodcut on title, woodcuts in the text.

Original blue paper wrappings.
The preface is dated from Newmarket, 3 October, 1809. This book is without the printer's imprint. The publisher's imprint on the title is the same as on the previous item.

Cooper, [W. D.] The History of North America: containing A Review of the Customs and Manners of the Original Inhabitants; the first settlement of the British Colonies, their rise and progress, from the earliest period to the time of their becoming united, free, and independent states. By the Rev. Mr. Cooper. New York: Published by Evert Duyckinck, 1809. [386]

Duodecimo, 72 leaves, A-M⁶.

Original half binding.
This edition is without the Contents tables published in the Lansingburgh edition of 1795 (no. 188). It is unillustrated.

[Cooper, W. D.] A New Roman History; from the Foundation of Rome, to the end of the Commonwealth. Embellished with four Copper-plate Cuts. Designed for the use of young Ladies and Gentlemen. Philadelphia: Printed for Mathew Carey, 1809. [387]

Duodecimo, 72 leaves, A-D¹⁸ (lacks one leaf in sig. A), engraved frontispiece and three plates.

Original half binding.
Another edition of The History of Rome contained in no. 363.

[Corp, Harriett.] An Antidote to the Miseries of Human Life, in the history of the Widow Placid and her daughter Rachel . . . Third Edition. New Haven: From Sidney's Press, for Increase Cooke, & Co., 1809. [388]

Duodecimo, 72 leaves, A-M⁶.

Original marbled boards.
A Quaker story.
Not in Smith: *Catalogue of Friends' Books.*
At the beginning is the Advertisement to the second London edition.

Early American Children's Books

THE COUNCIL OF DOGS. Illustrated with suitable engravings. Philadelphia: Brown & Merritt for Johnson & Warner, 1809. [389]

Sq. octavo, 8 leaves, sig. A⁸, 8 engravings, the first pasted down to the front cover.

Original wrappers with title on the front cover, advertisement on the back.
The text in rhymed couplets.
Copies were also issued in plain salmon wrappers.

EDGEWORTH, MARIA. The Barring Out; or, Party Spirit. By Maria Edgeworth, Author of Practical Education, and Letters for Literary Ladies. Second American Edition. Philadelphia: W. M'Culloch for Johnson & Warner, 1809. [390]

Duodecimo, 54 leaves, A-I⁶, engraved frontispiece.

Original half binding.
A school story originally written for inclusion in *The Parent's Assistant*.
At the end a list of Juvenile Works published by Johnson & Warner, three pages.

FLORA'S GALA. Illustrated with elegant engravings. Philadelphia: W. M'Culloch for Wm. Charles, 1809. [391]

Duodecimo, 8 leaves, A⁸, engraved frontispiece, and 5 full-page plates.

Original wrappers, upper with title (varying from that on title-page) lower with advertisement.
Weiss: *William Charles*, page eight.
William Charles is one of the most important and influential figures in the history of book production for children in America. Following his predecessor, Isaiah Thomas of Worcester, he copied with enormous success the English juveniles, and produced a series of charming engraved books in a square duodecimo, of which *Flora's Gala* is an early example. The plates in this work are plain as it was some years later (see note to *Pug's Visit to Mr. Punch*) that Charles conceived the idea of adding to the attractiveness of the volumes by issuing them with colored plates.
Both before and after his death his titles were sold by other firms as well as his own, and Charles items will be found with the imprints of Morgan and Yeager, Morgan and Sons, and others.
William Charles was by birth a Scot, and emigrated from Scotland to America in 1801 in order to escape prosecution for having caricatured some of the clergymen in the city of Edinburgh. He is known to have been living in New York in 1808, but must have moved to Philadelphia during that year, as books with the Philadelphia imprint bear that date. He died in 1820.

THE HISTORY OF THE HOLY BIBLE Abridged Embellished with Eight Elegant Copper Plate Prints. Philadelphia: Published by A. Dickinson, 1809. [392]

Duodecimo, 18 leaves, A-C⁶ (signature C wrongly marked D), engraved title and seven plates.

Original fancy wrappers.
The text is the same as in nos. 92 and 228 but without the preface, and containing the History of the Old Testament only.

JOHNSON'S NEW PHILADELPHIA SPELLING-BOOK: or, A Pleasant Path to Literature. Philadelphia: Benjamin Johnson, 1809.   [393]

Duodecimo, 48 leaves, A¹², B-G⁶, large woodcut on title and numerous woodcuts throughout the text.

Original half binding, with alphabets, woodcuts and imprint (dated 1809).
The date in the imprint on the title-page is 1808.
Contains alphabets, spelling lists, lists of homonyms, etc., with stories and extracts in prose and verse from the works of various children's authors including the Story of the Whistle by Benjamin Franklin.
Amongst the illustrations, which are by A. Anderson, are the Cataract of Niagara and the Falls of Passaick.
The compiler explains in the preface that the principal difference between this and the spelling books now in common use, will consist in the fairness of the paper, the size of the type, and the beauty of the ornaments.

JONES, JOHN PAUL. The Life, Travels, Voyages, and daring Engagements of Paul Jones: Containing numerous anecdotes of undaunted courage. To which is prefixed, The Life and Adventures of Peter Williamson, who was Kidnapped when an infant from his native place, Aberdeen, and sold for a slave in America. Albany: Printed by E. & E. Hosford, 1809.   [394]

Duodecimo, 48 leaves, A-H⁸,⁴.

Original wooden boards, and half binding.
The Life and Adventures of Peter Williamson begins on page (47), with caption title.
John Paul Jones, the celebrated American naval officer, was born in Kirkbean, Kirkcudbright, Scotland, in 1747. His name was originally John Paul, son of a father of the same name, but after a series of exciting and breath-taking adventures he arrived in Philadelphia in 1775, calling himself John Paul Jones, and with a commission as a senior lieutenant in the new continental navy. His middle life was as full of adventure as his boyhood, and he died in Paris at the age of 45.

KLEINE ERZÄHLUNGEN über Ein Buch mit Kupfern, oder leichte Geschichte für Kinder. Philadelphia: [Jacob Meyer] for Johnson and Warner, 1809.   [395]

24 mo, 22 leaves, the leaves before the strings marked A-C³, D², the leaves after the

strings unmarked, woodcut on title-page and numerous illustrations in text. The printer's imprint is at the end.

Original marbled boards.
A translation into German of *Little Prattle over a Book of Prints*, no. 372. The translation was made from the American edition, as it contains Benjamin Johnson's advertising
footnote, and the interpolation regarding the Fourth of July. The illustrations are woodcut copies of the copper-plate engravings in the earlier edition, with two additional cuts.
At the end is a leaf with alphabets and a syllabary.

MAIR, JOHN. Clavis Mairiana, or Key to Mair's Introduction to Latin
Syntax. Plane, ornate, apte, congruenterque scribamus. By a Young
Gentleman. New York: J. Seymour [for Thomas and James Swords]
1809.   [396]

Duodecimo, 88 leaves, A-O⁶, P⁴. List of *errors* at the end.

Original sheep.
John Mair was a Scottish schoolmaster.
The preface, dated from Rutland, Vermont, October 3, 1808, contains the information
that the key is compiled *by a boy, not yet fourteen years of age*, who is *too young to be very
ambitious of fame, if so humble a production could be followed by any.*

MILLS, ALFRED. A Short History of the Bible and Testament, with 48
Neat Engravings, Designed By Alfred Mills. [At the end:] Philadelphia:
John Bouvier for Johnson & Warner, 1809.   [397]

Duodecimo, 48 leaves, A-M⁴, 48 copper-plate engravings.

Original half binding.
A miniature book measuring 2½ by 2¼ inches.
Alfred Mills (1776-1833) was a famous English draughtsman, who specialized in illus-
trations to small books of juvenile instruction.

MOORE, J[OHN] HAMILTON. The Young Gentleman and Lady's Monitor,
and English Teacher's Assistant; being a Collection of Select Pieces
from our Best Modern Writers: calculated to Eradicate vulgar Preju-
dices and Rusticity of Manners: Improve the Understanding; Rectify
the Will; Purify the Passions; Direct the Minds of Youth to the Pur-
suit of proper Objects; and to facilitate their Reading, Writing, and
Speaking the English Language, with Elegance and Propriety. Particularly adapted for the Use of our eminent Schools and Academies, as
well as private Persons, who have not an Opportunity of perusing
the Works of those celebrated Authors, from whence this Collection is

made. Divided into small Portions, for the Use of Reading in Classes. By J. Hamilton Moore, Author of the Practical Navigator and Seaman's New Daily Assistant. Hudson: Ashbel Stoddard, 1809. [398]

Duodecimo, 186 leaves, A-Z, Aa-Hh⁶.

Original sheep, gilt.

At page 279 begins the appendix which includes passages in prose and verse, and a section on the Elements of Gesture, illustrated with full-page wood engravings.

The author is chiefly known to fame on account of the two works mentioned on the title-page.

THE PARLOUR SPELLING-BOOK. Philadelphia: Published by Benjamin Johnson, 1809. [399]

Duodecimo, 30 leaves, A¹², B-D⁶, large woodcut on title and woodcuts in the text by A. Anderson.

Original boards, with blue wrapper containing title with imprint and a woodcut pasted down on each side, the imprint on the front cover dated 1807, that on the back cover, as on the title-page, dated 1809.

Another edition of *Johnson's New Philadelphia Spelling Book*, no. 393, with a different title, the title-page being in other respects the same as in the earlier work, and having the same woodcut. This book has only 30 leaves, ending on page 60, and the back of the title is a blank, otherwise it is a page for page reprint of the former edition.

PILKINGTON, MARY. Biography for Boys; or Characteristic Histories, calculated To impress the Youthful Mind with an admiration of Virtuous Principles, and a Detestation of Vicious Ones. By Mrs. Pilkington. Philadelphia: [Lydia R. Bailey] for Johnson & Warner, 1809. [400]

Duodecimo, 72 leaves, including 2 blanks at the end, A-M⁶, engraved frontispiece by W. Rafe, containing five medallion portraits.

Original marbled boards, partly uncut.

Contains the biographies of seven good men, with the date of the death of each one, and his age at that time. The biographies all conclude with the obituary stanzas engraved upon the respective monuments. The book was first published in England in 1799.

The author, the daughter of a surgeon named Hopkins, was born in Cambridge in 1766. She wrote a large number of children's books to occupy her time whilst her husband, a naval surgeon, was at sea. She died in 1839.

PILKINGTON, MARY. Biography for Girls; or, Moral and Instructive Examples for The Female Sex. Fourth edition. By Mrs. Pilkington. Philadelphia: J. Adams for Johnson and Warner, 1809. [401]

Duodecimo, 68 leaves, including the last blank, A², B-M⁶.

Original boards.

First published in England in 1799.

The work is similar to the preceding, but contains the lives of six women. As in the previous item, the date of the death and the age of each subject is given, with the obituary verses engraved upon the tombstones.

SACRED BIOGRAPHY, exhibiting the History of the Old Testament. From a Plan Suggested by Dr. Watts. Philadelphia: Lydia R. Bailey for Johnson & Warner, 1809. [402]

16mo, 32 leaves, A-H⁴, 32 woodcut medallion portraits.

Original marbled wrappers, many edges uncut.

Contains short biographies, each accompanied by a medallion portrait of thirty-two prominent Old Testament characters, and a list of the chief events occurring during the lifetime of each one. The biographies are not always accurate; *Isaac*, we read, *was deprived of his Father's Blessing by the Stratagem of his Mother Rebekah, who caused it to be given to his Brother Jacob.* The last biography is that of Alexandra, the wife of Aristobulus, the only woman included in the collection.

A SHORT AND EASY INTRODUCTION TO UNIVERSAL GEOGRAPHY; By way of question and answer: Containing a general description of the earth, with a brief account of the situation, natural and political state of all the principal empires, kingdoms, and republics, throughout the known world. To which is prefixed A definition of all the common geographical terms, and a number of useful problems performed on the terrestrial globe. Intended for the use of young pupils in the science of geography. Philadelphia: Benjamin Johnson, 1809. [403]

Duodecimo, 108 leaves, A-S⁶, large folded table, woodcut frontispiece of an orrery.

Original half binding.

This work appears to be founded on that of Nathaniel Dwight, see no. 257.

[SWIFT, JONATHAN.] Voyages to Lilliput and Brobdingnag. By Lemuel Gulliver: First a Surgeon, and then a Captain of a Vessel. In two volumes. Vol. I. Voyage to Brobdingnag Complete. [Vol. II. Voyage to Lilliput Complete.] Philadelphia: for Mathew Carey, 1809. [404]

Two volumes, duodecimo, 56 and 60 leaves, sig. A-F, H-K⁶, L⁸; A⁴, B-I⁶, K⁸, engraved frontispiece by J. Bower in each volume.

Original marbled boards, rebacked linen, partly uncut.

This edition is unabridged, and has at the beginning the announcement from the Publisher to the Reader, by Richard Sympson, from the original edition.

Early American Children's Books

TALES UNITING INSTRUCTION WITH AMUSEMENT: Consisting of The Children who were fond of Climbing; Matty in the Flower-Garden; The Boys who tore their Clothes; and The Girl who was kind to the Poor. Ornamented with copper-plate engravings. Philadelphia: [Lydia R. Bailey] for Johnson & Warner, 1809. [405]

Duodecimo, 18 leaves, A-C⁶, 3 plates including the frontispiece.

Original wrappers, title on the front, advertisement on the back.

The title on the front cover reads: *Johnson & Warner's Juvenile Library, The Children who were fond of Climbing; and other Tales. No. 147. Market-Street Philadelphia.*

TALES UNITING INSTRUCTION WITH AMUSEMENT: Consisting of The Boy with a Bundle; The Boy who told Lies; Willy and his Dog Diver; and The Girl who was fond of Flowers. Ornamented with copper-plate engravings. Philadelphia: [Lydia R. Bailey] for Johnson & Warner, 1809. [406]

Duodecimo, 18 leaves, A-C⁶, 3 plates including the frontispiece.

Original wrappers, title on front and advertisement on back.

The title on the front cover reads: *Johnson & Warner's Juvenile Library, The Boy with a Bundle; and other Tales. No. 147, Market-Street Philadelphia.*

The plate for The Children who were fond of Climbing from the previous item is repeated in this number, and inserted in the story Willy and his Dog Diver. The name of the heroine of the last story, The Girl who was fond of Flowers, is Patty Primrose, which is the name of the heroine of a story with that title by Lucy Peacock; *Patty Primrose, or the Parsonage House*, see no. 555. This may indicate that Lucy Peacock was the author of these stories, although the two young ladies have nothing in common except their names.

[TAYLOR, ANN AND JANE.] City Scenes; or A Peep into London for Good Children. By the Author of Rural Scenes. Philadelphia: [Brown & Merritt] for James P. Parke, 1809. [407]

Duodecimo, 36 leaves, A-F⁶; engraved title and 36 leaves of engraved illustrations also with signatures as far as sig. D, each in 2 or 3 compartments.

Original half binding.

Contains descriptions in prose and verse, each accompanied by an illustration, of 103 common scenes in London. The original illustrations were by John Gilbert.

The book is concerned with London and no attempt has been made to change the original English text. This is consequently somewhat misleading at times to an American child. The statement in the account of a wharf (no. 3) that *sugar is the juice of a kind of cane, which grows in the West-Indies as commonly as corn grows in England,* is a case in point, for the word *corn* has a very different meaning for an American than it would have for an English child.

Early American Children's Books

We quote the description of a book-stall (no. 49) without comment: *Now this old gentleman has found a treasure; some rare and valuable book, for which he had been hunting at every book-stall in London for these twenty years; and here it is at last! worm-eaten through and through, to be sure, but then, as there is not another copy in England, he does not care. For my part, though I would not be disrespectful to an old gentleman, I cannot help thinking, that a good new book, upon some useful subject, would be more valuable; and where the pleasure can be, of having a thing merely because nobody else can get it, I cannot tell!*

Ann Taylor (1782-1866), afterwards Mrs. Gilbert, and her sister Jane (1783-1824), were famous both individually and jointly as authors of children's books, and had a great influence on the children's literature of the period, both in England and America. They were the daughters of the celebrated Isaac Taylor of Ongar, and were amongst the most famous members of that remarkable family.

WAKEFIELD, PRISCILLA. Juvenile Anecdotes, founded on facts. Collected for the Amusement of Children. By Priscilla Wakefield, author of Mental Improvement, Leisure Hours, &c. Philadelphia: Published by Johnson & Warner, 1809. [408]

Duodecimo, 89 leaves, A³, B-K⁹, L⁵.

Original half binding.
Contains thirty-three moral stories all concerning English children. One story *A New Method of Swimming* contains an anecdote of Benjamin Franklin, and Industrious Ambrose, the hero of the last story, owed part of his success to the American war.

WATTS, ISAAC. A Catechism for children. By Isaac Watts, D. D. Windham: Printed by John Byrne, 1809. [409]

Duodecimo, 24 leaves; A-D⁸,⁴.

Original wrappers.
Alphabets on the back of the title. Pages (5) to 12 contain *The First Catechism of the Principles of Religion: or, The Catechism for a young Child, to be begun at three or four years old*. This is followed on pages (13) to 42 by *The Second Catechism of the Principles of Religion: or The Catechism for Children, which they begin at seven or eight years old, according to their different capacities*. At the end are the Lord's Prayer, and four of the Divine Songs of Dr. Watts.

1810

BLOOMFIELD, ROBERT. The Fakenham Ghost a true Tale. Taken from Bloomfield's admired Rural Poems. Philadelphia: Johnson & Warner, n. d. [c. 1810.] [410]

Duodecimo, 18 leaves, without signatures, engraved throughout, with illustrations and lines of verse, printed on one side only.

Wrappers.

Early American Children's Books

BLOOMFIELD, ROBERT. The Fakenham Ghost a true Tale. Taken from Bloomfield's admired Rural Poems. [Philadelphia: Johnson & Warner, c. 1810.]   [411]

Duodecimo, 18 leaves, without signatures.

Another issue of the preceding number, the letterpress and the illustrations re-engraved. The imprint has been cut away from the title, but it was apparently the work of Johnson & Warner, c. 1810.

THE BLOSSOMS OF MORALITY. Intended for the amusement and instruction of young ladies and gentlemen. By the editor of The Looking-Glass for the Mind. With fifty-one engravings on wood. Philadelphia: Thomas and William Bradford, 1810.   [412]

Duodecimo, 102 leaves, A⁸, B-Q⁶, R⁴, woodcut on the title and woodcuts in the text.

Original sheep.

This, as the advertisement explains, is *a very free translation of some of the most interesting tales of Mons. Berquin, and other foreign writers.* It was originally a Newbery publication, and according to Charles Welsh, *was issued under J. Cooper's editorship.* Halkett and Laing, on the authority of the British Museum, ascribe it to the Rev. Charles Cooper, and in the list of books at the end of Mr. Harvey Darton's chapter on children's books in the *Cambridge History of English Literature* it is assigned to W. D. Cooper. See the note to no. 188.

The book contains twenty-four stories, the third of which, entitled *The Book of Nature*, contains the Newbery address: *My dear papa, said young Theophilus to his father, I cannot help pitying those poor little boys, whose parents are not in a condition to purchase them such a nice gilded library, as that with which you have supplied me from our good friend's near St. Paul's church.*

Two of the stories in this edition have American interest, the scene of one being in Connecticut and New York, and the other in Pennsylvania.

The woodcuts, which appeared for the first time in the second Newbery edition, are after Bewick, and according to the preface of that edition were the *last effort of his incomparable genius.*

[CORRY, JOHN.] Biographical Memoirs of the Illustrious General George Washington, Late President of the United States of America, and Commander in Chief of their Armies, during the Revolutionary War. Dedicated to the Youth of America. New Haven: Sidney's Press for I. Cooke & Co., 1810.   [413]

Duodecimo, 72 leaves, A-M⁶, woodcut frontispiece portrait, woodcut vignette on title-page.

Boards.
Sabin 16916.

Early American Children's Books

The last two pages are occupied by an article entitled *Character of Washington* (*By a Scotch Traveller*). The imprint reads: *From Sidney's Press. For I. Cooke & Co. Book-sellers, N. Haven*, 1810.

John Corry, topographer and miscellaneous writer, was a native of the north of Ireland. The dates of his birth and death are not known; he followed his profession of journalist in Dublin until about 1792 when he went to London. He was the author of numerous works, the greater number of which were published anonymously.

THE CRIES OF PHILADELPHIA: Ornamented with Elegant Wood Cuts. Philadelphia: John Bouvier for Johnson and Warner, 1810.   [414]

Duodecimo, 18 leaves, without signatures, woodcut on title, woodcut illustrations in the text.

Original wrappers, title on the front wrapper, advertisement on the back.
Not in Sabin.
Contains twenty-four Cries based on the Cries of New York. Each one has a woodcut illustration and descriptive, moral and instructive text in prose. With one or two substitutions and omissions the order is the same as in the Cries of New York published by Samuel Wood in 1814, many of the cuts, and portions of the text being also the same.
Certain attempts have been made to localize the interest. The description of watermelons does not contain the homily on stealing and is short and topical, *The melons brought to this market are from the state of New-Jersey . . . Pepper Pot, smoking hot* is a product peculiar to Philadelphia, and is not found in the Cries of other cities. *R- U-S-K, Fine light Rusk*, sold to be eaten hot with tea, is an opportunity for a long homily on industry, the lack of which *clothes with rags; covers with vermin; diseases the body; dulls the mind; ruins the character; tempts to evil; fills prisons; furnishes the gallows; and, in the coming world, Oh, the dreadful consequence!* Hot Muffins, another tea-table delicacy, is also accompanied by a homily on the dangers of tea parties, and the accompanying chat which *tends to injure the characters of the absent*; this statement is supported by a quotation from Dr. Franklin's *Way to Wealth*. The Cries of Oysters and of Clams are both localized by the insertion of Delaware Bay in the list of places where those delicacies are to be found. In *Very fine Images* the name of Philadelphia is substituted for that of New York, as the city to which the stone is brought.
On the back of the title is an account of the city of Philadelphia.
From Johnson & Warner's Juvenile Library, in the same series as nos. 405 and 406.

A DRAWING BOOK OF LANDSCAPES. Philadelphia: Johnson & Warner, 1810.   [415]

Quarto, consisting of a single sheet of paper folded into four, and engraved on one side, each leaf containing an engraved *Landscape* in two states, making eight in all.

Unbound as issued.

THE ECONOMY OF HUMAN LIFE, translated from an Indian manuscript, written by an ancient Bramin. To which is prefixed, an account of the manner in which the said manuscript was discovered: in a letter from an English gentleman, residing in China, to the Earl of * * * *. With thirty-two elegant cuts, by A. Anderson. Philadelphia: J. Bouvier for Johnson & Warner, 1810. [416]

Duodecimo, 2 parts in 1, 90 leaves, A-P⁶, 29 woodcuts by A. Anderson.

Original half binding.

Probably by the Earl of Chesterfield, but at first ascribed to Robert Dodsley.

The first part is divided into seven books and subdivided into chapters, each of which is headed by a woodcut, twenty-nine in all. There are no illustrations in the second part. This copy appears to be perfect with twenty-nine woodcuts, although the title calls for *thirty-two elegant cuts*. No other copy of this edition has been traced.

A poor reproduction of the woodcut on page 69 is used as the frontispiece to the *Story of Quashi*, printed at Newburyport by W. & J. Gilman, c. 1814, no. 510.

Pages 175 to 180 are occupied by a list of *Books for Youth, lately published, and for sale, by Johnson & Warner*.

ELMINA; or, The Flower that Never Fades. A Tale for Young People. Ornamented with Engravings. Albany: E. and E. Hosford, 1810. [417]

16mo, 16 leaves, first and last pasted down to wrappers, without signatures, full-page woodcut frontispiece and full-page woodcut on the last leaf, numerous woodcut illustrations in the text, alphabets on the back of the title.

Original wrappers, title and woodcut on the front, woodcuts in two compartments on the back.

A popular fairy story. It will be found also in the *American Primer*, no. 282. An edition with frontispiece and cuts by Bewick was published by Newbery in 1791, and the woodcut frontispiece to Dr. Watts's *Divine Songs* no. 201, is probably from that work.

DIE GEFAHR IN DEN STRASZEN. Nebst Einigen andern Erzählungen. Philadelphia: Jacob Meyer for Johnson and Warner, 1810. [418]

Duodecimo, 18 leaves, A-C⁶, woodcut on title.

Original salmon boards, partly unopened and uncut.

Contains seven stories in German. The woodcut on the title is by Anderson.

[GOLDSMITH, OLIVER.] The Vicar of Wakefield, a tale. Philadelphia: Brown & Merritt for Johnson & Warner, and for sale at their book-stores in Philadelphia; Richmond (Vir.) and Lexington (Ken.) 1810. [419]

Duodecimo, 72 leaves, A-M⁶, including 3 blanks at the end, engraved frontispiece by G. Fairman, and 4 full-page woodcut illustrations.

Original sheep.

This American edition which is printed in a small type calculated to ruin the eyesight of adult or child, has not removed the well known reference to John Newbery, the English

THE CRIES

OF

PHILADELPHIA :

ORNAMENTED WITH

ELEGANT WOOD CUTS.

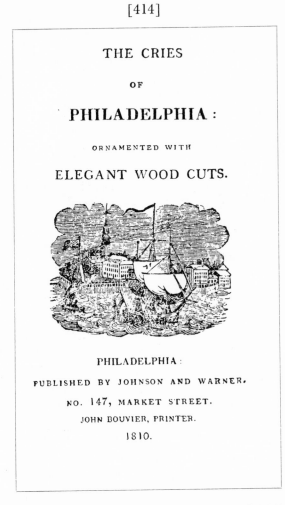

PHILADELPHIA :

PUBLISHED BY JOHNSON AND WARNER,

NO. 147, MARKET STREET.

JOHN BOUVIER, PRINTER.

1810.

Title-page from "The Cries of Philadelphia"

15

PEPPER POT.

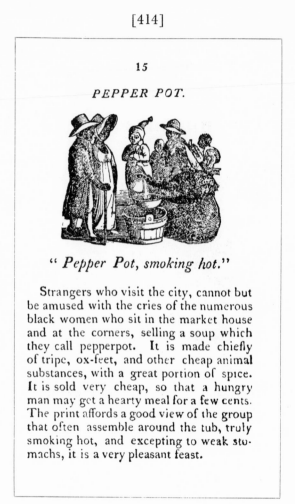

" *Pepper Pot, smoking hot.*"

Strangers who visit the city, cannot but be amused with the cries of the numerous black women who sit in the market house and at the corners, selling a soup which they call pepperpot. It is made chiefly of tripe, ox-feet, and other cheap animal substances, with a great portion of spice. It is sold very cheap, so that a hungry man may get a hearty meal for a few cents. The print affords a good view of the group that often assemble around the tub, truly smoking hot, and excepting to weak stomachs, it is a very pleasant feast.

Page from "The Cries of Philadelphia"

children's book publisher . . . *This person was no other than the philanthropic bookseller in St. Paul's church yard, who has written so many little books for children: he called himself their friend; but he was the friend of all mankind. He was no sooner alighted but he was in haste to be gone; for he was ever on business of the utmost importance, and was at that time actually compiling materials for the history of one Mr. Thomas Trip. I immediately recollected this good-natured man's red pimpled face . . .*

Gideon Fairman, the engraver, was born in Newtown, Fairfield County, Connecticut, in 1774. In 1796 he set up business for himself as an engraver in Albany, and removed to Philadelphia in 1810, the year of the publication of the present work. During a visit to London he was in partnership with Charles Heath, the celebrated English engraver, but eventually returned to Philadelphia, where he died in 1827.

KIMBER & CONRAD'S A B C BOOK, with pictures for children. Philadelphia: Kimber & Conrad, n. d. [c. 1810.]   [420]

Duodecimo, 12 leaves, woodcut on the title, 2 woodcuts on the reverse as frontispiece, woodcuts on each page of text.

Wrappers.

Contains alphabets and a syllabary. The pictures are all taken from other books and have no connection with the printed matter. At the end is the woodcut of a watch, with the warning lines:

> All of us my son are to die.
> If we do no ill we go to joy.
> The eye of God sees us all the day.

followed by a recommendation to go to Kimber & Conrad's and buy the Universal Primer.

LONDON CRIES FOR CHILDREN. With twenty elegant wood cuts. Philadelphia: John Bouvier for Johnson & Warner, 1810.   [421]

Duodecimo, 20 leaves, woodcut frontispiece, woodcut on title, a woodcut illustration for each Cry in the text. In verse and prose.

Original salmon wrappers.

> No Cries are sure of such renown,
> As those of famous London town.

This edition of the London Cries resembles those of Philadelphia and of New York in that each Cry is accompanied by a verse, and a long explanatory passage in prose. The information contained in the prose portions deals with many matters, and although the book is intended for children, the propaganda introduced into both the verse and prose passages is at times obviously intended for their parents. *Hot Cross Buns* for example, which closes

> But if flour should rise anew,
> To hot-cross buns we bid adieu,

and *The King's Speech*, the last two lines of which are

> But must new taxes yet continue,
> Still to increase the revenue?

Early American Children's Books

The passage on Newspapers, explanatory of *Extraordinary News!* contains much political propaganda: . . . *if the produce of the numerons [sic] taxes which abound in England were always suitably applied, there surely would not be an occasion of laying so many new ones on the industry of the inhabitants; nothing tends so much to reduce to poverty and misery the people of any country as the continuance of long and obstinate wars: always remember, this is one of the greatest evils with which mankind can be afflicted* . . .

[O'KEEFE,] ADELAIDE. Original Poems; calculated to improve the mind of youth, and allure it to virtue. By Adelaide. Part I. [Part II.] Ornamented with elegant engravings. Philadelphia: Brown & Merritt for Johnson & Warner, 1810; [Part II] Benjamin Warner, 1821.   [422]

Two volumes, sm. sq. octavo, each volume with 8 leaves, sig. A⁸, and 8 plates including the frontispieces, that to the first volume being signed by H. Charles; the first and last leaves in Part II are pasted down.

Original boards, titles on upper and advertisements on lower covers. The cover of Part II is that of the original edition, with the Johnson and Warner imprint dated 1809.

Adelaide O'Keefe (1776-1855) was the daughter of John O'Keefe, Irish dramatist and song writer. She was a prolific writer, but her fame rests chiefly on her verses for children. She was the author of thirty-four of the poems in *Original Poems for Infant Minds* (see no. 543), although she seems to have been unacquainted with the Taylors. The first edition of the present collection was published in London, probably in 1808; the illustrations are after those in the original edition.

[PERRAULT, CHARLES.] Cinderilla (*sic*); or, the Little Glass Slipper. Designed For the Entertainment of all good Little Misses. Ornamented with Engravings. Albany: E. & E. Hosford, 1810.   [423]

16mo, 16 leaves, without signatures, first leaf with frontispiece and last leaf pasted down to covers, woodcuts in text.

Original wrappers, upper with title and woodcut, lower with woodcuts in two compartments.

The woodcut illustrations are very poor copies of the English originals. On the back of the title are alphabets. The story begins on page (5) and ends on page 25; pages (26) to 31 are occupied by six riddles in rhyme, each with a woodcut illustration of the answer, and two of which have already appeared before, one in *The Puzzling Cap* and one in *A Pretty Riddle Book*.

[PHILLIPS, SIR RICHARD.] A View of the Character, Manners, and Customs of the North-Americans, comprehending an Account of the Northern Indians; of the Inhabitants of Oonalashka and Nootka Sound; of the five Indian Nations of Canada; of the inhabitants of the United States, &c. In which are displayed all the remarkable Curiosities which are to be found

𝕷𝖔𝖓𝖉𝖔𝖓 𝕮𝖗𝖎𝖊𝖘

FOR

CHILDREN.

WITH

TWENTY ELEGANT WOOD CUTS

PHILADELPHIA:

PUBLISHED BY JOHNSON & WARNER,

NO. 147, MARKET STREET.

JOHN BOUVIER, PRINTER,

1810.

Title-page from "London Cries for Children"

Page from "The Uncle's Present, a New Battledoor"

in those Countries. Ornamented with plates. By the Rev. J. Goldsmith, Vicar of Dunnington, and formerly of Trinity College, Cambridge. Philadelphia: J. Bouvier for Johnson and Warner, 1810. [424]

Duodecimo, 22 leaves, A⁴, B-D⁶, last leaf a blank, 3 full-page engraved illustrations including the frontispiece (pasted down to cover) by W. Rafe.

Original wrappers, title on the front, advertisements on the back.
Not in Sabin.
The Description of the Character, Manners, and Customs of the Inhabitants of the United States of North America occupies pages 17-23, and is extremely interesting reading . . . *People become old in America sooner than in Europe. Upon females the influence of the climate is still more sensible. When young they are generally beautiful, and more particularly so at Philadelphia*, the interpolation of the Philadelphia publisher doing credit to his civic pride. *The principal universities are that of Cambridge, in the state of Massachusetts, and those of New-York and Philadelphia*, the inclusion of the last mentioned city again demonstrating the civic pride of the publisher. *Some prose-writers of conspicuous merit have arisen in the United States; but poetry has not been cultivated with equal success . . . The most common vice of the inferior class of American people is drunkenness . . . In other respects there are certainly fewer crimes committed in America than among an equal number of people in Europe. Assassinations are not unknown, but they are very rare . . .*
The Rev. J. Goldsmith was one of the pseudonyms used by Sir Richard Phillips, see note to no. 349.

[PHILLIPS, SIR RICHARD.] A View of the Earth, containing an account of its Internal Structure; its Caves and Subterranean Passages; its Mountains, its Rivers and Cataracts. Together with A Brief View of the Universe. To which are added, Problems on the Globes, Directions for drawing Maps, and Tables of Latitudes and Longitudes. With plates. By the Rev. J. Goldsmith, Vicar of Dunnington, and formerly of Trinity College, Cambridge. Philadelphia: J. Bouvier for Johnson and Warner, 1810. [425]

Duodecimo, 28 leaves, A-D⁶, E⁴, 3 engraved plates by W. Rafe, including the folded frontispiece, many edges uncut.

Original salmon boards, the title repeated on the upper, publisher's advertisement on the lower.

PUG'S VISIT TO MR. PUNCH. Illustrated with eight whimsical engravings. Philadelphia: Wm. Charles, 1810. [426]

Duodecimo, 8 leaves, without signatures, entirely engraved and printed on one side only, an illustration and 4 lines of verse on each leaf.

Original wrappers, cover title, back wrappers gone.

Early American Children's Books

There is no title-page, the first page has a caption title. The illustrations which are from the English originals are plain, the book being issued before Charles had started to color the illustrations of his children's books. The original price was 12½ cents.

Not in Weiss: *William Charles*.

THE PULLET; or A Good Foundation for Riches and Honour. Philadelphia: Lydia R. Bailey for Johnson and Warner, 1810.   [427]

Duodecimo, 18 leaves, A-C⁶, 3 engraved plates including the frontispiece, all by W. Rafe.

Original wrappers, the front cover reading: *Johnson & Warner's Juvenile Library*, *The Pullet, or, A Good Foundation for Riches and Honor. No. 147, Market-Street, Philadelphia;* advertisement on the back.

THE UNCLE'S PRESENT, A New Battledoor. Philadelphia: Published by Jacob Johnson, 147 Market Street, n. d. [c. 1810].   [428]

Four leaves, the first and last pasted down to the covers, the 2 inner ones pasted together making 4 pages in all, containing 24 letters of alphabet cries in six compartments to a page; in the original covers with a flap reading *Come, read and learn*; the front and back cover have at the top, *Read, and be wise*, below this an alphabet, a woodcut by A. Anderson, numerals, and on the front cover the imprint of Benjamin Warner, 147 Market Street, without date; the lower cover has the lower case alphabet in roman and italic letters, a different woodcut, the numerals, and no imprint.

The Cries illustrating the alphabet are a very pretty set, and are probably an early set of Newcastle or York Cries by Bewick. They include Newcastle Salmon; Yorkshire Cakes, muffin or crumpet; and Great News in the London Gazette. The letters J and U are omitted in order to have 24 letters for the 24 compartments.

The battledore was an offshoot of the hornbook, and was printed on the double fold of stiff cardboard with the extra piece folded over in order to fit it for the double purpose it had to serve. In school it was used for teaching children the alphabet, whilst out of school it served as the battledore in the game of shuttlecock and battledore.

This form of battledore is supposed to have been invented in London about 1746 by Benjamin Collins, famous as the printer of the first edition of *The Vicar of Wakefield* at Salisbury.

VARIOUS MODES OF CATCHING. Philadelphia: J. Johnson, n.d. [c. 1810.] [429]

16mo, 16 leaves (misbound), without signatures, 16 illustrations including that on the title.

Original yellow and gold wrappers.

Contains much useful information for children on the various modes of catching, dealing at length with the different ways of catching fish, wild animals, birds, etc., in different countries, but also dealing with less important matters such as how to catch horses, how cats catch mice, how gardeners catch small boys stealing fruit from orchards, etc. Each form of catching is accompanied by a full-page engraved illustration.

Early American Children's Books

WATTS, ISAAC. Divine Songs, attempted in Easy Language, for the use of Children. By I. Watts, D. D. Utica: Seward and Williams, 1810. [430]

Duodecimo, 36 leaves, A-F⁶, woodcut vignettes, woodcut frontispiece to the Moral Songs.

Original half binding over wooden boards, marbled sides.

Stone: page 84.

This edition contains the preface. The Moral Songs has a separate title, which includes also *The Principles of the Christian Religion, Expressed in plain and easy Verse. By P. Doddridge*, with imprint; separate pagination and continuous signatures. The symbolic woodcut frontispiece to this part contains a representation of Britannia.

THE WAY TO GET MARRIED: and the Advantages and Disadvantages of The Marriage State; represented under the similitude of a Dream. To which is added, A Father's Legacy to his Daughters.—With a few excellent letters. Philadelphia: Published by Johnson and Warner, 1810. [431]

Duodecimo, A-I⁶, 54 leaves, woodcut frontispiece.

Original marbled boards, a few leaves with uncut edges.

A Father's Legacy to his Daughters begins on page 31, and has a separate title-page; the pagination and signatures are continuous.

It contains the preface, and the note on page 75: *These observations are happily inapplicable in America, although perfectly just in Great Britain.*

At the end are the two poems *The Trials of Virtue* and *The Martyr's Hymn*, which are also printed together in *The Lottery*, no. 337.

YOUTHFUL RECREATIONS. Philadelphia: Published by J. Johnson [c. 1810].

16mo, 16 leaves A¹⁶, engraved title-page, 15 engraved illustrations. [432]

Original yellow and gold wrappers, partly uncut.

A companion volume to *Various Modes of Catching*, no. 429 above.

The author has advanced ideas on the necessity of outdoor recreations for the benefit of the health of both rich and poor. Each game described is accompanied by a full-page engraved illustration. Hop-Scotch requiring no accessories is eminently suitable for the poor, and the author adds a footnote: *This exercise was frequently practised by the Greeks and Spartan women. Might it not be very useful in the present day, to prevent children having of chilblains? . . . Indeed, it is a pleasant sight to see cheerful, healthy children, and nothing contributes so much to make them so, as proper exercise in the open air, and keeping their hands and faces clean. We do not mean to say that children should never dirty their hands, but that the dirt should be frequently washed off again . . . Playing at Foot-Ball is a manly exercise, and though not proper for girls, it affords good exercise for boys on a cold day . . . in flying of a Kite . . . care should be taken not to raise it in or near to a public road, for thereby horses have been affrighted, their riders thrown and bruised . . . I Spie! Hi! This is a recreation but little known in London, except at the Blue-Coat, Charter-House, and Westminster*

Schools... Skipping over a Rope *is such an useful exercise, that we would have every boy and girl occasionally practise it in cold weather.*

No attempt has been made to Americanize this book, the references to England and London remaining untouched.

1811

BIBLE HISTORY. New York: S. Wood, 1811.   [433]

128 leaves, A-Q⁸, woodcut frontispiece, full-page woodcuts in the text. (This copy lacks 2 leaves in sig. H.)

Original sheep, gilt.
A *Thumb Bible* measuring 1⅞ by 1¼ inches.
The preface is based on that in the *Bible in Miniature* no. 145. The text is entirely different.

THE BOLD MARINERS. The Rambling Boy. And The Answer. Roslin Castle. To which is added The Answer. Flashy Tom. [?Philadelphia] January, 1811.   [434]

Duodecimo, 4 leaves, woodcut vignette of a ship on the title.

Unbound.
A chapbook collection of six ballads.

THE BOOK OF GAMES; or, a History of the Juvenile Sports practised at the Kingston Academy. Illustrated with Twenty-four copperplates. Philadelphia: A. Fagan for Johnson & Warner, 1811.   [435]

Duodecimo, 52 leaves, A-H⁶, I⁴ (A₄ missing), 24 engraved illustrations of the various games.

Original half binding.
Contains descriptions, built round a story, of twenty-four games, each accompanied by an illustration. The book is entirely English in interest, and no attempt at Americanization has been made. Benjamin Franklin is quoted in the chapter on bathing: *Do not be afraid. I have heard that Dr. Franklin used to say, that to be persuaded that you can swim, is almost all that is necessary to be able to do it.*

THE CASKET: or The Orphan's Portion. Philadelphia: J. Bouvier for B. & T. Kite, 1811.   [436]

36mo, 18 leaves, sig. A¹⁸, including the last blank pasted down, engraved frontispiece, 2 full-page plates, uncut.

Original blue wrappers, title (dated 1811) on upper, advertisement on lower.
The date in the imprint on the title-page is 1810.
The scene of the story is laid in Devonshire, England.

Early American Children's Books

EL DIRECTOR DE LOS Niños para Aprender á Deletrear y Léer; ó Metodo para facilitar los progresos de los Niños quando se mandan por la primera vez á la Escuela. Philadelphia: Matthew Carey, 1811.   [437]

Duodecimo, 54 leaves, A-I⁶, stipple frontispiece by Seymour, woodcuts in oval compartments.

Blue morocco.
First edition.
An abecedarium, syllabarium and *reading-easy* in Spanish. Lesson XVIII contains an alphabet, two letters to a page, and each one illustrated with a woodcut in an oval compartment. The rhymed alphabet in Lesson XX, also illustrated with oval woodcuts, is a translation into Spanish of *A was an Archer who shot at a frog.* The lines are for the most part in a different order from the English version owing to the differences in the languages. Several are merely transposed. The Archer himself, for example, has changed places with the Farmer, the Spanish version opening with *A era un Arador y seguia el arado,* and the line for the letter F is *F era un Flechero y tiró á una rana;* some few are the same in both languages, *C era un Capitan,* for example, O, *una oficiosa muger que vendia ostras y bacalao,* and V, *un Vinatero muy estúpido.* One or two of the rhymes at the end are not from the English edition. U was omitted from the original, but in this version is *Union, virtud y libertad;* X in English was Xpensive, but here is represented by Ximenes, who is popular in other rhymed English alphabets, and the Zany having gone to the letter T, his place is taken by Zacarias, who is thus in the position he occupies in most of the versions of the New England Primer.
Many of the woodcut illustrations are Newbery-Isaiah Thomas cuts.
The passages for reading contain the Lord's Prayer, the Creed, conversations, fables etc. The frontispiece represents a boy playing with a parachute. The imprint reads: *Philadelphia, en la Imprenta de Matio Carey, calle del Mercado, no.* 122, 1811.

[DORSET, CATHERINE ANN.] Think before you speak: or, the Three Wishes. A Tale. By the author of the Peacock at Home. Philadelphia: J. Bouvier for Johnson & Warner, 1811.   [438]

Duodecimo, 16 leaves, A-B⁸, 6 engraved plates including the frontispiece.

Original wrappers, title on upper dated 1811, advertisements on the lower. The imprint on the title-page is dated 1810.
The story is in verse, and, according to the preface, *is principally taken from the admirable Work of Madame de Beaumont* (Le Magazin des Enfans), *which formed almost the whole library and the delight of the children of the last generation* . . .
The plates are the same, printed in reverse, as those in the London edition of M. J. Godwin, 1809, except that in that edition they headed the text pages, whereas in this edition they are full-page. This edition, dated 1811, is included by Mr. Harry B. Weiss in his list of the works engraved by William Charles (page 10).
Catherine Ann Dorset (1750?-1817?) was the younger daughter of Nicholas Turner, and the sister of Charlotte Smith, also a famous author. She wrote several books for children which were all published anonymously.

Early American Children's Books

DWIGHT, NATHANIEL. A short but comprehensive system of the Geography of the world: by way of question and answer. Principally designed for Children and Common Schools. Revised, corrected and improved. By Nathaniel Dwight... Fifth Northampton Edition. Northampton: for Simeon Butler, 1811.   [439]

> Duodecimo, 108 leaves, A-S⁶.
>
> Original half sheep over wooden boards.
> Sabin 21523.
> For an earlier edition see no. 257.
> The printer's imprint at the foot of the title-page reads: *Greenfield, printed by J. Denio.*

THE HISTORY OF LITTLE GOODY TWO-SHOES. Ornamented with twenty-one original designs. Philadelphia: William Brown for Johnson & Warner, 1811.   [440]

> Duodecimo, 54 leaves, A-I⁶, woodcut frontispiece and woodcuts in the text.
>
> Original boards with the label of a Munroe and Francis (Boston) edition pasted on the front cover.
> This edition is without the Appendix, it closes with the *lines spoken extempore by a young gentleman.* The Introduction has been edited only slightly to the extent of omitting any name in the places where John Newbery followed by Isaiah Thomas had each introduced his own.
> The frontispiece to this edition represents the portrait of a boy, presumably Master Thomas Two-Shoes.

MILLS, ALFRED. Pictures of Roman History, in miniature, Designed by Alfred Mills, With Explanatory Anecdotes. Philadelphia: J. Bouvier for Johnson & Warner, 1811.   [441]

> Duodecimo, 49 leaves, 1 leaf for title, A-M⁴, 48 plates.
>
> Original boards with half title on the front cover, advertisements on the back.
> A miniature book measuring 2 5/16 by 2 1/8 inches, the plates are full-page.
> Copies of this book were also issued in plain boards; in one copy in the possession of the present collector the title on the cover has the misprint *Alered* in the name of the designer.
> The original edition of this work was published in England in 1809.

[MORE, HANNAH.] The Search after Happiness: A pastoral drama. To which is added, Joseph made known to his brethren: A sacred drama. Philadelphia: [Lydia R. Bailey] for Johnson and Warner, 1811.   [442]

> Duodecimo, 36 leaves, A-F⁶, engraved frontispiece by B. Tanner after Stothard.
> Original wrappers.

PICTURES

OF

ROMAN HISTORY,

IN MINIATURE,

Designed by ALFRED MILLS.

WITH

Explanatory Anecdotes.

PHILADELPHIA:
Published by JOHNSON & WARNER.
No. 147, Market Street.

J. Rouvier, Printer.

1811.

*Title-page from "Pictures of Roman
History, in Miniature"*

PICTURES

OF

GRECIAN HISTORY,

IN MINIATURE,

Designed by ALFRED MILLS.

WITH

DESCRIPTIONS.

PHILADELPHIA:

Published by Johnson and Warner,

No. 147, Market Street.

1812.

*Title-page from "Pictures of Grecian
History, in Miniature"*

THE

BIBLE.

The Ninth Edition.

Philadelphia:
Printed for W. Jones,
No. 30, N. Fourth St.
1798.

*Title-page from "The Bible.
The Ninth Edition.* 1798"

Dedication.

To his Excellency

G. WASHINGTON,

*President of the United
States of America.*

*Title-page from "The Bible.
The Ninth Edition.* 1798"

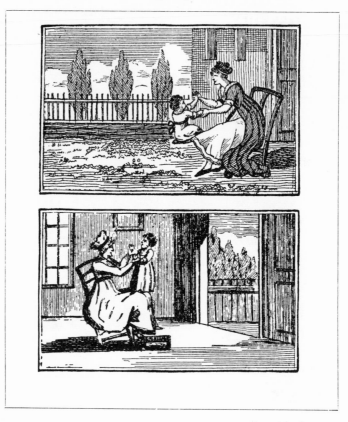

Page from "Old Dame Margery's Hush-A-Bye"

Early American Children's Books

The Search after Happiness is in verse; *Joseph made known to his Brethren* in prose. The dedication of the former piece to Mrs. Gwatkin is dated from Bristol, May 10, 1773.

In the preface to the Search after Happiness, the author explains that *it has been so hackneyed a practice for Authors to pretend, that imperfect copies of their works had crept abroad, that the Writer of the following Pastoral is almost ashamed to allege this, as the real cause of the present publication. This little Poem was composed several years ago (the Author's age eighteen)... She is sensible it has many imperfections, but if it may be happily instrumental in promoting a regard to Religion and Virtue in the minds of Young Persons... the end for which it was originally composed... will be fully answered.*

MUSICAL CATECHISM: in three parts. For the use of schools and private families. Third edition, with additions and corrections. Philadelphia: W. M'Culloch for D[avid] Hogan, 1811.   [443]

Sq. duodecimo, 30 leaves, A-B¹², C⁶ (last leaf blank), musical notation.

Original half binding.
The questions are on the recto, and the corresponding answers on the verso of each leaf, and therefore not opposite to each other.

[PHILLIPS, SIR RICHARD.] An Aesy Grammar of Geography, intended as a Companion and Introduction to the "Geography on a popular plan for Schools and Young Persons." With Maps. By the Rev. J. Goldsmith. A New Edition, Improved, by a Citizen of Philadelphia. Philadelphia: Lydia R. Bailey for Johnson & Warner, 1811.   [444]

Duodecimo, 102 leaves, A-R⁶, engraved frontispiece with volvelle.

Original half binding.
Not in Sabin.
The Rev. J. Goldsmith was one of the pseudonyms of Sir Richard Phillips, see note to no. 349.

POUPARD, JAMES. Metamorphosis; or, a Transformation of Pictures, with Poetical Explanations, for the Amusement of Young Persons. Philadelphia: Published by Jonathan Pounder, 1811.   [445]

For the first edition see no. 82.
This edition of the Metamorphosis is engraved on wood. In addition to the illustrations, ornaments and text as in the first edition, this edition has a title-page, and woodcut ornaments on the first and last leaves forming covers. The title reads as above, and has a woodcut of a man reading, seated under a tree, and the reference Micah, Ch. IV. 4. cut in white on a black background. The illustrations on the two leaves forming the covers are unsigned, and are in quite a different style from the Metamorphosis.
The signature of an early owner, Rachel Davenport, Williamsburg, occurs in several places.

Early American Children's Books

SIMPLE BALLADS; intended for the Amusement and Instruction of Children. Philadelphia: J. Bouvier for Johnson and Warner, 1811. [446]

Duodecimo, 54 leaves, A-I⁶, engraved frontispiece.

Original pink boards, title printed on front cover, advertisement on back.
Contains eighteen ballads. The intention of the author is outlined in the first poem

> ... I will try
> And recollect some pretty little tale;
> Not one of church-yards, ghosts, or spectres pale,
> Of ogre, giant, dwarf, or fairy elves,
> But little harmless beings, like yourselves.

This ideal is hardly maintained in all the ballads, the title of one being *The Ghost; or, Will with his Whisp*, of which the opening lines set the tone of the piece:

> Gloomy the night, but a few stars
> Shone forth and dimly in the skies,
> Drear was the way Hodge had to pass,
> By heath and wood it lies.

The English origin of the book is shown in the poem *The Little Patriot*, a patriotic piece extolling England.

[TAYLOR, ANN AND JANE.] Limed Twigs, to catch Young Birds. By the Authors of Original Poems, Rhymes for the Nursery, &c. &c. Part I. [Part II.] Philadelphia: Published by Johnson & Warner, 1811. [447]

Duodecimo, 2 parts in 1, 54 leaves, A-I⁶, including the last blank, frontispiece engraved by Charles.

Original boards.
Contains a series of graduated reading lessons in dialogue form, beginning with words of three letters, and ending with words of three and four syllables. The half title for the second part is at page (45). At the end is Hannah More's Ballad *Patient Joe; or, The Newcastle Collier*.
The original English edition was published in 1808.
This book is referred to by Mr. Weiss in his account of William Charles, but is not included in his list of Children's Books published or illustrated by him.

THE TRAGI-COMIC HISTORY OF THE BURIAL OF COCK ROBIN; with the Lamentation of Jenny Wren; The Sparrow's Apprehension; and the Cuckoo's Punishment. Being a Sequel to the Courtship, Marriage, and Pic-nic Dinner of Robin Red-Breast and Jenny Wren. Philadelphia: J. Bouvier for Johnson and Warner, 1811. [448]

Sq. octavo, 8 leaves of text in verse, 8 engraved plates, the first and last pasted down to covers.

Original wrappers.

This is not *Who killed Cock Robin*, but a poem on that story beginning:
> When Robin now lay dead,
> Before his Jenny's eyes . . .

Weiss: *William Charles*, page 11, states that this is probably a Charles item.

THE WHIM WHAM: or, Evening Amusement, for all ages and sizes. Being an Entire New Set of Riddles, Charades, Questions, and Transpositions. By a Friend to Innocent Mirth. Philadelphia: Sweeny & M'Kenzie for Johnson & Warner, 1811. [449]

Duodecimo, 18 leaves, including the last blank, engraved frontispiece by Charles.

Wrappers.
Contains a number of Riddles and Charades etc., as indicated on the title. The answers are at the end. The book is evidently of English origin. A work with a similar title printed in London by William Carton has different riddles.
This work is not mentioned by Mr. Weiss in his account of William Charles.

1812

THE ADVENTURES OF ROBERT EARL OF HUNTINGTON, commonly called Robin Hood, the Famous English Archer. Being a complete History of all the merry Adventures and valiant Battles, which he, Little John, and his bold Bow-men, performed and fought at divers Times and on various Occasions. Baltimore: Printed and sold by William Warner, 1812. [450]

Duodecimo, 56 leaves, A-F^{12,6}, G^2, woodcut on the title.

Original fancy boards.
Contains XXXI songs. The woodcut on the title was used again by Warner in his edition of *Robinson Crusoe*, 1815, no. 519. It appears to be copied from the cuts illustrating *The English Hermit* printed by John Marshall in London, circa 1790.

AESOP. Seventy-four select Fables of Aesop and other Fabulists, by R. Dodsley. In two parts. Philadelphia: Published by M. Carey, 1812. [451]

Duodecimo, 2 parts in 1, 49 leaves, A^7, B-H^6.

Original half binding.
The first part contains Fables from the Ancients, numbered I-LIV. The second part, the half title for which is on page (77), contains Fables from the Moderns, numbered I-XII. The book appears to be perfect, though the Contents list at the beginning calls for twenty fables. Each fable is headed by a woodcut in a frame, and has the Moral at the foot.
The first edition of Dodsley's Aesop, intended for children, was printed by John Baskerville in 1771. It was in three parts, and had a preliminary essay on the fable by Dodsley.

Early American Children's Books

The present edition is in two parts, and is without the essay. Some of the fables are original. This copy has the bookplate of — Lewis (the original given name scratched out and replaced by Montgomery in ink), engraved by J. Akin, see no. 283.

THE BLACK BIRDS NEST A Tale. Philadelphia: Published by Johnson & Warner, 1812. [452]

Duodecimo, 18 leaves, lettered A-C³ before the strings, unlettered after the strings, engraved title-page and numerous engravings in the text, some uncut edges.

Original tan wrappers, upper with title, imprint, and engraved illustration, lower with advertisement.
The title on the cover reads: *The Blackbird's Nest. A Tale for Youth.*
The same vignette was not used on every copy of the wrappers.

CATECHISM of the Protestant Episcopal Church, with Notes. To which is prefixed, An Address to Parents, Sponsors, & Guardians, by the Rev. Dr. Abercrombie. Also, Additional Questions; and Forms of Prayer on a variety of occasions, suited to aid the devotion of Young Persons. Selected from Dr. Abercrombie's Lectures on the Cathecism (*sic*). Philadelphia: David Hogan, 1812. [453]

Duodecimo, 12 leaves, without signatures.

Wrappers.
The Reverend James Abercrombie was born in Philadelphia in 1758. He graduated from the University of Pennsylvania, and eventually became an associate pastor of Christ Church, and Principal of the Philadelphia Academy. He died in 1841. His Address occupies pages 3 to 9.

CHESTERFIELD, LORD AND TRUSLER, JOHN. Principles of Politeness, and of Knowing the World: By Lord Chesterfield. With Additions, By John Trusler, D.D. Containing Every instruction necessary to complete the Gentleman and Man of Fashion, to teach him a knowledge of Life, and make him well received in all companies. For the Improvement of Youth: yet not beneath the attention of any. Walpole [N.H.]: Printed by J. G. Watts & E. Brooks at the office of I. Thomas & Co. January, 1812. [454]

16mo, 73 leaves, A-H⁸, I, K⁴, L¹.

Original wrappers.
Another edition of no. 100.

Early American Children's Books

THE CONTINUATION OF OLD DAME TRUDGE AND HER PARROT. Illustrated with whimsical engravings. Philadelphia: W. M'Culloch for Wm. Charles, 1812. [455]

Duodecimo, 8 leaves, engraved throughout and printed on one side only, an illustration and 6 lines of verse on each leaf.

Original wrappers, cover-title, and advertisements on the back.
There is no title-page, the cover appearing on the wrapper only; the illustrations are from the English edition.
Weiss: *William Charles*, page 7.
For the *Adventures of Old Dame Trudge and her Parrot*, see no. 547.

[DARTON, WILLIAM.] Little Truths, for the Instruction of Children. Vol. II. Philadelphia: Published by Johnson & Warner, 1812. [456]

Duodecimo, 24 leaves, A⁴, B⁸, C¹², engraved title-page with large vignette (pasted down to cover), 12 engraved illustrations in the text.

Original wrappers, title on front with large vignette, advertisement of children's books on the back.
Another edition of vol. II of no. 254 with different illustrations.

THE DIAMOND SONGSTER: Containing The most approved Lively Scottish Songs.—The Diamond Songster: Containing The most approved Humorous Irish Songs.—The Diamond Songster: Containing The most approved Humorous English Songs. Baltimore: B. W. Sower & co. for F. Lucas, jun'r, 1812. [457]

Three parts in 1 as issued, each part with 36 leaves, sigs. D-F¹², engraved title at the beginning.

Original calf, gilt, with the lettering M. T. on the front cover.
A miniature book measuring 2½ by 1½ inches.
Part I is the same as the second part of the following number.

THE DIAMOND SONGSTER: Containing The most approved Sentimental Scottish Songs. Baltimore: B. W. Sower & co. for F. Lucas, jun'r. 1812.

Duodecimo, 2 parts in 1, 72 leaves, A-F¹². [458]

Red morocco, gilt.
Continuous signatures but separate pagination for the two parts. The title to Part II (on D₁) reads: *The Diamond Songster: Containing The most approved Lively Scottish Songs*, with imprint as in the first part. Each part has an index.
A miniature book measuring 2⅜ by 1½ inches.
Part I is the same as the first part in the following number. Part II is Part I of the preceding number.

[173]

Early American Children's Books

THE DIAMOND SONGSTER: Containing The most approved Sentimental Scottish Songs.—The Diamond Songster: Containing The most approved Sentimental Irish Songs.—The Diamond Songster: Containing The most approved Sentimental English Songs. Baltimore: B. W. Sower & co., for F. Lucas, jun'r, 1812.   [459]

Three parts in 1 as issued, with separate signatures and pagination, each part with 36 leaves, A-C¹², engraved title at the beginning.

Calf, gilt, with lettering M. T. on the upper cover.
A miniature book measuring 2½ by 1⅜ inches.
Part I is the same as Part I in the preceding number.

HAYES, S. Stories For Little Children. By S. Hays. Part I. [Part II.] Philadelphia: Johnson & Warner, 1812.   [460]

Duodecimo, 2 volumes, 18 leaves each, engraved vignette on each title, engraved illustrations in the text.

Original wrappers, title on upper cover, advertisements on lower.
Contains fifteen moral stories with engraved illustrations. The date on the engraved tombstone in the fourteenth story is 1810, which may be the date of the first edition. Story the Sixth is the Starved Goldfinch, a favorite subject with children's story-writers of the period, see no. 381.
The name of the author is spelt Hayes on the covers.

THE HISTORY OF FORTUNIO, and his Famous Companions. Boston: Published by Isaiah Thomas, Jun., 1812.   [461]

36 mo, 18 leaves, first and last leaves pasted down to covers, woodcut frontispiece, vignette on title and numerous illustrations in text.

Original dark blue wrappers, upper with title and woodcut vignette, lower with advertisement of Juvenile Books.
The History of Fortunio was one of the Tales of Mother Bunch. It closes on page 25; on page (26) are two stanzas of verse entitled: *Summer,* headed by a woodcut, and on page (27) begins *Wishes. An Arabian Tale.*

[LAMB, CHARLES AND MARY.] Poetry for Children, entirely original. By the author of "Mrs. Liecester's (*sic*) School." Boston: E. G. House for West and Richardson, and Edward Cotton, 1812.   [462]

Duodecimo, 72 leaves, A⁴, B-M⁶, N².

Original half binding.
This is the first American edition. The first English edition was published in London in 1809. The printer's imprint is on the back of the title.

POETRY

FOR

CHILDREN,

ENTIRELY ORIGINAL.

BY THE AUTHOR OF
" MRS. LIECESTER'S SCHOOL."

BOSTON :

PUBLISHED BY WEST AND RICHARDSON,
AND EDWARD COTTON.

1812.

Title-page from "Poetry for Children"

TALES

FROM

SHAKSPEARE,

DESIGNED

FOR THE USE OF YOUNG PERSONS.

BY CHARLES LAMB.

IN TWO VOLUMES.
VOL. I.

PHILADELPHIA:

PUBLISHED BY BRADFORD AND INSKEEP; AND
INSKEEP AND BRADFORD, NEWYORK.

J. Maxwell, Printer.

1813.

Title-page from "Tales from Shakspeare, Designed for
the Use of Young Persons"

Early American Children's Books

In writing of the English edition of this work in 1827 to his friend Bernard Barton, who appears elsewhere in this Catalogue as part author of *Original Poems for Infant Minds*, 1816, no. 543, Charles Lamb refers to it as *the joint production of Mary and me*. With a few exceptions it has not been determined which pieces are by Charles Lamb, and which by his sister.

In a letter to Mrs. Norris written in 1832, Charles refers to this American edition: *The first volume printed here* (i. e. Poetry for Children) *is not to be had for love or money, not even an American edition of it, and the second volume, American also, to suit with it. It is much the same as the London one.*

THE LIVES AND CHARACTERS of the Principal Personages in the early part of The History of America. Philadelphia: Published by Bennett & Walton, 1812. [463]

Duodecimo, 52 leaves, A-H⁶, I⁴.

Original boards, title on front cover, advertisements on back.
Not in Sabin.
Contains the Lives of Christopher Columbus; Fernando Cortes; Montezuma; Pizarro, Almagro, & Luque.
The printer's imprint is on the back of the title: *Printed by John F. Gilbert, Frankford, Pa.*

MILLS, ALFRED. Pictures of Grecian History, in miniature, Designed by Alfred Mills. With Descriptions. Philadelphia: Johnson and Warner, 1812. [464]

24mo, 48 leaves, A-M⁴, 46 plates.

Original boards, half title on front cover, advertisement on back.
A miniature book measuring 2¹⁸⁄₁₆ by 2¼ inches.
A companion volume to *Pictures of Roman History*, no. 441.

THE NEW-YORK PRECEPTOR; or, Third Book. New York: Printed and Sold by Samuel Wood, 1812. [465]

Duodecimo, 36 leaves (first and last blanks pasted down to wrappers), irregular signatures, woodcut illustrations.

Original wrappers, title with woodcut and imprint on the upper, two woodcuts on the lower cover.
Not in Sabin.
Contains alphabets, syllabaries illustrated and unillustrated, and passages for reading, consisting chiefly of natural history subjects, and each with an illustration.
At the end are two descriptive alphabets, one with illustrations, and containing much valuable information: *Smoking the pipe and segar is a kind of amusement·that destroys much time and property; and injures the health of many.*
The same woodcuts were not used on the wrappers of all copies.

Early American Children's Books

A PICTURE BOOK, for Little Children. Philadelphia: Published by Kimber and Conrad, n. d. [c. 1812.]   [466]

Duodecimo, 12 leaves, without signatures, woodcut on title and 2 woodcuts on each page.

Yellow wrappers.
Measures 5⁹⁄₁₆ by 2¹⁰⁄₁₆ inches.

This book is exactly what it is stated to be on the title-page. It contains a series of woodcut illustrations, all taken from other books, and with a line or so of text beneath containing moral precept, advice, a truism or mere explanation. A cut of a mirror is labelled: *We cannot see ourselves in this Glass*; another equally obvious statement is attached to a cut of a tree: *Some trees bear fruit, but this one has none on now*; a group of young ladies is simply labelled *Nice Folks*; a picture of Robinson Crusoe and Man Friday has the exhortation *Do be kind to the poor black boy*, and on the same page is a kite which *should never be raised in the street*. Fashions have evidently changed since 1795, for the same pair of stays that Master Billy Bland presented to his school-girl sister Kitty is here labelled: *Give the Stays to Grandmother* (see no. 187); local interest is represented by a picture of *The Swedes Church*, and a Bible gives the publishers an opportunity for advertisement: *The bible is the best of all books. Children who can read in the bible, may go to Kimber & Conrad's Store and buy one for themselves.* On the back of the title are alphabets in hornbook form.

THE YOUTH'S CABINET OF NATURE, for the year; containing curious particulars characteristic of each month. Intended to direct young people to the innocent and agreeable employment of observing nature. New York: Samuel Wood, 1812.   [467]

Duodecimo, 28 leaves (first and last blanks pasted down to covers), woodcuts by Anderson.

Original boards.
On the verso of the title, below the preface is the following note: *Although calculated for the latitude and meridian of Great Britain, yet on an examination of this little book, the publisher was induced to believe, the Youth of Columbia might be profitably amused in a perusal of the same; he accordingly has given it an American impression, taking the liberty to make some notes on what he deemed exceptionable.*

1813

THE AMERICAN PRIMER; or, An easy introduction to Spelling & Reading. Fourth improved edition. Philadelphia: Mathew Carey, 1813.   [468]

Duodecimo, 18 leaves, woodcut on title, each page with a woodcut illustration in an oval compartment.

Original wrappers, woodcut oval vignette and title on upper, alphabets on lower.
This American Primer is not the same as that printed in Norfolk, 1803. On the title is an oval woodcut of the Archangel and Apollyon, alphabets in hornbook form on the back; the text consists of syllabaries and reading lessons, with an alphabet illustrated by oval wood-

cuts as the running headline to each page. Most of these cuts were used by Carey in his Spanish Primer, *El Director de los Niños*, 1811, no. 437.

BIBLE HISTORY. New York: S. Wood, 1813. [469]

128 leaves, A-Q⁸, woodcut frontispiece, several woodcuts in text.

Original sheep, gilt.
A Thumb Bible measuring 1⅛ by 1¼ inches.
Another edition of no. 433 with the same woodcuts. This copy is imperfect, lacking three leaves.

THE BUDGET; consisting of Pieces, both instructive and amusing, for Young Persons. Philadelphia: A. Fagan for Johnson & Warner, 1813. [470]

Duodecimo, 36 leaves, A-F⁶, first leaf pasted down to cover, woodcut frontispiece and numerous illustrations in the text.

Original yellow covers sprinkled with gold.
A collection of ten short stories, dialogues, etc.
In the story entitled The Ship, on page 28, the explanatory word in brackets in the following passage was probably added by the American editor: *Near two thousand years ago, when Julius Caesar came over to this island (England)* . . .
The woodcuts for this edition were by Alexander Anderson.

THE DEATH AND BURIAL OF COCK ROBIN: with the story of the Farmer's Daughters, to which is added, The Tragical Death of an Apple-Pye. Ornamented with Engravings. Albany: E. &. E. Hosford, 1813. [471]

16mo, 16 leaves, without signatures, first (with frontispiece) and last leaves pasted down to covers, woodcut illustrations.

Original cream wrappers, woodcuts.
Another edition of no. 305. The woodcuts are copied from those in the former edition with the exception of the frontispiece and the owl, and there is an additional cut in The Farmer's Daughters. At page 27, between *The Farmer's Daughters* and *An Apple Pie* is *The History of Ebouli Sina and a poor Woman*. There are no advertisements at the end.

EDGEWORTH, MARIA. To-morrow, or the Dangers of Delay. By Maria Edgeworth. New York: C. W. Bunce for Evert Duyckingk, (*sic*) 1813.

Duodecimo, 54 leaves, A-I⁶, woodcut on title-page. [472]

Original half binding.
The story is dated at the end, August, 1803. A footnote on page 91, relating to the story of the poisoning of pheasants by the leaves of Kalmia Latifolia reads in part: *In the severe winter of the year* 1790 *and* 1791, *there appeared to be such unequivocal reasons for believing*

that several persons in Philadelphia, had died in consequence of their eating pheasants, in whose crops the leaves and buds of the Kalmia Latifolia were found, that the mayor of the city thought it prudent and his duty to warn the people against the use of this bird . . . Vide a paper by B. Smith Barton, D. M. American Transactions, V. 51.

ENGLISH, CLARA. The Children in the Wood, An Instructive Tale; By Clara English. Philadelphia: Printed by Jacob Meyer, 1813. [473]

Duodecimo, 24 leaves, A-D⁶, woodcut vignette on title and woodcut illustrations.

Wrappers.

At the end the ballad beginning *Now, ponder well, you parents dear.*

This edition is illustrated with woodcuts which are copied from the copper-plate engravings in the edition of 1807, see no. 330.

[HELMUTH, JUSTUS HEINRICH CHRISTIAN.] Das Gute Kind, vor, in und nach der Schule. Philadelphia: Conrad Zentler, 1813. [474]

Duodecimo, 12 leaves, sig. A, woodcut vignette on title and woodcut illustrations in text.

Marbled paper wrappers.

In verse and prose.

This edition has a *Vorrede zur zweyten Auflage* dated from Philadelphia, den 1. October, 1813, in addition to the Vorrede to the first edition which is here repeated (see no. 211).

The woodcuts for this edition were probably by Anderson.

THE HISTORY OF INSECTS. And God made every thing that creepeth upon the earth. Gen. 1. 25. New York: Printed and sold by Samuel Wood, 1813. [475]

16mo, 16 leaves, without signatures, first and last leaves pasted down to covers, woodcut on title and woodcut illustrations in the text.

Original wrappers, title with woodcut on upper and two woodcuts on lower.

The alphabets in hornbook form on the first leaf, a quotation from Mrs. Barbauld on the back of the title. The work contains an introductory essay, and the descriptions with illustrations of fourteen insects. The information is of general interest, but there are at least two local references: the ant-hills made by ants are *commonly built in woody places: the brushy plains on Long-Island abound with them*: and again silkworms *are natives of China, and were brought into Italy . . . and some have been reared in the United States of America.*

On the last leaf Samuel Wood *Hereby informs the good little Boys and Girls, both of city and country, who love to read better than to play, that if they will please to call at his Juvenile Book-store, No. 357, Pearl-street, New-York, it will be his pleasure to furnish them with a great variety of pretty little books . . . Besides many from Philadelphia, New-Haven, and elsewhere, he has nearly fifty kinds of his own printing, and proposes to enlarge the number.*

Early American Children's Books

LAMB, CHARLES [AND MARY.] Tales from Shakespeare, designed for the use of young persons. By Charles Lamb. In two volumes. Vol. I. [II.] Philadelphia: J. Maxwell for Bradford and Inskeep; and Inskeep and Bradford, New York, 1813.   [476]

Two volumes, portrait of *Shakespear* by Edwin after Zoust as frontispiece to Vol. I. Vol. I, 142 leaves, A-Z⁶, Aa⁴. Vol. II, 154 leaves, [A]², B-Z, Aa-Cc⁶, Dd², the last a blank.

Original grey boards, title on the front, advertisement on the back, uncut.
First American edition.
The first English edition appeared in 1807, the adaptations having been written during 1805 and 1807 at the suggestion of William Godwin.
Six of the pieces were by Charles Lamb, and fourteen by his sister Mary.
In the preface Charles explains: *I have wished to make these Tales easy reading for very young children . . . For young ladies too it has been my intention chiefly to write, because boys are generally permitted the use of their fathers' libraries at a much earlier age than girls are . . . therefore, instead of recommending these Tales to the perusal of young gentlemen who can read them so much better in the originals, I must rather beg their kind assistance in explaining to their sisters such parts as are hardest for them to understand; and when they have helped them to get over the difficulties, then perhaps they will read to them (carefully selecting what is proper for a young sister's ear) some passage which has pleased them in one of these stories, in the very words of the scene from which it is taken . . .*

THE NEW TESTAMENT, in verse; or The history of our Blessed Saviour. Containing A brief account of his Birth, Life, Death, Resurrection, and Ascension, &c. Being a pleasant and profitable companion for Children. Philadelphia: Benjamin Johnson, 1813.   [477]

Duodecimo, 36 leaves, A-C¹², woodcut frontispiece, woodcuts in the text.

Original wrappers, title on upper cover.
Bates, page 14.
An edition of the *History of the Holy Jesus* with the first part of the title changed.
This edition contains The Child's Body of Divinity; St. Paul's Shipwreck; The Ten Commandments in Metre; the Cradle and other Hymns, and prayers.
On the blank recto of the frontispiece the signature of *Phebe Sharpless Book this the* 20 *of the* 6 *Month Eighteen hundred and sixteen* 1816. *Price* 12½ *Cts.*

PRETTY POEMS, in easy language, for the amusement of Little boys and girls. By Tommy Lovechild. Ornamented with Cuts. Hartford: Hale & Hosmer, 1813.   [478]

16mo, 16 leaves without signatures, woodcut frontispiece of Tommy Lovechild reading poetry, a woodcut illustration for each poem.

Early American Children's Books

Original yellow wrappers, title with woodcut on the front, advertisement on the back.

For a former edition see no. 380. This edition contains twenty-two poems, amongst the additions being *My Father* and *My Mother* by Ann Taylor. The remaining poems are one verse stanzas, each together with a woodcut illustration, occupying one page. The woodcuts, with four exceptions, are the same as in the earlier edition. Alphabets on the back of the title.

[WEBSTER, NOAH.] The Pirates. A Tale for the Amusement and Instruction of Youth. Embellished with cuts. To which is added: Several Select Pieces in prose and verse. Philadelphia: William Greer for Johnson & Warner, 1813.   [479]

Duodecimo, 54 leaves, A-I⁶, woodcut frontispiece, several full-page woodcut illustrations.

Original blue boards.
First edition.
This was apparently the only piece of fiction for the young produced by the great dictionarist and grammarian. The Select Pieces begin on page 47, those in prose are all taken from *The Prompter* (see no. 243); those in verse are not by Webster, they consist of four pieces, and at the end a *Whimsical Epitaph in a Church-Yard*:

> Reader, I've left this world, in which
> I had a world to do,
> Sweating and fretting to get rich;
> Just such a fool as you.

THE WONDERFUL HISTORY OF AN ENCHANTED CASTLE, kept by Giant Grumbo, the most humane and tender-hearted giant in the known world. Ornamented with Engravings. Albany: E. and E. Hosford, 1813. [480]

16mo, 16 leaves, without signatures, first and last pasted down to wrappers, woodcut frontispiece and woodcuts in text.

Original wrappers, title with woodcut vignette on upper, two woodcuts on lower.
The Enchanted Castle is governed by Giant Grumbo. It is occupied also by many good young gentlemen *For here (and I think it ought to be so in America,) the young masters are all very good natured and very mannerly*. The story contains a rhymed alphabet beginning:

> A is an ass, a poor dull lazy beast;
> His reward is a stick and a bramble his feast.
> B is a beauty, all cheerful and gay,
> But her beauty soon fades, like a flower in May.

Most of the woodcuts will be found in other books by other printers. The frontispiece of the Giant Grumbo himself is the King in the Silver Penny, printed by Parke in Philadelphia, 1807, and others of the cuts will also be found in that and in other books.

THE PIRATES.

A TALE

FOR THE AMUSEMENT AND INSTRUCTION OF

YOUTH.

EMBELLISHED WITH CUTS.

TO WHICH IS ADDED :

SEVERAL SELECT PIECES

IN PROSE AND VERSE.

———

Philadelphia :

PUBLISHED BY JOHNSON & WARNER.

WILLIAM GREER, PRINTER.

1813.

Title-page from "The Pirates"

108

WHIMSICAL EPITAPH

IN A CHURCH-YARD.

Reader, I've left this world, in which
  I had a world to do,
Sweating and fretting to get rich;
  Just such a fool as you.

Page from "The Pirates"

Early American Children's Books

1814

AESOP. Aesop's Fables: New York: Samuel Wood, 1814.   [481]

Duodecimo, 24 leaves without signatures, including the last blank; woodcut on title, a woodcut illustration for each fable by A. Anderson.

Bound with others in half dark blue morocco.
Contains twenty-two fables with their applications.

[BARBAULD, ANNA LETITIA.] Hymns in Prose, for the Use of Children. New York: Samuel Wood, 1814.   [482]

Duodecimo, 22 leaves, without signatures, woodcut vignette on title and numerous woodcuts in the text, by A. Anderson.

Bound with others in half dark blue morocco.
The *Hymns in Prose* are usually considered to be Mrs. Barbauld's best work.

BEAUTIES OF THE NEW-ENGLAND PRIMER. New York: Samuel Wood, 1814.   [483]

16mo, 16 leaves without signatures, the first and last pasted down, woodcut vignette on title, woodcut illustrations, alphabets on the back of the title.

Original wrappers, title and woodcut vignette on upper, 2 vignettes on lower.
Heartman 212 cites this copy only.
The editor of this edition has explained his object in a preface:
The New-England Primer of latter time, having become almost useless, unless on account of the Catechism, which is likewise printed in a separate pamphlet, it appears likely to become nearly if not quite obsolete. As it contains matter worthy of being preserved, the publisher has made a selection, with some alterations, and put it in the shape in which it now appears, hoping it will be acceptable to the children of the present day, and to those which may follow: and afford an opportunity to gather some good hints from a work that for generations has been a first book for their forefathers.
The selection includes the alphabet couplets; *I in the burying place may see*; Agur's Prayer; A Cradle Hymn; the account of the burning of John Rogers, and his poem of advice to his children; A Dialogue between Christ, a Youth, and the Devil, etc.
The alphabet couplets include some that have not been found in any previous edition in this collection:

Adam and Eve
Their God did grieve.
* * *
The paper Kite
Is boy's delight.
* * *
Queens and kings must
Lie in the dust.
* * *
Urns hold, we see,
Coffee and tea.

Early American Children's Books

BIBLE HISTORY. New York: S. Wood, 1814.   [484]

128 leaves, A-Q⁸, woodcut frontispiece and other woodcut illustrations.

Original leather with tie.
A Thumb Bible measuring 1⅞ by 1¼ inches.
Another edition of no. 433 with the same woodcuts.

The CRIES OF NEW-YORK. New York: Printed and sold by Samuel Wood, at the Juvenile Book-Store, No. 357, Pearl Street, 1814.   [485]

16mo, 24 leaves, without signatures, woodcut on the title.

Full blue levant morocco, padded with blanks.

Contains twenty-six Cries, each with a woodcut, a description in prose, and notes and comments by the editor. The New York Cries, first published in 1808, formed the model for the Philadelphia Cries, and a comparison between this edition, and the edition of the Cries of Philadelphia, no. 414 is interesting, each city having made efforts to localize the material. Many of the woodcuts are the same in the two editions. The editor has introduced a dissertation on thieving into the watermelon cry *Here's your fine, ripe Water-Milyons; Watermelons are raised in great plenty, and with ease; but the difficulty lies in preserving them from thieves. Strange, indeed, to tell; but so it is: there are many who would by no means take a cent from a neighbour's drawer, and yet will steal watermelons. . .*
The Cry of the Bell-Man

> This man on his cart,
>   As he drives along,
>   His bell doth swing,
>   Ding, dong, ding, dong.

is not in the Philadelphia Cries. The description closes: *Would not eating less animal food, and rather salt than fresh, drinking less spirituous liquors, and frequent bathing at suitable seasons, probably tend to the health and comfort of the people?* This is followed by a long note: *Query. Ought there not to be proper baths erected, that people of every class, age, and sex, in a decent manner, might be encouraged, free of expense, frequently to use them in the warm season. . .*
A Description of New-York is on the first leaf facing the title.

[DORSET, CATHERINE ANN.] The Peacock "At Home:" or Grand Assemblage of Birds. Written by Roscoe. Illustrated with Elegant Engravings. Philadelphia: W. M'Culloch for Wm. Charles, 1814.   [486]

Sq. octavo, 8 leaves of text (in verse), 7 full-page plates including the frontispiece.

Original wrappers with title on front cover and imprint of Wm. Charles, advertisements on the back.
Weiss: *William Charles*, page 8.
This popular poem for children was first published in London, in 1807 as *By a Lady* for no. 2 of Harris's Cabinet Series, illustrated by Mulready. This is the first American reprint; the plates are after those by Mulready.
The statement on the title-page that the poem is by Roscoe is an error. William Roscoe

was the author of the *Butterfly's Ball*, also published in 1807, and the *Peacock at Home* was written by Mrs. Dorset as a sequel. The poem was published anonymously, and the authorship not discovered until some years later.

The title on the cover reads the same as the title-page except that *Illustrated with Eight Plates* is substituted for *Illustrated with Elegant Engravings*. This is, however, an error, seven being the correct number.

Beneath the imprint on the cover title is the price, 18¾ cents.

FALSE STORIES CORRECTED. "Learn to unlearn what you have learned amiss." New York: Samuel Wood, 1814.   [487]

Duodecimo, 24 leaves, including one leaf of advertisement and the last blank, woodcut on the title and numerous woodcut illustrations in the text, by Anderson.

Bound with others in dark blue half morocco.

The work opens with an essay on the reprehensibleness of impressing the infant mind with wrong ideas, and *The Fakenham Ghost* by Robert Bloomfield is quoted in full to illustrate the effect of fear on the imagination.

The terrible effects of an improper education in our treatment of our less fortunate neighbours is then shown, and finally, the folly of believing in Mermaids, Fairies, harpies, griffons, that salamanders live in fire, in the phoenix, centaurs, Jack Frost, and Santaclaw (*sic*): *such a creature as Jack Frost never existed, any more than old Santaclaw, of whom so often little children hear such foolish stories; and once in the year are encouraged to hang their stockings in the chimney at night, and when they arise in the morning, they find in them cakes, nuts, money, &c. placed there by some of the family, which they are told Old Santaclaw has come down chimney in the night and put in. Thus the little innocents are imposed on by those who are older than they, and improper ideas take possession which are not by any means profitable.* The last example is the pelican, *which is a good example to idle parents, who neglect to labour, and are not provident for their offspring.*

FRANKLIN, BENJAMIN. Franklin's Way to Wealth; or, "Poor Richard Improved." Industry leads to Wealth. New York: Samuel Wood, 1814. [488]

Duodecimo, 22 leaves, woodcut illustrations.

Bound with others in half blue morocco.

This edition not in Ford: *Franklin Bibliography*.

At page (31) begins Advice to a Young Tradesman, from An Old One. By Dr. Benjamin Franklin, and at page (37) Pro Bono Publico. A New Way of Paying Old Debts; each with caption title.

The Introduction states that this edition was printed from a London one, from which it quotes the introduction, ending as follows: *And, shall we, brother Englishmen, refuse good sense and saving knowledge, because it comes from the other side of the water?*

G., J. A Small Help, offered to Heads of Families, for Instructing Children and Servants. By J. G. . . . To which is added, Directions for Self-Examination. Morris-Town: J. Mann for P. A. Johnson, 1814. [489]

Duodecimo, 20 leaves, first and last blanks pasted down to wrappers, partly unopened.

Wrappers.

GARDEN AMUSEMENTS, for Improving the Minds of Little Children. New York: Samuel Wood, 1814. [490]

Duodecimo, 24 leaves, woodcut vignette on title, woodcuts in the text.

Original wrappers, upper with title and woodcut vignette, lower with advertisement.

Contains much instruction built round a slight story. The editor explains in the advertisement that *This little treatise, (written and first published in the great emporium of the British nation, the country of our ancestors, on the other side of the Atlantic,) containing so many pleasing remarks for the juvenile mind, was thought worthy of an American edition.*

At the beginning of the story is a quotation from Milton, to which the editor has appended a footnote: *These two lines of the great poet, savor too much, I think, of what is termed, poetic license.* He is even more critical of Cowper, two of whose poems are quoted in full. The last stanza of *The Jackdaw* calls forth a grave reproof: *If by this verse, we are to understand the poet to mean, he would prefer the existence of a bird to a man, he certainly was in this instance, highly reprehensible; and, however we may esteem him as a wise, pious, and pleasing poet: yet, this sentiment was very improper, and a mark of human frailty . . .*

The illustrations are by A. Anderson. At the end are four pages of advertisement of school and children's books sold by Samuel Wood.

HABERMANN, JOHANN. Doct. Johann Habermanns Christliches Gebet-Büchlein, Enthaltend Morgen- und Abend-Segen auf alle Tage in der Woche. Nebst andern schönen Gebetern. Wie auch Magister Neumanns Kern aller Gebeter, und geistlichen Stundenwecker. Libanon: Joseph Schnee, 1814. [491]

Duodecimo, 78 leaves, A-N^6, including the last blank (one leaf torn out).

Original half calf.

THE HISTORY OF MOTHER TWADDLE, and the Marvellous Atchievments of Her Son Jack, by H. A. C. Philadelphia: Wm. Charles, 1814. [492]

Sq. duodecimo, 16 leaves, including frontispiece and title, engraved throughout and printed on one side only, 4 lines of verse and an illustration on each leaf.

Original wrappers, title on the front wrapper, advertisement on the lower.

The original issue of 1809 (the imprint on the title-page so dated) with new covers, dated 1814.

Not in Weiss: *William Charles.*

A rhymed version of the story of Jack and the Beanstalk. The title on the cover reads: *Jack and the Bean Stalk. The History of Mother Twaddle, and the Marvellous Achievements of her son Jack. Illustrated with Fifteen Engravings. Philadelphia: Published and sold wholesale by Wm. Charles, and may be had of all the booksellers. 1814. Price 25 cents.*

Early American Children's Books

The frontispiece is described by the couplet:

Here Jack, and his wife, and his Mother, is seen,
All dancing a jig round the wonderful bean.

HISTORY OF THE BIBLE. Boston: [Printed by Nathaniel Willis for] T. Bedlington & J. Ball, 1814. [493]

128 leaves, A-Q⁸, woodcut frontispiece and woodcut illustrations.

Original calf.
A Thumb Bible measuring 1⅝ by 1⅛ inches.
Another edition of the *Bible History* published by Samuel Wood, no. 433, with the same woodcuts.
The printer's imprint *Willis, Printer* is on the back of the title.

THE HUMOROUS ALPHABET. Newburyport: W. & J. Gilman, n. d. [c. 1814.] [494]

16mo, 8 leaves, without signatures, the last with advertisements, woodcut of a lion on the title and numerous woodcuts in text.

Original cream wrappers.
The book is Irish: *Come here vid yourself, you little O'Shaugnessy, bring your primmer in your hand, and your copper in your fist—blow your nose, and hold up your head like a man: arrah, now, don't be hunting the flies across the ceiling, but cock your eye, and look straight at your book.* The lesson on the alphabet follows, partly in prose and similar in style to the above, and partly in verse. At the end is a woodcut of *little O'Shaughnessy, shewing his sisters how well he can read,* the cut being headed *Come Read and Learn* from the Battledore.
On the back of the title are alphabets and numbers; the woodcuts in the book have all been used in other works.

THE INSTRUCTIVE ALPHABET. New York: Samuel Wood, 1814. [495]

Duodecimo, 24 leaves, without signatures, including the first blank, woodcut on the title (the alphabet in white on black), woodcut illustrations in the text.

Bound with others in dark blue half morocco.
Prefaced to the work is an alphabet in easy verse beginning:

A t early dawn of day arise,
B less first the Ruler of the skies;
C omb, wash, and cleanse, and ev'ry day
D ress, read, or work, ere thou dost play.

The Instructive alphabet follows, each object being accompanied by a woodcut, four lines of verse, and a long description in prose.

K The Kite

The school boy, with his paper Kite,
Is best pleas'd when high its flight.
With Kites philosophers like boys,
The thunder's lightning court like toys.*

Early American Children's Books

The asterisk refers to a footnote: *Allusion to Dr. Franklin's experiments of the electrical kind.* The description of the Rat closes: *The Europeans first introduced these animals into America, about the year 1544, and they have become the pest of the continent. If America has lent the Europeans any of her evils, it may be said that by her exportation of Rats into America, the account of injuries is fully balanced.*

At the end is a poem *The Negro's Complaint.*

JUVENILE MONITOR; or The New Children's Friend. Translated from the German. First American Edition. Boston: A. Bowen for Bradford and Read, 1814. [496]

Duodecimo, 60 leaves, A-K⁶ (this copy lacks C₆), woodcut illustrations in the text.

Original paper wrappers over wooden boards, upper cover with title and vignette, lower with advertisement.

Contains twenty-seven short stories and dialogues.

The editor in the preface expresses the opinion that in absorbing the morals contained in this book *the acquisition of Wisdom, Experience, and Virtue, at so cheap and easy a rate, must be deemed an advantage of the highest importance.*

Many of the cuts are by Anderson.

THE LIFE AND DEATH OF TOM THUMB, The Little Giant, ornamented with cuts. Boston: N. Coverly, jun., 1814. [497]

16mo, 8 leaves, without signatures, woodcut illustrations.

Original wall paper wrappers.

In this edition Chapter II is omitted entirely, that being the chapter which originally contained the name of John Newbery, and was thus copied by John Norman in his edition of 1790, no. 150, whereas Samuel Hall in his edition of 1794, no. 185, substituted his own name for that of the English publisher.

This edition has the alphabet on the back of the title, and at the end a poem to a dove, with a woodcut illustration.

[MORE, HANNAH.] Parley The Porter. An Allegory. New York: Samuel Wood, 1814. [498]

Duodecimo, 9 leaves.

Unbound, as issued, stitched.

Signed at the end Z, the initial used as a signature by Hannah More.

[MORE, HANNAH.] The Shop-Keeper turned Sailor: or, the folly of going out of our element. Ornamented with Cuts. Philadelphia: Printed for Benjamin Johnson, 1814. [499]

Duodecimo, 12 leaves, A¹², woodcuts.

Original green wrappers, title and woodcut on the front, a list of Repository Tracts on the back.

The last few pages of Part IV, which in the original version referred to conditions in England, have in this edition been revised and edited. This revised portion begins on page 22 with the line

When Freemen, wearied with their lot,

which in the original version read

When Britons, wearied with their lot,

For the original version see no. 342.

MOTHER GOOSE'S MELODY, or Sonnets for the Cradle. Windsor (Vt.): Jesse Cochran, 1814. [500]

16mo, 16 leaves, without signatures, first and last leaves pasted down to wrappers, woodcut frontispiece in 2 compartments, woodcuts in the text.

Original wrappers, title and woodcut on the front, woodcut on the back.

Contains a selection of nursery songs, chiefly extracted from Mother Goose's Melody, but without the notes and maxims, without the second part containing the Lullabies of Shakespeare, and without the preface.

The text of many of the songs has been revised in many cases.

Songs not from Mother Goose include *Father and I went down to Camp*, and *Little boy Blue*.

At the end is a counting out rhyme *Intry mintry cutry corn*, and a rhymed alphabet beginning A *Stands for Age, and for Adam, and Awl*. Many of the woodcuts have been used in other books.

THE NEW ENGLAND PRIMER. Or, an easy and pleasant guide to the art of reading. Also, The Assembly of Divines and the Episcopal Catechisms. New York: C. W. Bunce for Samuel A. Burtus, 1814. [501]

16mo, 36 leaves, A-I⁴, alphabet and John Rogers woodcuts, first and last leaves pasted down to covers.

Original wrappers.

Heartman 211.

This edition has no frontispiece, the title is on the verso of the first leaf (pasted down). The alphabet couplets are as in the edition of John Babcock at Hartford, 1800, no. 261. Both the Shorter and the Episcopal Catechisms are included.

THE NEW-ENGLAND PRIMER; or, an easy and pleasant Guide to the Art of Reading. Adorned with cuts. To which is added, The Catechism. Walpole, N. H.: I. Thomas & Co., 1814. [502]

16mo, 32 leaves, A-D⁸, woodcut frontispiece, alphabet woodcuts, and the cut for John Rogers.

Original half leather and blue boards.

Heartman 210.

The alphabet rhymes contain one quatrain which has not appeared in any previous edition in this collection:

> Of sturdy Oak,
> That stately tree,
> The ships are made
> That sail the sea.

OLD DAME MARGERY'S HUSH-A-BYE: Embellished with fifteen elegant engravings on copper-plates. Philadelphia: Ann Coles for Johnson & Warner, 1814. [503]

Sq. octavo, 8 leaves of text, engraved frontispiece, 7 plates each in 2 compartments.

Original salmon boards.

Contains nursery rhymes from Mother Goose and other sources. The town in the rhyme See-Saw, Sacradown has reverted to London in this edition,

> See-saw, Sacradown,
> Which is the way to London-town?

It will be remembered that the early American editions of Mother Goose substituted Boston for London. *O my kitten, my kitten* has become *Oh! my chicken, my chicken.*

A rhymed alphabet begins

> A was an Archer, you saw on the heath;
> B was a Beauty that shew'd her white teeth.

This is possibly a Charles item.

[?OLIVER, DANIEL.] The Foreign Visitant: containing interesting observations and remarks, made by an inhabitant of Terra Incognita, on the character and manners of the inhabitants of this earth; particularly in relation to the Lord's Day. Second edition, with alterations and additions. Boston: T. B. Wait & Sons for the Proprietor, 1814. [504]

Duodecimo, 36 leaves, 1-6⁶, woodcut frontispiece, 2 woodcut tailpieces.

Original half binding.

This allegory was deposited at the Clerk's office in the District of Massachusetts by Daniel Oliver, the proprietor, who was probably the author. Daniel Oliver (?1752-1840) was a minister in Beverly, Massachusetts. He was the author of several religious works.

REMARKS ON CHILDREN'S PLAY. New York: Samuel Wood, 1814. [505]

Duodecimo, 23 leaves, without signatures, woodcut on title and woodcuts in the text.

Bound with others, in half dark blue morocco.

Gives an account of forty-two children's games, each with a woodcut illustration. Many of the descriptions are edited from other works, and some of the cuts have also appeared in other books (see for example *The Seasons* by the same publishers, no. 507).

In his remarks on the See-Saw the compiler quotes Saltzman as having said it was a favourite amusement of the ladies of the Russian Empire, and adds *It is probable, it would be considered laughable in an American lady; but it is quite as rational as nursing a Lap-Dog.*

Riding Down Hill is *not only a laborious, but it is a dangerous play, and is, as Dr. Franklin says, "paying too much for the whistle."*

Some of the illustrations are copied from the London edition of *Youthful Sports* published by Darton & Harvey.

SCRIPTURAL STORIES, for very young children. By the Author of "The Decoy, Natural History of Quadrupeds," &c. With elegant wood-cuts. London printed. Philadelphia: Reprinted for Kimber and Conrad, 1814. [506]

Duodecimo, 36 leaves, A-F⁶, woodcut frontispiece and several woodcut full-page illustrations.

Original yellow wrappers.

THE SEASONS. New York: Samuel Wood, 1814. [507]

16mo, 23 leaves, without signatures, including a leaf of advertisement at the end, woodcut on title in 4 compartments, woodcut illustrations in text.

Bound with others in dark blue half morocco.

Contains accounts of the occupations suitable to each season of the year, with verses at the end of each season.

The preface contains an exposition of the realistic school of thought for children, and deplores the fact that *Stories of fairies, enchanted castles, hobgoblins, romances, and the like, must fill the infant mind with improper ideas. There is matter enough which is true, extraordinary, entertaining and innocent.—Then, why fill their minds with such as Tom Thumb, Giant Grumbo, House that Jack Built, Cinderilla, Gulliver's Travels, and such like?*

The remarks on Flying the Kite, one of the occupations for summer, contain the usual warning: *caution is necessary in raising them in streets or highways, lest horses in carriages take fright at them, which might cost lives or limbs.* Gathering Apples, an autumn occupation, is an opportunity for a homily on drink: *Cider is a cheap, pleasant, and wholesome drink, much to be prefered to strong spirits, which are wonderful in their operations; for they will unroof barns, fill broken windows with pillows and old clothes, pull down fences, make cattle lean, children ragged and ignorant, break the hearts of tender mothers, and affectionate wives, bring disease and shame, fill gaols and state prisons, and often bring to the gallows; and it is feared, to eternal ruin. . . .* Playing at Marbles, another autumn recreation, also contains the usual warning, it is *a common and innocent play, provided the children do not make it a game, to win each other's marbles. This ought never to be done, as it encourages a spirit of covetousness, and frequently cheating, and may lead to larger gaming, with cards, dice, &c.*

SELECT FABLES, in prose and verse. New York: Samuel Wood, 1814. [508]

Duodecimo, 24 leaves, woodcut on title and woodcut illustrations.

Original yellow wrappers, title with woodcut on upper, advertisement on lower.

The fables are from various sources; each is accompanied by a woodcut illustration.

Early American Children's Books

THE SEVEN WONDERS OF THE WORLD; And other Magnificent Buildings, &c. New York: Samuel Wood, 1814. [509]

> Duodecimo, 22 leaves, woodcut on title and woodcut illustrations in the text.
>
> Bound with others in dark blue half morocco.
> The *other Magnificent Buildings* are St. Paul's and the Monument in London; St. Peter's, Rome; the Sphynx, and Pompey's Pillar. At the end is a list of Juvenile Books, printed and sold by Samuel Wood.

THE STORY OF QUASHI; or, The Desperate Negro. To which is added, The Story of Sinbad the Sailor and The Elephants. Together with the Story of Mendaculus. Newburyport Edition. Newburyport: W. & J. Gilman, n. d. [c. 1814.] [510]

> Duodecimo, 12 leaves, first and last pasted down to covers, woodcut emblematic frontispiece, woodcut illustrations in the text.
>
> Original wrappers, upper with title and woodcut, lower with woodcut.
> The Story of Quashi ends on page 9; its frontispiece by Anderson, which is also on the upper cover, was used in the *Economy of Human Life* printed for Johnson and Warner in Philadelphia, 1810, no. 416. The Story of Sinbad the Sailor and the Elephants begins on page 11, preceded by a frontispiece, and followed on page 19 by an account of the Elephant; The Story of Mendaculus begins on page 20.

[TAYLOR, ANN AND JANE, *and others.*] Poems for Children. New York: Samuel Wood, 1814. [511]

> Duodecimo, 21 leaves, (A)^5, B^{16}, woodcut on title, woodcut illustrations in the text.
>
> Bound with others, in half dark blue morocco.
> All the poems in this collection are from *Original Poems, for Infant Minds*, by Jane and Ann Taylor, Adelaide O'Keefe and others, see no. 543. The greater number in this edition are by the Taylors, but at least two (The Child's Monitor and The Butterfly) are by Adelaide O'Keefe.

[TAYLOR, ANN.] The World Turn'd Upside Down, or the Wonderful Magic Lantern. Illustrated with humourous engravings. Part II. Philadelphia: W. M'Culloch for Wm. Charles, 1814. [512]

> Sq. octavo, 8 leaves of text, 8 plates, the first and last pasted down to wrappers.
>
> Original wrappers with title on the front and advertisements on the back.
> On the cover title the description of the engravings reads *whimsical* and not *humourous*. Weiss, *William Charles*, p. 11.
> The idea for this work was taken from the French *Images Populaires* of the eighteenth century. In the original London edition of this version for children (Tabard and Co., 1810), the name of Ann Taylor appears on the title as the author, but her sister Jane and her brother Jefferys had also a share in the production.

Early American Children's Books

Mr. Weiss, in *Joseph Yeager, Early American Engraver, Publisher of Children's Books, and Railroad President*, states that a signed plate by Yeager appeared in the William Charles edition of *The World Turn'd Upside Down*, 1814. None of the plates in this example of Part II is signed.

Joseph Yeager was an outstanding figure in the history of American Children's Books, both as an engraver, and as a publisher in partnership with William Morgan. According to Mr. Weiss he was born in 1792, probably in Philadelphia. He died in that city in 1859.

For a note on the Morgan and Yeager partnership, see no. 631.

TRUE STORIES RELATED. By a friend to little children. New York: Samuel Wood, 1814. [513]

23 leaves, woodcut on the title and numerous woodcut illustrations in the text.

Bound with others in dark blue half morocco.

The short preface is an exposition of the realistic school of thought for children.

Many . . . have been guilty of poisoning the infant and vacant mind, with not only false, but ridiculous and baneful Stories . . . What advantage can be derived from the Stories of Hobgobblins, Enchanted Castles, Fairies, Sylphs, Magical Wands, Wishing Caps, &c. &c. &c. . . such stuff as the battle of Tom Thumb with the Bumble-Bee, the exploits of Gulliver among the Lilliputians, the Descent of Sinbad into the Valley of Diamonds, &c. . . What but a depraved taste, poisoned by habit, could make a blooming youth prefer Novels, Plays, and Romances, to the Sacred Records, and other useful writings . . .

The ten stories which follow are *simple narrations of plain facts* intended to replace the *magazine of trash*, with which the children's minds have been stored; some of these are taken from the Bible and others are tales of contemporary American life.

The first one, *Wicked and Unmannerly Children*, is the history of the children mocking Elisha, and being destroyed by bears, which took place *A long time ago, long before Old Columbus crossed the trackless deep, in quest of a new Continent, or Western World.* The Hymn of Dr. Watts on this subject is quoted in full.

Amongst the other tales are *Disobedience, Punishment, and Repentance; Daniel in the Lion's Den; The Crane with a Broken Leg*, which inhabited a Mill-Pond *about 20 miles from New-York, a little east of New-Rochelle; The dangerous effects of fear in the Water*, a story of Long Island; *The Danger and Sad Effects of Gun-Powder; The sad effects of Wrestling.*

VILLAGE ANNALS, containing Austerus and Humanus. A sympathetic tale. Embellished with fine engravings. Philadelphia: Griggs & Dickinsons, for Johnson & Warner, 1814. [514]

Duodecimo, 18 leaves, sig. A, woodcut frontispiece, 6 large woodcuts (leaves otherwise blank), first and last leaves pasted down.

Original blue wrappers.

WATTS, ISAAC. Songs, Divine and Moral, for the Use of Children. By Isaac Watts. New York: Samuel Wood, 1814. [515]

Duodecimo, 23 leaves (this copy lacks 2 leaves, pp. 39-42), woodcut on the title and woodcut illustrations in the text.

Bound with others in dark blue half morocco.
Not in Stone.
The illustrations are by Anderson. On the last leaf is *The Drum* by Scott.

THE YOUTH'S CABINET OF NATURE, for the year; containing Curious Particulars characteristic of Each Month. Intended to direct young people to the innocent and agreeable employment of observing nature. New York: Samuel Wood, 1814. [516]

Duodecimo, 26 leaves, woodcut illustrations in the text.

Original wrappers, title with woodcut vignette on upper, advertisement on lower.
A reprint of no. 467 with very slight variations in the text.

1815

COWPER, WILLIAM. The Diverting History of John Gilpin; shewing how he went farther than he intended, and came safe home again. Illustrated with Humourous Engravings, on Copperplate. Philadelphia: Wm. Charles, 1815. [517]

Sq. octavo, 8 leaves, sig. A⁸, and 7 full-page copper-plates including the frontispiece.

Original wrappers with title on the front cover and advertisements on the back; the date of the imprint on the wrapper is 1810. *Price 25 cents.*
This copy is the only one located by Weiss in *William Charles.*
The first line of the last verse of this popular ballad has suffered a change in order to make it more suited to the young American reader. As written by Cowper it read *Now let us sing, long live the King;* in this edition it reads *Let's sing—"Long live our President."* The rest of the ballad is unchanged. This line was not changed in the edition printed by Jacob Johnson, 1807, no. 328.

[COWPER, WILLIAM.] The Humourous Story of Mrs. Gilpin's Return from Edmonton. Being the Sequel to Johnny Gilpin. Illustrated with Humourous Engravings, on Copperplate. Philadelphia: Wm. Charles, 1815. [518]

Sq. octavo, 8 leaves of text without signatures, 6 plates (plain).

Original wrappers, title on front cover, including imprint with date, advertisements on the back. On the cover-title the word *Humourous* is spelt *Humorous* in the first instance, and *Homorous* in the second.
The price, *plain,* 18 3-4 *Cents. Coloured,* 25 *Cents,* is quoted beneath the imprint on the title-page and on the cover-title.
This copy is the only one located by Weiss in *William Charles.*

Early American Children's Books

[DEFOE, DANIEL.] The Life and most Surprising Adventures of Robinson Crusoe, of York, Mariner. Containing A full and particular Account, how he lived twenty eight Years in an uninhabited Island on the Coast of America: How his Ship was lost in a storm, and all his Companions drowned; and how he was cast upon the Shore by the wreck; with a true Relation how he was at last miraculously preserved by Pirates. Faithfully epitomized from the three volumes. Baltimore: Printed by William Warner, 1815.   [519]

Duodecimo, 72 leaves, A-H¹², ⁶, woodcut frontispiece in 2 compartments on the verso of the half title.

Original fancy boards.

One of the woodcuts in the frontispiece was used previously by Warner in his edition of *Robin Hood*, 1812, no. 450.

The text of the first part follows very closely that of the edition printed for Benjamin Gomez in 1795 (no. 190).

THE HAPPY SEQUEL, or, The History of Isabella Mordaunt. A tale for young people. New York: Van Winkle & Wiley for William B. Gilley, 1815.   [520]

Duodecimo, 44 leaves, including the half title, 1-6⁶, 7⁸, engraved frontispiece by Scoles.

Original half binding.

In the absence of any explanation from the author, the publisher announces that the narrative is *in his opinion, perspicuous in its plot, natural in its incidents, and unexceptionable in its morality*.

The first edition was published in London by J. Harris in 1814.

THE HERMIT OF THE FOREST, and the Wandering Infants. A rural fragment. Embellished with cuts. Hartford: Printed by Sheldon & Goodwin [Stereotyped by J. F. & C. Starr], n. d. [1815.]   [521]

16mo, 16 leaves without signatures, first and last pasted down to covers, woodcut frontispiece, woodcut on the title, and illustrations in the text; advertisement of children's books on the last·leaf.

Original wrappers, title on the upper cover, two woodcuts on the lower.

Alphabets on the back of the title; the woodcuts in this edition are not the same as in the earlier editions in this collection, nos. 236 and 276.

The Hermit of the Forest ends on page 28. The next leaf is occupied with a description of the Rose, headed by a woodcut of that flower.

The firm of Sheldon & Goodwin existed as such only in the year 1815, having succeeded the firm of Hudson & Goodwin in the latter part of that year. It was dissolved in a short time and followed in November by Sheldon and Goodrich on the one side, and George Goodwin's Sons on the other.

THE HISTORY AND ADVENTURES OF LITTLE ELIZA, A Companion to Little William; Illustrated with a Series of Elegant Figures. Philadelphia: J. Bioren for William Charles, 1815. [522]

Duodecimo, 4 leaves of text in verse, 8 full-page plates (plain), including the frontispiece.

Original wrappers with the title (imprint of Wm. Charles dated 1814) on the front cover and advertisements on the back.

This issue not in Weiss: *William Charles*.

In the original edition of this book, printed by R. Harrild for J. Aldis in London, without date, the illustrations consisted of colored cut-out figures. The plates of the present edition are copied from these, but are not cut out. It is noticeable that in the English edition Little Eliza was a companion to Little Fanny, whereas in this American edition she is a companion to Little William. On the title-page, between the title proper as quoted above and the imprint, is a stanza of twelve lines on the frontispiece, headed *Eliza in the Garden reading a little Book*, which is the first verse of the poem, and which is not repeated in the body of the book.

The title on the cover is without this stanza, and the wording in other respects differs very slightly from the title-page. At the foot is the price: *plain* 18 3-4 *Cents—Colored*, 25 *Cents*, followed by the date, 1814.

The story of Little Eliza, who is of an age to play with dolls, is a common one in books of this period. She is stolen by gypsies, and becomes a Fortune Teller, a Match Girl, a Beggar, a Water-Cress Seller, and a Cottage Maid, before she is eventually restored to her parents.

THE HISTORY AND ADVENTURES OF LITTLE WILLIAM, a companion to Little Eliza; Illustrated with a series of Elegant Figures. Philadelphia: J. Bioren for William Charles, 1815. [523]

Duodecimo, 4 leaves of text in verse, 8 full-page plates (plain).

Original wrappers, title on upper cover (date of imprint 1814, the *Price, plain* 18 3-4 *Cents—Colored*, 25 *Cents.*); advertisements on the back.

This issue not in Weiss: *William Charles*.

This book is also copied from the English edition with the plates changed from the cut-out style to plain full-page plates. As in Little Eliza, the first verse of the text is printed on the title-page, with the heading *William at Home with his Parents*. The frontispiece represents William with his kite, and the other illustrations picture him at various stages of his career. William ran away from the Blue Coat School, became a sailor, went to war with France, and played a Hero's part, was promoted to be a Midshipman, and enjoyed the wars and the excitements of his life until his ship was wrecked, fortunately on his native shore. William was the only soul saved, and he now began to repent having run away from school; he became a shepherd and a ballad singer and was eventually restored to his parents.

Page from "The History and Adventures of Little Eliza"

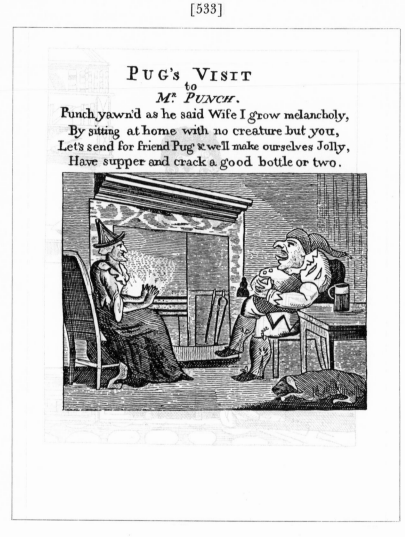

Page from "Pug's Visit to Mr. Punch"

HISTORY OF THE BIBLE. Boston: Nathaniel Willis, 1815. [524]

128 leaves, A-Q⁸, woodcut frontispiece, woodcuts in the text.

Original sheep.
A Thumb Bible measuring $1\frac{7}{8}$ by $1\frac{3}{16}$ inches.
Another edition of no. 493 with the same woodcuts.

LITTLE POEMS FOR CHILDREN. Windsor, (Vt.): Printed by Jesse Cochran, 1815. [525]

16mo, 16 leaves without signatures, first and last leaves pasted down on the wrappers, woodcut frontispiece.

Original wrappers, title and woodcut within a border on the front cover, woodcut within a border on the back.
Contains ten poems by Jane and Ann Taylor and others. The last poem is entitled *The Book*, and is a plea for proper treatment.

* * *

O do not turn my corners down!
Tho' little dogs have ears,
As I'm a book of high renown,
Affront me not my dears.

* * *

On the last leaf, pasted down, is the printer's advertisement:

If little children, as they grow,
To study are inclin'd,
Let them to Jesse Cochran go,
The pleasing means to find.

In useful and instructive books,
For little children dear;
With pretty cuts, and as they look,
Choice stories will appear.

LITTLE POEMS FOR CHILDREN. Windsor, Vt.: Printed and Sold by Jesse Cochran, 1815. [526]

16mo, 16 leaves, without signatures, the first and last pasted down on the wrappers, woodcut frontispiece.

Original wrappers, with title and woodcut on the front and woodcut on the back (different from preceding issue).
This edition contains five additional poems to the preceding item, including *The Thief* (by Isaac Watts), and *The Drum*, by Scott, the last being the only one to which the name of the author is attached. Jesse Cochran's rhymed advertisement is at the end, as in the previous number.

Early American Children's Books

MASON, WILLIAM. The Pious Parent's Gift, or A plain and familiar Sermon, wherein the Principles of the Christian Religion, are proposed, and clearly represented to the minds of Children. Each part of which is accompanied with Select Verses, From the Works of Dr. Watts... To which is added, The Closet Companion: and the Swearer's Prayer. Hartford: B. & J. Russell for O. D. Cooke, 1815.   [527]

Duodecimo, 36 leaves, A-F⁶, woodcut frontispiece, separate title-page with imprint for The Closet Companion, pagination and signatures continuous.

Original wrappers, being the covers for an edition of 1814 contained in *Serious Advice to persons who have been sick*, with cover-title, advertisement on the back.

Chapter headings will show the scope of the work: Part V. *Containing a very pretty story of a dear little child who loved her Saviour; how good she was, how holy and happy she lived, and how comfortably she died.* Part VI. *In which little Children are told of their misery and danger, what sad enemies they have who will try to keep them from Jesus Christ, their only Friend and Saviour.*

The title-page for The Closet Companion is on page (43), and the text occupies pages 45-56. It is signed at the end G. B. (?George Burder). On page (57), with caption title begins Serious Advice to a person recovered from Sickness, and on page 69 A Thanksgiving after Recovery from Sickness.

The author of this work was not the famous William Mason, poet and friend of Gray, but was a contemporary of the same name (1719-1791), who was a native of Rotherhithe, Surrey. He was a justice of the peace and a magistrate, and the author of several religious works.

MAVOR, WILLIAM [FORDYCE]. The Mother's Catechism; or First Principles of Knowledge and Instruction, for Very Young Children. By William Mavor, L.L.D. Author of Travels, and many other popular Works. Leicester: Printed by Hori Brown, 1815.   [528]

Duodecimo, 28 leaves, 1-4⁶, 5⁴.

Unbound, stitched, as issued.

The preface to this work is addressed *To Christian Mothers*. It explains the author's object, and expresses the opinion that *if mothers and nurses will use it in the manner prescribed, much benefit may arise from its introduction into the nursery.*

In the catechism which follows, the questions are asked by the children and the replies given by the mother. At the end is a selection of the Divine Songs of Dr. Watts.

William Fordyce Mavor, a celebrated compiler of educational works, schoolmaster and clergyman, was a native of Aberdeenshire. He was born in 1758, and died at Woodstock in 1837.

MOSELY, WILLIAM. The New Token for Children: or, A sequel to Janeway's: Being An authentic account, never before published, of the conversion exemplary lives, and happy deaths of Twelve Children. By

[145]

Title-page from
"The Bible in Miniature"
[c.1790]

[204]

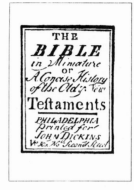

Title-page from
"The Bible in Miniature"
[1796]

[524]

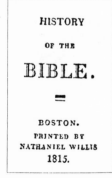

Title-page from
"History of the Bible"

[637]

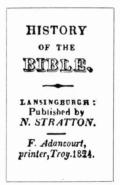

Title-page from
"History of the Bible"

*Page from "The History of Little Red Riding-Hood.
In Verse"*

Early American Children's Books

William Mosely, Minister of the Tabernacle, Hanley, Fourth edition revised. Philadelphia: A. Griggs & K. Dickinson for W. W. Woodward. 1815. [529]

Octavo, 71 leaves, A⁷-B-I⁸, the publisher's advertisement of Toy and Chap Books on the last page.

Original marbled boards.

The preface explains that *from the concern which the Editor feels for the spiritual and eternal welfare of youth in general, and for his own children in particular, he has been induced to publish this* New Token.

It contains the accounts of the conversion and happy deaths of twelve children in England whose ages range from five to sixteen years.

THE NEW-ENGLAND PRIMER improved, For the more easy attaining the true Reading of English. To which is added, The Assembly of Divines & Episcopal Catechisms. New York: T[homas] & J[ames] Swords, 1815. [530]

Sm. 16mo, 32 leaves, aB-D⁸, woodcuts.

Unbound as issued.

Heartman 216.

In addition to the usual matter contained in the New England Primer, including the two Catechisms, this edition has incorporated other pieces, namely, the Description of a Good Boy, and the Description of a Bad Boy (in prose), and The Good Girl, and The Naughty Girls (in verse).

The alphabet couplets are all early with the exception of the letter K, which is post-Revolution, *Kings should be good*, *Not men of blood*, and the letter W, which is the Washington couplet. The woodcut for *The Cat doth play*, *And after slay* represents the cat playing the fiddle to five dancing mice.

THE NEW-ENGLAND PRIMER, improved; or, An easy and pleasant Guide to the Art of Reading. To which is added, The Assembly's Catechism. Adorned with cuts. Boston: James Loring, n. d. (between 1815 and 1830.) [531]

Octavo, 32 leaves, A-D⁸, first and last pasted down, woodcut illustrations.

Original wooden boards, covered with paper, leather back.

Heartman 343.

This edition contains many of the features found in the early editions, with few additions. The alphabet couplets are in an early state with the exception of the letter K which is the one for *Proud Korah's Troop*.

THE PIOUS PARENT'S PRESENT: containing, A Father's Advice to his Son; A Father's Advice to his Daughter; An Epistle by William Massey;

Early American Children's Books

The Advantages and Disadvantages of the Marriage State, &c.; and The Life of Armelle Nicolas. New York: Samuel Wood, 1815.　　　[532]

Duodecimo, 36 leaves, 1-6⁶, first and last leaves blank and pasted down to covers, 2 woodcut frontispieces.

Original tan wrappers, upper with title, lower with advertisement.
Each part has a half title. The original *Father's Advice to his Son* was written by Patrick Scot. *The Father's Advice to his Daughter* is a reprint of the old didactic poem see no. 157.
An Epistle, written by William Massey, in the County of Surrey, England, inscribed to those Young Men, who had their education under his care is also in verse. William Massey (1691-1764?) was at one time the Latin usher in a boarding school at Wandsworth, Surrey.
The author of *The Advantages and Disadvantages of the Marriage State* was John Johnson (1706-1791), an English baptist minister and founder of the Johnsonian baptists.

Pug's Visit to Mr. Punch. Illustrated with eight whimsical engravings. Philadelphia: Wm. Charles, 1815.　　　[533]

Duodecimo, 8 leaves, engraved throughout, and printed on one side only, each leaf with a colored illustration and 4 lines of verse.

Original wrappers, cover title, advertisement on back.
Weiss: *William Charles*, p. 10.
A re-issue of no. 426 with colored plates.
There is no title-page, the full title appearing on the wrappers only, the first leaf having a caption title.
William Charles was the first printer in Philadelphia to realize the added charm of colored plates in children's books, and from 1814 onwards most of his juveniles were issued in the two states, plain and colored, the prices for the colored copies being higher than for the plain.
The method of producing colored plates for this class of book must have enhanced the charm for young readers.
A number of children, usually in their early teens, were each given a paint brush, and a supply of paint of a certain color, the child then being responsible for the application of his own color on each copy where it belonged. This method accounts for the variations in quality which will be noticed in many of the Charles items with colored plates.

Whimsical Incidents, or the Power of Music, a poetic Tale: by a near Relation of Old Mother Hubbard. [Philadelphia: William Charles, 1815].　　　[534]

Sq. octavo, 16 leaves, including the engraved title, engraved throughout, each leaf with an illustration and 4 lines of verse, printed on one side of the paper only.

Original wrappers, engraved title and illustration on front cover, back cover plain. The title on the wrapper reads: *Whimsical Incidents: or The Power of Music, A Poetic Tale. A Present for the New-Year*, 1816.
Weiss: *William Charles*, p. 11.
The original English edition was issued in 1805.

Early American Children's Books

[WYNNE, JOHN HUDDLESTONE.] Choice Emblems, natural, historical, moral and divine, For the Improvement and Pastime of Youth; displaying the beauties and morals of the ancient fabulists: The whole calculated to convey the Golden Lessons of Instruction under a new and more delightful dress. Hartford: Published by Oliver D. Cooke, 1815. [535]

16mo, 38 leaves, the last a blank, woodcut frontispiece.

Original tan wrappers, upper with title reading slightly differently from that on the title-page, and containing the words *Originally written for the amusement of a Young Nobleman. From the eleventh London edition*, and the imprint dated 1814; publisher's advertisement on the back wrapper.

Contains XXXIII Emblems, each with a Moral and an Application, written in verse and prose. The printer's imprint is below that of the publisher on the title-page: *Seth Richards, printer—Middletown*.

John Huddlestone Wynne, miscellaneous writer, was born at Southampton in 1743, and died in St. Bartholomew's Hospital, London, in 1788. The first English edition of the *Choice Emblems*, 1772, contained the name of the nobleman for whom they were written: *Written for the Amusement of Lord Newbattle*.

1816

BIBLE HISTORY. Leicester: Hori Brown, 1816. [536]

122 leaves, 1-15⁸, 16², last blank pasted down, woodcut frontispiece.

Original leather.
A Thumb Bible measuring 1¾ by 1⅛ inches.
Another edition of no. 433. This edition has the frontispiece, but is otherwise unillustrated.

[DEFOE, DANIEL.] The Wonderful Life and Surprising Adventures of that renowned hero, Robinson Crusoe, who lived twenty-eight years on an uninhabited island, Which he afterwards Colonised. New York: J. C. Totten for Evert Duyckinck, 1816. [537]

Duodecimo, 72 leaves, A-F¹², woodcut frontispiece of a ship, woodcuts in the text.

Original sheep.
The text of this edition is the version printed by Hugh Gaine in the first American edition, 1774, no. 77. Robinson Crusoe ends on page 106. On page 107 begin Cowper's *Verses supposed to be written by Robinson Crusoe, During his solitary abode in the desolate island*. Pages 110-114 contain *The Youth's Amusement*, consisting of seventeen short stories.

AN ENTERTAINING HISTORY of two pious Twin Children, Who were stolen from their Christian Parents by a Jew, and sold to the Turks as

Slaves; And with their Father, were marvellously saved from death. First edition. Translated from the German. To which is added Little Charles, or the Good Son. New-Market: Printed in S. Henkel's Printing Office, 1816. [538]

Duodecimo, 18 leaves, A-C⁶, including the frontispiece pasted down to front cover, woodcut illustrations.

Original fancy wrappers.
Not in the Bibliography of Virginia (Bulletin. Virginia State Library).
The story ends on page 18. Pages 19-25 are occupied by an essay on the lessons to be learned from it, headed *Dear Reader!* This is followed by a hymn, and on page (28), with caption title, begins *Little Charles, or The Good Son* who lived with his family in *a house- on the borders of a wood, in one of the most wild and desolate parts of the State of New, Jersey.*

GREGORY, RICHARD. My Son A Poem By Richard Gregory. Illustrated with engravings. Philadelphia: Wm. Charles, 1816. [539]

Sq. duodecimo, 6 leaves, engraved throughout and printed on one side only, an illustration between 2 stanzas of verse on each leaf.

Original wrappers, title on the front and advertisements on the back.

There is no title-page, the title occurs on the wrapper only.
This copy is the only one located by Weiss in *William Charles.*
One of the large crop of poems written in imitation of Ann Taylor's famous verses *My Father* and *My Mother.* The cover-title ascribes this poem to Richard Gregory, and it is therefore assigned to him, although the attributions on the titles of the Charles items are not always correct. This poem falls far below the standard of Ann Taylor's verses:

> Who never did. (as says report,)
> Unite in any cruel Sport,
> Or with mischievous Boys resort?
> MY SON

> * * *

> When sick (my old Domestic) lay,
> Who did a kind attendance pay,
> And read to sooth his Grief away?
> MY SON

THE NEW-ENGLAND PRIMER, improved; For the more easy attaining the True Reading of English. To which is added The Assembly of Divines' Catechism. Lansingburgh: Printed by Tracy & Bliss, 1816. [540]

Duodecimo, 36 leaves, A-F⁸,⁴, woodcuts; this copy has 29 leaves only, lacking all after E₅.

Original grey wrappers.

Early American Children's Books

Heartman 222 locates the A. A. S. copy only.
Contains much of the original material of the early editions of the New England Primer.
The alphabet couplets are as in James Loring's Boston edition, no. 531, with different woodcuts.

THE NEW-ENGLAND PRIMER, improved; or an easy and pleasant guide to the art of reading. Adorned with Cuts. Also, The Assembly of Divines' Catechism. Norwich: Printed by Russell Hubbard, 1816. [541]

Duodecimo, 36 leaves (A)-B¹⁸, first and last leaves pasted down on cover, woodcuts in the text.

Red wrappers.
Heartman 223.
In addition to the alphabet couplets, which are the same as in the preceding item, this edition contains a set of twenty-four alphabet cuts in compartments, twelve on a page, each with the name of the object represented. These cuts are the same as in *The Child's New Spelling Primer*, printed in Dublin in 1799 by T. Wilkinson, and probably appeared in many books. In this set Y stands for Young Lamb, as in *The Silver Penny*, no. 354. It is noticeable that *Young Lamb* is printed in italics, the other twenty-three names being in roman letter. This may have been in order to save space, or it may have been the editor's acknowledgment of the weakness of the illustration.

THE NEW-YORK PRECEPTOR; or, Third Book. New York: Printed and sold by Samuel Wood & Sons, 1816. [542]

Duodecimo, 36 leaves (first and last blanks pasted down to covers), woodcuts.

Original wrappers, title with woodcut vignette on front, two woodcuts on back.
The same designs were not used on the wrappers of every copy of this book.
For an earlier edition see no. 465.

ORIGINAL POEMS, for infant minds. By several young persons. In two volumes. Ornamented with twenty elegant woodcuts... Volume I. [II.] Philadelphia: W. Brown for Solomon W. Conrad, 1816. [543]

Duodecimo, 2 volumes in 1. Vol. I, 60 leaves, A-K⁶; Vol. II, 66 leaves, A-L⁶; woodcut illustrations.

Original sheep.
The *several young persons* were Ann Taylor, Jane Taylor, Isaac Taylor, Bernard Barton and Adelaide O'Keefe; the greater number of the poems are signed at the end.
This is one of the most influential books of poetry in the history of children's literature. The first edition was published by Harvey and Darton in London, 1804.

[PARNELL, THOMAS, AND GOLDSMITH, OLIVER.] The Hermit and The Traveller. New York: Samuel Wood & Sons, 1816. [544]

Duodecimo, 24 leaves, irregular signatures, illustrated with woodcuts.

Original tan wrappers, upper with title and woodcut vignette, lower with advertisement. The titles on the title-page are in oval compartments, white lettering on black. The two poems mentioned are followed by *Prejudice* by Adelaide O'Keefe. The American editor has endeavoured to make the text clear to the understandings of children by the use of explanatory footnotes: *Little children are desired to consider this pleasing and beautiful Poem* [The Hermit], *not as a real fact, but a beautiful allegory of the ways of the Almighty with his creatures.* Many of the comments on *The Traveller* are intended to counteract the English feeling of the poem, and it was in order to provide an antidote to this feeling that *Prejudice* was printed with it, as is explained in the footnote to the line *I see the lords of human kind* pass by:* * *The writer of this was a British subject. As a parallel, see the little boy's song, page 45, headed Prejudice, taken from Original Poems, and the wise and happy conclusion occasioned by the Father's observations to his Child.* The description of the *tangled forests* and *dang'rous ways* of North America is thus annotated: *Abundantly altered by the hand of industry, and American enterprise, a peaceful asylum from European oppression.*

TRENCK, FREDERICK, BARON. The Life of Baron Frederick Trenck, Containing his adventures, and also his excessive sufferings during ten years imprisonment at the fortress of Magdeburgh, by command of the late King of Prussia. Translated from the German, by Thomas Holcroft. Poughkeepsie: P. & S. Potter for Paraclete Potter, 1816.   [545]

Duodecimo, 67 leaves, A-L⁶, M¹.

Original half binding.
The first German edition of the *Life of Baron Trenck* was published in Berlin and Vienna in thirteen volumes in 1787. The first edition of Holcroft's translation was published in London in 1798.
On page 123 is an interesting reference to America: *From the year 1774 to 1777, I chiefly spent my time in journeying through England and France. I was intimate with Dr. Franklin, the American minister; also with the counts St. Germain and Vergennes who made me advantageous proposals to go to America; but I was prevented accepting them by my affection for my wife and children.*
Thomas Holcroft (1745-1809) was a famous English dramatist, novelist and translator, and the friend of Thomas Paine and William Godwin.

1817

A B C-UND BILDER-BUCH, A B C-and Picture-Book. New Market, Va.: Printed in S. Henkel's printing-office, 1817.   [546]

Octavo, 8 leaves, sig. A, woodcut on the title, woodcut illustrations in the text.

Original grey wrappers, large woodcuts on both covers.
Not in the Bibliography of Virginia (Bulletin. Virginia State Library).
The text is in German and English. It contains alphabets and syllabaries, with alphabet woodcuts and large woodcut illustrations of animals, etc. The German imprint reads: *Neu-Market, Virg. gedruckt in S. Henkel's Druckerey.*
For a note on the press see no. 384.

Early American Children's Books

THE ADVENTURES OF OLD DAME TRUDGE AND HER PARROT. Illustrated with Whimsical Engravings. Philadelphia: Wm. Charles, 1817. [547]

Sq. octavo, 8 leaves printed on one side only, and engraved throughout, a stanza of text and an illustration (plain) on each leaf.

Original wrappers, cover-title, advertisements on the back (damaged in this copy).
Weiss: *William Charles*, page 7 (this copy only).
There is no title-page, the title appearing on the wrapper only. For the Continuation of Old Dame Trudge and her Parrot, see no. 455. A promise of the Continuation is given in the last lines of the Adventures:

> If by chance her adventures should ere come to light,
> The whole of the tale I'll immediately write,
> And you'll get it at every Book Store.

THE ARITHMETICAL TABLES. Most of which must necessarily be committed to Memory, before any considerable progress can be made in learning Arithmetic. Philadelphia: Published by Kimber & Sharpless [1817]. [548]

Duodecimo, 10 leaves, A^{10}.

Original paper wrappers, title on the front cover reading: *Kimber & Sharpless' Arithmetical Table Book, for children. Philadelphia: published by Kimber & Sharpless, No. 93, Market Street.* [*Price 6 cents.*] On the back cover is printed the Multiplication Table.
The last chapter of the book is on roman numbers, and the final sentence reads:
MDCCCXVII one thousand eight hundred and seventeen, 1817, presumably the year in which the book was printed. On page 13 is a Table *To reduce divers Coins, to Pounds, Pennsylvania currency.*

[BERQUIN, ARNAUD.] The History of Caroline; or, a lesson to cure Vanity. Adorned with cuts. New Haven: Sidney's Press, 1817.   [549]

16 mo, 14 leaves, without signatures, woodcut illustrations.

Unbound, original stitching.
A translation of one of the stories of *L'Ami des Enfants.*
This edition has the alphabet on the back of the title, and three poems at the end, entitled Charity, Pity, and Contemplation. The illustrations, some of which in this copy have been touched with color by hand, do not all belong to this story, and one at least is from the fairy tale Elmina.

DAME TROT AND HER COMICAL CAT. Illustrated with Sixteen Elegant Engravings. Philadelphia: Wm. Charles, 1817.   [550]

Sq. octavo, 16 leaves, engraved throughout, printed on one side only, and a stanza of verse and an illustration on each leaf.

Original wrappers, cover-title.
Weiss: *William Charles*, page 7 (this copy only).
There is no title-page, the title appearing on the cover only.

Early American Children's Books

[ELLIOTT, MARY.] My Father. A Poem for Children. New York: Published by Samuel Wood & Sons, 1817. [551]

Sq. duodecimo, 6 leaves, engraved throughout, and printed on one side only; title-page with vignette, each leaf with two stanzas of verse and an illustration (plain).

Original wrappers, title with imprint and a vignette on the upper, an engraving of a horse race on the lower. The imprint on the title-page is undated, the date appears on the wrapper only.

This is not the well known poem with this title by Ann Taylor, first published in *Original Poems for infant minds*, but an imitation by Mary Elliott in the same metre.

It was one of seven poems (My Father, My Mother, My Brother, My Sister, My Uncle, My Aunty, My Mammy), first published by Darton in London in 1811 or 1812, with the title *Grateful Tributes*.

In this edition the poem has ten stanzas. The number of stanzas varies in different editions.

One verse betrays the fact that fathers from time immemorial, seem to have shared at least one well-known characteristic:

> And when my kite I wished to try,
> Who held the string to make it fly,
> While pleasure sparkled in my eye?
> My Father.

The accompanying illustration represents Father flying the kite, pleasure sparkling in his eye, whilst the small son looks somewhat wistfully on.

The format of the book is similar to the publications of William Charles.

Mary Elliott, an Englishwoman, who wrote also under her maiden name of Mary Belson, was one of the most prolific writers for children of the period, and her works were equally popular in America and in England.

[HUGHES, MARY.] Aunt Mary's Tales, for the Entertainment and Improvement of Little Boys. Addressed to her nephews. First American from the third London edition. New York: Forbes & Co. for D. Bliss, 1817. [552]

Duodecimo, 90 leaves including the last blank, A-P⁶.

Original half binding.

Contains The Rival Friend, and The Ghost.

In her dedication to her nephews the author begins: *Your alarm, my dear boys, lest your sisters were to be the exclusive objects of my attention, is very gratifying to my feelings, as a proof of the value you set on my endeavours to amuse. The two following stories are more particularly your own; though, as virtue and knowledge have no right to a distinction of sexes, what is serviceable to the one, will not, I hope, be unacceptable to the other.*

Mary Hughes, formerly Robson, was the author of a large number of children's books, mostly published anonymously, and all showing strongly the influence of Maria Edgeworth. In 1818 she and her husband emigrated to this country, and Mrs. Hughes opened a school for young ladies in Philadelphia.

JULIA AND THE PET-LAMB; or, Good Temper and Compassion rewarded. Philadelphia: Lydia R. Bailey for Solomon W. Conrad, 1817.   [553]

Duodecimo, 26 leaves, A-C⁶, D⁸, engraved frontispiece and 2 engraved illustrations.

Original wrappers, title on upper, advertisement on lower.
This story has evidently been printed directly from an original English edition, and no attempt at Americanization has been made.

MY TIPPOO. A Poem Illustrated with Engravings. Philadelphia: Published and sold by Wm. Charles, 1817.   [554]

Square duodecimo, 6 leaves, engraved throughout and printed on one side only, each leaf with two stanzas of verse and an illustration, the illustrations colored.

Original wrappers, cover-title, lower cover with advertisement.
Weiss: *William Charles*, page 10 (this copy only).
There is no title-page, the title appearing on the wrapper only. The illustrations are in octagonal compartments. The subject of the poem is a dog.

> When first a puppy Tippoo came,
> Companion of each childish game,
> Who,—on my heart held stronger claim?
>   THAN TIPPOO.

[PEACOCK, LUCY.] Patty Primrose; or, The Parsonage House. By the author of "A Visit for a Week," &c. &c. Philadelphia: Published by Benjamin Warner, 1817.   [555]

Duodecimo, 36 leaves, A-F⁶, engraved frontispiece.

Original wrappers, title on the upper, advertisement on the lower.
A story of Yorkshire, England, first published by Harvey and Darton in London, 1816.
Lucy Peacock was a bookseller and author who kept a shop in Oxford Street, London, and wrote tales for children, for the most part published anonymously.

[PEDDER, James.] The Yellow Shoe-Strings; or, the Good Effects. Of Obedience to Parents. Philadelphia: [A. Bowman] for Benjamin Warner, 1817.   [556]

Duodecimo, 24 leaves, A-D⁶, engraved folded frontispiece and 2 full-page engraved illustrations.

Original wrappers, upper with title and imprint dated 1817, lower with advertisement.
The date on the title-page is 1816. The printer's imprint is at the end.
The author describes in his introduction, signed J. P., how the story was related to his own children, who begged that it might be *written out* for their amusement. It *is now transcribed for the amusement of that most interesting part of society*, obedient children. At the end is *The Beggar's Song*, two stanzas of verse.

TALES OF THE ROBIN, and other Small Birds; Selected from the British Poets, For The Instruction and Amusement of Young People. By Joseph Taylor, Compiler of the General Character of the Dog, Wonders of the Horse, &c. &c. Philadelphia: M'Carty & Davis for Wm. Charles, 1817. [557]

Duodecimo, 72 leaves, A-M⁶, engraved frontispiece and five full-page plates, all colored by hand.

Original half binding.
Weiss: *William Charles*, page 10.
An anthology of verse on the robin and small birds. The name of the author, when known, is given after each poem, and in the list of Contents at the end. *Tales of the Robin* fill pages (3) to 36 and on page 37 is the heading *Small Birds*. Little seems to be known about the compiler, the original editions of whose works were published by Benjamin Tabart in London.

TRUE STORIES RELATED. By a friend to little Children. New York: S. Wood & Sons, 1817. [558]

Duodecimo, 24 leaves, including first and last blanks pasted down to wrappers, woodcut on title-page, woodcuts in text.

Original wrappers, title and woodcut on upper, two woodcuts on lower.
Another edition of no. 513 with slight variations in the text, and two additional woodcuts.

VAUX, FRANCES BOWYER. Henry. A Story, intended for Little Boys and Girls, from Five to Ten Years Old. By Frances Bowyer Vaux. First American Edition. Philadelphia: Published and Sold by Wm. Charles, 1817. [559]

32mo, 30 leaves including title and half-title, the 15 leaves before the strings lettered A-E³, folded frontispiece, 2 full-page plates, all colored.

Original half binding.
Not in Weiss: *William Charles*.
In common with many books of its class this story was originally written for the benefit of the author's nephew. In the preface, dated from Ipswich (England), January, 1815, the author acknowledges the influence of Miss Edgeworth, and explains that the manuscript was originally offered for publication on the recommendation of Mrs. Wakefield.

1818

BARBAULD, ANNA LETITIA. Lessons for Children. In four parts. By Mrs. Barbauld. Improved by cuts, designed by S. Pike, and engraved by Dr. Anderson. Philadelphia: Lydia R. Bailey for Benjamin Warner, 1818. [560]

Duodecimo, 52 leaves, A-H⁶, I⁴ (the last a blank), woodcut illustrations in the text.

Original grey boards.

In this edition the ages of the children for whom the various parts are intended do not correspond exactly with the earlier editions.

[BERQUIN, ARNAUD.] The History of Bertrand. A Poor Laborer, and his Little Family. Montpelier: Published by E. P. Walton, 1818.   [561]

Sm. octavo, 16 leaves, A-B⁸, woodcut frontispiece and woodcut illustrations in the text.

Original tan covers, title and woodcut on the upper, 2 woodcuts on the lower.

In addition to The History of Bertrand the book contains also The History of a Passionate Boy, and The History of Cleopatra, or The Reformed Little Tyrant, all stories from *L'Ami des Enfants* by Arnaud Berquin.

The History of Bertrand is nearer to Berquin's original story than is the version in *The Peasant's Repast*, no. 361, and in this case the child martyr is a boy.

The frontispiece is a poor copy of The Dreamer, the frontispiece to *The Pilgrim's Progress*.

BROWN, JOHN. A Short Catechism, for Young Children. By John Brown, Late Minister of the Gospel at Haddington. Morristown, N. J.: Printed for Peter A. Johnson, 1818.   [562]

Duodecimo, 12 leaves, A-C⁴, first (blank) and last leaves pasted down to cover.

Original wrappers.

On the last page are the Morning and Evening Prayers for a Child, and the Lord's Prayer.

John Brown of Haddington, Scotland (1722-1787), was a remarkable personality, and became a famous author and minister. As a herd boy he taught himself Latin, Greek and Hebrew; he became a travelling chapman, a soldier and a schoolmaster; he joined the Burgher Church in 1747 and became minister to the Burgher Congregation at Haddington in 1750, an appointment which he kept until his death in 1787, in spite of an invitation to minister to the Dutch Church in New York.

[BUNYAN, JOHN.] Bunyan's Pilgrim's Progress, Versified: for the Entertainment and Instruction of Youth. By George Burder, Author of Village Sermons, &c.. Hartwick: L. & B. Todd, 1818.   [563]

Duodecimo, 36 leaves, A-F⁶.

Original half binding.

In the preface, dated from Islington, Dec. 17, 1803, the editor explains that he *conceived that the Pilgrim, in verse, would be peculiarly acceptable to young persons, that it would entertain them more than in prose, and make a more durable impression on their memory.*

The poem opens:

'Twas in the silent watches of the night,
When airy visions please us or affright,
Fast lock'd in sleep's embrace, I dreamt a dream;—
The Pilgrim's journey was the fruitful theme.

The verses supposed to be sung by the Pilgrims on various occasions, and printed in italics, are, according to the editor, copied from the original work, with little alteration.

At the end is Newton's Pilgrim's Song.

George Burder (1752-1832) originally intended to be an artist and took lessons in drawing from Isaac Taylor, the father of Jane and Ann Taylor. Eventually he became a congregationalist minister, and was instrumental in forming the Religious Tract Society, a development of the committee for the distribution of the Cheap Repository Tracts, see no. 258. He was also one of the founders of the British and Foreign Bible Society.

HOCH-DEUTSCHES LUTHERISCHES ABC-und Namen-Büchlein für Kinder welche anfangen zu lernen. Verbesserte Ausgabe. Philadelphia: Conrad Zentler für Daniel Bräutigam, 1818. [564]

A reprint of no. 334 with the same covers.

[HOFLAND, BARBARA.] The Son of a Genius; a tale, for the use of youth. By the author of The History of an Officer's Widow and Family, Clergyman's Widow and Family, Daughter-in-law, etc. etc. Second American edition. New York: A. Paul for David Bliss, 1818. [565]

Duodecimo, 126 leaves, 1-21^6, woodcut illustrations in the text.

Original half binding.

Barbara Hofland (1770-1844) was the daughter of Robert Wreaks, a manufacturer in Sheffield, England. She was twice married but was compelled to write for a living, to support herself and her son. *The Son of a Genius*, originally published in 1812, is her best known work, and is in part autobiographical.

LITTLE, WILLIAM. Reading made Easy: or, A New Guide to Spelling & Reading. In four parts. 1st. Containing various Alphabets, and nearly two hundred Spelling and Reading Lessons, by regular gradations, from the most easy to the difficult, and in which the words are divided and accented according to the purest pronunciation. 2d. A Vocabulary of Words nearly alike in Sound, but different in Spelling and signification. 3d. Lessons in Reading and Reciting. 4th. Outlines of Geography; a Sketch of Grammar; Abbreviations; Arithmetical Tables; and Prayers for the use of Schools. The whole rendered Pleasing and Impressive, by Neat and Appropriate Cuts. By William Little, A. M. New York: Benjamin G. Jansen for W. B. Gilley, 1818. [566]

Duodecimo, 48 leaves, A-H⁶, woodcut frontispiece in 2 compartments and numerous woodcuts in the text, first and last leaves pasted down to covers.

Original salmon wrappers, upper with title and woodcut vignette, lower with advertisement and alphabet.

At the beginning is a set of alphabet cuts in twenty-four compartments. These are the same as in Joseph Guy's *British Spelling Book*, London, C. Cradock and W. Joy, 1814, and the woodcut frontispiece is copied from the engraved frontispiece in that work.

This book was deposited in the Office of the Southern District of New-York on the twenty-ninth of August, in the forty-second year of the Independence of the United States of America, by Daniel D. Arden, *the right whereof he claims as proprietor.*

[MORE, HANNAH.] The History of Mr. Fantom, the New Fashioned Philosopher, and His Man William. Philadelphia: Benjamin Johnson, 1818. [567]

Duodecimo, 12 leaves, sig. A, woodcut frontispiece.

Original wrappers, the upper with the title and imprint, bearing the name of Dickinson as printer, dated 1818, the lower with advertisement; partly unopened.

The date in the imprint on the title-page is 1817.

One of the Cheap Repository Tracts. The story is signed Z, the letter used by Hannah More to denote her authorship.

The Man William came to a bad end, and on page 20 begins, with caption title, *The Last Words, Confession, and Dying Speech of William Wilson, who was executed at Chelmsford for Murder.*

The author's description of the tragedy is terse: *Poor William was turned off just a quarter before eleven, and may the Lord have mercy on his soul!* This is followed by a poem *The Day of Judgment; or, The Grand Reckoning.*

MURRAY, LINDLEY. A First Book for Children. By Lindley Murray. Author of "English Grammar adapted to the Different Classes of Learners." Fifth Edition with Cuts. Philadelphia: Griggs & Co. for Benjamin Warner, sold also at his stores, Richmond, (Virg.) and Charleston, (S. C.) 1818. [568]

Duodecimo, 36 leaves, A-F⁶, first and last (a blank) leaves pasted down; woodcut frontispiece, woodcuts in the text.

Original blue wrappers, the upper cover with the half-title, a woodcut vignette, and the date 1815, the lower with the publisher's advertisement.

Contains alphabets, syllabaries and passages for reading, with illustrations.

Lindley Murray, one of the most famous grammarians of the English language, was a native of Pennsylvania. He was born in Swatara in 1745, and lived in America until 1784, when he emigrated to England, and never returned to his native country. He settled at Holgate near York, and died there in 1826.

Early American Children's Books

THE NEW-ENGLAND PRIMER, or an easy and pleasant guide to the art of reading. To which is added, the Catechism. Concord, N. H. Published and sold by I. and W. R. Hill, at their Book Store, 1813. Baltimore: Cushing & Jewett, 1818. [569]

24mo, 24 leaves, A-B¹², woodcut frontispiece, woodcut on title and woodcuts in the text, first and last leaves pasted down to covers.

Original grey wrappers, title with imprint on the front, woodcut vignette on the back. Heartman 202.

This is the edition put out by I. and W. R. Hill at Concord, N. H. in 1813, with new covers. The title-page bears the Concord imprint, with date 1813, the covers the Baltimore imprint dated 1818.

The alphabet couplets are the same as in the Walpole edition of 1814, which this edition originally preceded by a year. The cuts are also from the same originals printed in reverse.

A NEW HIEROGLYPHICAL BIBLE, for the amusement and instruction of Children; being, A Selection of some of the most useful lessons and interesting narratives, from Genesis to the Revelations. Embellished with familiar figures and striking emblems, Neatly Engraved. To the whole is added, A sketch of the life of our Blessed Saviour, and The Holy Apostles, &c. New York: Samuel Wood & Sons, and Samuel S. Wood & Co., Baltimore, 1818. [570]

Duodecimo, 36 leaves, 1-6⁶, 2 engraved frontispieces representing the Tree of Grace and the Tree of Wrath, emblematic woodcuts throughout the text, probably by Anderson.

Original half binding; marbled sides and red leather back.

This is a completely revised edition of no. 181. The compiler's preface has been retained, and the publisher of the present edition has added a note: *The publisher of the present edition of the Hieroglyphical Bible, has often been pleased at least, if not edified by reading it. He has endeavoured, by procuring neat cuts and fine paper, to furnish an edition more likely to attract the attention, and to please the young mind. He has omitted some parts of the old, which contained hieroglyphics of beings to which we cannot attach form or shape, as calculated to give gross and incorrect ideas; others, because the emblems were not sufficiently striking to be understood by the infant mind.*

[SHERWOOD, MARY MARTHA.] The History of Little Henry and His Bearer. Third American Edition. Catskill: Croswell & Son for Nathan Elliott, 1818. [571]

Duodecimo, 27 leaves, A⁸, B¹⁰, C⁹.

Original tan wrappers, title on upper cover, advertisement on lower.

The story of a little English orphan in India, who, from the age of five, was brought in the space of a year and a half *from the grossest state of heathen darkness and ignorance to a competent knowledge of those doctrines of the Christian religion which are chiefly necessary to salvation*, and who then proceeded to convert his bearer.

At the end are six pages of Hymns for Infant Minds [by Ann and Jane Taylor].

The popularity of this work which was first published anonymously in 1814 has been compared to that of *Uncle Tom's Cabin*. It was translated into French, Hindustani, Chinese, Cingalese and German.

The author was born in Stanford, Worcestershire, in 1775, and spent some time in India during the time her husband's regiment was stationed there. She died in 1851. She was the elder sister of Lucy Lyttleton Cameron, author of *The Polite Little Children*, and other works to be found in this catalogue.

STORIES FOR GOOD CHILDREN or, A Birth-Day Present. Hartford: Sold by Cooke & Hale, n. d. [c. 1818.] [572]

Sm. octavo, 8 leaves without signatures, woodcuts in the text.

Original wrappers.
A miniature book, measuring 2⅜ by 2 inches.
The principal story concerns Emma, the small daughter of *Mr. Thompson, a Gentleman of respectability, who resided at his seat in a Village, on the banks of the River Thames*, nevertheless the editor has made an attempt to hold the interest of American children by a personal and local appeal: *I hope there is no little Girl in Hartford, or in the State of Connecticut, who will be guilty of disobeying the orders of her Parents: The little reader will not, I am sure.* For an edition of this story without the local interpolation, see the *Story of William and Ellen*, 1827.

Messrs. Cooke and Hale were in partnership during the years 1818 and 1819.

1819

DAME PARTLET'S FARM: containing an account of the great riches she obtained by industry, the good life she led, and alas good reader! her sudden death; to which is added, a hymn, written by Dame Partlet, just before her death, and an epitaph for her tomb stone. Philadelphia: J. Bouvier for Johnson and Warner, 1819. [573]

Duodecimo, 30 leaves, A-E⁶, last leaf pasted down to cover, woodcut illustrations.

Original wrappers, title and woodcut on the front, advertisements on the back. The imprint reads: *From the Juvenile Library, No. 171, Market Street, Philadelphia.* 1819. *Griggs & Co. Printers.*

This is Johnson and Warner's edition of 1810 with new covers; the imprint on the title-page bears the date 1810.

This book is a copy of the original edition printed in London by John Harris, successor to Newbery, in 1804. As in so many of the Johnson imitations the traces of the original Harris and Newbery have been only partially removed or revised, resulting in a curious mixture of Newberyism and Johnsonianism.

The advertising poem on the second leaf begins:

> At Johnson's store, in Market-street,
> A sure reward, good children meet.

On page 28, however, *the Rector, at his own expense, gave a larger book every New Year's Day, which he got from the Corner of St. Paul's Church Yard*, and the books mentioned throughout are all English publications.

The story itself is pure Newbery, as the names alone are sufficient to indicate. Dame Partlet herself is a *very near relation to that renowned person Goody Two Shoes*, and we are introduced to Mr. Coverup, the sexton; Mr. Screwdown, the undertaker; Mr. Singclear, the parish clerk; Miss Deborah Crabface, the Rector's maiden aunt by the mother's side; and many others.

The Life of Dame Partlet is followed by the description of her farm (with half-title), which is in verse, an account of her funeral, and a hymn and an epitaph in verse.

The woodcut illustrations are by Anderson.

[DAY, THOMAS.] The Forsaken Infant; or entertaining history of Little Jack. New York: Printed and sold by J. C. Totten, 1819. [574]

Duodecimo, 24 leaves, A-D⁶, first and last (a blank) pasted down to covers, woodcut frontispiece, woodcut on title, illustrations in the text.

Original wrappers, title with woodcut of a ship on the upper, full-page woodcut on the lower.

An abridgement of one of the most popular tales of the famous author of *Sandford and Merton*. It was originally written for Stockdale's *Children's Miscellany* in 1788, and afterwards published separately. The original cuts were by Bewick.

HISTORY OF THE BIBLE. Boston: [Parmenter & Balch] for T. Bedlington, 1819. [575]

128 leaves, A-Q⁸, woodcut frontispiece and woodcut illustrations in the text.

Original sheep.

A Thumb Bible measuring 1⅛ by 1⅞ inches.

Another edition of no. 493 with the same woodcuts. The printers' imprint is on the back of the title.

HOCH-DEUTSCHES REFORMIRTES A B C und Namen Büchlein, für Kinder, welche anfangen zu lernen. Germantown: M. Billmeyer, 1819. [576]

Octavo, 16 leaves, A-B⁸, first and last leaf pasted down to cover, woodcut alphabet pictures on verso of title.

Original half binding, alphabet and four line stanza on front cover within ornamental borders, full-length woodcut of David playing a harp, on back cover, signed D.

A German Primer. The text is practically the same as in the editions of the *Hoch-Deutsches Lutherisches A B C*, with a different set of alphabet woodcuts.

[?LEATHLEY, MRS.] The Story of Joseph and his Brethren, in three parts. Written for the benefit of youth. To which is added, The History of Charles Jones. Wilmington: R. Porter, 1819.   [577]

Duodecimo, 53 leaves, A-H⁶, I⁵.

Unbound.
The History of Charles Jones, with caption title, begins on page (80).

MAVOR, WILLIAM [FORDYCE]. The Catechism of Health; containing simple and easy rules and directions for the Management of Children, and observations on the conduct of health in general. For the use of schools and families. By William Mavor, LL. D. Author of Travels, and many other popular works. With Alterations and Improvements. New York: Published by Samuel Wood & Sons and Samuel S. Wood & Co., Baltimore, 1819.   [578]

Duodecimo, 34 leaves, 1-5⁶, 6⁴.

Original blue wrappers, title on upper, advertisement on lower.
The author acknowledges his indebtedness for the general plan of his work to a *German work of greater length, under a similar title.*

MAVOR, WILLIAM [FORDYCE]. Catechism of Universal History. For the use of schools and families. By William Mavor, LL. D. Author of Travels, and many other popular works. With Alterations and Improvements. New York: Published by Samuel Wood & Sons, by Samuel S. Wood & Co., Baltimore, 1819.   [579]

Duodecimo, 36 leaves, 1-6⁶, some edges uncut.

Original blue wrappers, upper with title, lower with advertisement.
Covers the whole of the period from the creation of the world, 4004 B. C. to the time of writing.

MURRAY, LINDLEY. A First Book for Children. By Lindley Murray. Author of "English Grammar adapted to the different classes of learners." Fifth edition with cuts. Philadelphia: Griggs & Co. for Benjamin Warner, 1819.   [580]

Duodecimo, 36 leaves, first and last pasted down to covers, A-F⁶, woodcut frontispiece, woodcuts in the text.

Original wrappers, upper with title and woodcut, imprint dated 1819, lower with advertisement.
The date on the title-page is 1818. The book is a re-issue of the 1818 edition with new wrappers.

A SET OF FLOWERS, Alphabetically Arranged, for Little Children. New York: Samuel Wood & Sons, and Samuel S. Wood & Co. Baltimore: 1819. [581]

Duodecimo, 12 leaves, without signatures, woodcut on the title and a woodcut on each page of the text.

Original yellow wrappers, title with woodcut vignette on upper, two vignettes on lower cover.

As stated on the title-page, the flowers are in alphabetical order, and each has a woodcut illustration, and a prose description beneath. The illustration on the title-page represents a Yellow-Lnpin (*sic*).

The text appears to have been revised for American children from an original English edition. Of the English Poppy we read: *This plant grows in our own country as well as in England;* in the account of the Hyacinth: *So highly are some of the varieties prized in England . . .*

WATTS, ISAAC. Divine Songs for Children . . . To which is added, Dr. Watts' Plain and Easy Catechisms: together with a collection of Prayers, &c. Designed and arranged for Sunday Schools. New Haven: Printed and published by A. H. Maltby & Co., 1819. [582]

Duodecimo, 36 leaves, A-F⁶.

Original marbled wrappers; uncut.
Stone, page 86.
This edition has the introduction; it is unillustrated. The publishers' advertisement is on the back of the title.

WORLDS DISPLAYED: for the benefit of young people, by a familiar history of some of their inhabitants. Philadelphia: Lydia R. Bailey for The Philadelphia Female Tract Society, 1819. [583]

Duodecimo, 26 leaves, A-D⁶, E².

Original blue wrappers, title on upper, advertisement on lower.
The design of this little book is to impress the minds of young people with the importance of time and eternity, and to exhibit the close connexion that there is betwixt them.

THE YOUNG ROBBER; or Dishonesty Punished. To which is added, Mr. Goodman and his Children, The Way to be Good and Happy, and The Ditch. New York: J. C. Totten, 1819. [584]

Duodecimo, 24 leaves including the last blank, A-D⁶, first and last leaves pasted down to covers, woodcut frontispiece, woodcut illustrations in text.

Original wrappers, upper with title, lower with woodcut.

The Young Robber occupies pages 7 to 29, and closes with the poem by Isaac Watts, entitled The Thief; Mr. Goodman and his Children begins on page (30); The Way to by Good and Happy, on page (37), and The Ditch, on page (44). The woodcuts are by Anderson.

1820

AN ADDRESS TO CHILDREN. Mount Pleasant: S. Marshall, 1820. [585]

Duodecimo, 6 leaves.

Unbound, stitched.

The Address is signed *From a Sincere Lover of Children*. Following this are two hymns by Philip Doddridge, and a catechism, which *it is desired that all children who may be presented with this little book, will commit to memory*.

This book was printed by Stephen Marshall, the printer of the *Westchester Herald* in the office of that newspaper in the village of Sing-Sing, now Ossining. The name of the township was Mount-Pleasant, and Sing-Sing on the Hudson was the principal village, and the place where all the printing was done.

BEAUTIES OF THE NEW-ENGLAND PRIMER. New York: Samuel Wood & Sons, and Samuel S. Wood & Co. Baltimore, 1820. [586]

16mo, 16 leaves, without signatures, first and last pasted down to wrappers, woodcut on title and woodcuts in the text.

Original wrappers.
Heartman 254.
Another edition of no. 483.

[CAMERON, LUCY LYTTLETON.] The Polite Little Children. By the author of "The History of Margaret Whyte," "The Two Lambs," &c. First American edition. Andover: Mark Newman, 1820. [587]

Duodecimo, 10 leaves, including the last blank; in this copy the leaf opposite the title (probably with a frontispiece) has been torn out.

Original tan wrappers.

Lucy Lyttleton Cameron (1781-1858) was a famous writer of religious stories for children. She was the younger sister of Mrs. Sherwood, author of Little Henry and his Bearer, and other works to be found in this catalogue.

EARLY INSTRUCTION, recommended in a narrative of the life of Catherine Haldane; with an address to parents on the Importance of Religion. New Haven: Sidney's Press for J. Babcock & Son, 1820. [588]

Sm. octavo, 16 leaves, without signatures, large woodcut frontispiece, first and last leaves pasted down to covers.

Original grey wrappers, title and woodcut on the upper, advertisement on the lower.

A juvenile funeral elegy. Catherine was a Scottish child, who died a pious death at the age of nine. *No particular impression appeared to be made on Catherine's mind by the word of God, till she was five years of age*, but after that she began *to be much more concerned about religion than formerly*. It is probable, however, that she would have lived a natural and healthy life had it not been for her mother . . . *Her complaints increasing, her mother told her she thought her dying . . . In April her mother took her into a room by herself, and asked her if she should pray with her, and told her she was dying . . .*

Pages 20 to 31 are occupied by the author's remarks addressed partly to children and partly to parents.

The publishers' advertisement is on the back of the title.

FABLES FOR YOUNG LADIES. From the Best Authors. Cabinet Edition. Philadelphia: [Griggs & Dickinson] for D. Hogan, 1820.   [589]

16 mo, 80 leaves, A-K⁸, with a half title.

Original half binding, title on the upper cover, advertisement of *Paul and Virginia* on the lower; uncut and unopened.

The preface, consisting of an essay on the Fable, is dated March, 1820. The printers' imprint is on the back of the title.

The work is divided into four parts, consisting of Enchanted Plants; Fables of Flora, by Dr. Langhorne; Fables, by Edward Moore, and Fables from Various Authors; the first three have half titles.

[HENDLEY, GEORGE.] An Authentic Account of the Conversion, Experience, and Happy Deaths, of Ten Boys. Designed for Sunday Schools. New Haven: Sidney's Press, for John Babcock & Son, New Haven; S. & W. R. Babcock, Charleston; and M'Carty & Davis, Philadelphia, 1820.   [590]

Sm. octavo, 16 leaves without signatures, woodcut frontispiece.

Original wrappers with the title *Biography of Boys*, a vignette and the imprint on the upper cover, and an advertisement on the lower.

Contains the accounts of the deaths of the boys extracted from George Hendley's *Memorial for Children*, see no. 317. The *Conclusion* has been rewritten and lengthened.

MAVOR, WILLIAM FORDYCE. Catechism of Botany; or, an easy introduction to the Vegetable Kingdom: for the use of schools and families. By William Mavor, L.L.D. Author of Travels, and many other popular works. New York: Published by Samuel Wood & Sons, and Samuel S. Wood & Co., Baltimore: 1820.   [591]

Duodecimo, 36 leaves, 1-6⁶, last leaf blank, and pasted down to back cover.

Original wrappers, title on upper, advertisement on lower.

[MORE, HANNAH.] The Pilgrims, and Parley the Porter: two Allegories. New York: Published by Samuel Wood & Sons, and by Samuel S. Wood & Co., Baltimore: 1820. [592]

Duodecimo, 24 leaves, woodcut frontispiece, woodcut illustrations in the text, many of which in this copy have been colored by hand.

Original wrappers, title on the upper, advertisement on the lower.
Parley the Porter begins on page (29), with half title.

THE NEW-ENGLAND PRIMER, improved. Or, an easy and pleasant Guide to the Art of Reading. To which is added, The Assembly's Catechism. Hartford: George Goodwin & Sons, 1820. [593]

16mo, 32 leaves, A-D⁸, first and last pasted down to wrappers, woodcut frontispiece, woodcuts in the text, advertisement on the last leaf.

Original wrappers.
Heartman 252.
The alphabet couplets are as in the Lansingburgh edition of 1816, no. 540.

[TAYLOR, ANN AND JANE.] Hymns for Infant Minds. By the author of Original Poems, Rhymes for the Nursery, etc. "We use great plainness of speech." Newburgh: Printed by Uriah C. Lewis, for himself and Junius S. Lewis, Catskill, 1820. [594]

Duodecimo, 36 leaves, 1-6⁶, first and last pasted down to covers, woodcut of David with a harp on the title-page, woodcut frontispiece in an oval compartment with two stanzas of verse beneath.

Original wrappers, title-page repeated on the upper, advertisement on the lower.
Originally published in England in 1810. The *Advertisement* contains a tribute to Dr. Watts.
The work contains LXXI Hymns, the last of which is headed *Written by William Cowper, Esq.*

[TAYLOR, ANN AND JANE.] A Selection of Hymns, for Infant Minds. Boston: Sylvester T. Goss, 1820. [595]

Duodecimo, 20 leaves, with signatures A-E before the strings, unlettered after the strings, woodcut vignette on the title.

Wall paper wrappers.
A selection of thirty-nine hymns from the *Hymns for Infant Minds* (see the previous item).

Early American Children's Books

THE YOUNG CHILD'S A, B, C; or, First Book. New York: Samuel Wood & Sons, and Samuel S. Wood & Co., Baltimore. [c. 1820.]   [596]

Sq. octavo, 8 leaves, woodcut vignette on title and woodcuts throughout the text.

Original tan wrappers, with title and woodcut on front, woodcut on back.

This edition has variations from the first edition (no. 325) both as to text and woodcuts. There is no printer's imprint at the end.

1821

THE AFFLICTED VILLAGER, or some account of M. M—who has been sixteen years confined to her bed. In Four Letters to Eliza. To which is added, an account of the remarkable suferings (*sic*) of John Williams. New York: Samuel Wood & Sons, and Samuel S. Wood & Co., Baltimore, 1821.   [597]

Duodecimo, 24 leaves, the last a blank, woodcut illustrations.

Original tan wrappers, title on the front cover, publishers' advertisements, dated Second-month, 1821, on the back.

The Advertisement contains the information that *this good little work was first published in Scotland*, and that M. M. is a real person.

The American publishers, have taken the liberty to leave out some parts, and made some alterations in the language of others, but in no case have they changed the language of the sufferer, or that respecting her situation.

At the end of the narrative, which is in letter form, are *Hymns, suited to the subjects of the foregoing Letters*, pages 38 to 41.

On page 42 begins *Memoir of John Williams' remarkable affliction. By Robert Eastburn, of New-Brunswick, New-Jersey.*

THE ALPHABET OF GOODY TWO SHOES. Philadelphia: Published by Benjamin Warner, 1821.   [598]

Duodecimo, 26 leaves, printed on one side only, an illustration and 4 lines of descriptive verse for each letter of the alphabet, one on each leaf, first leaf with title, and last leaf pasted down to covers.

Original yellow wrappers, with engraved vignette on the upper, the title reading: *The Alphabet of Goody Two Shoes; by learning which she soon got rich.*

The alphabet rhymes are original and amusing:

> C, is a Cheese,
>   But don't ask for a slice
> For it serves to maintain
>   A whole nation of mice.
>
> H, was a Hoyden,
>   Not like you or me,
> For she tumbled about
>   Like the waves of the sea.

Early American Children's Books

BUNYAN, JOHN. Bunyan's Pilgrim's Progress, from this world to that which is to come, exhibited in a Metamorphosis, or a transformation of pictures. To which is added, The Christian's Triumph over Death, &c. Designed and published by J. W. Barber. Hartford: P. B. Goodsell, 1821. [599]

The 5 leaves of this Metamorphosis fold to form 15 woodcut illustrations. This copy has the title on the first leaf, and numbered verses in prose on the last headed *Death and Judgment* with a woodcut, the last verse being unfinished.

According to Mr. Harry B. Weiss in his article on *Metamorphoses and Harlequinades* there should be paper covers, the first with a title, and the last with an illustration of the Bunyan Church in Bedford, England.

John Warner Barber was born in 1798 at Windsor, Connecticut, and became a famous historian, author and engraver. According to Mr. Weiss in the article cited above, *one of his first publications was Bunyan's Pilgrim's Progress, for which he engraved the woodcuts.*

BURDER, GEORGE. Early Piety; or, Memoirs of Children, eminently serious. Interspersed with familiar Dialogues, Prayers, Graces, and Hymns. By George Burder. Baltimore: R. J. Matchett, for Armstrong and Plaskitt, 1821. [600]

16mo, 40 leaves, 1, 2^{16}, 3^8, 4 pages advertisement at the end; pages 73-76 contain the Appendix to the third edition.

Original wrappers, title and woodcut on upper, advertisements on lower cover.

In his preface, dated 1812 and addressed to *My dear young Reader*, the author of this work betrays for the first time in this class of literature some doubt as to the effect that reading of the pious deaths of young children might have on the behaviour of young living children still attracted by life.

This little book is written with a design and a desire, at once to profit and please you; by shewing in the examples of children, young as you are, the great happiness and advantage of real and early piety. . . Many of them died very young; (not that they died the sooner because they were good; but being good, they were the sooner fit to die;) . . .

[CAMERON, LUCY LYTTLETON.] The History of Fidelity and Profession. An Allegory. By the author of 'The Raven and the Dove,' 'The Two Lambs,' &c. &c. New York: Published by Samuel Wood & Sons, and Samuel S. Wood & Co., Baltimore: 1821. [601]

Duodecimo, 18 leaves, including the last blank, engraved frontispiece by Scoles.

Original blue boards, with title on the front and advertisements on the back.

An allegory, the purpose of which is explained at the end: *O ye young ones, who read the story of Fidelity and Profession, learn hence to restrain your busy, active, wandering thoughts. Teach them to labour at the Grotto of Repentance, the Hill of Faith, the Vineyard of Charity, and the Arbour of Hope. . .*

[CAMERON, LUCY LYTTLETON.] The History of Susan and Esther Hall; or, A religious life the only happy one. By the author of "The History of Margaret Whyte." Philadelphia: J. Harding for the Protestant Episcopal Sunday and Adult School Society, 1821. [602]

Duodecimo, 74 leaves, A-M⁶, A², woodcut frontispiece.

Original half binding.

THE COUNCIL OF DOGS. Illustrated with suitable engravings. Philadelphia: Published by Johnson & Warner, 1809. Philadelphia: Published by Benjamin Warner, 1821. [603]

Original wrappers, front cover with title and imprint of Johnson & Warner, dated 1809, lower with advertisement.

The edition of 1809 (no. 389) reissued in 1821. The later date and imprint are at the foot of the frontispiece.

THE DIVERTING AMUSEMENT of the House that Jack Built, being the Particulars of the Wonderfull Incidents that took place therein. Philadelphia: Benjamin Warner, 1821. [604]

Duodecimo, 12 leaves, first with title (imprint dated 1821) and last with text, pasted down to covers, illustrations and text engraved throughout, leaves printed on one side only, the text in italic letter.

Original salmon wrappers, upper with title, imprint reading *Philadelphia: Published by Johnson & Warner*. 1812. *Price* 19 *Cents*.

GROTZ, CHRISTOPHER. The Art of Making Fireworks, Detonating Balls, &c. Containing Plain and Easy Directions for Mixing and Preparing the Ingredients, and Making and Finishing the most simple Devices in this Ingenious Art: Together with how to make and fill Air and Fire Balloons; And How to prepare and make Detonating Balls, Spiders, Segars, Boots and Shoes, Waterloo Crackers, &c. By Christopher Grotz, Real Engineer. New-York: W. Grattan for S. King, 1821. [605]

Duodecimo, 12 leaves, engraved frontispiece (colored) by Prud'homme.

Half red morocco; original wrappers bound in, the upper with the publisher's advertisement of pamphlets in the same series.

A book intended for the instruction of boys in the art of making all kinds of fireworks including *Ingenious Devices; Fancy Devices for the Water;* etc. At the end are *Amusements with Fulminating Silver* containing instructions for the manufacturing of devices calculated to give violent shocks to the unwary and to make any boy a nuisance to his relatives and friends.

Early American Children's Books

These include a trick to make a drawer, on being opened or shut, *explode with a loud report, to the no small discomfiture of the person at the drawer;* another to cause a chair to explode on being sat upon; instructions how to *cause some sport* by arranging for smokers' pipes and *segars* to explode on being lighted, and other equally fascinating and unpleasant devices.

JAMES TALBOT. Printed for the trustees of the publishing fund. Cambridge: Hilliard and Metcalf, Nov. 1821.   [606]

    Octavo, 19 leaves, 1-3⁶, 4¹.

    Original tan wrappers, uncut, title on the front cover, advertisements on the back.
    The tone of this story can be judged by the opening sentence: *"Is there no hope, sir?"* *said Lucy, following the Doctor softly to the door. "I am afraid not, my dear," replied the kind physician...*

JOHNSON'S PHILADELPHIA PRIMER. Or, a first book for children. Philadelphia: Published by Benjamin Warner, 1821.   [607]

    Duodecimo, 18 leaves, without signatures, woodcut on title and numerous woodcuts in the text.

    Wrappers, uncut and unopened.
    Contains alphabets, syllabaries, illustrated and unillustrated, and passages for reading. The woodcuts are by A. Anderson, and include a fine set of alphabet cuts of birds.

MARSHALL, MRS. A Sketch of my Friend's Family, intended to suggest some practical hints on Religion and Domestic Manners. By Mrs. Marshall, Author of Henwick Tales. Fifth Edition. In every work, regard the Writer's end. Hartford: [P. B. Goodsell for] Oliver D. Cooke, 1821.   [608]

    16mo, 66 leaves, 2 leaves without signatures (frontispiece and half title), 1-8⁸, including the last blank, full-page cuts.

    Original boards, title on front cover and publisher's advertisement on back, partly unopened.
    There were at least two issues of the covers, the wording of the title and the advertisement on the back being different in each case. The printer's imprint is on the back of the title. The half title is headed *Miniature Edition.*

MAVOR, WILLIAM [FORDYCE]. Catechism of Animated Nature; or an easy introduction to the Animal Kingdom. For the use of Schools and Families. By William Mavor, L.L.D. Author of Travels, and many other popular works. With Alterations and Improvements.—Catechism of General Knowledge; or, a brief Introduction to the Arts and Sciences.

Early American Children's Books

For the use of Schools and Families... Catechism of Geography, or an Easy Introduction to the Knowledge of the Globe and its Inhabitants. For the Use of Schools and Families... New-York: Published by Samuel Wood & Sons, and by Samuel S. Wood & Co., Baltimore, 1821. [609]

Three volumes, duodecimo, each with 36 leaves, 1-6⁶.

Original wrappers, titles on upper covers, advertisements on lower.

The first work *aims only at giving such a view of this extensive subject, as may lead the youthful and inquisitive mind to farther researches.*

The subjects in the *Catechism of General Knowledge* are treated in alphabetical order from Agriculture to Zoology. The author was evidently a man that hath no music in his soul: Q. *What is music? A. An agreeable and very fascinating luxury; useless to any real purpose of life, but extremely gratifying to the ear... Q. Is not music much cultivated in this country? A. It certainly is cultivated much more than it deserves, and frequently at the expense of more valuable acquisitions.*

The *Catechism of Geography* contains instruction on the countries of the world, with an account of their natural manufactures, and the character of their respective inhabitants.

The inhabitants of the United States *are reputed to be proud and independent. Frugality, industry, and attachment to liberty, are the leading parts of their character. The English are comely in their persons, lovers of liberty; an industrious and commercial people, enterprising and active, but reserved in their manners. The Irish are polite and hospitable, but hasty in their disposition. Some political discouragements have repressed their native energies; but, it is to be hoped that the union with England, will in time be productive of the greatest advantages to them, and render their island, what it naturally is, the seat of commerce, manufactures, and plenty.*

MURRAY, LINDLEY. A First Book for Children. By Lindley Murray, author of "English Grammar adapted to the different classes of learners." Sixth edition with cuts. Philadelphia: Griggs & Dickinson for B. Warner, sold also at his store, Richmond, (Vir.) and by William P. Bason, Charleston, (S. C.) 1821.   [610]

Duodecimo, 36 leaves (A)-F⁶, first and last leaves pasted down to covers, woodcut frontispiece, woodcut illustrations.

Original blue boards, title with woodcut on the front cover (imprint dated 1819), advertisement on the back.

A reprint of the former editions.

[PERRAULT, CHARLES.] The History of Little Red Riding-Hood. In verse. Illustrated by Engravings. Second American edition. Philadelphia: Mary Charles, 1821.   [611]

Duodecimo, 6 leaves of text in verse, 12 full-page colored plates, including the half title.

Original wrappers, title on the front wrapper with the imprint of Morgan and Sons, undated, and their advertisement on the back.

Weiss: *William Charles*, page 9, does not locate a copy.

At the end is a *Moral*, part of which is quoted on the front wrapper:

> This Story demonstrates that Children discreet,
> Should never confide in each Stranger they meet;
> For often a Knave in an artful disguise,
> Will mark out an innocent prey for his prize;
> Take warning, dear Children, before 'tis too late,
> By Little Red Riding-Hood's tragical fate.

The poem is based on the story by Charles Perrault.

The prices printed at the foot of the cover have been changed in ink, and raised from
12½ cents plain, and 18¾ coloured to 25 cents plain, and 37½ cents coloured.

PETER PRIM'S PROFITABLE PRESENT to the little Misses and Masters of the
United States.
"One-Two—
"Come buckle my shoe."
Illustrated with neat engravings. Philadelphia: Published by Morgan
& Sons, n. d. [c. 1821.]   [612]

Sq. octavo, 8 leaves, engraved throughout and printed on one side only, a colored
illustration on each leaf, with verse below.

Original wrappers, cover-title with the imprint of Morgan & Sons, and their advertisement on the back wrapper.

Weiss: *William Charles*, page 10.

There is no title-page, the title appearing on the cover only. At the foot of the first page
of the text is the imprint: *Philadela. Pub. and Sold by W. Charles.*

Another copy has a different issue of the wrappers. The advertisements on the back are
the same, differently set up.

Mr. Weiss does not record the two issues of the wrappers.

PETER PRY'S PUPPET SHOW. Part the Second. "There is a time for all
things, A time to work, and a time to play." Philadelphia: Mary Charles,
1821.   [613]

Sq. octavo, 8 leaves engraved throughout and printed on one side only, the first with
a vignette-frontispiece enclosing the half title with the quotation, each of the others with
an illustration above a 4 line stanza of verse, the illustrations colored.

Original wrappers, cover-title (without the quotation), on the back a list of books recently
published by Mary Charles. The lining of the back wrapper has come loose, and contains
a list of books published by Wm. Charles.

Weiss: *William Charles*, page 10.

The illustration to the first verse of text was used in *The Horse's Levee or The Court of
Pegasus intended as a Companion to the Butterfly's Ball, and the Peacock ".At Home."* London,

J. Harris, Successor to E. Newbery, 1808. We have not seen a copy of that work, merely a reproduction of this illustration, and are unable to say whether the other illustrations are from the same work or not.

Another copy has different wrappers, bearing the imprint of Morgan & Sons, without date. In this copy the cover-title reads Part the II, not Part the Second, and has the quotation.

Weiss, page 10.

PUG'S VISIT TO MR. PUNCH. Illustrated with eight whimsical engravings. Philadelphia: Morgan & Sons, n. d. [c. 1821.]   [614]

Sq. octavo, 8 leaves, engraved throughout and printed on one side only, a colored illustration and 4 lines of verse on each leaf.

Original wrappers, with the imprint of Morgan & Sons, undated, and their advertisement on the back.

The book was originally issued by William Charles in 1810 and again in 1815, see nos. 426 and 533. The remainders were reissued by Morgan & Sons, with their wrappers, probably about 1821.

Weiss: *William Charles*, page 10.

Another copy has a different issue of the wrapper, though probably issued about the same time. The advertisements on the back are the same though differently set up.

THE TRAGICAL WANDERINGS AND ADVENTURES OF GRIMALKIN the eldest son of Dame Trot's Cat. Philadelphia: Mary Charles, 1821.   [615]

Sq. octavo, 8 leaves, engraved throughout and printed on one side only, each with a colored illustration and a stanza of 6 lines. The first page has a caption title; the full title appears on the wrapper only.

Original wrappers, cover-title, advertisement of Mary Charles on the back.

This edition not in Weiss: *William Charles*, who lists an edition of 1815.

THE TRAGI-COMIC HISTORY OF THE BURIAL OF COCK ROBIN; with the Lamentation of Jenny Wren; the Sparrow's Apprehension; and the Cuckoo's Punishment. Being a Sequel to the Courtship, Marriage, and Pic-nic Dinner of Robin Red-Breast and Jenny Wren. Philadelphia: S. Probasco for Benjamin Warner, 1821.   [616]

Sq. octavo, 8 leaves of text, 8 plates, first and last pasted down to cover.

Wrappers.

In verse.

For the first edition see no. 448.

ONE   TWO

Come buckle my Shoe.

You lazy Elf!

Pray do it yourself.

Philadel.ᵃ Pub. and Sold by W.Charles.

Page from "Peter Prim's Profitable Present"

Here's johnny Bull From England come,
Who boast's of being a sailor,
But yankey tars will let him know,
He'll meet with many a Failure.

Page from "Peter Pry's Puppet Show"

WAKEFIELD, PRISCILLA. A Brief Memoir of the Life of William Penn. Compiled for the use of young persons. By Priscilla Wakefield. New York: Mahlon Day, No. 84, Water Street, 1821.　　　[617]

Duodecimo, 28 leaves, A-C⁶, D¹⁰, first and last (a blank) pasted down to covers. Woodcut frontispiece by A. Anderson.

Original wrappers, upper with title, lower with *Lines by Dr. Roscoe, of Liverpool, on receiving from Dr. Rush, of Philadelphia, a piece of the tree, under which William Penn made his Treaty with the Indians. The tree had been blown down in* 1812, consisting of six four-line stanzas of verse.

The frontispiece by Anderson represents William Penn's Treaty with the Indians, and has an account beneath of the *wide-spreading elm, in that part of Philadelphia now called Kensington*, under which it was made.

The same frontispiece, with a much shorter description beneath, is in the *Book of Cuts* printed in 1823 by the same publisher, no. 621.

1822

THE HISTORY OF BETSEY BROWN, the Robber's Daughter. Showing the utility of Sunday Schools. Albany: G. J. Loomis and Co., 1822.　　[618]

Duodecimo, 18 leaves.

Original blue wrappers, title and woodcut vignette on upper, large woodcut on lower. The same woodcuts are not used on the wrappers of all copies.

At the end, in verse, *The Pious Child's Song.* (*From the Guardian.*)

[PERRAULT, CHARLES.] Cinderella; or the Little Glass Slipper. Illustrated with Elegant Engravings. Philadelphia: Published and sold by Mary Charles, 1822.　　　[619]

Sq. octavo, 8 leaves of text, 8 colored plates.

In the wrappers for the original edition issued by William Charles in 1815, the imprint so dated, and the title reading: *Cinderella; or The Little Glass Slipper: Beautifully versified; Illustrated with Elegant Figures, to dress and undress.*

Weiss: *William Charles,* page 7.

This is an arrangement in verse of Charles Perrault's famous story, and the first stanza is one of explanation and apology:

> Of famed Cinderella
> In prose is made known,
> How by goodness and virtue
> She came to a throne.
> Such a lesson we cannot
> Too often rehearse;
> So young folks, now accept
> Of her story in verse.

The figures in this edition of 1822 are not *to dress and undress*. The frontispiece is signed J. Y. *sc* [i. e. Joseph Yeager].

1823

AIKIN, J[OHN.] The Calendar of Nature; designed for the Instruction and Entertainment of Young Persons. By J. Aikin. New York: Samuel Wood & Sons; and Samuel S. Wood & Co., Baltimore: [c. 1823.] [620]

Duodecimo, 54 leaves, 1-9⁶, woodcut frontispiece and a woodcut illustration for each month by A. Anderson.

Original half binding.
In prose interspersed with verse.
The dedication is addressed from Warrington, May 20, 1784, to Mrs. Barbauld, the famous sister of the author.
At the end of *The Calendar of Nature* is *The Rural Calendar* consisting of a poem for each month of the year, which is followed by *An Account Of the origin of the names of some months of the year* . . . and other matter.
The American editor has been careful to point out in a footnote the difference in the meaning of the word *corn* in the United States and in England.

BOOK OF CUTS, designed for the Amusement and Instruction of Young People. New York: Printed and sold by Mahlon Day, No. 372 Pearl-street, 1823. [621]

Duodecimo, 12 leaves without signatures, the first and last pasted down to covers, woodcut frontispiece, woodcut vignette on the title and a woodcut illustration on each leaf of the text, by Anderson.

Original wrappers, title on the front cover, two woodcuts on the back.
Contains five short extracts from the story of Joseph; an abridgement in eight parts of *The Blackbird's Nest* (see no. 452) and other extracts, each with an illustration.
The frontispiece is the picture of William Penn's Treaty with the Indians, as in Priscilla Wakefield's *Brief Memoir of the Life of William Penn*, 1821, no. 617, but with only four lines of description beneath.

[CERVANTES, MIGUEL SAAVEDRA DE.] The Adventures of Don Quixote, De la Mancha, Knight of the Sorrowful Countenance, and his Humourous Squire, Sancho Pancha; with the particulars of his numerous challenges, battles, wounds, courtships, enchantments, feats of chivalry, &c. &c. &c. New York: Published by W. Borradaile, 1823. [622]

Duodecimo, 11 leaves, A⁶, B⁵, folded engraved frontispiece in 4 compartments.
Half dark green morocco.
This abridgement is in chapbook form.

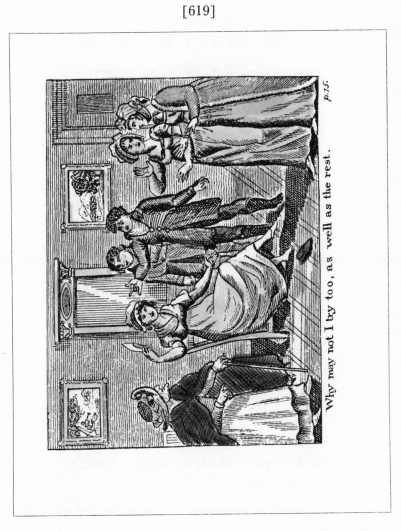

Page from "Cinderella; or the Little Glass Slipper"

THE GAMUT IN VERSE.

Said Ann to her sister Maria one day,

If you wish it, my dear, I will teach you to
play;

I'll hear you your notes, each day if you're
good,

And make them quite easy to be understood,

But first you'll observe, what is clear to
be seen,

Those five straight black lines, and

four spaces between,

Page from "The Gamut and Time Table, in Verse"

Early American Children's Books

COTTIN, MARIE. Elizabeth; or, The exiles of Siberia, being a true and affecting display of filial affection. By Madame Cottin. Translated from the French. New York: Published by W. Borradaile, 1823.   [623]

Duodecimo, 26 leaves, A-D⁶, E², engraved frontispiece, colored.

Boards.

Marie Cottin (called Sophie), née Risteau, a famous French novelist, was born in Paris in 1770. *Elisabeth; ou les exiles de Siberië*, her last and most famous tale, was first published in 1806; she died in the following year.

THE EXTRAORDINARY LIFE AND ADVENTURES OF ROBIN HOOD, Captain of the Robbers of Sherwood Forest. Interspersed with The History of Little John and his Merry Men All. New York: Published by W. Borradaile, 1823.   [624]

Duodecimo, 14 leaves, irregular signatures, engraved frontispiece by Prud'homme (colored).

Boards.

A chapbook version in prose, with two songs from the Garland at the end.

GREGORY, JOHN. A Father's Legacy to his Daughters. By the late Dr. Gregory, of Edinburgh. Troy: Printed and published by W. & J. Disturnell, 1823.   [625]

Duodecimo, 48 leaves, 1-6⁸, engraved frontispiece (colored), and engraved title with vignette.

Original half binding.

This edition contains the preface. On four leaves at the end is printed Goldsmith's ballad, *Edwin and Angelina* (from *The Vicar of Wakefield*).

HISTORY OF THE BIBLE. Troy: Printed and published by W. & J. Disturnell, 1823.   [626]

128 leaves, A-Q⁸, woodcuts.

Original black leather, gilt.

A Thumb Bible measuring 1⅞ by 1¼ inches.

Another edition of no. 433.

This edition has a different frontispiece and a number of different cuts in the text, although some of the same cuts are used.

JONES, JOHN PAUL. The interesting Life, Travels, Voyages, and Daring Engagements of the celebrated Paul Jones; containing numerous anecdotes of undaunted courage, in the prosecution of his bold enterprizes.

To which is added, The song written on the engagement between the Good Man Richard, and the English frigate Serapis, New York: Published by W. Borradaile, 1823. [627]

Duodecimo, 14 leaves, A-B⁶, C², folded engraved frontispiece.

Dark blue half morocco.

Another edition of no. 394 without the Life of Peter Williamson.

MORE, HANNAH. Sacred Dramas: chiefly intended for Young Persons. The subjects taken from the Bible . . . By Hannah More. To which are Added, The Search after Happiness: A Pastoral Drama. By the same Author. Philadelphia: Published by David Hogan, 1823. [628]

Sm. octavo, 96 leaves, A-M⁸, with a general half title (Sacred Dramas. By Hannah More. Cabinet Edition.), and a separate half title to each drama.

Original half binding, title on the upper cover, and a list of Cabinet Editions published by D. Hogan on the lower.

Contains: Moses in the Bulrushes; David and Goliath; Belshazzar, Daniel, and The Search after Happiness.

THE NEW-ENGLAND PRIMER improved: or, An Easy and Pleasant Guide to the Art of Reading. To which is added, the Shorter Catechism, As composed and agreed upon by the Reverend Assembly of Divines at Westminster. Adorned with cuts. Amherst: Published by Charles Wells, 1823. [629]

Duodecimo, 32 leaves, including 2 blanks at the beginning (A)², B-C¹², D⁶, woodcut frontispiece in two compartments, the upper representing a girl seated at a piano, the lower the usual one of a boy and girl at prayer, woodcuts in the text.

Original half binding of wooden boards covered with grey paper, leather back.

Heartman 270.

PRAYERS FOR CHILDREN AND YOUTH; with an Historical Catechism of the Life of Jesus Christ. Salem: [W. & S. B. Ives] for Whipple & Lawrence, 1823. [630]

Duodecimo, 2 parts in 1, 54 leaves, 1-4⁶, 5⁴; 1², 2-5⁶, a separate title-page for the Historical Catechism.

Original half binding, title on the upper cover, advertisement on the lower.

Tapley: *Salem Imprints*, page 474.

Contains prayers and catechisms for young children, including an abridgement of the catechism of Dr. Watts. The printers' imprint is at the end.

Early American Children's Books

1824

[ELLIOTT, MARY.] My Father A Poem. Illustrated with engravings. Philadelphia: Published and sold by Morgan and Yeager, 1824. [631]

Sq. duodecimo, 6 leaves, engraved throughout and printed on one side only, an illustration between two stanzas of verse on each leaf, the illustrations colored.

Original wrappers, cover-title, advertisement on the back wrapper.
This issue not in Weiss: *William Charles*, although it is marked in the list of Children's Books published by Morgan and Yeager as having been described in that work.
There is no title-page, the title appears on the cover only. The price *Plain* 12½ *cents Colourd* (*sic*) 18¾ *cents*.
This edition is very similar to that of Samuel Wood, 1817, no. 551. It has the last two stanzas, omitted from the earlier edition, and the order of two stanzas is transposed. A comparison of the illustrations in the two editions is interesting. In the Morgan and Yeager issue the plates are printed the reverse way and the mother has been entirely suppressed from the two plates in which she appeared in the Wood edition. Moreover in at least one of the plates the sex of the child is changed, and is represented as a girl instead of a boy.
The exact dates of the partnerships of the firms of Morgan and Yeager and of Morgan and Sons are not known, neither firm appearing in the Philadelphia directories. The two firms specialized in the toy books previously published by William Charles, and the greater number of their publications are undated. The present work bears the date 1824, the earliest date to appear on any of the Morgan and Yeager toy book imprints, and, as will be seen from this catalogue, several other dated books appeared in this year. The last book described in this catalogue published by Morgan and Sons bears the date 1834.
For a note on Joseph Yeager see no. 512. The name of William H. Morgan, the senior partner of both firms, appears in the Philadelphia directories as a carver and gilder as early as 1815.

FINCH, C. The Gamut and Time Table, in verse. For the instruction of children in the Rudiments of music. By C. Finch. Embellished with sixteen beautiful engravings. Philadelphia: Morgan & Yeager, 1824. [632]

Octavo, 16 leaves, without signatures, engraved throughout and printed on one side only, illustrations colored, musical notation.

Original wrappers, cover-title, publishers' advertisement on the lower wrapper.
Weiss: *William Charles*, page 8, gives no imprint, and says *Probably a Charles item*.
There is no title-page, the title appearing on the wrapper only; the price is *col.* 37½, *plain* 25 *cents*; the first leaf has a full-page frontispiece.
The work contains elementary instruction in music in verse. Several pianos are depicted in the illustrations, of which one is inscribed *Willig. Maker*, another, *Carr's Music Store*, and a third has simply the name *Blake*.

GREGORY, RICHARD. My Daughter A Poem By Mr. Rd. Gregory. Illustrated with Elegant Engravings. Philadelphia: Published and sold by Morgan & Yeager, 1824. [633]

Early American Children's Books

Duodecimo, 6 leaves, engraved throughout and printed on one side only, two stanzas of verse and one illustration (colored) on each leaf.

Original wrappers, cover-title, advertisements on the back cover; the wrappers are pasted on to the covers of *The Adventures of Old Dame Trudge and her Parrot*, William Charles, 1817.

Weiss: *William Charles*, page 9.

There is no title-page, the title appearing on the cover only.

The attribution to Richard Gregory on the cover-title of this work may be accurate, though it is sometimes ascribed to Mary Elliott, author of *My Brother, My Sister, My Uncle* and similar poems written in imitation of *My Mother* by Ann Taylor. The illustrations in the present edition are the same as those in the London edition of circa 1815. That to the verse

> Who'll mournfully attend my Bier,
> Who shed the sympathetic Tear,
> And falt'ring say, *"my Bliss lies here"?*
>   My Daughter!

is particularly interesting, with its representation of the grave scene, and the two undertaker's mutes walking away from the grave, leaving behind the bereaved daughter, and an extremely youthful grave digger.

GREGORY, RICHARD. My Son A Poem By Richard Gregory. Illustrated with Engravings. Philadelphia: Published and sold Wholesale and Retail by Morgan and Yeager, 1824.   [634]

Duodecimo, 6 leaves, engraved throughout and printed on one side only, 2 stanzas of verse and the illustration (colored) on each leaf.

Original wrappers, title on the front cover, advertisements on the back.

This issue not in Weiss.

The edition of 1816 (no. 539) by William Charles, with new covers. The Morgan and Yeager covers are precisely the same as the original Charles covers with the exception of the name of the publishers and the date. The imprint on these covers is printed in smaller type than that used by Charles for his own name, and includes the address of the firm omitted in the earlier issue. The misprint in the statement of the price is repeated: *Price Plain* 12½ *cents Colourd* 18¾ *cents.*

GUESS AGAIN or Easy Enigmas & Puzzles, For Little Folks. Second Edition. Enigma 6. Philadelphia: Published Wholesale by Morgan & Yeager, n. d. [c. 1824.]   [635]

Duodecimo, 18 leaves, A-C⁶, engraved title and frontispiece, both colored.

Original engraved wrappers, the upper cover with the title-page repeated, the lower with the frontispiece, both uncolored.

Weiss: *William Charles*, page 8.

The frontispiece and engraving on the back wrapper represents an old lady asking two children the Enigmas and Puzzles from a book:

MY FATHER

Who in my Childhood's earliest day,
Before my tongue one word could say,
Would let me with his watch-chain play.
My Father.

When seated on my Mother's knee,
Who used to play at peep with me
Hiding, where Baby could not see?
My Father.

Page from "My Father A Poem"

Who'll mournfully attend my Bier,
Who shed the sympathetic Tear,
And faltring say, "*my Bliss lies here*"?
                    My Daughter!

Who faithful as the tender dove,
Will treat my memory with love,
And hope to meet in Heaven above?
                    My Daughter!

Page from "My Daughter A Poem"

Come give it up and let me see,
It is— it is— what can it be!
On the wall is a hanging bookcase labelled *W. Charles's Library for Little Folks.*
Several of the Enigmas show the provenance of the book. Enigma 29 for example:

* * *

In gold and pearls am often seen,
And bob about our gracious Queen;
By her oft lent to George our King,
She'll own me for a useful thing.

* * *

THE HISTORY OF GOODY TWO-SHOES. Embellished with Elegant Engravings. Philadelphia: Stavely & Bringhurst for Ash & Mason, 1824. [636]

16mo, 16 leaves, A-B^8, 4 engraved plates including the frontispiece, colored.

Original blue wrappers.
This is the story of Little Goody Two-Shoes rewritten and abridged.

HISTORY OF THE BIBLE. Lansingburgh: for N. Stratton, [Printed at Troy by F. Adancourt,] 1824. [637]

Duodecimo, 128 leaves, A-Q^8, woodcut frontispiece and other illustrations.

Original calf.
A *Thumb Bible* measuring 1¼ by 1⅜ inches.
Another edition of no. 626 with the same woodcuts. The printer's imprint is below that of the publisher on the title-page.

THE HOUSE THAT JACK BUILT. This is the House that Jack built. [Philadelphia:] Published and sold Wholesale and Retail by Morgan & Yeager, n. d. [c. 1824.] [638]

Duodecimo, 18 leaves, including the first and last blanks, engraved throughout and printed on one side only, an illustration with the text beneath on each leaf.

Original wrappers, uncut.
Not in Weiss: *William Charles. The History of the House that Jack Built* is included in Mr. Weiss's list of Children's Books published by Morgan and Yeager.
The tenth leaf containing the *Priest all shaven and shorn* has the caption *Continuation of the House that Jack Built.* In this copy the leaf with *Jack with his hound and his horn* has been omitted, and in its place is the *Cock that crowed in the morn* (repeated).
The book is uncut, and the wrappers appear to be original, though they are plain, and unlike the usual Morgan and Yeager wrappers.

Early American Children's Books

THE LITTLE FARMER, a companion for the Little Poulterer. Designed for the Instruction of Children. By a Lady. Embellished with neat Copperplate Engravings. Philadelphia: Morgan & Yeager, n. d. [c. 1824.] [639]

Duodecimo, 8 leaves of text, 6 leaves with full-page colored plates, including the frontispiece.

Original wrappers, with title on the front cover reading: *The Little Farmer, or Moral and Instructive Lesson, s. (sic) with Plates*; a vignette and the imprint of Morgan and Yeager, and their advertisement on the back.

Weiss: *William Charles*, page 9, notes the title as being *Advertised on the back cover-page of the History of Little Fanny, published by Mary Charles in* 1821, but does not locate a copy.

Contains accounts of various animals to be found on a farm, partly quoted from Bewick's *History of Quadrupeds*, built round a slight story. The book is purely English, and no attempt has been made at localization.

LITTLE NANCY, or, the Punishment of Greediness. A moral tale. Embellished with engravings. Philadelphia: Published by Morgan & Yeager, n. d. [c. 1824.] [640]

Sq. duodecimo, 4 leaves of text in verse, 4 full-page plates including the frontispiece (plain).

Original wrappers, title on upper, advertisement on lower.
Weiss: *William Charles*, page 9.

THE LITTLE POULTERER. Designed for the Instruction of Children. By a Lady. Embellished with neat copperplate engravings. Philadelphia: Published by Morgan & Yeager, n. d. [c. 1824.] [641]

Sq. octavo, 8 leaves of text, engraved frontispiece and 5 full-page plates illustrating specimens of poultry.

Original wrappers, title with engraved vignette on the front cover, advertisements on the back. On the front cover the word *Poultrer* is so spelt.
Weiss: *William Charles*, page 9.

MEMOIRS OF THE LITTLE MAN, and the Little Maid. So wonderfully contrived, as to be either sung or said. Illustrated with curious Engravings. Philadelphia: Morgan & Yeager, 1824. [642]

Duodecimo, 12 leaves, each engraved on one side only, with text in verse and colored plates.

Page from "The History of Goody Two Shoes"

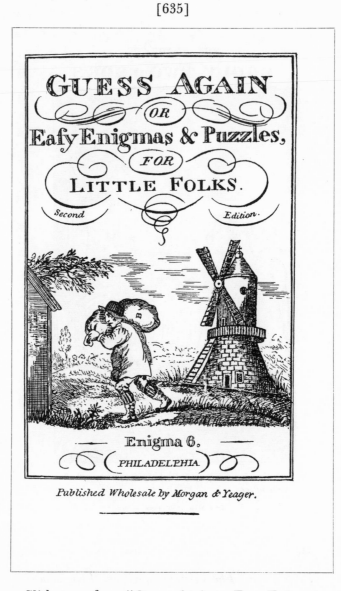

Title-page from "Guess Again or Easy Enigmas & Puzzles, for Little Folks"

Original wrappers, cover-title, engraving on back wrapper, advertising *A New Edition of the Little Man and the Little Maid.*

This edition not in Weiss: *William Charles.*

The illustrations are the same (in reverse) as those in the edition published in London by B. Tabart & Co., 1808.

MILK FOR BABES, or A Catechism in Verse: for the use of Sunday Schools... Second edition. Philadelphia: I. Ashmead & Co., for the Sunday and Adult School Union; A. Claxton, agent, 1824. [643]

Duodecimo, 14 leaves, including the last blank.

Original blue wrappers, title on the upper cover.
The questions are printed in italics, and the answers are in verse:

> 1. Q. *WHO is the maker of all things?*
>
> *A.* Th' Almighty God, who reigns on high;
> He form'd the earth, he spread the sky,
> And fashion'd in their various forms,
> Angels and men, and beasts and worms.

At the end are *Verses on the Bible* and a *Hymn, on the Scriptures.*

MY GOVERNESS A Poem. Illustrated with Engravings. Philadelphia: Published and sold by Morgan & Yeager, n. d. [c. 1824.] [644]

Duodecimo, 6 leaves, engraved throughout and printed on one side only, an illustration (colored) and two stanzas of verse on each leaf.

Original wrappers, cover-title, advertisement on the back.
Weiss: *William Charles*, page 9.
There is no title-page, the title appearing on the wrapper only. The price is *plain* 12½ *Cents. Coloured* 18¼ *Cents.*
Each verse has a title: The School; The Task; The Reprimand; The Work; Prayer; Praise; The Sampler; The Gift; Breaking-Up; Going Home; Return to School; The Farewell.
The exigencies of rhyme lead at times to a certain inconsequence of ideas. The Sampler and The Gift, on the same page, read as follows:

> *THE SAMPLER.*
> Who made the Scholar proud to show,
> The sampler work'd to friend and foe,
> And with Instruction fonder grow?
> My Governess.
>
> *THE GIFT.*
> Who first fine work and needle gave,
> And learnt me many an hour to save,
> And told of Heaven and earthly grave?
> My Governess.

THE NEW-ENGLAND PRIMER, improved; or, an easy and pleasant guide to the Art of Reading. To which is added The Assembly's Catechism. Adorned with cuts. Exeter: Printed by Samuel T. Moses, 1824. [645]

16mo, 32 leaves, A-D⁸, first and last leaves pasted down to covers, woodcut frontispiece, woodcut illustrations.

Original wrappers, leaf of hymnal printed over with marbled paper design.
Heartman 275.
The text of this edition is the same as that in the edition printed at Hartford, 1820, no. 593 with different woodcuts.

THE NEW-ENGLAND PRIMER, improved, or, an easy and pleasant Guide to the Art of Reading. To which is added, The Assembly's Catechism. Stereotyped by A. Chandler & Co. Newark: Benjamin Olds, 1824. [646]

16mo, 32 leaves, (the first leaf with frontispiece is lacking in this copy), the last pasted down to the wrapper, woodcuts.

Original blue wrappers, (front one missing).
Heartman 276.
The text is the same as in the previous number with different woodcuts.

OUR SAVIOUR. A Poem By a Christain (*sic*) Illustrated with Engravings. Philadelphia: Published and sold by Morgan and Yeager, 1824. [647]

Duodecimo, 6 leaves engraved throughout and printed on one side only, one illustration and two stanzas of verse on each leaf, the illustrations colored.

Original wrappers, cover-title, Morgan & Yeager's advertisement on the back.
Not in Weiss: *William Charles*, who cites the first edition of 1816.
There is no title-page, the title being on the wrapper only.
The author of this poem was perhaps wise to remain anonymous.

> Who was it that (high heav'ns decree)
> Brought Wise men from the East to see
> The Son of God—in Galilee?
> OUR SAVIOUR.

* * *

> Who for us yeilded (*sic*) up his breath,
> Seem'd by all nature mourn'd in death!
> While lightnings rent the earth beneath?
> OUR SAVIOUR.

TOY-BOOKS. The History of Animals. The Ill-Natured Little Boy. New Haven: Sidney's Press [for J. Babcock and Son, New Haven, and S. Babcock & Co., Charleston, S. C]. 1824. [648]

Two volumes, duodecimo, each volume with 12 leaves measuring 4 by 3½ inches, woodcut frontispiece, vignette on titles and illustrations in text, first and last leaves pasted down to covers.

Original yellow wrappers, title and woodcut on the upper, large woodcuts on the lower covers.

The publishers' imprint with an advertisement is on the back of each title.

The History of Animals contains descriptions of nine animals, each with an illustration.

The picture on the back wrapper of *The Ill-Natured Little Boy* represents a scene from Blue-Beard.

UPTON, MR. My Childhood A Poem By Mr. Upton. Illustrated with Engravings. Philadelphia: Published and sold by Morgan and Yeager, n. d. [c. 1824.]   [649]

Duodecimo, 6 leaves, engraved throughout and printed on one side only; caption title, illustration and one stanza on the first leaf, an illustration and two stanzas on the other leaves, the illustrations colored.

Original wrappers, cover-title, Morgan and Yeager's advertisement on the back; the covers are pasted to the covers of *The Deserted Boy, or The Cruel Parents*, by the same publishers.

Weiss: *William Charles*, page 9.

Each page has a descriptive headline: Perfect Inocence (*sic*); Going Alone; Gaining Knowledge; Fearful of Correction; Pleasure and Amusement; Youthful Vigour.

The identity of Mr. Upton is not known.

Perfect Inocence reads:

> When first my eyes discovered day,
> And quite a senseless lump I lay,
> What did my wond'ring looks display?
>> My Childhood.

Fearful of Correction:

> When first the rattle charm'd my ear,
> Or rod but nam'd created fear,
> What was it caus'd the glist'ning tear?
>> My Childhood.

> When nurs'ry tales 'bout "Buggaboo"
> Have made me shrink, and startle too,
> What made me think such *nonsense* true?
>> My Childhood.

THE YOUNG CHILD'S PRAYER BOOK. Part II. Boston: O. Everett, 1824.

16mo, 15 leaves, including the first and last blanks, 1⁸, 2⁷.   [650]

Unbound.

For the continuation see *The Child's Prayer-Book*, 1827.

The advertisement at the beginning states the design of the selection — *to furnish a simple manual for children, suitable to acquaint them with some of the topicks, and assist them in the practice, of devotion.*

1825

THE BABES IN THE WOOD, in verse. An affecting tale. A new edition, corrected and enlarged by a friend to youth. To which is added, Lines addressed to a Friend on Long-Island, on the death of her very promising Daughter, aged nearly four years. New York: Mahlon Day, 372, Pearl-street, 1825. [651]

Sm. octavo, 16 leaves, first leaf with woodcut frontispiece and last leaf pasted down to cover, woodcut vignette on title and numerous woodcut illustrations in the text.

Original wrappers, half-title and repetition of frontispiece on the upper, large vignette on the lower.

At the beginning is a preface containing the moral. The work consists of the ballad *Come ponder well, you parents dear*, considerably edited and revised, followed by the Conclusion (page 20) which does not form part of the original ballad.

The *Lines, Addressed to a Friend on Long-Island, on the death of her very promising daughter, aged nearly four years. By R. W.* begins on page 27, preceded by a frontispiece. It is not mentioned by Wegelin in *Early American Poetry*.

[CAMERON, LUCY LYTTLETON.] Marten and his Two Little Scholars at a Sunday School. By the Author of "The Two Lambs," &c. Revised by the Committee of Publication. Philadelphia: American Sunday School Union, 1825. [652]

Duodecimo, 72 leaves, A-M⁶, woodcut frontispiece by Gilbert, 2 leaves of advertisement at the end.

Original boards, title on upper cover with imprint *A. Claxton, agent. I. Ashmead & Co. Printers.* 1824.

The work is signed at the end *L*.

THE CHILDREN'S COMPANION, or Entertaining Instructor for the youth of both sexes; designed To Excite Attention, and inculcate virtue. Selected from the works of Berquin, Genlis, Day, and others. New York: [R. Tyrell] for S. King, 1825. [653]

16mo, 64 leaves, A-D¹⁶, engraved frontispiece and plates colored by hand, advertisements at the end.

Original half binding.

Contains fifteen stories and dialogues. The printer's imprint is on the back of the title.

THE COMIC ADVENTURES OF OLD MOTHER HUBBARD AND HER DOG. Illustrated with Fifteen elegant Copperplate Engravings. By S. M. C. Philadelphia: Morgan & Yeager, n. d. [c. 1825.] [654]

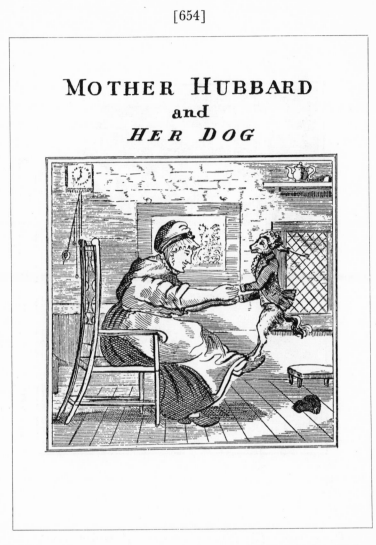

MOTHER HUBBARD
and
HER DOG

Page from "The Comic Adventures of Old Mother Hubbard and Her Dog"

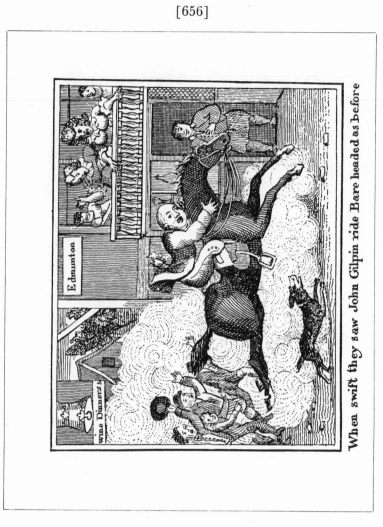

*Page from "The Humorous Story of Mrs. Gilpin's
Return from Edmonton"*

Sq. octavo, 8 leaves, engraved throughout and printed on one side only, one verse of text and an illustration (colored) on each leaf, caption title and frontispiece on the first leaf.

Original wrappers, cover-title, Morgan & Yeager's advertisement on the back. The price at the foot of the front cover is 37 *cents coloured*, 25 *cents plain*.

Not in Weiss: *William Charles*. The title is included in Mr. Weiss's list of *Children's Books Published by Morgan and Yeager*, made up mainly from the lists advertised on the back covers of *The Peacock 'At Home': or Grand Assemblage of Birds*, and other works.

CONTINUATION OF OLD DAME TRUDGE AND HER PARROT. Illustrated with Whimsical Engravings.

> Now old Goody Trudge with her Parrot began
> To lay down a simple, but excellent plan,
> By which they might still be together:
> "Whene'er," said the dame, "I on visiting go,
> "Perch'd safe on my shoulder, my Poll shall go too,
> "Provided it be not bad weather."

Philadelphia: Morgan & Yeager, n. d. [c. 1825.] [655]

Sq. octavo, 8 leaves, engraved throughout, and printed on one side only, an illustration (colored) and a 6 line stanza on each leaf.

Original wrappers, cover-title, advertisement on the back wrapper.

Weiss: *William Charles*, page 7.

The poem in this book is not *The Continuation of Old Dame Trudge*, but *The Adventures of Old Dame Trudge*, see no. 547, and the first verse of this poem is printed on the cover-title. The mixed title on the wrapper, the only place where the title appears, would prove that the error must have been made at the time of printing. For a copy of *The Continuation of Old Dame Trudge* with the genuine text of that poem see no. 455.

[COWPER, WILLIAM.] The Humorous Story of Mrs. Gilpin's Return from Edmonton. Being the Sequel to Johnny Gilpin. Illustrated with Humorous Engravings, on Copperplate. Philadelphia: Printed and sold Wholesale, by Morgan and Sons, n. d. [c. 1825.] [656]

Sq. octavo, 8 leaves of text, 6 plates (colored).

Original Morgan & Yeager wrappers, the title on the front, with Morgan & Yeager's imprint, and their advertisement on the back. The covers are pasted on to covers of the *Drawing Books* of William Charles as linings. The title-page has the imprint of Morgan and Sons.

This issue not in Weiss: *William Charles*.

The price at the foot of the title-page is *plain*, 18¾ *cents—coloured* 25 *cents*, on the wrapper 25 *cents coloured*, 18 *cents plain*.

For the edition of William Charles, see no. 518.

Early American Children's Books

THE DISASTROUS EVENTS WHICH ATTENDED JOE DOBSON. Illustrated with Appropriate Copperplate Engravings.

> Whilst they partook their dainty meal,
> Joe sullenly confess'd,
> He was convinc'd that wives could do
> The household business best.

Part Second. Philadelphia: Morgan & Yeager, n. d. [c. 1825.] [657]

Sq. octavo, 8 leaves, engraved throughout and printed on one side only, 4 lines of verse and an illustration (colored) on each leaf.

Original wrappers, cover-title; advertisement on the back wrapper; uncut, and partly unopened.

Weiss: *William Charles,* page 9, lists this title thus: *Joe Dobson. Advertised on back cover-page of The History of Little Fanny published by Mary Charles in* 1821.

It is not included in his list of *Children's Books published by Morgan and Yeager.*

This book has no title-page, the title appearing on the wrapper only. The first leaf has the caption *A Continuation of Joe Dobson;* below which the verse

> He went to hang the cloaths to dry,
> It was a lovely day,
> But oh, alas! a Magpie came,
> And stole his Wig away.

Beneath the verse is an illustration of this incident.

The title of the English edition of this book, which contained both parts, published by J. Harris in 1807, was *Cobler! stick to your last; or, The Adventures of Joe Dobson, exhibited in sixteen Elegant Copper-Plate Engravings. by B. A. T.*

DORSET, CATHARINE ANN. The Peacock "At Home:" or Grand Assemblage of Birds. Written by Roscoe. Illustrated with elegant engravings. Philadelphia: Published and sold Wholesale by Wm. Charles, and may be had of all the Booksellers. 1814. W. M'Culloch, Printer. Philadelphia: Morgan & Yeager, n. d. [c. 1825.] [658]

The edition of 1814 of William Charles, put out by Morgan & Yeager probably about 1825. Weiss: *William Charles,* page 10.

EDWIN AND HENRY; or, Holiday Times: containing original, moral, and instructive Tales, for the improvement of youth. New Haven: Sidney's Press for J. Babcock & Son and S. Babcock & Co. Charleston: 1825. [659]

16mo, 16 leaves, without signatures, first leaf pasted down; woodcut frontispiece, woodcuts in the text.

Original tan wrappers, upper with half-title, the date and a woodcut, publishers' advertisement on the lower.

Publishers' advertisement of Books for Children on the back of the title.

[660]

FRONTISPIECE.

A CATARACT

Is a high fall of water in a river, which may
be heard at the distance of several miles; as
the Falls of Niagara, in the United States: the
noise is sometimes heard at York in Upper Canada, a distance of 50 miles: the most sublime
scene is presented to the observer, when he
views the Cataract from below; it is considered
one of the greatest natural curiosities in the World.

Page from "The Elements of Geography Made Easy"

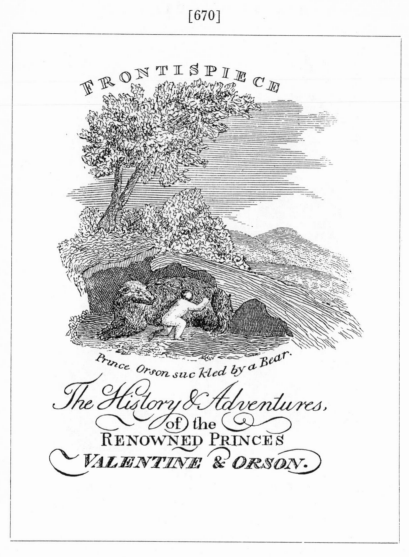

FRONTISPIECE

Prince Orson suckled by a Bear.

The History & Adventures,
of the
RENOWNED PRINCES
VALENTINE & ORSON.

Page from "The History & Adventures
of Valentine & Orson"

Early American Children's Books

THE ELEMENTS OF GEOGRAPHY MADE EASY. Embellished with neat coloured Copperplate Engravings. Designed to render a General Knowledge of the Elements of Geography and Maps, so plain and easy, as to come witin (*sic*) the capacity of our most Juvenile Readers. Philadelphia: Published by Morgan & Yeager, n. d. [c. 1825.]   [660]

Duodecimo, 12 leaves, engraved throughout and printed on one side only; an illustration and text on each leaf, the illustrations colored.

Original wrappers, cover-title, publishers' advertisement on the back.
Not in Weiss: *William Charles.* Not included in Mr. Weiss's list of Children's Books published by Morgan and Yeager.
The book appears to be of English origin, but has been considerably Americanized for the benefit of young American readers. Some of the descriptions relate entirely to England; A Coast or Shore, for example, and A Cliff, the examples given of the latter being *the Cliffs of Flamborough, in Yorkshire; Margate, Ramsgate, and Dover, in Kent; &c.* The examples of Islands begin with Great Britain and Ireland (which form the subject of the illustration) and end with *Nantucket and long Island on the Coast of the United States of North America.*
Some of the examples have been almost completely Americanized: A Bay *is a great inlet of land; as the Bay of Biscay, on the Western coast of France. A Bay is likewise a station or road for ships to anchor in; as the Chesapeak and Delaware Bay; the Chesapeak is 200 miles in length, and affords many commodious harbors...*

[ENGLISH, CLARA.] The Affecting History of the Children in the Wood.
        He bargain'd with two ruffians rude,
            Who were of furious mood,
        That they should take these children young,
            And slay them in a wood.
Troy: Printed and published by J. Disturnell, 1825.   [661]

Duodecimo, 18 leaves, A-C⁶, first and last pasted down to cover, woodcut frontispiece, woodcut on the title, and illustrations in the text.

Original wrappers, title with woodcut on the front, the publisher's advertisement, dated from Troy, September, 1825, on the back.
The text, which is in prose and verse, is an abridgment of the version arranged by Clara English, see no. 330, without the interpolated stories (The Boy and the Robin, The Little Girl and the Eagle, etc.). At the end is the ballad beginning *Now, ponder well you parents dear.*

THE ENTERTAINING & INTERESTING STORY, of Alibaba the Wood Cutter with the Death of the Forty Thieves, and the Overthrow of their Protector Orcobrand, the Evil Genius of the Forest. Philadelphia: Published by Morgan & Yeager, n. d. [c. 1825.]   [662]

Early American Children's Books

Sq. octavo, 12 leaves, engraved throughout and printed on one side only; the first leaf with the frontispiece, the second leaf with the title; the remaining ten leaves have each an illustration (colored) with a headline above, and a 6 line stanza of verse below.

Original wrappers, the upper with the title, the lower with the publishers' advertisement. The title on the wrapper reads: *The Forty Thieves, and the Overthrow of their Protector, Orcobrand, the Evil Genius of the Forest. Illustrated With Copperplate Engravings. Philadelphia: Published by Morgan & Yeager, at their Juvenile Bookstore. Price* 31 *cents coloured,* 18 *cents plain.*

This issue not in Weiss: *William Charles,* and not included in his list of *Children's Books published by Morgan and Yeager.*

Another copy has the covers of Morgan & Sons.

The title on the front wrapper and the advertisement on the back are differently set up, and the name Morgan & Yeager is replaced by that of Morgan & Sons in both places where it occurs.

Weiss: *William Charles,* page 8, cites this issue.

THE ENTERTAINING HISTORY OF JOBSON & NELL. Illustrated with Humorous Engravings.

> Near the sign of the Bell
> Liv'd Jobson and Nell,
> And cobbling of shoes was his trade;
> They agreed very well,
> The neighbours did tell,
> For he was a funny old blade.

Philadelphia: Published by Morgan & Yeager, n. d. [c. 1825.]   [663]

Duodecimo, 12 leaves, engraved throughout and printed on one side only, an illustration (colored) and a 6 line stanza of verse on each leaf.

Original wrappers, cover-title, advertisements on the back.
Weiss: *William Charles,* page 7.

There is no title-page, the title appearing on the wrapper only, and a caption title on the first leaf of the text. Mr. Weiss describes the New York Public Library copy as lacking the title-page, but there seems to be no doubt that the present copy was issued without a title-page.

THE GLASS OF WHISKEY. Philadelphia: American Sunday-School Union, n. d. [c. 1825.]   [664]

4 leaves, woodcut of grapes on title and 4 woodcuts in text.

Original yellow wrappers, title repeated on upper cover with the grapes printed the reverse way up, a woodcut of a watch on the lower.
Measures 2¾ by 1¾ inches.

There is a bottle. It has something in it which is called whiskey. Little reader, I hope you will never taste any as long as you live. It is a poison. So is brandy, so is rum, so is gin,

[664]

THE

GLASS OF WHISKEY.

PHILADELPHIA:
AMERICAN SUNDAY-SCHOOL UNION,
No. 146 Chestnut Street.

Title-page from
"The Glass of Whiskey"

[743]

THE

PENNY PRIMER.

" I've read my pretity book all through,
How much of your's, dear Jane, have you?
A penny primer I have got,
At Mahlon Day's, it too was bought "

NEW-YORK:
Printed and Sold by Mahlon Day
At the New Juvenile Book-store
No. 374, Pearl-street.

Title-page from
"The Penny Primer"

[750]

THE
STRAY
LAMB.

In New-York, that famous city,
Many books like this are sold,
And for such 'twould be a pity,
One cent only to withhold.

NEW-YORK:
Printed and sold by Mahlon Day,
At the New Juvenile Book-store,
No. 376, Pearl-street.

Title-page from
"The Stray Lamb"

[746]

A
PLEASING TOY
FOR
GIRL OR BOY.

I'm for the child,
Who is active in play,
And thorough at work;
That's the best way.

NEW-YORK:
Printed and sold by Mahlon Day,
At the New Juvenile Book-store,
No. 376, Pearl street.

Title-page from
"A Pleasing Toy for Girl or Boy"

THE INFANT'S GRAMMAR 6

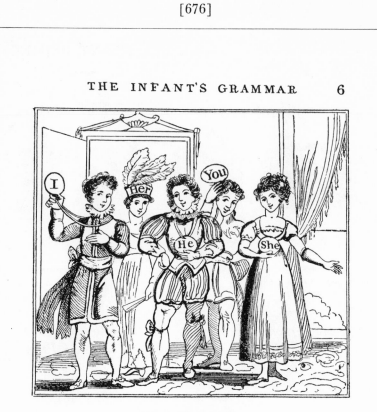

THE PRONOUNS.

At this moment a bustle was heard at the door
From a Party of PRONOUNS, who came by the score.
And what do you think?   Why I vow and declare
THEY would pass for the Nouns who already were there.
And THEIR boldness was such, as I live IT is true,
ONE declar'd HE was I, and ONE call'd HIMSELF YOU.
THIS, THAT, and the OTHER, THEY claim'd as THEIR own,
But WHO THEY are really, will shortly be known.

Page from "The Infant's Grammar"

and many other drinks. They are called strong drink. They are so strong that they knock people down, and kill them. . . . For the purposes of propaganda it seems unfortunate to have admitted the taste was so good. Hugh was given something to drink as a small child. *When Hugh got bigger, he remembered that the taste was pleasant, and he wanted some more,* and Hugh eventually became a confirmed drunkard. Another little boy *went to a closet where there was a jug of rum. He tasted it. He liked it. He tasted a little more. Then he drank a good deal. At last he became drunk, and fell over, and lay there till he died. He was found dead by the jug of rum.* We rejoice to learn that he would not be kept out of Heaven, however, for *he did not know what he did,* unlike poor Hugh. *O, how shall I keep from being a drunkard? I will tell you, Never drink a drop of any thing that makes people drunk.*

GRAPHICAL REPRESENTATION of the Coronation Regalia of the Kings of England; with the degrees and Costume of different Ranks. Illustrated with twelve Copperplate Engravings. Philadelphia: Published by Morgan and Yeager, n. d. [c. 1825.]   [665]

Duodecimo, 12 leaves, engraved throughout, and printed on one side only, full-page frontispiece on the first leaf, the other leaves each with an illustration, usually in two compartments representing two ranks or dignitaries, with descriptive text beneath, the illustrations all finely colored.

Original wrappers, cover-title, publishers' advertisement on the back.
Not in Weiss: *William Charles.* Not in Mr. Weiss's list of Children's Books published by Morgan and Yeager.
There is no title-page, the title appearing on the wrapper only.
This work was probably inspired by the *Book of Ranks and Dignitaries* of Charles Lamb, first published in 1805.

THE HISTORY AND ADVENTURES OF LITTLE ELIZA, A Companion to Little William. Illustrated with a Series of Elegant Figures. . . Philadelphia: Published and Sold Wholesale by William Charles, and may be had of all the Booksellers. J. Bioren, Printer. 1815. Philadelphia: Morgan & Yeager, n. d. [c. 1825.]   [666]

Duodecimo, 4 leaves of text, in verse, 8 full-page colored plates.

Original wrappers, title and imprint of Morgan & Yeager on the front, and their advertisement on the back.
Weiss: *William Charles,* page 8.
The edition of William Charles of 1815, see no. 522, put out by Morgan & Yeager without date, but probably about 1825.

THE HISTORY AND ADVENTURES OF LITTLE HENRY, a companion to Little Fanny, exemplified in a series of figures, Engraved on Copperplate. Philadelphia: Published by Morgan & Yeager, 1825.   [667]

Sq. octavo, 8 leaves of text, 7 engraved plates, colored.

Original wrappers, title on the front cover, advertisement on the back.
Weiss: *William Charles*, page 8.
From the English edition published in 1810 by S. and J. Fuller, and with the same illustrations, which, however, in the English edition were cut-out figures with movable parts.

In the English editions of these books, Little Eliza and not Little Henry, was the companion to Little Fanny. The stories of Little Henry and Little Fanny have so many points in common, that it seems quite appropriate that they should be companions.

Little Henry was stolen by a gipsy, and after being a beggar, then a sweep, an occupation in which he

> In Portman Square a deal of fame acquires,
> For Mistress Montague the youth admires,

a drummer boy, a cabin boy, etc., he eventually reached a high position in the navy,

> Thus loading, by achievements brave and bold,
> His brows with laurel, and his purse with gold.

Unlike Little Fanny's mother, the parents of Little Henry were ignorant of his whereabouts during all these adventures, and *by day they weep, in sighs they pass the night*, until

> At last dame Fortune on his parents smiles,
> Who after various cares and various toils,
> Find out the ship which Henry's talents grace,
> And once more hold him fast in their embrace.

The title on the wrapper varies from that on the title-page; it is undated, and quotes the first verse of the text.

THE HISTORY AND ADVENTURES OF LITTLE WILLIAM, a companion to Little Eliza; Illustrated with a series of Elegant Figures . . . Philadelphia: Published and sold Wholesale, by Morgan and Sons, n.d. [c.1825.] [668]

Duodecimo, 4 leaves of text, 8 full-page plates, colored.

Original wrappers, title on the front cover, differing from that on the title-page. The first verse of the text quoted on the title-page is replaced by the last verse, and the imprint is that of Morgan & Yeager, whose advertisement is on the back.
This issue not in Weiss: *William Charles*.
For other editions see no. 523, and the following item.

THE HISTORY AND ADVENTURES OF LITTLE WILLIAM, a Companion to Little Eliza . . . Philadelphia: Printed and Sold Wholesale by William Charles, and may be had of all the Booksellers. J. Bioren, Printer, 1815. Morgan & Yeager, n. d. [c. 1825.] [669]

This is the edition printed for William Charles in 1815, with plain plates, see no. 523, reissued with fresh covers by Morgan & Yeager about 1825. The covers are the same as those of the previous item.
This issue not in Weiss: *William Charles*.

Early American Children's Books

THE HISTORY AND ADVENTURES OF VALENTINE & ORSON. Illustrated with twelve Copperplate Engravings.

> Pepin of France his sister gave
> To Greece's Emperor great and brave;
> Whose breast by jealousy inflamed,
> His guiltless Queen disgraced and shamed.
> She from his palace turned astray
> To seek to France her lonely way.

Philadelphia: Published by Morgan & Yeager, n. d. [c. 1825.]   [670]

Duodecimo, 12 leaves, engraved throughout and printed on one side only; the frontispiece and half title on the first leaf, text with a large illustration and a headline on each of the eleven leaves, the illustrations colored.

Original wrappers, cover-title, advertisements on the back. The price is 31 *cents coloured*, 18 *cents plain*.
Weiss: *William Charles*, page 8.
A poetical version of this famous romance. The first stanza is quoted on the cover-title.

THE HISTORY OF BIRDS. New Haven: Sidney's Press, [for J. Babcock & Son] 1825.   [671]

Duodecimo, 12 leaves, woodcut frontispiece, woodcut of a peacock on the title and illustrations in the text, first and last leaves pasted down to covers.

Original yellow wrappers, title, with imprint dated 1825, and a wood engraving on the upper; large wood engraving on the lower.
The date in the imprint on the title-page is 1824; the publishers' advertisement is on the back of the title.
The work contains a descriptive account of nine birds, with illustrations.

THE HISTORY OF LITTLE FANNY, exemplified in a series of figures, Engraved on Copperplate. Second Edition. Philadelphia: Published by Morgan & Yeager, 1825.   [672]

Duodecimo, 8 leaves of text in verse, 7 engraved plates, colored.

Original wrappers; title on the front cover, with the words *Second Edition*, but with the imprint of Mary Charles dated 1821, and a list of books which *Mary Charles has recently publihed* (sic) on the back.
This issue not in Weiss: *William Charles*.
The illustrations are the same as in the London edition published by S. and J. Fuller, fourth edition, 1810, except that in the English edition the figures were cut out, and had movable parts.
Whatever the author's intention may have been in this story, the results could hardly fail to be disastrous, both on the mind of the small reader, and on her relations with her

mother. Little Fanny, who is of an age to play with dolls, is stolen from her nurse for her fine clothes, when out against her mother's wishes, and becomes *a dirty beggar girl*. This state apparently lasted for some time, and *with vice she dwelt, which doubled all her pain*. Eventually Fanny is rescued and becomes an errand girl, crying *fish to sell*. In the course of time she leaves the fish business for milk and eggs, and thinking of home and her mother *down her cheeks descends the trembling tear*. After all this misery we are amazed to read that

> Had she but known her mother's watchful eye
> Follow'd her close, and was for ever nigh,
> Longing once more her daughter to embrace,
> Hang on her neck, and kiss her smiling face,
> Whilst prudence still withheld maternal love,
> Till longer trial Fanny's virtue prove.

Eventually Fanny is restored to the bosom of her family by being sent to deliver butter at her mother's house.

Another copy has a different issue of the wrappers, with the imprint of Morgan & Sons, and their advertisement on the back.

These wrappers have not the words *Second Edition* as the Mary Charles wrappers in the previous item, but in their place is printed the moral of the story:

> "Turn not away, attend to pity's call;
> "But learn from this the evils that befall
> "Those who their mothers learn to disobey,
> "And venture, 'gainst her will, from home to stray."

The book itself is the same issue as the previous item.
Weiss: *William Charles*, page 8.

HISTORY OF THE BIBLE. Sandy-Hill, N. Y.: Published by Hart & Hare, & J. Wright, 1825. [673]

128 leaves, A-Q⁸, woodcut frontispiece and several woodcut illustrations.

Original sheep, gilt.
A *Thumb Bible* measuring 2 by 1$\frac{5}{8}$ inches.
Another edition of no. 637 with the same woodcuts.

HORWOOD, CAROLINE. The Deserted Boy; or, Cruel Parents. A Tale of Truth. Calculated to promote benevolence in children. Illustrated with Engravings. By Miss Horwood. Philadelphia: Published and sold by Morgan and Yeager, n. d. [c. 1825.] [674]

Sq. duodecimo, 6 leaves of text in verse, 4 full-page colored plates including the frontispiece.

Original wrappers; title on the front: *The Deserted Boy; or, Cruel Parents. A Moral Tale. Embellished with Beautiful Engravings. By Miss Horwood. Philadelphia: Published and sold by Morgan & Yeager. Price plain*, 12½ *cts.—coloured*, 18¾ *cts;* advertisement on the back. The covers are pasted on to the wrappers of William Charles's Drawing Book as linings. Not in Weiss: *William Charles*. This title, not seen, is included in Mr. Weiss's List of Children's Books published by Morgan and Yeager.

Early American Children's Books

HORWOOD, CAROLINE. Little Emma and her Father. A lesson for proud children. Written by Miss Horwood. Philadelphia: Published by Morgan & Yeager, n.d. [c. 1825.]   [675]

Sq. octavo, 8 leaves of text, 4 plates, including the frontispiece, all tinted in colors; and another copy, with plain plates.

Original wrappers, title on the front: *Little Emma and Her Father. Or, the Effects of Pride*, and the imprint; advertisement on the back.

Weiss: *William Charles*, page 9 (NYPL. copy with colored plates).

Little Emma's father lost all his money, and Emma had then to work for her bread, a just retribution for her treatment of her father's servants during the days of his affluence, for she had treated them *with disdain*, ignoring her father's teaching that it was God who made them poor, and forced to work for bread.

Emma became a milk maid, but eventually joined a gypsy band, and after much ill treatment, was left to a repentant death:

> And soon young Emma on the ground,
>   All cold and stiffen'd lay;
> But may the awful words she spake,
>   On that her dying day,
>
> A warning prove to ev'ry child,
>   Who is too proud to mind
> The counsels of their eldest friends,
>   And of their parents kind.

THE INFANT'S GRAMMAR. Baltimore: Published by F. Lucas, Jr., n.d. [c. 1825.]   [676]

Duodecimo, 13 leaves, first leaf pasted down inside front cover, engraved throughout, title-page with large colored vignette, colored illustrations at the head of each page, leaves printed on one side only.

Original wrappers, upper with: *The Infant's Grammar, or a Pic-Nic Party of the Parts of Speech*, with imprint, within ornamental border, lower with advertisement.

On the first leaf is the explanatory Introduction, in verse, beginning:

> One day, I am told, and, as it was cold,
>   I suppose it occurr'd in cold weather,
> The NINE PARTS OF SPEECH, having no one to teach,
>   Resolv'd on a PIC-NIC together.

This is followed by the title with a colored plate representing the Picnic. Each of the eleven succeeding leaves deals with a personified part of speech in verse, with an illustration at the head of each one.

JUVENILE LIBRARY, containing the Adventures of Valentine and Orson. Ali Baba, or The Forty Thieves. Bruce's Travels in Abyssinia, and Mother Bunch's Fairy Tales. New York: Published by S. King, 1825.   [677]

16mo, 4 parts in 1, 72 leaves, A-E⁴, A-C⁴, D² (D₂ a blank), A², B-E⁴, A-E⁴, 3 engraved frontispieces, in colors.

Original half binding.

Each part with separate title-page, signatures, and pagination; a leaf of advertisement at the end of Bruce's Travels.

The first two stories have *Prefatory Remarks* at the beginning, and are profusely annotated with footnotes throughout. In the story of Ali Baba the morals of the hero occasionally place the annotator in a difficult position, from which he has to extricate himself as best he may: *The only excuse we can make for Ali Baba's taking what did not belong to him is, that it was the property of robbers who had taken it from the owners by force; his conduct however cannot be fully justified.* The pouring of boiling oil into the jars by Morgiana is considered completely justifiable: *To kill another in self-defence is lawful.*

JUVENILE PASTIMES or Sports for the Four Seasons. Part II. Embellished with twenty-eight neat copper-plate engravings. Philadelphia: Morgan & Yeager. [c. 1825.] [678]

Sq. octavo, 8 leaves, printed on one side only, text and illustrations engraved throughout, illustrations in colors.

Original wrappers, cover-title, lower cover with advertisement. For part I, see no. 775.

Not in Weiss: *William Charles.* Not included in Mr. Weiss's list of Children's Books published by Morgan and Yeager.

There is no title-page, the title appearing on the wrapper only. This part contains descriptions in verse, each accompanied by a charming illustration in colors, of the various pastimes or sports for Autumn and Winter. We have not seen a copy of the English edition, but some adjustment must have been made, as in the last picture

> With colours flying, drum and fife,
> They mimic Soldiers to the life,

the flying colors are the Stars and Stripes.

LIGHTS OF EDUCATION, or, Mr. Hope and his family: A narrative for young persons. By a Lady. Baltimore: J. Robinson for E. J. Coale, 1825. [679]

Duodecimo, 88 leaves, (A)², B-P⁶, Q², engraved frontispiece.

Original half binding.

Mr. Hope, a gentleman of fortune of Orange County, in the State of New York, was the father of five children, and tells them each stories of a moral or instructive nature.

THE LITTLE TRAVELLER; or, a sketch of the Various Nations of the World; representing The Costume, and describing the Manners and Peculiarities of the Inhabitants. Embellished with fifteen beautifully-coloured engravings. By J. Steerwell, Jun. R. N. Baltimore: Published by J.S.Horton. Sold by W. R. Lucas & R. N. Wight, n.d.[c. 1825.] [680]

16mo, 16 leaves without signatures, full-page frontispiece, and 14 illustrations in the text, all in colors.

Original wrappers, title on the front cover, headed: No.10. Child's Library; a list of the publications in the Child's Library on the back.

The book opens with an account, accompanied by an illustration, of the party of young relatives to whom James Steerwell is about to describe his travels. The nations described and illustrated are Laplanders, Highlanders, Dutch, Greeks, Turks, Tartars, Persians, Chinese, East Indians, Negroes, American Indians, Otaheitians and Sandwich Islanders.

An edition of this work was published in London by A. K. Newman and Co., without date (c. 1820).

A MEMOIR OF THOMAS HAMITAH PATOO, a native of The Marquesas Islands; who died June 19, 1823, while a member of the Foreign Mission School, in Cornwall, Conn. Andover: Published by the American Tract Society, 1825. [681]

Duodecimo, 24 leaves, 1-2¹², woodcut bust portrait as frontispiece, signed *H. Page, del. et sc.* on the block, woodcut illustrations.

Original wrappers, upper with title within ornamental woodcut border, lower with advertisement of children's books published by the American Tract Society, of which this is no. 19.

The imprint on the title has no date, the date being on the front wrapper.

At the end are five pages of Hymns.

MEMOIRS OF ELIZA THORNTON; containing a narrative of her life and happy death. The Pious Sisters, An interesting Sabbath School Anecdote. Concord, N. H. Published by Jacob B. Moore, 1825. [682]

Duodecimo, 12 leaves, a frequently used woodcut of an open Bible on the title.

Original wrappers, title (imprint dated 1825) and a woodcut of a cat in an oval compartment on the upper, advertisement on the lower.

The imprint on the title-page is dated 1824.

The story of Eliza Thornton is a funeral elegy after the manner of Hannah Hill junʳ., Janeway's *Token*, and similar works. Eliza died at the age of twelve on Tuesday, March 25, 1817. The woodcut at the end of the story is a representation of her funeral.

The *pious sisters* were natives of Philadelphia, and at the time of writing the story *These young females are still living, and still as much engaged in the cause of Christ as ever.*

At the end are hymns (by Dr.Watts) with a woodcut tailpiece of a girl seated at a spinet, which will be found also in the *New England Primer* published by Charles Wells at Amherst in 1823, no. 629.

Early American Children's Books

[MURRAY, HANNAH, AND MARY MURRAY.] The American Toilet. New York: Imbert's Lithographic Office, n. d. [c. 1825.] [683]

16mo, 20 leaves, lithographed throughout and printed on one side only.

Wrappers.

Contains illustrations of nineteen articles of the toilet, each with a flap concealing the name of a virtue, a headline above, and a stanza of explanatory verse beneath.

The first article is *The Enchanting Mirror*, the mirror being raised from the frame reveals the word *Humility*, the accompanying verse beginning: *This curious Glass will bring your faults to light.* The second article is *A Wash to Smooth Wrinkles*, contained in a jar, the lid of which conceals the word *Contentment*, with the lines below:

> A daily portion of this Essence use,
> T'will smooth the brow and tranquil Joy infuse.

The original London edition from which this book was copied was entitled *The Toilet*, and was first printed in 1821.

THE NEW-ENGLAND PRIMER, improved For the more easy attaining the true Reading of English. To which is added The Assembly of Divines' Catechism. Rochester, N. Y.: E. Peck, 1825. [684]

Duodecimo, 36 leaves, A-C¹², first and last leaves pasted down to cover, woodcuts.

Original tan wrappers, title on upper, advertisement on lower.
Heartman 278 locates this copy only.
This edition contains a rhymed alphabet beginning:

> A was an Angler, and fish'd with a hook,
> B was a Blockhead, and ne'er learnt his book.

PICTURE OF NEW-YORK. New York: Printed and sold by Mahlon Day, No. 372, Pearl-street, 1825. [685]

Sm. octavo, 8 leaves, woodcut on the title, woodcut frontispiece, cuts in the text.

Original wrappers, title on the front wrapper as on the title-page with the addition of the lines:

> Here you have a picture small,
> Of New-York, far renown'd;
> But recollect, when it you've read,
> Where others can be found.

Mahlon Day's advertisement on the back wrapper.

The publisher of this book has contrived to introduce his advertisement into the text in the most approved Newbery style. After describing the shipping of New York, the cartage of the merchandise brought by the ships is explained, *some they carry to the splendid stores in Pearl-street . . . Here the merchants from all parts of the United States, select such articles as they may want . . . some call at* DAY's JUVENILE BOOK-STORE, *for little books for little folks, among which is this little volume, also the Field Daisy, Little Stories, New-York Cries in Rhyme, Youthful Sports, Two Lambs, Life of Joseph, Happy Waterman, all with pretty*

Early American Children's Books

pictures in them, and a long list of others, too tedious to mention. This passage is accompanied by a woodcut of *Mahlon Day's Juvenile Book Store,* [no.] 372 [Pearl Street]. The cut on page 10 is signed on the block *Day & Turner, Print.*

THE PILGRIMS, or First Settlers of New England. Baltimore: Published by F. Lucas, Jr. Philadelphia: Ash & Mason, 1825. [686]

Duodecimo, 14 leaves, engraved throughout and printed on one side only, first and last leaves pasted down to covers, an illustration with a headline, and 2 stanzas of descriptive verse on each leaf. This copy lacks 2 leaves, having 12 only.

Original wrappers, title on the upper, with a woodcut of Liberty in a circular compartment, and the imprint of J. Murphy.

The scenes described are Bishops and Pilgrim's (*sic*); Leaving England; Landing at Plymouth; Clearing the Forest; The Pilgrims Home; Indian and Looking Glass:

> And scared would see his form and air,
>   In looking glass reflected;
> Then search behind it, as if there
>   Himself might be detected.

Indian War; Drunken Indians; Coming of Friends; Progress of Improvement; Anniversary of Landing.

The Pilgrims can be distinguished throughout in the illustrations, even during their fights with the Indians, by the high Puritan hats which they unfailingly wear.

The imprint on the title-page is not dated; the engraved symbolical vignette on that page contains an open Bible, on a leaf of which is *Entered according to Act of Congress by F. Lucas Jʳ. of the State of Maryland, Octʳ. 31st. 1825.* John Murphy, whose imprint appears on the wrappers, acquired the business of F. Lucas in 1837, and it is to be presumed put out the remainder about that year, with his own wrappers.

THE PLEASING TOY. Wendell, Mass.: J. Metcalf, 1825. [687]

Eight leaves, woodcut on the title, and cuts in the text.

A toy book measuring 3¼ by 2 inches, unbound as issued.

The book contains an incomplete alphabet, illustrated with woodcuts and descriptive verse, the greater number of which have previously appeared in other books. The illustration for *Youth* represents a boy flying a kite. The verse for *Tree* still shows English influence, or the influence of the New England Primer, for it is the royal oak, and not just a plain oak, which is described. Alphabets are on the back of the title.

1826

EDGEWORTH, MARIA. Moral Tales for Young People. By Maria Edgeworth, Author of the Parent's Assistant, Tales of Fashionable Life, &c. In three volumes. Vol. I. New York: J. C. Totten, for W. B. Gilley, 1826. [688]

Duodecimo, 114 leaves, 2 leaves without signatures, A-S⁶, T⁴ (last a blank), woodcut frontispiece and title with woodcut vignette.

Original half binding.

The imprint on the printed title bears the date 1819, that on the woodcut title-page 1826. Contains Forester, and The Prussian Vase, and a preface by Richard Lovell Edgeworth, the author's father. The woodcut illustrations are by Anderson.

THE NEW-YORK CRIES, in rhyme. New York: Mahlon Day, No. 376, Pearl-street, 1826. [689]

Duodecimo, 12 leaves, woodcut vignette of a sailing-ship on the title, and a woodcut illustration at the head of each page of text.

Green half morocco.

These New York Cries are entirely different from the Cries of New York published by Samuel Wood in 1814, no. 485. The set contains nineteen cries. Each cry has a woodcut illustration in a frame, and is amplified by four lines of verse, and a long footnote in prose, containing geographical and historical information, and in some cases moral precept. On the verso of the first leaf (recto blank) is a description of New York.

The Cry of *Sand O!* will illustrate the quality of the book:

SAND O!
"S-A-N-D! Here's your nice white S-A-N-D!"
Sand, O! white Sand, O!
Buy Sand for your floor;
For so cleanly it looks
When strew'd at your door.

This Sand is brought from the seashore in vessels, principally from Rockaway Beach, Long Island... Almost every little girl or boy knows that it is put on newly scrubbed floors, to preserve them clean and pleasant.

But since people have become rich, and swayed by the vain fashions of the world, by carpeting the floors of their houses, there does not appear to be so much use for Sand, as in the days of our worthy ancestors.

Mahlon Day, the publisher, must have removed from no. 372 Pearl Street to no. 376 in the same street in 1825 or 1826. Books bearing the former address are dated 1825, and on the present work, dated 1826, the address is 376 Pearl Street. He moved again to no. 374 Pearl Street in 1833.

TRENCK, FREDERICK, BARON. The Life, Adventures & Uncommon Escapes of Frederick, Baron Trenck, the Prussian: detailing, his entrance into the Prussian army; reception by the King; wonderful escapes from confinement; and imprisonment in a dungeon, loaded with 68 pounds of iron chain; With only Bread and Water for his Support! The many Years of Suffering he passed in this horrid Cell; his repeated attempts to escape, till at last he recovers his liberty. Written by himself. New York: Samuel Forbes, 1826. [690]

Duodecimo, 12 leaves, A-B⁶.

Boards. A chapbook version.

Early American Children's Books

THE YOUTH'S FRIEND; and Scholar's Magazine, nos. 30, 33, 36. Philadelphia: American Sunday-School Union, 1826. [691]

Octavo, woodcuts in text. 3 numbers, published respectively in June, September and December, 1826.

Original wrappers with cover-title and advertisements, uncut. On the title it is stated that the magazine is published monthly by the American Sunday School Union, No. 13 North Fourth Street, and that the price is Twenty Five cents a year, *when paid in advance and called for at the Depository.*

1827

BOLLES, WILLIAM. A spelling book: containing exercises in Orthography, Pronunciation, and Reading. By William Bolles. Second edition. New-London: S. Green for William Bolles, 1827. [692]

Duodecimo, 78 leaves, (1)-(13)^6, woodcuts.

Original half binding.
Contains alphabets, a syllabary, passages for reading, lists of homonyms, vocabularies, &c. The author states in his preface, dated from New-London, October, 1826, that *the plan of the work, it is believed, is entirely new.*

THE CHILD'S PRAYER BOOK. Boston: Nathan Hale, 1827. [693]

Duodecimo, 16 leaves, 1^6, 2^6, 3^4.

Original marbled wrappers.
On the back of the title is the advertisement, announcing that *The following compilation is a sequel to the Young Child's Prayer Book. It is intended to be put into the hands of children, from ten to twelve years old.*
On the flyleaf is the inscription *James Lawrence. April 7th,* 1831. *from the Reverend J. G. Palfrey.*
For the Young Child's Prayer Book, see no. 650.

ELLIOTT, MARY. The Two Edwards; or, Pride and Prejudice Unmasked. By Mary Elliott. Philadelphia: Thomas T. Ash, 1827. [694]

Duodecimo, 90 leaves, A-P^6, engraved frontispiece.

Original half binding.
First published by William Darton in London, 1823. The frontispiece in this edition is the same as that in the London edition. Inserted in this copy is an engraved presentation leaf.

HISTORY OF THE BIBLE. Hartford: Published by Julius Gilman, 1827.

89 leaves, 1-11^8, 12^1, woodcut frontispiece and woodcut illustrations. [695]

Cloth. A *Thumb Bible* measuring 1$\frac{1}{8}$ by 1$\frac{1}{2}$ inches.
Another edition of no. 433 with the cuts re-engraved.

Early American Children's Books

MALLÈS DE BEAULIEU. The Modern Crusoe. A Narrative of the Life and Adventures of a French Cabin Boy, who was shipwrecked on an Uninhabited Island. Translated from the French of Mad. Malle de Beaulieu. First American Edition. Boston: James Loring, 1827. [696]

Duodecimo, 110 leaves, A², B-T⁶, woodcut frontispiece.

Original half binding, title repeated on the upper cover.

A translation of *Le Robinson de Douze Ans*, one of the most popular of the stories inspired by Robinson Crusoe, and the most famous of the juvenile works of its author, a French writer of children's tales. Madame Mallès de Beaulieu died at Nontron (Dordogne) in 1825.

The translator's preface is signed F. L., Battersea, Eng.

[MANT, ALICIA CATHERINE.] A Boat to Richmond: or, The Excursion. By the author of "Ellen, the Young Godmother;" "The Young Naturalist;" &c. &c. Boston: Munroe and Francis, and New York: C.S. Francis, n. d. [c. 1827.] [697]

Duodecimo, 26 leaves, first leaf pasted down inside front cover, sigs. 17-20⁶, 21², woodcut frontispiece, woodcut on title, and one engraving in the text, illustrations colored by hand.

Original tan wrappers, upper with the title and an engraved illustration, the seal of Munroe & Francis' Juvenile Library on the lower.

MANT, ALICIA CATHERINE. The Young Naturalist; A tale. By Alicia Catherine Mant, Author of "Ellen, the Young Godmother," "Tales for Ellen," &c. Boston: Munroe and Francis, New York: C. S. Francis, 1827. [698]

Duodecimo, 114 leaves, A-T⁶, including the last blank.

Original half binding; title and wood engraving on the upper, seal of Munroe & Francis' Juvenile Library on the lower cover; red leather back.

On the second leaf is the advertisement to the second edition.

MEN AND MANNERS, in verse. Concord: Printed and sold by J. B. Moore, 1827. [699]

Duodecimo, 10 leaves, woodcut of a beehive on title, full-length woodcut of the figure of a man in the costume of his country at the head of each page.

Original wrappers, title with woodcut on the upper, advertisement on the lower.

Contains illustrations of the people of eighteen nations, each one with two stanzas of descriptive verse. The peoples described are: Persian; Dutchman; African, who, in his native land *roves in liberty, Far from tyrant white's control;* Russian; Laplander; Otaheitan; *The* Spaniard *tall, in manners grave; The indolent* Turk *on his mattress reclining; The in-*

dustrious German, who *boasts not a noble or patriot mind, Or manners that highly adorn; The love of his country is chiefly confin'd, To the spot where his father was born;* Italian, who *for music and painting is famed;* Highlander, whose *country boasts the product too, Of hero, and of bard;* Englishman, who *deems the little spot that gave him birth, Superior to all countries on the earth;* Indian, *swift on his foot and dextrous with his bow;* Zealander; Tartar, *a hunter, warrior, foe to labour he;* Chinese, who *dates his era far before the flood;* Kamschatkan, *the lazy Kamschadale, Of squaddy form, in manners mild;* and the Frenchman, who *loves to sing and dance.*

NEW-JERSEY SUNDAY SCHOOL JOURNAL. Vol. I. From July to December, 1827. Princeton, N. J.: D. A. Borrenstein [1827]. [700]

> Octavo, 50 leaves, including the first blank, (A)², B-G⁸, 2 woodcuts in the text.
>
> Original half binding.
> Contains Vol. I. nos. 1-6.

[POLLOK, ROBERT.] Helen of the Glen. A tale for youth. New York: W. E. Dean for Orville A. Roorbach, 1827. [701]

> Duodecimo, 72 leaves, including last blank, A-M⁶, engraved frontispiece, signed *O. H. Throop, Sc. N. Y.*
>
> Original half binding, title printed on the front cover, advertisements on the back.
> A story of the covenanters in Scotland.
> Robert Pollok (1798-1827) was a native of Renfrewshire, Scotland. This book, with other works treating of the same subject, was published anonymously, and never acknowledged by the author.
> The only fact recorded by Stauffer, *American Engravers upon Copper and Steel*, concerning O. H. Throop, the engraver of the frontispiece, is that he was an engraver of landscapes and vignettes, and had his office at 172 Broadway, New York City.

SHERWOOD, MARY MARTHA. The History of Henry Milner, A Little Boy who was not brought up according to the fashions of this world. By Mrs. Sherwood, Author of the "Stories explanatory of the Church Catechism," &c. Princeton Press: Published by D. A. Borrenstein, 1827. [702]

> Duodecimo, 92 leaves, with signatures AB⁸, C¹⁰, E⁸, FG¹⁰, KL⁸, M², NO⁸, P⁴, title within an ornamental border.
>
> Boards, g. e.
> One of Mrs. Sherwood's most famous stories, first published in 1822.

SHERWOOD, MARY MARTHA. Julian Percival. By Mrs. Sherwood, Author of "Little Henry and His Bearer," &c. &c. Salem: [W. Palfray, jr. and J. Chapman for] Whipple & Lawrence, 1827. [703]

Duodecimo, 18 leaves, A-C⁶, first leaf with frontispiece, and last leaf pasted down inside covers, vignette on title.

Original wrappers, title with *First American Edition* and a vignette on the upper, advertisement on the lower. The printers' imprint is on the back of the title.

SHERWOOD, MARY MARTHA. Juliana Oakley. A Tale. By Mrs. Sherwood. Revised by the Committee of Publication. Second Edition. Philadelphia: Stereotyped by L. Johnson for the American Sunday School Union, 1827. [704]

Duodecimo, 44 leaves, A-G⁶, H², first leaf blank.

Original pink boards, with the title and a woodcut on the upper cover, with the addition of *No. 212. VIII Series*, publisher's advertisement on the lower.

STORY OF WILLIAM AND ELLEN. Wendell, Mass.: J. Metcalf, 1827. [705]

Sm. octavo, 8 leaves, woodcut on title and illustrations in the text.

Original wrappers, title with woodcut on the upper, woodcut on the lower.
The alphabet on the back of the title. The story of William and Ellen closes on page 12, pages 13 to 16 are occupied by the *Story of Emma Thompson*, a little girl who *never paid attention to what was said to her;* for another edition of which see no. 572.

1828

BLACKFORD, MRS. The Eskdale Herd-Boy, a Scottish Tale, for the instruction and amusement of young persons. By Mrs. Blackford, Author of 'The Scottish Orphans,' 'Arthur Monteith,' &c. First American edition. New York: [Vanderpool & Cole for] Wm. Burgess, Jun., 1828. [706]

Duodecimo, 99 leaves, *⁶, 1-15⁶, 16³, including 1 leaf of advertisements at the end, engraved frontispiece.

Original half binding, title on the front boards, advertisements on the back.

[ELY, JOHN.] The Child's Instructer; consisting of easy lessons for children on subjects which are familiar to them, in language adapted to their capacities. By a teacher of little children in Philadelphia. New York: S. Marks, for Daniel D. Smith, 1828. [707]

Duodecimo, 54 leaves, A-I⁶, woodcut vignette on title, and at the end, some edges uncut.

Original half binding.
For a copy of the second edition, Philadelphia, 1793, see no. 168. The present edition omits the words Volume I from the title-page.
Below the date on the title-page is the printer's imprint: *S. Marks, Printer, Peekskill,* N.Y.

EVENINGS IN BOSTON. First Series. Second Edition. Boston: I. R. Butts
& Co., for Bowles and Dearborn, 1828.   [708]

Duodecimo, 64 leaves, 1^{10}, $2-7^9$, woodcut frontispiece, woodcut vignette on the
title-page.

Original half binding, the title within an ornamental border on the front cover, an engraving (printed upside down) of Bowles & Dearborn's Store on the back.

THE EXTRAORDINARY LIFE AND ADVENTURES OF ROBIN HOOD, Captain of
the Robbers of Sherwood Forest. Interspersed with The History of
Little John and his Merry Men All. New York: Published by S. King,
1828.   [709]

Octavo, 15 leaves, engraved frontispiece by Prud'homme (colored).

Original brown paper wrappers, uncut, short title on the upper, with the price 12½ cents,
followed by a list of pamphlets, &c., printed and sold by S. King, continued on the lower.
Another edition of no. 624.

GOOD EXAMPLES FOR CHILDREN.
                  On God for all events depend;
                  You cannot want if God's your friend.
New York: Printed and sold by Mahlon Day, no. 376, Pearl-Street,
1828.   [710]

Sm. octavo, 8 leaves, woodcut on the title-page, woodcut illustrations in the text.

Original orange wrappers, the title-page repeated on the upper, with the addition of the
number I in the upper right-hand corner, two woodcuts in oval compartments, labelled
respectively *Merchant* and *Sailor* on the lower. Inside the front wrapper is the Frontispiece
(so labelled), and inside the back are alphabets.
The Good Examples consist of six moral stories, the first of which, entitled *Truth Com-
mended*, is the story of George Washington, the hatchet, and the cherry-tree.
On the back of the title is a poem by Dr. Watts.

HISTORY OF ANIMALS. Wendell, Mass.: J. Metcalf, 1828.   [711]

Sm. duodecimo, 12 leaves, including the wrappers, and a first and last blank, woodcut on the title-page, woodcuts in the text.

Original wrappers, title with woodcut on the front cover, woodcut on the back.
The book is of English origin. It contains accounts of eight animals, the last being the
Hog, of which the description concludes: *The male is called a boar, the female a sow, and
the young ones pigs. Their flesh is pork, which, when salted and dried is bacon.* Alphabets
are on the back of the title.

Early American Children's Books

JACK HALYARD, and Ishmael Bardus. Wendell, Mass.: J. Metcalf, 1828. [712]

4 leaves, measuring 3 3/16 by 2 inches, alphabets on the back of the title, woodcut illustrations.

Original wrappers, title *Jack and Ishmael*, with a woodcut and the imprint, undated, within a border on the front, woodcut of a zany on the back.

An essay against teaching children the rhymes of Mother Goose, and fairy stories. The opening paragraph states that *Hardly any two boys were more different than Jack Halyard and Ishmael Bardus*. Jack Halyard is merely used as a contrast to the foolish Ishmael, and the essay does not concern him. The reference is possibly to the remarkable hero of *The Story of Jack Halyard*, contained in the *Analytical Spelling Book* by John Franklin Jones, published in 1823.

The reading that pleased Ishmael the best was a little picture book, called the "Melodies of Mother Goose." It was a parcel of silly rhymes, made by some ignorant people in England, about a hundred years ago. The book was written in bad English, and full of plumping wrong stories, from beginning to end... Now we wish to caution every little boy and girl in the United States against believing such foolish stories, or even listening to them...

The illustrations are not new to this work.

LOVE OF ADMIRATION, or Mary's Visit to B—. A moral tale. By a Lady. New Haven: [Durrie, Peck & Co.] for A. H. Maltby, 1828. [713]

Duodecimo, 80 leaves, 1-13⁶, 14².

Original half binding.
Dedicated to Mrs. H. F. W———— of New-Haven, Conn. The initial on the title probably stands for Boston.
The printers' imprint is on the back of the title.

M'CARTY'S AMERICAN PRIMER. Being a selection of words the most easy of pronunciation. Intended To facilitate the Improvement of Children in Spelling. Philadelphia: Published and sold by M'Carty & Davis, (successors to the late Benjamin Warner,) stereotyped by J. Howe, n.d. [c. 1828.] [714]

Duodecimo, 18 leaves, large woodcut on title, woodcut illustrations in the text.

Original blue wrappers, title with an eagle woodcut on the upper, *Questions for Children* on the lower, varying in different copies.

Contains alphabets, with and without woodcut illustrations, syllabaries, woodcut illustrations of several animals and birds, with short explanatory passages, divided into syllables for reading.

MOTHERLESS MARY; or the Interesting History of a Friendless Orphan, who Being, at her Mother's Death, left entirely destitute, is taken to the parish workhouse; Through an Act of Honesty, she is placed in the family of Mrs. Bouverie: Where she becomes, unintentionally, the Rival of Miss Bouverie, by whose Stratagems she is Decoyed to London: The perilous situation she is placed in there, And the singular Events by which Mary discovers her father: The history of her mother, And the Circumstances which led to her distress, and unfortunate Death. The termination of Mary's troubles, and her happy union with Henry Bouverie. New York: Published by S. King, 1828.   [715]

> Duodecimo, 16 leaves, B-C⁶, D⁴, engraved frontispiece, in colors.
>
> Boards.
> The frontispiece is in the style of a fashion plate in *Godey's Lady's Book*.

PICTURES OF BIBLE HISTORY, with Suitable Descriptions. Wendell, Mass.: Printed and sold by J. Metcalf, 1828.   [716]

> Duodecimo, 10 leaves, without signatures, woodcut frontispiece on verso of front wrapper, woodcut illustration on each page.
>
> Original wrappers, title *Scripture History*, with woodcut and imprint (undated) on the front cover (the back cover missing).
> The text is the same as that in *A Short History of the Bible and Testament* with engravings by Alfred Mills, no. 397, though only a certain number of the chapters of that work have been reprinted in this edition.

A PLAIN AND EASY CATECHISM, suitable for Children of a tender age. And Adapted to the Use of Families and Sabbath Schools. By a Lady of New-Jersey. Princeton, N. J.: D. A. Borrenstein for the Princeton S. School Union, 1828.   [717]

> Octavo, 8 leaves, without signatures, woodcut on the title.
>
> Original wrappers.
> The Note at the beginning states that the Catechism is prepared by a lady of long experience in teaching children, and that *for many of the questions the author is indebted to a little work published some years since by a gentleman of South Carolina.*

[SANDERS, ELIZABETH.] Conversations principally on The Aborigines of North America. Salem: W. & S. B. Ives, 1828.   [718]

> Duodecimo, 90 leaves, A-P⁶.
>
> Original tan wrappers, title repeated on the front cover, advertisement on the back.
> First edition.
> Sabin 16206.
> The introduction explains that the object of the book is *to engage the sympathy of the youth of our country in favour of our Aborigines.*
> On the back of the title is: *Printed at the Salem Observer Office.*

Early American Children's Books

SCRIPTURE HISTORY, Abridged. In which it is designed to give Children such a taste of the writings of the inspired penmen, as may engage them diligently to Study the Sacred Scriptures. Waterville: William Hastings, 1828. [719]

16mo, 27 leaves, A¹⁸, B⁹.

Wrappers.
At the end is a hymn entitled *Excellence of the Bible*.
This is a reprint of *The Holy Bible Abridged*, for the first American edition of which see no. 92.

THE STORY OF ALADDIN; or, The Wonderful Lamp. New York: S. King, n. d. [c. 1828.] [720]

Duodecimo, 10 leaves only (lacks 2), engraved frontispiece, colored, uncut.

Original blue wrappers, title and advertisements on the upper, the advertisements continued on the lower.
This book has no title-page, cover and caption titles only.
In the same series as *Robin Hood* no. 709.

VALENTINE AND ORSON: or, The Surprising Adventures of Two Sons of the Emperor of Greece. A new edition, embellished with cuts. New York: Published by S. King, n. d. [c. 1828.] [721]

Duodecimo, 18 leaves, engraved frontispiece in two compartments, colored.

Boards.
The advertisement explains that *In former editions of this history, the language has been so uncouth, and some passages so indelicate, as to render it unfit for the perusal of the rising generation. These objections, however, are now completely obviated; as the present edition has been not only carefully revised, but the most scrupulous attention has been paid to render it both interesting and instructive.*

VARIETY; or, Stories for children. With twenty-four engravings. Founded on facts. Dedicated to the author's little friends Kate and Fanny. First American from the Second London Edition. New York: [Gray & Bunce for] W. B. Gilley, 1828. [722]

Duodecimo, 66 leaves, 1-11⁶, 12 colored plates including the frontispiece, each in two compartments.

Original boards and half red morocco, title on the upper, advertisement on the lower. The plates are copied from those in the original English edition. The printers' imprint is at the end.

Variety;

OR,

STORIES FOR CHILDREN.

WITH

TWENTY-FOUR ENGRAVINGS.

FOUNDED ON FACTS.

DEDICATED TO THE AUTHOR'S LITTLE FRIENDS KATE AND FANNY.

First American from the Second London Edition.

New-York:
W. B. GILLEY, 94 BROADWAY.
1828.

Title-page from "Variety; or, Stories for Children"

Page from "*Variety; or, Stories for Children*"

Early American Children's Books

1829

A CHOICE COLLECTION OF RIDDLES & CHARADES, by Peter Puzzlewell, Esq. Embellished with neat Engravings. Cooperstown: H. & E. Phinney, 1829. [723]

14 leaves, pasted on to 7 wooden boards, measuring 3⅞ by 2⅝ inches, the boards taped together to form a *Jacob's Ladder*. The leaves on the first board have a short title on the front, with the imprint and an engraving on wood of Fortune, and alphabets on the back; the full title is on the next leaf, with the imprint, and wood engraving of an organ; the ten Riddles and Charades are in verse, and each one is accompanied by an illustration; on the last leaf are two wood engravings.

[ELLIOTT, MARY.] The History of Tommy Two Shoes. Philadelphia: Published by W. Johnson, 1829. [724]

Sq. duodecimo, 12 leaves, the first and last pasted down to the wrappers, sig. A, woodcut frontispiece, woodcut on the title, woodcut illustrations in the text.

Original wrappers, the upper with a short title, the date misprinted 1889, and a woodcut in an oval compartment, the lower with a woodcut.

An abridged edition, imperfectly edited. In this version Tommy brings the treasure chest to America, and *as he was now possessed of sufficient wealth, and had it in his power to fix in any part of the United States he pleased, he took a straight course for the city of Philadelphia, knowing it to be a genteel, healthful, pleasant, and plentiful situation, where he spent his remaining days in ease and honor; and as he was determined to be as good as he was great, he attended divine service every day at the minister.*

The choice of Philadelphia as a permanent residence reflects credit on the publisher, but the mention of the *minister* was probably more suited to the town selected by Master Two-Shoes in the original version.

The story of the philosopher, whose treasure he obtained, begins on page 18, with a caption title.

Most of the woodcuts are to be found in other books. That on the title-page is on the wrapper of the *History of Animals* published by J. Metcalf in Wendell, Mass. in the previous year (no. 711).

[GOODRICH, SAMUEL GRISWOLD.] Stories about Captain John Smith, of Virginia; for the instruction and amusement of Children. Hartford: [P. Canfield for] H. & F. J. Huntington, 1829. [725]

Duodecimo, 50 leaves, 1-7⁶, 8⁸, woodcut illustrations in the text.

Original half binding.
Sabin 27920.
The printer's imprint is on the back of the title-page.

Early American Children's Books

THE IMPROVED NEW-ENGLAND PRIMER: or, An easy and pleasant Guide for the Instruction of Children. Containing, many explanatory notes, and references to the Scriptures. To which is annexed, The Shorter Catechism, As composed and agreed upon by the Reverend Assembly of Divines at Westminster in England, in the year 1649. With explanations of difficult words and phrases in the answers. Concord: George Hough, 1829. [726]

Sm. sq. octavo, 24 leaves, 1-3⁸, woodcuts.

Original pink wrappers, title and large woodcut on upper.
Heartman 296.

In his advertisement at the beginning, the compiler, who is anonymous, explains that *the first edition of the present Compilation was printed in the year* 1823, *in which the publisher had the use of several ancient as well as modern editions*... *Out of the whole, however, the Compiler collected about every article that was contained in the New-England Primer as printed so long ago as the year* 1770... *The Compiler has added, in this edition, to the sketch of the martyrdom of Rev. John Rogers, in the year* 1555, *some notice of two of his descendants who arrived and settled in New-England; which must be peculiarly interesting and gratifying to all those especially who can trace their connexion with so respectable an ancestry.*

The alphabet couplets and the catechism are fully annotated. The woodcuts are copied from those in earlier editions. In this edition the oak that sav'd His Royal Majesty is noble, and not royal, as in the earlier editions.

THE LITTLE ROGUE. Boston: [Putnam & Hunt for] Marsh & Capen and Putnam & Hunt, 1829. [727]

Sq. octavo, 8 leaves, woodcut frontispiece.

Original wrappers, title with woodcut on the front, advertisement on the back.
The printers' imprint is on the back of the title.

MAYHEW, EXPERIENCE. Narratives of the Lives of Pious Indian Children, who lived on Martha's Vineyard more than one hundred years since. By Experience Mayhew, A. M. Preacher to the Indians of Martha's Vineyard at that time. Carefully revised from the London edition, originally printed for Samuel Gerrish, bookseller in Boston, New-England, 1727. Boston: Published at James Loring's Sabbath School Bookstore [1829]. [728]

Duodecimo, 54 leaves, (A)⁴, B-I⁶, K², woodcut frontispiece.

Original half binding, the sides of tan boards, with the title on the upper, enclosed in an ornamental border, advertisement on the lower, leather back.
Sabin 47125.

This book, on the lines of Janeway's *Token*, is a reprint of the fourth division of the Indian Converts.

Early American Children's Books

THE NEW-ENGLAND PRIMER, improved, for the more easy attaining the true Reading of English. Adorned with cuts. To which is added, The Episcopal and The Assembly of Divines' Catechisms. New-York: Pinted for the Bookselles (*sic*), 1829. [729]

Duodecimo, 36 leaves, half title with *A Divine Song* (5 stanzas) on verso, wood-cuts.

Unbound, stitched, as issued.
Heartman 292: [1], 2, 3 *in twelves quired.*
This copy has one quire only, and is stitched in the middle of the book. The fifth leaf has the signature 1*, the seventh, 2, the eleventh, 2*, the thirteenth, 3, the seventeenth, 3*, after which there are no signature marks.

[ROBBINS, ELIZA.] Tales from American History; containing the Principal Facts in the life of Christopher Columbus. For the use of young persons. By the author of American popular Lessons. New York: Published by William Burgess, 1829. [730]

Duodecimo, 134 leaves, 6 leaves without signatures, 1-21⁶, 22², engraved frontispiece, title, and one engraving in the text, 4 pages advertisement at the end.

Half morocco.
First edition.
Sabin 71807.
Dedicated from New York, March 16, 1829, to Edward Lyman, James Howe, and John Revere, by their aunt. The author explains in the preface that the work is *part of a design similar in its purpose to the Tales of a Grandfather.*
Eliza Robbins, the daughter of Edward Hutchinson, a lawyer, was born in 1786. She became famous as a teacher and author of children's books, and died at Cambridge, Massachusetts, in 1853.
The plates are by Gimber after Agate. According to Stauffer, *American Engravers upon Copper and Steel*, Stephen H. Gimber was born in England and there learned to engrave, *but he was working at his profession in New York as early as* 1830.

A SERIES OF EASY LESSONS on the Lord's Prayer. Hartford: P. Canfield for D. F. Robinson & Co., 1829. [731]

Sm. sq. octavo, 24 leaves, 2 leaves without signatures, the first a blank, the second with the frontispiece, 1-2⁸, 3⁶.

Original tan wrappers, title on the upper, advertisement on the lower, and title on the back.

THE YOUTH'S NATURAL HISTORY OF ANIMALS. New York: Solomon King, 1829. [732]

Duodecimo, 12 leaves, A-B⁶, first and last pasted down to covers, woodcut frontispiece, vignette on the title, and illustrations in the text.

Original green wrappers, the title-page repeated on the upper (without the date), advertisement on the lower.

Another edition of the *History of Animals*, no. 648, with the same woodcuts but a different frontispiece.

The publisher's advertisement occurs as part of the imprint: *Of whom may be had the greatest variety of Toy Books, Christmas Pieces, and Pamphlets, in the United States.*

1830

AMERICAN TRACT SOCIETY. The History of Ann Lively and her Bible; Little Verses for Good Children; A New Picture Book; The Shepherd Boy; The Pleasing Instructer (*sic*); A Pretty Picture Book; The Twelve Months of the Year; The Fourth Commandment; Good Examples for Good Children; Morning and Evening; etc. New York: Published by the American Tract Society; n. d. [c. 1830.]   [733]

Sm. octavo, each volume with 8 leaves, the first and last serving as wrappers, woodcuts.

Unbound as issued.

These volumes are from the publications of the American Tract Society. Each of those listed has the title on the recto of the first leaf, and a woodcut, with the price ½ *cent.* on the last. The text begins on the verso of the first leaf, except in *The Shepherd Boy*, which has alphabets and a woodcut on that page. Each volume is paginated on the outer margin for the tract, and on the inner for the series.

The tracts contain stories from various sources, and extracts in verse from the writings of Dr. Watts and other children's authors.

A poem entitled *The Bible* is constructed on the same principle as *My Father, My Mother*, etc.

What can support my drooping head,
When I am laid on my death-bed?
THE BIBLE.

The series is fully illustrated with woodcuts. Some of the earlier numbers were issued in 1829. This collection contains a number of the American Tract Society's publications for children, issued from 1829 to 1833.

BARBAULD, ANNA LETITIA. Barbauld's Hymns. New-York: Printed and sold by Mahlon Day, No. 376, Pearl-street, n. d. [c. 1830.]   [734]

Four leaves, measuring 3⅛ by 2 inches, a woodcut on the title, and a woodcut on each page of the text.

Original wrappers, title on the front cover, and a list of school books on the back.
Contains portions of Mrs. Barbauld's *Hymns in Prose*.

THE CHILD'S FIRST STEP up the Ladder of Learning; or, Easy Lessons for the Infant Mind. New York: Printed and sold by Mahlon Day, No. 376, Pearl-street, n. d. [c. 1830.]   [735]

Eight leaves, measuring 3⅝ by 2¼ inches. This copy has 7 leaves, the pagination numbers beginning at 3; it is probable that the first leaf, missing, had the title.

Original wrappers, title on the front with a picture of Mahlon Day's Book Store.

Contains alphabets, syllables, passages for reading and woodcuts. All the woodcuts have been used previously in other books.

In the cut of Mahlon Day's Book Store on the wrapper, the street number is 372, from which address Day removed to no. 376 Pearl-street in 1825 or 1826. In the two editions of the *Picture of New-York*, nos. 685 and 745, the earlier edition has the number 372 on this cut, but in the later it has been changed to 376.

[ELLIOTT, MARY.] My Sister. A Poem.

Some lads are very idle boys,
They love their kite and ball,
They do not read these little toys,
They do not learn at all:
While one cent only is the price,
For books so very good and nice.

New York: Printed & Sold by Mahlon Day, No. 376, Pearl-street, n. d. [c. 1830.]   [736]

Four leaves, measuring 3 by 1¹⅜ inches, woodcuts.

Original wrappers (the front wrapper in this copy gone), advertisement of school books on the back.

This poem was originally issued in *Grateful Tributes* first published by W. Darton in 1811 or 1812; see note to no. 551.

A GEOGRAPHICAL PRESENT; being descriptions of the several Countries of Europe. Compiled from the best authorities. With representations of the various inhabitants in their respective costumes. New York: [R.& G.S.Wood for] William Burgess, Juvenile Emporium, 1830. [737]

Duodecimo, 72 leaves, 1², 2-12⁶, 13⁴, 12 colored plates, including the frontispiece.

Original half red morocco.

Based on the work of Mary Anne Venning entitled *A Geographical Present being descriptions of the principal countries of the world*, originally published in London by Darton & Harvey.

The printers' imprint with the address 265 Pearl-St., is on the back of the title.

HARRY WINTER; the Shipwrecked Sailor Boy. To which is added The Oak at Home. New York: Printed and sold by Mahlon Day, No. 376, Pearl-street. 1830.   [738]

Early American Children's Books

Duodecimo, 12 leaves, first and last pasted down, woodcut on the title-page, woodcut frontispiece and illustrations in the text.

Original wrappers, the title with a vignette within borders on the upper, advertisement of children's books on the lower.

The preface to the first story is signed M. D. (?Mahlon Day.) The story concerns a family living near Banborough Castle, in Northumberland (England). The second story begins on page (15) with the caption title: *The Oak "At Home," An Allegory.* [From the Boston Juvenile Miscellany.] It is signed M. H., and dated from Marblehead, Mass. 1828.

JUVENILE PASTIMES, IN VERSE.

> Come Boys and Girls, come out to play,
> The moon doth shine, as bright as day;
> Come with a whoop, come with a call,
> Come with a good will, or not at all.

Stereotyped by James Conner, New York. New-York: Printed & sold by Mahlon Day, No. 376, Pearl-street, n. d. [c. 1830.]   [739]

Eight leaves, measuring 3$\frac{11}{16}$ by 2$\frac{3}{16}$ inches, a woodcut on the title-page, a woodcut illustration of a pastime on each page of text.

Original wrappers, the title repeated on the front cover, a list of school and toy books on the back.

Contains descriptions in verse of fourteen games, with comments in prose. The illustrations have all appeared in other books, some were used by Day in *The Child's First step up the Ladder of Learning*, no. 735.

In this edition, not only is the usual danger connected with flying the kite pointed out, but the pastime is declared to be against the law: *In the spring, the boys of New-York fly their kites, and one may see several at a time high in the air. But still it is against the law, for horses are often frightened by them.*

A LITTLE PRESENT.

> This fine pretty present,
> A nice pleasing toy,
> Is made for a good girl,
> Or a brave little boy.

New-York: Printed and sold by Mahlon Day, No. 376, Pearl-street, n. d. [c. 1830.]   [740]

Four leaves, measuring 3 by 1$\frac{7}{8}$ inches, a woodcut on the title, and on each page of the text.

Wrappers.

The woodcuts are of animals and are accompanied by lines of descriptive verse, beneath which, in the bottom margins, are alphabets and numerals. On the last page are two woodcuts, representing a canister of China tea, and a cask of flour.

A

GEOGRAPHICAL PRESENT;

BEING

DESCRIPTIONS

OF THE

SEVERAL COUNTRIES

OF

EUROPE.

COMPILED FROM THE BEST AUTHORITIES.

WITH

REPRESENTATIONS OF THE VARIOUS INHABITANTS IN
THEIR RESPECTIVE COSTUMES.

NEW-YORK:

PUBLISHED BY WILLIAM BURGESS,
JUVENILE EMPORIUM,
97 Fulton-street.

1830.

Title-page from "A Geographical Present"

Man & Woman of Catalonia,
Dancing the Fandango.

Page from "A Geographical Present"

Early American Children's Books

THE LITTLE PRIMER.

New-York Cries,
And many more,
Can be bought
At Day's Book-store.

New-York: Mahlon Day, no. 376, Pearl-street, n. d. [c. 1830.] [741]

Four leaves, measuring 3⅛ by 1¹¹⁄₁₆ inches, woodcut on the title.

Original wrappers, the title-page repeated on the upper cover, cut of *A Meeting House* on the lower.
Contains the alphabet, words of two and three letters, the Ten Commandments in rhyme, and the Lord's Prayer.

LITTLE SUSAN AND HER LAMB. A story for children. Boston: Wait, Greene and Co., n. d. [c. 1830.] [742]

Three leaves.

Original yellow wrappers, the title repeated on the front cover, a woodcut on the back.

THE PENNY PRIMER. New York: Printed and sold by Mahlon Day, No. 376, Pearl-street, n. d. [c. 1830.] [743]

Four leaves, measuring 3 by 1¹⁵⁄₁₆ inches, woodcut on the title-page, and woodcuts in the text.

Original wrappers, the title repeated on the front cover, a list of schoolbooks on the back. Contains alphabets, numerals, and a passage for reading.

PETER PARLEY'S STORY OF THE STORM. Boston: [Waitt & Dow for] Carter & Hendee, 1830. [744]

Duodecimo, 9 leaves, woodcut frontispiece, colored, full-page woodcut illustration, and a vignette on verso of the last leaf.

Original yellow wrappers, title with the woodcut illustration repeated on the front, advertisement on the back.
The author of this work was not Samuel Griswold Goodrich, author of *Peter Parley's Tales*, and the originator of that pseudonym. A note below the copyright notice on the verso of the first leaf reads: *This tale, written in imitation of the Tales of Peter Parley, is not by the author of those Tales; it is, however, classed with the series, as being similar in size and design.*
The printers' imprint is below the copyright notice on the back of the title.

PICTURE OF NEW-YORK.

> Here you have a picture small,
> Of New-York, far renown'd;
> But recollect, when it you've read,
> Where others can be found.

Stereotyped by James Conner, New-York. New York: Printed & sold by Mahlon Day, no. 376, Pearl-street, n. d. [c. 1830.]   [745]

8 leaves, measuring 3⅜ by 2 inches, woodcut frontispiece and woodcuts in the text.

Blue morocco, gilt, padded with blanks.

This book is another edition of the *Picture of New-York* issued by Mahlon Day from 372, Pearl-street, in 1825, see no. 685. The woodcuts are the same as in the earlier edition except that in the picture of the store on page 12, the number has been changed to 376.

The text has slight variations in order to bring it up to date. In the earlier edition the ships mentioned as steering towards Amboy and New-Brunswick were the *William Penn*, or the *Legislator*, and the *James Kent* went to Albany; in the present edition the *Emerald* or the *Etna* steer towards Amboy and New-Brunswick, and the *Chief Justice Marshall* goes to Albany. The list of books which can be obtained at Day's Juvenile Book-Store (page 13) has not been chauged.

In the former edition Day's advertising rhyme was on the wrapper and not on the title-page; in the present edition it is on the title-page.

A PLEASING TOY FOR GIRL OR BOY.

> I'm for the child,
> Who is active in play,
> And thorough at work;
> That's the best way.

New-York: Mahlon Day, No. 376, Pearl-street. n. d. [c. 1830.]   [746]

4 leaves, measuring 3⅛ by 2 inches, woodcut on the title-page, and on each page of text.

Contains rhymes on the different games beginning *Who'll play Blind Man's Buff?* I, *says Catharine Luff* on the principle of *Who killed Cock Robin?* Each page has a woodcut illustration of the game described. This is a different work from the following item.

A PLEASING TOY, FOR GIRL OR BOY. Wendell, Mass.: J. Metcalf, 1830.
                                        [747]

Sm. octavo, 8 leaves without signatures, woodcut on the title, woodcut on each page of the text.

Original wrappers.
A similar work to no. 687, but with variations in both text and cuts.

Early American Children's Books

A PRESENT TO CHILDREN. By the Author of "Ditties for Children, Poetic Tales, Good Girl's Soliloquy." &c. &c. New York: Samuel Wood and Sons, and Baltimore: Samuel S. Wood & Co. [c. 1830.]   [748]

Sq. octavo, 16 leaves, including the first blank, without signatures, 8 woodcut illustrations in the text.

Original wrappers, title on the front and advertisements on the back wrapper.
Contains eight poems.
On the flyleaf is written: *Warren A. Draper—For attention to Study and good behaviour at School. W.Foord.*

THE SEVEN CHAMPIONS OF CHRISTENDOM. St.George of England. St.Denis of France. St.James of Spain. St. Anthony of Italy. St. Andrew of Scotland. St. Patrick of Ireland. St. David of Wales. New York: S. King, 1830.   [749]

Duodecimo, 24 leaves, 1-4⁶, engraved frontispiece, in 2 compartments, colored, by Throop.

Boards.
A chapbook edition; the text is quite different from that in nos. 245 and 295.

THE STRAY LAMB.
> In New-York, that famous city,
>   Many books like this are sold,
> And for such 'twould be a pity,
>   One cent only to withold.

New York: Mahlon Day, No.376, Pearl-street, n. d. [c. 1830.]   [750]

4 leaves, measuring 3 by 1¹³⁄₁₆ inches.

Original wrappers, title-page repeated on the front cover, advertisements on the back.

THE WONDERFUL EXPLOITS OF GUY, Earl of Warwick. With original plates. Philadelphia: William H. Morgan [c. 1830].   [751]

Sq. octavo, 8 leaves, engraved throughout and printed on one side only, half title and a colored illustration on the first leaf, a 4 line stanza and a colored illustration on each of the other leaves.

Original wrappers, cover-title, advertisements on back wrapper.
Weiss: *William Charles*, page 11.
A rhymed version of the exploit of this famous hero in killing the *monstrous cow*. On the half title the word Exploit is in the singular.

Early American Children's Books

1831

THE AFFECTING HISTORY OF THE CHILDREN IN THE WOODS.
> Peruse this little book, and you will find,
> How much the love of gold depraves mankind.

(Second Series—No. 8.) Concord: Published by Hoag & Atwood, 1831.

Sm. octavo, 8 leaves, woodcut on the title, and cuts in the text. [752]

Original blue wrappers, title on the upper, woodcut on the lower, woodcuts inside both covers.

Another edition of the version of the story printed by S. Trumbull at Stonington-port, 1800, no. 250, with different woodcuts.

AMENDMENT; or, Charles Grant and his Sister. By the author of Hugh Lattimere, Little Quaker, Rowland, Messingham, Tell Tale, Refermation (*sic*), Disobedience, &c. New York: Published by J. A. Clussman, 1831. [753]

Duodecimo, 18 leaves, A-C⁶, engraved frontispiece and 3 engraved illustrations.

Boards.

Extracted from an anonymous story entitled *The Little Prisoners or Passion and Patience* first printed in London in 1828.

ANDERSON, RUFUS. Memoir of Catharine Brown, a Christian Indian, of the Cherokee Nation. Prepared for the American Sunday School Union by Rev. Rufus Anderson, and revised by the Committee of Publication. Philadelphia: American Sunday School Union [1831]. [754]

Duodecimo, 70 leaves, including the last blank, A-K⁶, L¹⁰, several woodcut illustrations.

Red half morocco.

Sabin 1420.

Loosely inserted is a folded sheet with the Cherokee Alphabet, the Lord's Prayer in Cherokee, etc.

The author was minister of Wenham, Massachusetts, and the *Preface to the Original Work* is dated from the Missionary Rooms, Boston, Mass. Dec. 1824.

The American Sunday School Union which was established in Philadelphia in 1824, issued numerous books suitable for the Sunday reading of children. Only such in this collection which have genuine American interest have been included in this catalogue.

BOOK OF FIGURES.
> You first must learn your A, B, C,
> And then the figures, 1, 2, 3.

Early American Children's Books

New-York: Printed and sold by Mahlon Day, No. 376, Pearl-street, n. d. [c. 1831.] [755]

A Toy Book of 4 leaves measuring 3 by 1⅞ inches, woodcut on the title, and a woodcut on each page of text.

Original wrappers, title on the front cover, two woodcuts on the back.
A version of *One, Two, Come tie my shoe*. The illustrations are the same, in smaller size, as those for *Peter Prim's Profitable Present*, no. 612, another edition of the same rhyme.

GALLAUDET, THOMAS H. The Child's Book on The Soul. Part first. By Rev. T. H. Gallaudet, Late Principal of the American Asylum for the Deaf and Dumb. Second edition, improved. With questions, adapted to the use of Sunday Schools, and of infant schools. Hartford: Published by Cooke and Co., 1831. [756]

Sm. sq. octavo, 64 leaves, 1-8⁸, woodcut on the title, numerous full-page woodcut illustrations printed on one side of leaf only.

Original half binding, title with woodcut on the upper, advertisement on the lower cover.
Thomas Hopkins Gallaudet, 1787 to 1851, was a native of Philadelphia. In 1816 he established a school for deaf mutes at Hartford, Conn., the first institution of its kind in the United States.

GOLDSMITH, OLIVER. Doctor Goldsmith's Celebrated Elegy, on that glory of her sex, Mrs. Mary Blaize. Baltimore: Published by Joseph N. Lewis, 1831. [757]

Duodecimo, 12 leaves, text and illustrations engraved throughout and printed on one side only, illustrations colored.

Original yellow wrappers, title on the front, advertisement on the back.
The first leaf bears the half title, with colored vignette. The illustrations are copied (with variations) from those in the original London edition by T. Harris, 1808.

THE HISTORY OF GOODMAN RORY the Woodman, and his Family. New York: George W. Burgess, n. d. [1831.] [758]

Octavo, 14 leaves including the last blank; engraved throughout and printed on one side only; a colored vignette on the title-page, and a colored illustration at the head of each page of text (in verse).

Original orange wrappers, title on the upper.

HISTORY OF THE BIBLE. Bridgeport: J. B. & L. Baldwin, 1831. [759]

Duodecimo, 96 leaves, A-M⁸, woodcut frontispiece, and numerous woodcut illustrations.

Original calf.
A Thumb Bible measuring 2 by 1⅞ inches.
Another edition of nos. 433, etc., with a different set of woodcuts.
Another copy has the imprint: New-London: Published by W. & J. Bolles, 1831.

LITTLE JANE, or Playing with Fire. New York: Published by J. A. Clussman [c. 1831].   [760]

4 leaves, measuring 3⅜ by 2 inches; woodcut on the title, a woodcut at the head
of each page of the text, except the first.

Original wrappers, title on the upper, with a woodcut of an eagle and the advertising
rhyme:
> One cent only will buy this book,
> With pictures fair, on which to look.

The imprint on the wrapper reads: *Published by R. L. Underhill & Co. Bath, N. Y.* Advertisement of books at one cent each on the back.
Jane set the house on fire, *and as they lived more than six miles from New-York, no fire-*
engines could reach them.

MASON, WILLIAM. Crumbs from the Master's Table; or, select sentences,
Doctrinal, Practical, and Experimental. By W. Mason. New York:
D. Appleton, 1831.   [761]

24mo, 96 leaves, 1-12⁸.

Original cloth, with the original paper label on the back.
A miniature book, measuring 2⅝ by 2 inches.
The first book printed by the House of Appleton. The imprint reads: New-York:
D. Appleton, Clinton-Hall. Stereotype Edition, 1831.

OALTON, ANN ELIZABETH. Clara and Albina or, the Ill Effects of Prejudice. A Juvenile Tale by Ann Elizabeth Oalton. New York: Published
by J. A. Clussman, 1831.   [762]

Duodecimo, 18 leaves, A-C⁶, and two plates, one of which is used twice.
Boards.

A PEEP AT THE VARIOUS NATIONS OF THE WORLD. A concise description
of the Inhabitants. Embellished with several Engravings. Second Series—No. 6. Concord: Published by Hoag & Atwood, 1831.   [763]

14 leaves, pasted on 7 wooden boards measuring 4 by 2½ inches, attached by tapes
in the form known as a *Jacob's Ladder.*

Page from "Dr. Goldsmith's Celebrated Elegy,
on Mrs. Mary Blaize"

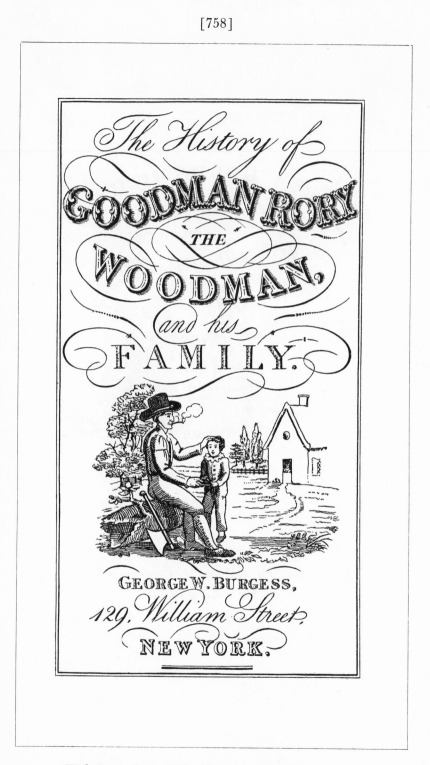

*Title-page from "The History of Goodman Rory
the Woodman, and his Family"*

Contains descriptions, each with a woodcut, of the people of eight countries. At the beginning and the end are woodcut illustrations of North American Indians, and of South American Indians.

PUNCTUATION PERSONIFIED, or pointing made easy. By Mr. Stops. Steubenville: Published by J. & B. Turnbull, 1831. [764]

Octavo, 10 leaves without signatures, printed on one side only, a colored illustration and a stanza of verse on each leaf, six colored vignettes on the last page.

Original blue wrappers, title on front and advertisements on back wrapper.

A similar production to Madame Leinstein's *Punctuation personified; or, the Good Child's Book of Stops.* On the verso of the first leaf is the half-title, below which an illustration and stanza of verse headed *Introduction* explanatory of the paragraph mark. The succeeding leaves deal with the various punctuation marks, one on each leaf except the last which contains descriptions in compartments of a collection of marks including the asterisk, the apostrophe, quotation marks, etc.

SOPHIA MORTON. Second edition. Boston: Leonard C. Bowles, 1831. [765]

Duodecimo, 34 leaves, 1-5⁶, 6⁴, including wood-engraved frontispiece and title with vignette at the beginning, and a blank leaf at the end.

Original half binding.

Dedicated *to the little girl of eight years old, for whom this story was first written.*

THE STORM. A Juvenile Tale, With four Coloured Engravings. First American edition. New York: J. A. Clussman, 1831. [766]

Duodecimo, 18 leaves, including last blank, A-C⁶, frontispiece and 3 plates in aquatint.

Boards.

SUSAN AND EDWARD; or, A Visit to Fulton Market.

With what high joy do children young
Behold the varied sight—
As each new object strikes their view,
'Tis seen with fresh delight.
O then, may wisdom's blessed way,
Be their choice from day to day.

New-York: Printed and sold by Mahlon Day, No. 376, Pearl-street, n. d. [c. 1831.] [767]

A Toy Book of 8 leaves, measuring 3⅝ by 2¼ inches, woodcut on the title, woodcuts in the text.

Original wrappers; title-page repeated on the front, a list of Reading Books on the back. The preface, which contains an account of the various markets of New-York, is dated New York, 1831.

WATTS, ISAAC. Divine Songs, attempted in Easy Language, for the use of Children. By I. Watts, D.D... Utica: William Williams, 1831.   [768]

Duodecimo, 36 leaves, A-F⁶, woodcut vignettes.

Original wrappers, with title reading: *Watts' and Doddridge's Songs*, and the imprint dated 1831.

Not in Stone.

At D₁ the title· *Moral Songs, attempted in Easy Language, for the use of Children. By I. Watts, D. D. . . . To which are added, The principles of the Christian Religion, Expressed in plain and easy Verse. By P. Doddridge, D. D.* with imprint. This part has separate pagination, though the signatures are continuous.

Seward and Williams' edition of 1810 (see no. 430) with new covers. Both the title-pages bear the 1810 imprint.

1832

[BERQUIN, ARNAUD.] Louisa's Tenderness to the little Birds, In Winter. (Third Series. No. 12.) Concord: Published by M. G. Atwood, 1832.   [769]

Sm. octavo, 8 leaves, woodcut vignette, woodcut frontispiece and illustrations in the text (colored in this copy).

Original cream wrappers, title with a woodcut within borders on the upper cover, a woodcut within borders on the lower.

Translated from one of the stories in *L'Ami des Enfants*. The woodcut on the lower cover was used in many books.

[DORSET, CATHARINE ANN.] Think before you speak; or the Three Wishes; a poetic tale. First American from the second London edition. Philadelphia: William W. Weeks for Morgan and Sons, 1832.   [770]

Sq. octavo, 16 leaves, A-B⁸, 6 engraved plates including the frontispiece, all colored.

Original wrappers with the imprint of Morgan & Yeager: Think before you speak, or, the Three Wishes. Illustrated with numerous Copperplate Engravings.

> I grant to you and your fair dame
> The three first wishes that you name;
> Think what will best your atate (*sic*) amend,
> And claim it from your grateful friend.

Philadelphia: Published by Morgan & Yeager, At the Juvenile Bookstore, No. 114, Chestnut Street, first door below the Post-Office. Price, plain, 18¾ cents—coloured 25 cents.

Weiss: *William Charles*, page 10.

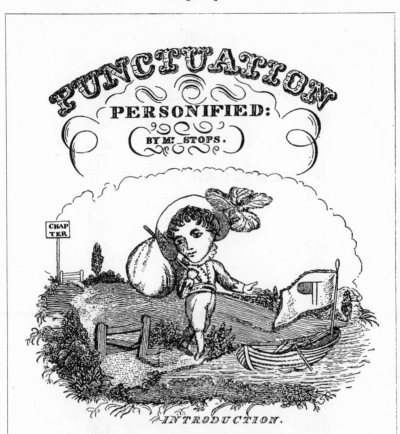

PUNCTUATION
PERSONIFIED:
BY Mr. STOPS.

INTRODUCTION.

The PARAGRAPH, which here you view,
Always announces something new;
Distinct from   what was read before,
As is the water from the shore.
This mark in Scripture oft is found,
As thriving best on sacred ground,
But here 'tis plac'd for your instruction.
To answer as an introduction.

Page from "Punctuation Personified"

THE

NEW-YORK CRIES,

IN RHYME.

NEW-YORK:

PRINTED & SOLD BY MAHLON DAY,

At the New Juvenile Book-store,

No. 376, Pearl-street.

. . . .

1826.

Title-page from
"The New-York Cries, in Rhyme"

Early American Children's Books

For an earlier edition of this work, which is stated on the title-page to be the first American edition, see no. 438.

THE GOOD BOY. Wendell, Mass.: John Metcalf, 1832. [771]

Sm. octavo, 8 leaves, woodcuts in the text.

Original yellow wrappers, title and the woodcut on page 15 on the front, a woodcut on the back cover.

A description of the qualities of the ideal *good boy*, alphabets on the back of the title.

[GOODRICH, SAMUEL GRISWOLD.] Peter Parley's Tales about the State and City of New York. Illustrated by a map and many engravings. For the use of schools. New York: Published by Pendleton and Hill, 1832. [772]

16 mo, 80 leaves, 1-10⁸, large folded engraved map of New York State, woodcut frontispiece, vignette on title and numerous illustrations in the text.

Original half binding of cream boards and red leather back.

At the end is a Catalogue of Entertaining and Useful Books for Children and Youth, six pages.

The Tales of Peter Parley are amongst the most celebrated in the history of American children's literature. The originator of the name, and author of a great number of the Peter Parley books was Samuel Griswold Goodrich, a native of Ridgefield, Connecticut (born 1793). He was a strong exponent of the realistic school of thought for children, condemning such stories as Little Red Riding Hood, Puss in Boots, Blue Beard, Jack the Giant Killer, as *tales of horror, commonly put into the hands of youth, as if for the express purpose of reconciling them to vice and crime.* He was strongly influenced by Hannah More's *Moral Repository*, see no. 235, which he describes as the first work he read with real enthusiasm, and it was in conversation with Miss More on her famous tract *The Shepherd of Salisbury Plain* (no. 345) when on a visit to England, that he *first formed the conception of the Parley Tales.*

Eventually Goodrich became a publisher in Hartford, and there began the publication of the famous Peter Parley volumes. The success of these books resulted in many imitators, and books not by Goodrich came out over the pseudonym of Peter Parley. In 1837 Nathaniel Hawthorne used the name for his *Peter Parley's Universal History on the basis of Geography.*

THE HISTORY OF JOSEPH.

> When once the sacred tie is broke
> 'Tween brothers of one kin,
> The heart grown cold and desolate,
> Its actions lead to sin.

Stereotyped by A. Chandler. New York: Printed and Sold by Mahlon Day, No. 376, Pearl-street, n. d. [c. 1832.] [773]

A Toy Book of 8 leaves, measuring 3½ by 2⅛ inches, woodcut illustrations.

Early American Children's Books

Original wrappers.

A footnote on page 10 corrects the false impression which would be made on the mind of an American child by the use of the word *corn* to denote the food bought by Joseph's brethren: *Not Indian corn; for that grain was not known in those days.* Corn, *as expressed in the Bible, means wheat, rye, barley, &c.; the same meaning they give it now in Europe. But in America, when we use the word* Corn, *we mean "Indian Corn," distinct from wheat, rye, barley, oats, &c. which, with Indian Corn, we class under the general name of* grain.

HISTORY OF THE DELAWARF (*sic*) AND IROQUOIS INDIANS formerly inhabiting the Middle States. With various anecdotes, illustrating their manners and customs. Embellished with a variety of original cuts. Written for the American Sunday School Union, and revised by the Committee of Publication. Philadelphia: American Sunday-School Union [1832]. [774]

Duodecimo, 78 leaves, A-N^6, woodcut frontispiece and woodcuts in the text.

Original marbled boards, linen back with original label.
Pilling, page 231. Sabin 32165.

JUVENILE PASTIMES, or Sports for the Four Seasons. Part I. Embellished with twenty-eight neat copperplate engravings. Providence: Cory, Marshall and Hammond. [c. 1832.] [775]

Duodecimo, 8 leaves, engraved throughout, verses and vignettes (colored) on each leaf, printed on one side only.

Original wrappers, cover-title, advertisements on the back wrapper.

This is Part I of a book of which a copy of Part II will be found published by Morgan and Yeager circa 1825. This part deals with the sports and pastimes for Spring and Summer. As in Part I some adjustment has been probably made from the English edition, unless Boston in Lincolnshire was referred to in the lines for *Sailing the Ship.*

> Who, said Charles will take a trip
> To Boston, in my trim built Ship?

The English national game is left untouched

> Cricket's the noblest game of all
> That can be play'd with bat and ball.

On the inside covers are manuscript notes by an owner, dated 1832.

THE LITTLE PRESENT for A Good Child. Wendell, Mass.: John Metcalf, 1832. [776]

Sm. octavo, 8 leaves, woodcut vignette on title, 2 woodcuts on each page.

Original yellow wrappers, title with woodcut vignette and the number 10 on the upper, woodcut on the lower.

[274]

Alphabets on the back of the title. Each page contains a rhymed couplet, with a wood-cut illustration for each line, all of which have appeared in other books.

[TAYLOR, JANE.] Select Rhymes for the Nursery.
> I had three cents to spend—
> I ran to DAY's with glee,
> To get a picture book;
> And here I've got it—see!

New-York: Mahlon Day, No. 376, Pearl-street, 1832.   [777]

16mo, 8 leaves, the frontispiece printed on the inside front cover, and the last leaf of text on the inside back cover, woodcuts.

Original wrappers, title on the front with the number 10, advertisements on the back.
This selection includes Twinkle, twinkle little star. The first American edition was published by Munroe and Francis, Boston, n. d.

TOY BOOKS. History of the Giants; The Lion's Den; Sam Patch; Tom Thumb. Philadelphia: Published by Willard Johnson, 1832.   [778]

A set of four toy books, each with 8 leaves, measuring 2½ by 2¼ inches, first and last leaves pasted down to covers, woodcut frontispieces, woodcuts in the text.

Original wrappers, titles with dated imprints on the front covers, woodcuts on the back.
The text and illustrations are all reprinted from other books. Each volume has the alphabet and numerals on the back of the title. *History of the Giants* contains descriptions with illustrations of seven giants, followed by rhymes from Mother Goose, and a hymn. *The Lion's Den* contains rhymes from Mother Goose and other sources, including verses to be found in *Jacky Dandy's Delight*, no. 130, each accompanied by an illustration. *Sam Patch* also has rhymes from Mother Goose, and *Tom Thumb* contains an abridged Life of Tom Thumb. Several varieties of the wrappers of these books are extant, both with regard to color, and the woodcut vignettes.

TOY BOOKS. The Medley.—The Sailor Boy. Or the first and last voyage of Little Andrew. Concord: Fisk & Chase, 1831. Concord: John W. Moore & Co. 1832.   [779]

2 volumes, 8 leaves, each measuring 3½ by 2⅜ inches, woodcuts on the titles and in the text.

Original wrappers, upper covers with titles, woodcuts, and imprint; lower covers with woodcuts.
The Medley contains a series of short articles for children, fully illustrated, on common objects, including the American Flag; the wind-mill, illustrated from mills in Boston; the cannon, with descriptions of the firing on Washington's birthday; the Fourth of July, etc.
Both volumes are the 1831 editions of Fisk & Chase, reissued by John W. Moore & Co. in 1832.

Early American Children's Books

THE YOUNG VOYAGER TO THE SOUTH SEAS: Part I-[II.] New Haven: [Hezekiah Howe & Co. and Whitmore & Minor] for Durrie & Peck, 1832. [780]

16mo, 2 volumes, each with 48 leaves, signatures 1-6⁸, woodcut frontispiece and woodcut illustrations in the text.

Original half binding, leather back.

The book is offered to the children and youth of our country, in the hope, that this short story, plainly told, may interest them for the Missionary cause in the islands of the sea.

Part I has on the title: *Visit to the Georgian and Society Islands.* Part II: *Scenes in the Georgian Islands.*

1833

A BRIEF MEMOIR of the Life of Dr. Benjamin Franklin. Compiled for the use of young persons. New York: Printed and sold by Mahlon Day, No. 376, Pearl-street, 1833. [781]

Duodecimo, 36 leaves, 1-6⁶, woodcut frontispiece, woodcut on title with portrait head, several woodcuts in the text.

Original half binding.

Ford 822 has only the edition of 1824.

[HOWLAND, MISS A.]. Rhode-Island Tales. By a Friend to Youth, of Newport R. I. New-York: Printed and sold by Mahlon Day, No. 374, Pearl-street, 1833. [782]

Duodecimo, 36 leaves (1)-6⁶, including three blanks, woodcut frontispiece and illustrations.

Original boards, cloth back, title printed on the upper, and advertisements on the lower cover.

Not in Sabin. Not in Wegelin.

In verse. The last poem is entitled *Twilight.* It consists of eleven stanzas, of which the last two contain Day's advertising rhyme, followed by a picture of his store (with figures concealing the number), and a footnote as to his removal connected with the last line by an asterisk.

> And here behold in fair array,
> A part of this her work,
> Printed and sold by Mahlon Day,
> Who lives in famed New-York.
>
> In Pearl-street stands his handsome store,
> The number we affix,
> In figures marked above the door,
> Three hundred Seventy-Six*.

*Removed in 1833, to No. 374, first door below.

The woodcuts are by Anderson, many of them will be found in other books by other publishers.

Early American Children's Books

THE LITTLE SOLDIERS; or, Holiday Sports. Dedicated to all good boys. Embellished with plates. New Haven: Sidney's Press for S. Babcock, 1833. [783]

Duodecimo, 12 leaves, woodcut frontispiece, woodcut on the title and illustrations in the text.

Original yellow wrappers, title with woodcut on the upper cover, advertisements on the lower.

MOTHER GOOSE'S MELODIES. The only Pure Edition. Containing all that have ever come to light of her memorable writings, together with those which have been discovered among the MSS. of Herculaneum. Likewise every one recently found in the same stone box which hold the Golden Plates of the Book of Mormon. The whole compared, revised, and sanctioned, by one of the annotators of the Goose Family. With many new engravings. Entered, according to Act of Congress, in the year 1833, by Munroe & Francis, in the Clerk's office, of the District Court of Massachusetts. New York and Boston: C. S. Francis and Company, [1833]. [784]

Sq. duodecimo, 48 leaves, A-(H)⁸,⁴, numerous woodcut illustrations, advertisement on the last page.

Original pink wrappers with half titles and wood engravings on both sides, the imprint of Munroe & Francis, Boston, n.d. on the upper cover.

Contains the Songs and Lullabies of Mother Goose, without the Lullabies of Shakespeare, and without the notes and maxims. A large number of additional songs, not in the original edition are inserted. *See saw, sacradown* has the reading *Boston town*, otherwise the English references have been retained. Norwich has been replaced by the phonetical spelling *Norridge*.

The illustrations, many of which are signed, are by various artists, including Alexander Anderson, Abel Bowen (1790-1850), Nathaniel Dearborn (1786-1852, at one time apprenticed to Bowen), Benjamin F. Childs, Avery, and others.

This copy has the signature C. S. Francis in pencil on the title-page.

NEW-ENGLAND PRIMER. A New and improved edition. The New-England Primer, Improved, for the more easy attaining the true Reading of English. Adorned with Cuts. To which is added The Episcopal and The Assembly of Divines' Catechisms. New York: M. Day, 374 Pearl-st. Published for the Booksellers, n.d. [c. 1833.] [785]

16mo, 36 leaves, first and last pasted down to wrappers, no signatures, woodcut frontispiece, woodcuts in the text.

Original paper wrappers, partly uncut.

Heartman 358 with a different collation. The present copy has one gathering, unsigned.

Mahlon Day moved from No. 376 to No. 374 Pearl Street during the year 1833; the book was not printed therefore before that date.

THE NEW-ENGLAND PRIMER, improved; or, an easy and pleasant Guide to the Art of Reading. To which is added, The Assembly's Catechism. Stereotyped by A. Chandler & Co. Pittsburgh: Published by Cook & Schoyer, 1833. [786]

16mo, 32 leaves, (24 leaves without signature marks, D⁸), first and last pasted down to covers, woodcut illustrations.

Original olive green wrappers, with title on the front, advertisements on the back.

TAYLOR, JANE. A Day's Pleasure: to which are added Reflections on a Day's Pleasure. By Jane Taylor. New York: Mahlon Day, No. 376, Pearl-street, 1833. [787]

Duodecimo, 12 leaves (first and last pasted down to covers), woodcut frontispiece, woodcuts on the title, and in the text.

Original wrappers, title and woodcut vignette on the upper, advertisements on the lower.

In this edition the imprint on the cover with the address No. 376, Pearl-street is not dated. The remainders were re-issued in 1836 with new covers bearing the address, 374 Pearl-street, and the date.

Mahlon Day removed from No. 376 to No. 374 Pearl-street in 1833.

WILLIAMS, JOHN. The Redeemed Captive: A narrative of the Captivity, Sufferings, and Return of the Rev. John Williams, Minister of Deerfield, Massachusetts, who was taken prisoner by the Indians on the destruction of the town, A. D. 1700. For Sabbath Schools. New York: Published by S. W. Benedict & Co., 1833. [788]

16mo, 58 leaves, 1-7⁸, 8², wood engraved frontispiece, and 1 full-page wood engraved illustration, many lower edges uncut.

Original half binding of marbled boards, and blue leather back.

This edition not in Field.

1834

[AIKIN, JOHN AND BARBAULD, ANNA LETITIA.] The Farm-Yard Journal. For the amusement and instruction of children. Cooperstown: Stereotyped, printed and sold by H. & E. Phinney, 1834. [789]

16mo, 16 leaves, including half title with alphabets on verso, woodcut on the title, and numerous woodcuts in the text.

Original pink wrappers.
This story is extracted from *Evenings at Home* by John Aikin in collaboration with his sister, Mrs. Barbauld. The preliminary letter from Richard Markwell to *Dear Tom*, dated July 1, 1807, is in this edition addressed from Westchester, probably an addition of an American editor.

CITY CRIES AND LONDON SIGHTS. New York: Printed and sold by Mahlon Day, No. 374, Pearl-street, n. d. [c. 1834.] [790]

A Toy Book of 4 leaves, measuring 3⅛ by 1⅞ inches, a woodcut on the title-page and on each page of the text.

Contains four *Cries* and three *London sights*, each accompanied by a woodcut and a stanza of descriptive verse.

> In London, that enormous town,
> Are sights most grand and rare,
> You'll see great wonders all around,
> Making one's eyes to stare.
> There are Lions bold, and Tigers too,
> And Elephants so high,
> Great Ostriches, and Camels tall,
> And Crocodiles that cry.

[FENN, ELEANOR, LADY.] Cobwebs to Catch Flies; or dialogues in short sentences, adapted to childern (*sic*) from the age of three to eight years. New York: Mahlon Day, 374 Pearl-Street, 1834. [791]

Duodecimo, 54 leaves, 1-9⁶, woodcut of a cobweb on the title, and numerous woodcut illustrations in the text, advertisements on the last leaf.

Original yellow boards, title-page repeated on the upper cover, advertisement on the lower.
Cobwebs to catch Flies was originally published in London, and contains much useful information and moral precept chiefly in the form of graded dialogue. The illustrations in this edition are not copied from those in the English edition. On page 36 is the woodcut illustration of Mahlon Day's Juvenile Book Store, with the street number 372, from which address Day removed in 1825 or 1826 to No. 376 Pearl-street.
Lady Fenn, formerly Eleanor Frere, was the wife of Sir John Fenn, the famous antiquary. She wrote various works for the young of an educational nature, either anonymously, or over the names Mrs. Lovechild or Mrs. Teachwell. She died in 1813.

SELECT HYMNS FOR YOUTH. New York: Printed and sold by Mahlon Day, No. 374, Pearl-street, 1834. [792]

Duodecimo, 12 leaves, without signatures, first and last leaf pasted down on covers, woodcut frontispiece, woodcut vignette on title (both colored), and woodcut illustrations throughout the text.

Yellow wrappers, title on the front, and advertisements on the back.

Contains XXI hymns selected from the works of Dr. Watts, Ann and Jane Taylor and others. Many of the woodcuts were originally by Anderson.

The address in the imprint on the wrappers is No. 376 Pearl-street, from which house Mahlon Day removed to No. 374 in 1833 (see the note to Miss Howland's Rhode Island Tales, no. 782). The wrappers therefore must have been printed originally for an earlier edition.

STORIES FOR THE NURSERY; in Words of one and two Syllables. By a mother, for the use of her own children. Embellished with neat coloured copperplate engravings. Philadelphia: [Weeks, for] Morgan & Sons, 1834. [793]

Duodecimo, 24 leaves (A)-D⁶, 6 full-page colored plates, including the frontispiece.

Original wrappers, with title on the front cover, imprint reading: *Philadelphia. Published by William H. Morgan*, advertisements on the back.

Not in Weiss: *William Charles.*

The printer's imprint is on the back of the title.

1835

COBB, LYMAN. Cobb's Toys. First Series, nos. 3 and 10; Second Series, nos 1-11; Fourth Series, nos. 2 and 3. Chambersburgh and Lewistown, (Pa.) Hickok & Blood; and Hickok & Stark, 1835, 6. [794]

Original wrappers.

First Series, each number with four leaves. An additional copy of no. 3, another issue, printed at Sandy Hill, N. Y. by Griffin and Moffat. The Preface to this series is dated from New York, May 1, 1835.

Second Series, 11 volumes, each with 8 leaves. The Preface dated from New York, June 1, 1835.

This celebrated series of Toy Books is a development of the hornbook, battledore, and primer. The various numbers contain alphabets, syllabaries, and reading-easies, all fully illustrated with woodcuts, the readings consisting of stories on natural history subjects and common objects.

Lyman Cobb, a famous educator, was born in Lenox, Mass., about 1800 and died in 1864.

DELAFAYE-BRÉHIER, JULIE. New Tales for Boys. By Madame Delafaye, Author of the "Six Tales of Youth," &c. With engravings. Boston: Munroe and Francis, n. d. [c. 1835.] [795]

Early American Children's Books

Duodecimo, 60 leaves, including 2 leaves of advertisements at the beginning, A-I⁶, K⁴, woodcut frontispiece, woodcut on the title, and 3 full-page illustrations.

Original half sheep, sides with the title on the upper and advertisement on the lower.

Translated from the French of Madame Delafaye-Bréhier. The Tales are: The Stolen Ass; The Old Cloak; The Little Don Quixotes, and The School for Prodigals, each with a frontispiece.

THE HISTORY OF JACK THE GIANT KILLER, containing the whole of his wonderful exploits. Embellished with Ten Engravings. New-York and Philadelphia: Published by Turner & Fisher, n. d. [c. 1835.]   [796]

Duodecimo, 12 leaves, 1-2⁶, woodcut frontispiece and illustrations.

Original blue wrappers, title-page printed on the upper cover, and the frontispiece repeated on the lower.

Jack the Giant Killer was a native of Cornwall, and according to Andrew Lang is England's one authentic fairy hero. His detrimental effect on the infant mind has been deplored by exponents of the realistic school of thought from time immemorial (see, for example, the quotation from the preface to the *Bag of Nuts ready cracked*, no. 231); the present editor, however, has succeeded in finding a suitable moral to the story: *Thus terminates the history of Jack the Giant Killer; which, if it be useless as an example of giant killing now, when giants are not to be found; yet may be of advantage in reminding us, that all great objects can be obtained only by diligent perseverance.*

A KID, A KID. Or the Jewish Origin of the celebrated Legend The House that Jack Built. New York: Mahlon Day, No. 374 Pearl-street, 1835.   [797]

Sm. octavo, 8 leaves, a woodcut on the title-page, and at the head of each page of the text.

Half red morocco.

The Hebrew nursery rhyme, now a part of the Passover service, which is supposed to be the origin of the well known English accumulative nursery song, The House that Jack Built, but which bears a much stronger resemblance to The Old Woman and her Pig, another English accumulative song.

The Introduction gives an account of the origin of the rhyme taken from the London Congregational Magazine, and at the foot of each page is the Interpretation.

The last leaf contains a poem of seven stanzas entitled *The Ocean*, with the explanation, *The following fine verses, on a truly sublime and poetic subject, are from an Irish magazine.*

KNECHT, LEONHARD. Eine Auswahl Reim-Gebäte. Ausgezogen aus: Starks, Zollikoffers und Schmolkens Gebätbüchern und der Himmelsleiter, von Leonhard Knecht. Erste Auflage. Millgrave, Buschkill Township: Samuel Siegfried for the author, 1835.   [798]

16mo, 48 leaves, without signatures.

Original wrappers.

The imprint reads: *Millgrave, Buschkill Taunschip, gedruckt von Samuel Siegfried; für den Verfasser*, 1835.

THE LADDER OF LEARNING; to be ascended Early in the Morning. Embellished with numerous neatly coloured engravings. Pittsburgh: Published by Cook and Schoyer, 1835. [799]

Duodecimo, 12 leaves, printed on one side only, first and last pasted down to covers, woodcut frontispiece, signed *T. Sandy, sc.* on the block, vignette on title, and woodcut at head of each page of text, all colored.

Original tan wrappers with title on the upper, full-page wood engraving on the lower: *Returning from School.*

An accumulative piece, constructed on the same principle as the House that Jack Built.

THE LITTLE FISHERMAN.

I'm for the boy

Who minds his book,

Who seldom gets

His line and hook.

New York: Mahlon Day & Co., No. 374, Pearl-street, and Baker, Crane & Co., 158 Pearl-street, n. d. [c. 1835.] [800]

A toy book of 4 leaves, measuring 3⅞ by 1⅞ inches, woodcuts.

Original yellow wrappers, the title repeated on the upper, advertisement on the lower. This copy is misbound and the covers are attached back to front.

MOTHER GOOSE'S MELODIES. The Only Pure Edition. Containing all that have ever come to light of her Memorable Writings, together with those which have been discovered among the MSS. of Herculaneum. Likewise, every one recently found in the same stone box which hold the golden plates of the Book of Mormon. The whole compared, revised, and sanctioned, by one of the annotators of the Goose family. Entered according to Act of Congress in the year 1833, in the clerk's office of the District Court of Massachusetts. Boston: Printed and published by Munroe and Francis, and C. S. Francis, New-York, 1835. [801]

Sq. octavo, 47 leaves, A²⁻⁸, B-F⁸, numerous woodcut illustrations.

Original wrappers, the title with the imprint and the date 1835 and a woodcut on both sides. The imprint on the title-page is not dated.

This edition shows many differences from no. 784, also licensed in 1833. On the back of the title is a *Family Dedication*, addressed *To His Excellency The Greatest and best Gander in the Country; To his Cabinet, that roast our family so nicely; And to my large Flock of Cousins throughout the Union;—To the Fellows of all the Antiquarian, Scientifical, Philosophical, Etymological, Explanatory, Critical, Comical, and every other learned and unlearned Institution; And last, though not least, To all worthy Members of Household Nursery Societies. . .*

The order of the songs is different from that in no. 784, and some songs are included not in the other edition, with notes signed G. G. (Gilbert Gosling). The illustrations are the same. The word Norwich has gone back to the original English spelling.

OALTON, ANN ELIZABETH. The Adventures of Poll Pry, the Learned Parrot; an account of her officious ways; including her birth, education, adversity, prosperity, and death. By Anne Elizabeth Oulton. "Beg pardon—hope I don't intrude."—Paul Pry. Boston: Munroe & Francis; New York: Charles S. Francis, 1835. [802]

Duodecimo, 90 leaves, 1-15⁶, woodcut frontispiece, and woodcut illustrations.

Original stamped cloth.
First edition.
Contains explanatory notes consisting of long extracts from the works of Audubon and others. In an earlier work, no. 762, the name of the author on the title-page is spelled as in the heading, and not as on the title-page of this work.

THE PENNY PRIMER.
"I've read my pretty book all through;
How much of your's, dear Jane, have you?
A penny primer I have got,
At Mahlon Day's, it too was bought."
New York: Mahlon Day, No. 374, Pearl-street. [c. 1835.] [803]

4 leaves, measuring 3¼ by 1⅞ inches, woodcut on the title-page, woodcuts in the text.

Original yellow wrappers, the title repeated on the upper, advertisement on the lower. Contains alphabets, two pages with woodcuts and ornaments, and a passage for reading.

THE PROGRESSIVE PRIMER; adapted to Infant School instruction. Embellished with appropriate Cuts. By Mrs. Goodheart. Copy Right secured according to Law. Concord: [White & Fisher for] Moses G. Atwood, 1835. [804]

Duodecimo, 18 leaves, woodcut frontispiece, title within an ornamental border, woodcuts in text, first and last leaves pasted down to wrappers.

Original yellow wrappers, title with woodcut vignette on the upper, full-page woodcut of a deer on the lower.

Contains alphabets, syllabaries, with and without woodcut illustrations, and passages for reading; the illustrations are not new to this work. The printers' imprint is below that of the publisher on the wrapper, but does not occur on the title-page.

SIGOURNEY, LYDIA HUNTLEY. Tales and Essays for Children. By Mrs. L. H. Sigourney. Hartford: [F. Cnafield (*sic*) for] F. J. Huntington, 1835. [805]

Sm. quarto, 64 leaves (-)², 1-15⁴, 16², vignette on the title-page, and at the end.

Original green cloth.

First edition.

Contains eleven stories, most of them connected with New England, and a hymn.

The printer's imprint is on the back of the title.

Lydia Huntley Sigourney (1791-1865), formerly Lydia Huntley, was born in Norwich, Connecticut, and lived there, where at the age of nineteen she established a school for girls, and at Hartford, until her death. She was the author of numerous works in prose and poetry.

TOY-BOOKS. Little John; the Industrious Boy.—Simple Verses; with Pretty Pictures. New Haven: S. Babcock, 1835. [806]

2 volumes, each with 4 leaves, measuring 2⅞ by 1¾ inches, woodcuts in the text.

Original wrappers, the titles with woodcuts on the upper, and woodcuts on the lower.

TOY-BOOKS. Tom Thumb's Picture Alphabet; in rhyme.—The Little Sketch-Book; or useful objects illustrated.—The Book of the Sea; for the Instruction of Little Sailors. New York: Kiggins & Kellogg, n. d. [c. 1835.] [807]

3 toy books of 4 leaves each, measuring 3⅛ by 2 inches, woodcuts.

Original wrappers, upper covers with the titles headed First Series.—No. 1., No. 8., and No. 12. respectively, the lower covers with advertisements.

The rhymed alphabet in Tom Thumb's Picture Alphabet begins:

> A is an Angler,
>   Young, but expert;
>
> B is a Butcher,
>   Who wears a red shirt.

Little John;

THE

INDUSTRIOUS BOY.

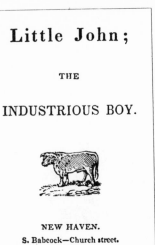

NEW HAVEN.
S. Babcock—Church street.
1835.

*Title-page from "Little John;
the Industrious Boy"*

Simple Verses;

with

PRETTY PICTURES.

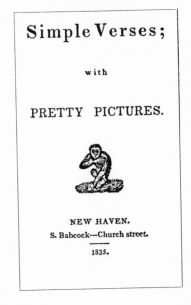

NEW HAVEN.
S. Babcock--Church street.
1835.

*Title-page from "Simple Verses;
with Pretty Pictures"*

FIRST SERIES. No 8.

THE LITTLE

SKETCH-BOOK;

OR

USEFUL OBJECTS ILLUSTRATED

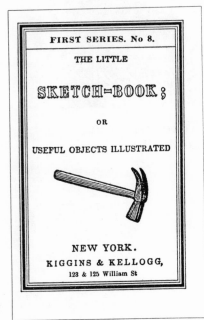

NEW YORK.

KIGGINS & KELLOGG,
123 & 125 William St

*Title-page from
"The Little Sketch-Book"*

FIRST SERIES.—No 12.

THE

BOOK OF THE SEA;

FOR THE INSTRUCTION OF

LITTLE SAILORS.

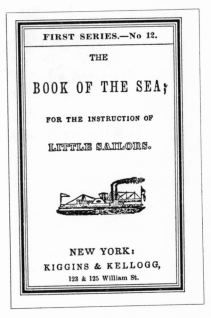

NEW YORK:

KIGGINS & KELLOGG,
123 & 125 William St.

*Title-page from
"The Book of the Sea"*

The sportive Needle quick to thread,
The verdant green they nimbly tread.

One Boy's the Horse, the Yoke the next,
The Horseman's place I like the best.

Page from "Juvenile Pastimes"

[WRIGHT, ALFRED, AND BYINGTON, CYRUS.] Triumphant Deaths of Pious Children. In the Choctaw Language. By Missionaries of the American Board of Commissioners for Foreign Missions. Boston: Crocker & Brewster, for the Board, 1835. [808]

Duodecimo, 27 leaves, A-C⁹, several pages of hymns at the end, in Choctaw, with English headings.

Original marbled wrappers.
First edition.
Pilling, page 100.

1836

[CHILD, LYDIA MARIA.] The First Settlers of New-England: or, Conquest of the Pequods, Narragansets and Pokanokets: as related by a mother to her children, and designed for the instruction of youth. By a Lady of Massachusetts. Boston: Munroe and Francis and Charles S. Francis, New York, 1836. [809]

Duodecimo, 144 leaves, 1-24⁶, engraved frontispiece, 2 leaves of advertisements at the end.

Original boards, title with date on the upper, leather back.
The title-page is undated, the date being taken from the imprint on the cover.
Lydia Maria Child (formerly Francis), famous as a children's author, and as a champion of anti-slavery, was born in Medford, Massachusetts, in 1802, and died at Wayland in the same state, 1880.

[DAVIS, JOHN.] Captain Smith and Princess Pocahontas, an Indian tale. New edition, revised and corrected. Dayton: Published by B. F. Ells and E. M. Strong and sold by E. M. Strong, Dayton, Ohio, 1836. [810]

Sm. octavo, 56 leaves, 1-7⁸.

Original half binding of green boards and sheepskin.
For the first edition see no. 302. This edition does not contain the List of Subscribers to the first edition, but has at the end *Historical Sketches*, pages 108-112.

[DEFOE, DANIEL.] The Life and Adventures of Robinson Crusoe, embellished with engravings, by Wm. Robertson. Ithaca, N.Y.: Mack, Andrus & Woodruff, 1836. [811]

Duodecimo, 80 leaves, 1-13⁶, 14².

Original half binding.
At the end are Cowper's *Verses, supposed to be written by Alex. Selkirk...*

Early American Children's Books

NEW-YORK SCENES: designed for the Entertainment and Instruction of City and Country Children. New York: Mahlon Day, No. 374 Pearl-street, 1836. [812]

Duodecimo, 12 leaves, first and last pasted down to front and back covers, wood-cuts by A. Anderson, tailpiece having his signature.

A re-issue of the edition of 1833, with new covers.

The imprint on the title-page bears the date 1833, with the address 376 Pearl Street.

The scenes, many of which are illustrated with woodcuts, include Trinity Church, Broadway; City Hall, Park; Police Office, City Hall; a Fire Engine; etc.

On the cover is a picture of a balloon.

A notice at the beginning, signed M. D., and dated 11th mo. 1832, explains *The first edition of this little work was printed several years ago. Since which time, divers changes have been made in the rooms of the City Hall, but this circumstance will not disturb the moral intended to be conveyed to children.*

PETER PIPER'S PRACTICAL PRINCIPLES of plain and perfect Pronunciation. Philadelphia: Willard Johnson, 1836. [813]

Sm. octavo, 16 leaves, A-B⁸, the first with frontispiece and last (a blank) pasted down to covers; woodcut on the title, and a woodcut illustration on each page of the alphabet, all in colors.

Original orange wrappers, title and woodcut on the upper, two woodcuts on the lower (varying in different copies).

The Preface states that *Peter Piper, without Pretension to Precocity or Profoundness, Puts Pen to Paper to Produce these Puzzling Pages, Purposely to Please the Palates of Pretty Prattling Play fellows. . . He Prays Parents to Purchase this Playful Performance, Partly to Pay him for his Patience and Pains; Partly to Provide for the Profit of the Printers and Publishers; but Principally to Prevent the Pernicious Prevalence of Perverse Pronunciation.*

At the end is a Hymn.

The original edition was published by J. Harris in St. Paul's Churchyard, London. The first American edition was published by Carter Andrews and Company in Lancaster, Massachusetts, about 1830.

The woodcuts in the present edition are all beautifully colored. The milestone beside which *Francis Fribble figured on a Frenchman's Filly* is lettered *Bolton* 4 M. This probably refers to Bolton, Mass., a small town near Lancaster, the home of the first American edition, and not to Bolton in Lancashire, England.

[RASPE, RUDOLF ERIC.] The Travels and Adventures by Sea and Land, of Baron Munchausen. Containing his Expedition into Africa—Destroys a Thousand Lions—Feasts of Live Bulls—Is Scalp't and Roasted by savages in the Wilds of North America—The Baron wrecked on an Island of Ice—Builds a Cast Iron Bridge of one Arch from the interior of Africa to England. Also, an account of his Celebrated Voyage to the

Cover from "Peter Piper's Practical Principles
of plain and perfect Pronunciation"

P p

Peter Piper picked a peck of pickled Peppers:
Did Peter Piper pick a peck of pickled Pep-
pers?
If Peter Piper picked a peck of pickled Pep-
pers,
Where's the peck of pickled Peppers Peter
Piper picked?

*Page from "Peter Piper's Practical Principles
of plain and perfect Pronunciation"*

Moon and Dog-Star. Humbly dedicated, without permission, to his illustrious Grandson the Hon. Basil H... ! Munchausen, R. N. Twenty-fourth American edition, Enlarged, corrected and improved. Baltimore: Lucas & Wight, 1836.   [814]

Duodecimo, 36 leaves, 1-6⁶.

Original boards, title with vignette and imprint on the front cover, linen back, vignette and advertisement on the back.

The date on the title-page is 1835, and the name of the printer does not occur.

Rudolf Eric Raspe (1737-1794) was a German by birth, who became disgraced in his own country, and fled to England. Some of his malpractices in Scotland are said to have given Scott the idea of Dousterswivel in *The Antiquary*. Baron Munchausen existed in real life, and the account of his adventures by Raspe, which received many additions by others, acquired a world-wide popularity, and was translated into many languages.

THE WASHINGTON PRIMER, or First Book for Children. Philadelphia: Willard Johnson, 1836.   [815]

Duodecimo, 18 leaves, A-C⁶, woodcut with portrait of Washington on the title, and numerous woodcuts in the text.

Original blue wrappers, title and large woodcut of an eagle and a snake on the upper, *A Hymn* on the lower consisting of four 4-line stanzas.

A primer containing alphabets, syllables, woodcuts, passages for reading, etc., the cuts being chiefly of natural history objects.

WRIGHT, REV. ASHER. Diuhsáwahgwah Gayádoshăh. Gówahás Goyádoh. Sgăóyadih Dówănandenyo. Neh Nadigéhjihshohoh dodísdoăgoh; Wastók tadínageh. [Boston: Crocker & Brewster,] 1836.   [816]

Duodecimo, 22 leaves, 1-3⁶, 4⁴, woodcut frontispiece and illustrations.

Original marbled covers.
Pilling, page 175.
An elementary reading book in the Seneca language. At the end is a Seneca and English vocabulary, alphabetically arranged. The last leaf has the colophon in English.

INDEXES

Index of Authors and Titles

The References are to the Numbers in the Catalogue

Index of Authors and Titles

Index of Authors and Titles

Index of Authors and Titles

Index of Authors and Titles

Index of Authors and Titles

Index of Authors and Titles

Moral Tales for young people. New York, 1826.   688

Tomorrow, or the dangers of delay. New York, 1813.   472

Edwin and Henry, or Holiday times. New Haven, 1825.   659

Elegy on the Death and Burial of Cock Robin. Phila., 1805.   305

Another edition. Albany, 1813.   471

Elements of Geography. *see* Phillips, Sir Richard.

Elements of Geography made easy. Phila., 1825.   660

Elliott, Mary. The History of Tommy Two Shoes. Phila., 1829.   724

My Father. New York, 1817.   551

Another edition. Phila., 1824.   631

My Sister. New York, 1830.   736

The Two Edwards. Phila., 1827.   694

Elmina; or The Flower that Never Fades. Albany, 1810.   417

also in The American Primer.   282

Ely, John. The Child's Instructor. Phila., 1793.   168

Another edition. New York, 1828.   707

English, Clara. The Children in the Wood. Phila., 1807.   330

Another edition. ibid., 1813.   473

Another edition. Troy, 1825.   661

Entertaining and Interesting story of Ali Baba the woodcutter. Phila., 1825.   662

Entertaining Fables for the instruction of children. Worcester, 1794.   173

Entertaining History of Jobson and Nell. Phila., 1825.   663

Entertaining History of two pious twin children. Newmarket, 1816.   538

Entertaining, moral, and religious repository. Elizabethtown, 1798.   235

Essay on Punctuation. *see* Robertson, Joseph.   141

Evenings in Boston. Boston, 1828.   708

Exhibition of Tom Thumb. Worcester, 1787.   116

Extraordinary Life and Adventures of Robin Hood. New York, 1823.   624

Another edition. ibid., 1828.   709

see also Robin Hood.

Fables ancient and modern. *see* Godwin, William.   331

Fables for young ladies. Phila., 1820.   589

Fall of Adam. *see* More, Hannah.   259

False stories corrected. New York, 1814.   487

Farmer's Daughters. *see* The Death and Burial of Cock Robin.

also in The Sugar Plumb.   123

and The Wisdom of Crop the Conjuror.   186

Farm-Yard Journal. *see* Aikin, John and Barbauld, A. L.   789

Father's Advice to his child. Exeter, 1792.   157

Another edition. *in* The Pious Parent's Present.   532

Father's Advice to his Son. *in* The Pious Parent's Present.   532

Father's Gift. Phila., 1804.   294

see A Mother's Remarks on a set of cuts.   288

Fénélon, François de Salignac de la Mothe. On Faithfulness in little things. New York, 1801.   268

Fenn, Eleanor. Cobwebs to catch flies. New York, 1834.   791

Fenning, Daniel. The American Youth's Instructor. Dover, 1795.   191

Few drops of choice honey. *see* Lane, Jeremiah.   176

Fielding, Henry. Remarkable History of Tom Jones. Salem, 1799.   244

Finch, C. The Gamut and the Time Table. Phila., 1824.   632

First, second, and third chapter of accidents. *see* Darton, William.   291

First settlers of New England. *see* Child, Lydia Maria.   809

Fisher, George. The American Instructor. Phila., 1748.   31

Flora's Gala. Phila., 1809.   391

Foreign Visitant. *see* Oliver, Daniel.   504

Forsaken Infant. *see* Day, Thomas.   574

Fortune-Teller. Phila., 1793.   169

Fortune-Teller. *see* More, Hannah.   341

Forty Thieves. *see* Ali Baba.

Fourth Commandment. *see* American Tract Society.   733

Index of Authors and Titles

Index of Authors and Titles

Index of Authors and Titles

Index of Authors and Titles

Index of Authors and Titles

Index of Authors and Titles

Index of Authors and Titles

Index of Authors and Titles

Index of Authors and Titles

Index of Authors and Titles

Index of Authors and Titles

Index of Authors and Titles

Index of Authors and Titles

Index of Authors and Titles

Index of Authors and Titles

Index of Authors and Titles

Index of Printers and Publishers

The References are to the Numbers in the Catalogue. The Dates in all cases are subject to revision.

Index of Printers and Publishers

Index of Printers and Publishers

Index of Printers and Publishers

Index of Printers and Publishers

Index of Printers and Publishers

Index of Printers and Publishers

Index of Printers and Publishers

Index of Printers and Publishers

Index of Printers and Publishers

Index of Printers and Publishers

Index of Printers and Publishers

Index of Printers and Publishers

Index of Printers and Publishers

Index of Printers and Publishers

Index of Printers and Publishers

Index of Printers and Publishers

Index of Printers and Publishers

Index of Printers and Publishers

Index of Printers and Publishers

Index of Printers and Publishers

Index of Printers and Publishers

Index of Printers and Publishers

Index of Printers and Publishers

Index of Printers and Publishers

Index of Printers and Publishers

Index of Printers and Publishers

Index of Printers and Publishers

Index of Printers and Publishers

Index of Printers and Publishers

List of Printers, Publishers and Booksellers

Adams, James; Wilmington, Del.
Adams, John; Phila., Pa.
Adancourt, F.; Troy, N. Y.
Aitken, Robert; Phila., Pa.
Alexander & Phillips; Carlisle, Pa.
Allen, John; Boston, Mass.
Andrews, Loring; Albany, N. Y.
Appleton, Daniel; New York, N. Y.
Armstrong & Plaskitt; Baltimore, Md.
Ash, Thomas T.; Phila., Pa.
Ash & Mason; Phila, Pa.
Ashmead, I. & Co.; Phila., Pa.
Atwood, Moses G.; Concord, N. H.
Avery, Joseph; Boston, Mass. and Plymouth, Mass.
Avery, Mary; Boston, Mass.
Babcock, John; Hartford, Conn.
Babcock, John & Son; New Haven, Conn.
Babcock, S.; New Haven, Conn.
Babcock, S. & Co.; Charleston, S. C.
Babcock, S. & W. R.; Charleston, S. C.
Bache, Benjamin Franklin; Phila., Pa.
Bailey, Francis; Phila., Pa.
Bailey, Lydia R.; Phila., Pa.
Bailey, Robert; Phila., Pa.
Baker, Crane & Co.; New York, N. Y.
Baldwin, J. B. & L.; Bridgeport, Conn.
Barber, John Warner; Hartford, Conn.
Barclay, Andrew; Boston, Mass.
Bärtgis, Matthias; Frederickstown, Md.
Bartram, Archibald; Phila., Pa.
Bason, William P.; Charleston, S. C.
Battelle, E.; Boston, Mass.
Bedlington, T.; Boston, Mass.
Bedlington, T., & J. Ball; Boston, Mass.
Belcher & Armstrong; Boston, Mass.
Bell, Robert; Phila., Pa.
Benedict, S. W. & Co.; New York, N. Y.
Bennett & Walton; Phila., Pa.

Billmeyer, Michael; Germantown, Pa.
Bingham, Caleb; Boston, Mass.
Bioren, John; Phila., Pa.
Bliss, David; New York, N. Y.
Bolles, William; New London, Conn.
Bolles, W. & J.; New London, Conn.
Bonsal & Niles; Wilmington, Del. and Baltimore, Md.
Bookbinders Society; New York, N. Y.
Boone, Nicholas; Boston, Mass.
Borradaile, William; New York, N. Y.
Borrenstein, D. A.; Princeton, N. J.
Bouvier, John; Phila., Pa. and Hamiltonville, Pa.
Bowen, A.; Boston, Mass.
Bowles, Leonard C.; Boston, Mass.
Bowles & Dearborn; Boston, Mass.
Bowman, A.; Phila., Pa.
Boyle, John; Boston, Mass.
Bradford, Andrew; Phila., Pa.
Bradford, Thomas & William; Phila., Pa.
Bradford, William; Phila., Pa.
Bradford, William; New York, N. Y.
Bradford & Inskeep; Phila., Pa.
Bradford & Read; Boston, Mass.
Bragg, Samuel, jun.; Dover, N. H.
Brautigam, Daniel; Phila., Pa.
Brisban & Brannan; New York, N. Y.
Brower, Abraham, jr.; New York, N. Y.
Brown, Hori; Leicester, Mass.
Brown, William; Phila., Pa.
Brown & Merritt; Phila., Pa.
Bryant & Denio; Greenfield, Mass.
Brynberg, Peter; Wilmington, Del.
Bull, John; New York, N. Y.
Bunce, C. W.; New York, N. Y.
Bunce, George; New Haven, Conn.
Burd & Boden; Charleston, S. C.

List of Printers, Publishers and Booksellers

Burgess, George W.; New York, N. Y.
Burgess, William; New York, N. Y.
Burtus, Samuel A.; New York, N. Y.
Bushell, J., and J. Green; Boston, Mass.
Butler, Simeon; Northampton, Mass.
Buttolph, Nicholas; Boston, Mass.
Butts, I. R. & Co.; Boston, Mass.
Byrne, John; Windham, Conn.
Cady, Ebenezer P.; New London, Conn.
Campbell, Robert; Phila., Pa.
Campbell, Samuel; New York, N. Y.
Canfield, Philemon; Hartford, Conn.
Carey, Mathew; Phila., Pa.
Carey & Co.; Phila., Pa.
Carey, Stewart and Co.; Phila., Pa.
Carlisle, David; Boston, Mass.
Carr, Robert; Phila., Pa.
Carter Andrews and Company; Lancaster, Mass.
Carter & Hendee; Boston, Mass.
Chandler, A. & Co.; New York, N. Y.
Charles, Mary; Phila., Pa.
Charles, William; Phila., Pa.
Charless, Joseph; Phila., Pa.
Chattin, James; Phila., Pa.
Cist, Carl; Phila., Pa.
Clap, W. T.; Boston, Mass.
Claxton, A.: Phila., Pa.
Clussman, J. A.; New York, N. Y.
Coale, E. J.; Baltimore, Md.
Cochran, Jesse; Windsor, Vt.
Coles, Ann; Phila., Pa.
Collins, Isaac & Son; New York, N. Y.
Conner, James; New York, N. Y.
Conrad, Solomon W.; Phila., Pa.
Cook & Schoyer; Pittsburgh, Pa.
Cooke, Increase & Co.; New Haven, Conn. and Hartford, Conn.
Cooke, Oliver D.; New London, Conn. and Hartford, Conn.
Cooke & Co.; Hartford, Conn.
Cooke & Hale; Hartford, Conn.

Cory, Marshall and Hammond; Providence, R. I.
Cotton, Edward; Boston, Mass.
Coverly, Nathaniel; Boston, Mass. and Salem, Mass.
Coverly, N. & J.; Salem, Mass.
Crocker & Brewster; Boston, Mass.
Croswell & Son; Catskill, N. Y.
Crukshank, Joseph; Phila., Pa.
Crukshank, J. & J.; Phila., Pa.
Cummings and Hilliard; Boston, Mass.
Curtis, John; Phila., Pa.
Cushing & Jewett; Baltimore, Md.
Davis, Cornelius; New York, N. Y.
Day, Mahlon; New York, N. Y.
Dean, W. E.; New York, N. Y.
Denio, J.; Greenfield, Mass.
Dickins, John; Phila., Pa.
Dickinson, A.; Phila., Pa. and Whitehall, Pa.
Dickinson, K.; Phila., Pa.
Dickinson & Heartt; Phila., Pa.
Disturnell, J.; Troy, N. Y.
Disturnell, W. & J.; Troy, N. Y.
Douglas, Nathan; Poughkeepsie, N. Y.
Douglas & Nichols; Danbury, Conn.
Dunham, J. M.; Boston, Mass.
Dunlap, William; Phila., Pa.
Durell, William; New York, N. Y.
Durrie & Peck; New Haven, Conn.
Duyckinck, Evert; New York, N. Y.
Duyckinck, E. & Co., New York, N. Y.
Edes, Benjamin & Sons; Boston, Mass.
Edes & Gill; Boston, Mass.
Edwards, John; Boston, Mass.
Edwards, Joseph; Boston, Mass.
Elder, J.; Harrisburg, Pa.
Eliot, Benjamin; Boston, Mass.
Elliot, John; Boston, Mass.
Elliott, Nathan; Catskill, N. Y.
Ells, B. F. and E. M. Strong; Dayton, Ohio.

List of Printers, Publishers and Booksellers

Etheridge, Samuel; Charlestown, Mass.
Everett, O.; Boston, Mass.
Fagan, A.; Phila., Pa.
Fanshaw, Daniel; New York, N. Y.
Fisk & Chase; Concord, N. H.
Fleet, Thomas; Boston, Mass.
Fleet, Thomas and John; Boston, Mass.
Forbes, Samuel; New York, N. Y.
Forbes & Co.; New York, N. Y.
Fowle, Z.; Boston, Mass.
Fowle and Draper; Boston, Mass.
Francis, Charles S.; New York, N. Y.
Francis, C. S. & Company, New York, N. Y. and Boston, Mass.
Franklin, Benjamin; Phila., Pa.
Franklin, B. and D. Hall; Phila., Pa.
Franklin, James; Boston, Mass.
Gaine, Hugh; New York, N. Y.
Gilbert, John F.; Frankford, Pa.
Gilley, William B.; New York, N. Y.
Gilman, Julius; Hartford, Conn.
Gilman, W. & J.; Newburyport, Mass.
Gomez, Benjamin; New York, N. Y.
Goodsell, P. B.; Hartford, Conn.
Goodwin, George & Sons; Hartford, Conn.
Goss, Sylvester T.; Boston, Mass.
Grattan, W.; New York, N. Y.
Graves, B.; Phila., Pa.
Gray, Benjamin; Boston, Mass.
Gray & Bunce; New York, N. Y.
Green, Bartholomew; Boston, Mass.
Green, B., & J. Allen; Boston, Mass.
Green, Henry; Phila., Pa.
Green, Samuel; New London, Conn.
Green, Thomas and Samuel; New Haven, Conn.
Green, Timothy; New London, Conn. and Boston, Mass.
Green, T. & J.; New London, Conn.
Greenleaf's Printing Office; Boston, Mass.

Greer, William; Phila., Pa.
Griffin & Moffat; Sandy Hill, N. Y.
Griggs & Co.; Phila., Pa.
Griggs & Dickinson; Phila., Pa.
Hale, Nathan; Boston, Mass.
Hale & Hosmer; Hartford, Conn.
Hall, Samuel; Boston, Mass.
Hall and Sellers; Phila., Pa.
Hancock, Thomas; Boston, Mass.
Harding, J.; Phila., Pa.
Hart & Hare; Sandy Hill, N. Y.
Hasselbach, Nicolaus; Chesnut Hill, Pa.
Hastings, W.; Waterville, Me.
Haven, J. P.; New York, N. Y.
Heaton & Williams; Providence, R. I.
Henchman, Daniel; Boston, Mass.
Henkel, Andreas N.; Newmarket, Va.
Henkel, Salomon; Newmarket, Va.
Hickock & Blood; Chambersburg, Pa.
Hickock & Stark; Lewistown, Pa.
Hill, I. and W. R.; Concord, N. H.
Hilliard & Metcalf; Cambridge, Mass.
Hilliard, Gray, Little and Wilkins; Boston, Mass.
Hoag & Atwood; Concord, N. H.
Hodge, Robert; Boston, Mass.
Hoff & Derrick; Phila., Pa.
Hoff, J., & H. Kämmerer; Phila., Pa.
Hogan, David; Phila., Pa.
Horton, J. S.; Baltimore, Md.
Hosford, E. & E.; Albany, N. Y.
Hosmer & Goodwin; Litchfield, Conn.
Hough, George; Concord, N. H.
House, E. G.; Boston, Mass.
Howe, Hezekiah & Co.; New Haven, Conn.
Howe, J.; Phila., Pa.
Hubbard, Russell; Norwich, Conn.
Hubbard, Thomas; Norwich, Conn.
Hudson and Goodwin; Hartford, Conn.
Humphreys, James; Phila., Pa.
Huntington, F. J.; Hartford, Conn.

Huntington, H. & F. J.; Hartford, Conn.

Hurtin & Commardinger; New York, N. Y.

Hutchins, James R.; Worcester, Mass.

Imbert's Lithographic Office; New York, N. Y.

Inskeep and Bradford; New York, N. Y.

Ives, W. & S. B.; Salem, Mass.

James, Joseph; Phila., Pa.

Jansen, Benjamin G.; New York, N. Y.

Jansen, Reynier; Phila., Pa.

Johnson, Benjamin; Phila., Pa.

Johnson, B. and J.; Phila., Pa.

Johnson, B., and T. Barton; Reading, Pa.

Johnson, Jacob; Phila., Pa., Whitehall, Pa., and Richmond, Va.

Johnson, Joseph; Wilmington, Del.

Johnson, L.; Phila., Pa.

Johnson, Peter A.; Morristown, N. J.

Johnson, Willard; Phila., Pa.

Johnson & Warner; Phila., Pa., Lexington, Ky. and Richmond, Va.

Johnston and Justice; Phila., Pa.

Jones, W.; Phila., Pa.

Jones, Hoff & Derrick; Phila., Pa.

Jordan, A. C. & Co.; Norfolk, Va.

Keatinge, Henry S.; Baltimore, Md.

Kiggins & Kellogg; New York, N. Y.

Kimber and Conrad; Phila., Pa.

Kimber & Sharpless; Phila., Pa.

King, Solomon; New York, N. Y.

Kirk, Thomas; Brooklyn, N. Y.

Kite, Benjamin and Thomas; Phila., Pa.

Knecht, Leonhard; Millgrave, Pa.

Kneeland and Adams; Boston, Mass.

Kneeland, Daniel, and J. Kneeland; Boston, Mass.

Kneeland, Samuel; Boston, Mass.

Kneeland, S., and T. Green; Boston, Mass.

Kollock, Shepard; Elizabethtown, N. J.

Larkin, Ebenezer; Boston, Mass.

Lawrence, Daniel; Phila., Pa.

Leavitt, Jonathan; New York, N. Y.

Leibert, Peter; Germantown, Pa.

Lewis, Joseph N.; Baltimore, Md.

Lewis, Junius S.; Catskill, N. Y.

Lewis, Uriah C.; Newburgh, N. Y.

Lincoln & Gleason; Hartford, Conn.

Longworth, D.; New York, N. Y.

Loomis, G. J. and Co.; Albany, N. Y.

Loring, James; Boston, Mass.

Loudon, A.; Carlisle, Pa. and Whitehall, Pa.

Loudon, Samuel; New York, N. Y.

Lucas, F. jr.; Baltimore, Md.

Lucas & Wight; Baltimore, Md.

M'Alpine, William; Boston, Mass.

M'Carty & Davis; Phila., Pa.

M'Culloch, John; Phila., Pa.

M'Culloch, W.; Phila., Pa.

Mack, Andrus & Woodruff; Ithaca, N.Y.

Maltby, A. H. & Co.; New Haven, Conn.

Mann, Herman; Dedham, Mass.

Mann, J.; Morristown, N. J.

Manning, T. S.; Phila., Pa.

Marks, S.; Peekskill, N. Y.

Marsh & Capen; Boston, Mass.

Marshall, Stephen; Mount Pleasant, N. Y.

Matchett, R. J.; Baltimore, Md.

Maxwell, J.; Phila., Pa.

Mecom, Benjamin; Boston, Mass.

Mein, John; Boston, Mass.

Mein & Fleeming; Boston, Mass.

Mentz, George W.; Phila., Pa.

Mentz, William; Phila., Pa.

Merritt, Samuel; Phila., Pa.

Metcalf, John; Wendell, Mass.

Meyer, Jacob; Phila., Pa.

Miller, Henry; Phila., Pa.

Mitchell, Edward; New York, N. Y.

List of Printers, Publishers and Booksellers

Moore, Jacob B.; Concord, N. H.
Moore, John W. & Co.; Concord, N. H.
Morgan, William H.; Phila., Pa.
Morgan and Sons; Phila., Pa.
Morgan and Yeager; Phila., Pa.
Moses, Samuel T.; Exeter, N. H.
Munroe and Francis; Boston, Mass.
Murphy, John; Baltimore, Md.
Mycall, John; Newburyport, Mass.
Negus, E.; Boston, Mass.
Newman, Mark; Andover, Mass.
Nichols, Francis; Boston, Mass.
Noel, Garrat; New York, N. Y.
Norman, John; Boston, Mass.
Norman, William; Boston, Mass.
Olds, Benjamin; Newark, N. J.
Oliver, Daniel; Boston, Mass.
Oram, James; Trenton, N. J. and New York, N. Y.
Palfray, W. jr. and J. Chapman; Salem, Mass.
Parke, James P.; Phila., Pa.
Parmenter and Balch; Boston, Mass.
Patten, Nathaniel; Hartford, Conn.
Paul, A.; New York, N. Y.
Peck, E.; Rochester, N. Y.
Pendleton and Hill; New York ,N. Y.
Perry, Joanna; Boston, Mass.
Perry, Michael; Boston, Mass.
Phillips, Eleazer; Charlestown, Mass.
Phillips, Gillam; Boston, Mass.
Phillips, John; Boston, Mass.
Phillips, Samuel; Boston, Mass.
Phinney, Elihu; Cooperstown, N. Y.
Phinney, H. & E; Cooperstown, N. Y.
Plowman, Thomas L.; Phila., Pa.
Porter, R.; Wilmington, Del.
Potter, Paraclete; Poughkeepsie, N. Y.
Potter, P. & S.; Poughkeepsie, N. Y.
Pounder, Jonathan; Phila., Pa.
Pratt, Luther & Co.; Lansingburgh, N. Y.

Preston, Samuel; Amherst, N. H.
Probasco, Simon; Phila., Pa.
Proctor, Nathaniel; Boston, Mass.
Putnam & Hunt; Boston, Mass.
Rakestraw, Joseph; Phila., Pa.
Ranlet, Henry; Exeter, N. H.
Reed, A.; Hartford, Conn.
Rice, H. & P.; Phila., Pa.
Richards, Seth; Middletown, Conn.
Robinson, D. F. & Co.; Hartford, Conn.
Robinson, J.; Baltimore, Md.
Rogers and Fowle; Boston, Mass.
Roorbach, Orville A.; New York, N. Y.
Russell, B. & J.; Hartford, Conn.
Sampson, Chittenden & Croswell; Hudson, N. Y.
Sanno, Friedrich; Carlisle, Pa.
Saur, Christopher; Germantown, Pa.
Schnee, Joseph; Lebanon, Pa.
Scott, Joseph T.; Phila., Pa.
Scott, J. W.; Phila., Pa.
Seward and Williams; Utica, N. Y.
Seymour, J.; New York, N. Y.
Sheldon & Goodwin; Hartford, Conn.
Shober and Loudon; New York, N. Y.
Sidney's Press; New Haven, Conn. and Hartford, Conn.
Siegfried, Samuel; Millgrave, Pa.
Smith, Daniel D.; New York, N. Y.
Snowden and M'Corkle; Chambersburg, Pa.
Southwark Office; Phila., Pa.
Southwick, Solomon; Newport, R. I.
Sower, B. W. & Co.; Baltimore, Md.
Sower, Christopher; see Saur, Christopher.
Sower, David; Norristown, Pa.
Spencer, Thomas; Albany, N. Y.
Spooner, Judah Paddock; Fairhaven, Vt.
Spotswood, William; Boston, Mass.
Springer, James; New London, Conn.
Starr, J. F. & C.; Hartford, Conn.

List of Printers, Publishers and Booksellers

Stavely & Bringhurst; Phila., Pa.
Steiner und Kämmerer; Phila., Pa.
Steuart Andrew; Phila., Pa.
Stewart, Peter; Phila., Pa.
Stewart & Cochran; Phila, Pa.
Stoddard, Ashbel; Hudson, N. Y.
Strattan, N.; Lansingburgh, N. Y.
Strong, E. M.; Dayton, Ohio.
Sweeny & M'Kenzie; Phila., Pa.
Sweitzer, Henry; Phila., Pa.
Swords, T. and J.; New York, N. Y.
Thomas, Isaiah; Boston, Mass. and
   Worcester, Mass.
Thomas, Isaiah, jun.; Boston, Mass. and
   Worcester, Mass.
Thomas, Isaiah, and Company; Boston,
   Mass.
Thomas, I. & Co.; Walpole, N. H.
Thomas, Isaiah, and Son; Worcester,
   Mass.
Thomas and Andrews; Boston, Mass.
Thomas and Carlisle; Walpole, N. H.
Thomas, Andrews & Penniman; Albany,
   N. Y.
Thomas & Sturtevant; Worcester, Mass.
Thomas & Tappan; Portsmouth, N. H.
Thomas & Whipple; Newburyport,
   Mass.
Thomas, Son and Thomas; Worcester,
   Mass.
Tiebout & O'Brien; New York, N. Y.
Tiffany, Silvester; Lansingburgh, N. Y.
Timothy, Peter; Charleston, S. C.
Todd, L. & B.; Hartwick, N. Y.
Totten, J. C.; New York, N. Y.
Tracy & Bliss; Lansingburgh, N. Y.
True, Benjamin; Boston, Mass.
Trumbull, John; Norwich, Conn.
Trumbull, Samuel; Stoningtonport, Conn.
Tuckniss, Henry; Phila., Pa.
Turnbull, J. & B.; Steubenville, Ohio.
Turner, W.; New York, N. Y.

Turner & Fisher; New York, N. Y. and
   Philadelphia, Pa.
Tyrell, R.; New York, N. Y.
Underhill, R. L. & Co.; Bath, N. Y.
Uranian Press; Phila., Pa.
Vance, J. & Co.; Baltimore, Md.
Vanderpool & Cole; New York, N. Y.
Van Veghten & Son; Schenectady, N. Y.
Van Winkle & Wiley; New York, N. Y.
Wait, Thomas B.; Portland, Me.
Wait, Thomas B. & Sons; Boston, Mass.
Wait, Greene and Co.; Boston, Mass.
Waitt & Dow; Boston, Mass.
Walton, E. P.; Montpelier, Vt.
Warner, Benjamin; Phila., Pa., Charleston,
   S. C., and Richmond, Va.
Warner, William; Baltimore, Md.
Warner & Hanna; Baltimore, Md.
Watts, J. G. & E. Brooks; Walpole,
   N. H.
Weeks, William W.; Phila., Pa.
Wells, Charles; Amherst, N. H.
West, John; Boston, Mass.
West, John and David; Boston, Mass.
West and Richardson; Boston, Mass.
Whipple & Lawrence; Salem, Mass.
Whitcomb, Chapman; Leominster, Mass.
White, James; Boston, Mass.
White, J., and C. Cambridge; Boston,
   Mass.
White, Timothy; Boston, Mass.
White & Fisher; Concord, N. H.
Whitmore & Minor; New Haven, Conn.
Williams, William; Utica, N. Y.
Willis, Nathaniel; Boston, Mass.
Wilson, James; Wilmington, Del.
Wood, R. & G. S.; New York, N. Y.
Wood, Samuel; New York, N. Y.
Wood, Samuel & Sons; New York, N. Y.
Wood, Samuel S. & Co.; Baltimore, Md.
Woodhouse, William; Phila., Pa.
Woodward & Green; Middletown, Conn.

List of Printers, Publishers and Booksellers

Woodward, W. W.; Phila., Pa.
Wright, J.; Sandy Hill, N. Y.
Wrigley & Berriman; Phila., Pa.
Young and M'Culloch; Phila., Pa.

Young, Stewart and M'Culloch; Phila., Pa.
Young, William; Phila., Pa.
Zentler, Conrad; Phila., Pa.

Bibliography

ASHTON, JOHN. Chapbooks of the Eighteenth Century. London, 1882.

BARRY, FLORENCE VALENTINE. A Century of Children's Books. London, 1922.

BATES, ALBERT CARLOS. History of the Holy Jesus.

Bibliographical Essays, A Tribute to Wilberforce Eames. (Cambridge, Mass.) 1924.

Cambridge History of American Literature, Vol. II, Chapter 7, by Algernon Tassin, New York and Cambridge, 1918.

Cambridge History of English Literature, Vol. XI, Chapter 16, by F. J. Harvey Darton, Cambridge, 1914.

CAMPBELL, WILLIAM J. The Collection of Franklin Imprints in the Museum of the Curtis Publishing Company. Philadelphia, 1918.

Catalogue of the American Library of George Brinley. Hartford, Conn., 1878-1893.

DARTON, F. J. HARVEY. Children's Books in England. Cambridge, 1932.

EAMES, WILBERFORCE. Early New England Catechisms. Worcester, 1898.

EARLE, ALICE MORSE. Child Life in Colonial Days. New York, 1932.

EVANS, CHARLES. American Bibliography. Chicago, 1903-1931.

FIELD, E. M. The Child and His Book. London, n. d.

FORD, PAUL LEICESTER. The Journals of Hugh Gaine, Printer. New York, 1902.

Goody Two-Shoes. A Facsimile Reproduction of the edition of 1766. With an Introduction by Charles Welsh. London, 1881.

GUMUCHIAN & CIE. Les Livres de l'Enfance du XVe au XIXe Siecle. Paris, 1930.

HALSEY, ROSALIE V. Forgotten Books of the American Nursery. Boston, 1911.

HEARTMAN, CHARLES F. The New England Primer issued prior to 1830. P.P. 1922.

HEARTMAN, CHARLES F. Checklist of Printers in the United States from Stephen Daye to the close of the War of Independence. New York, 1915.

HILDEBURN, CHARLES R. Issues of the Pennsylvania Press in Pennsylvania. Philadelphia, 1885-1886.

JOHNSON, CLIFTON. Old-Time Schools and School-Books. New York and London, 1904.

LITTLEFIELD, GEORGE EMERY. The Early Massachusetts Press. Boston, 1907.

LIVINGSTON, LUTHER S. A Bibliography of the first editions in book form of the writings of Charles and Mary Lamb. New York, 1903.

LUCAS, E. V. Forgotten Tales of Long Ago. London, 1906.

MOSES, MONTROSE J. Children's Books and Reading. New York, 1907.

Bibliography

Mother Goose's Melody. By Colonel W. F. Prideaux. London, 1904.

NICHOLS, CHARLES LEMUEL. Bibliography of Worcester. Worcester, 1819.

NOLAN, J. BENNETT. The First Decade of Printing in Reading, Pennsylvania. Reading, 1930.

PEARSON, EDWIN. Banbury Chapbooks. London, 1890.

PILLING, JAMES CONSTANTINE. Bibliographies of Indian Language. Washington Government Printing Office, 1887-1894.

Rhode-Island Imprints, 1727-1800. Providence, 1915.

SABIN, JOSEPH, Dictionary of Books relating to America, 1492-1932. New York, 1868-1932.

SMITH, JOSEPH. A Descriptive Catalogue of Friends' Books. London, 1867.

STAUFFER, DAVID McNEELY. American Engravers on Copper and Steel. Grolier Club, New York, 1907.

STONE, WILBUR MACEY. Divine and Moral Songs of Isaac Watts.

STONE, WILBUR MACEY. The Thumb Bible of John Taylor. Brookline, Mass., 1928.

TAPLEY, HARRIET SILVESTER. Salem Imprints. Salem, 1927.

TRUMBULL, JAMES HAMMOND. List of Books Printed in Connecticut, 1709-1800. Hartford, Conn., 1904.

TUER, ANDREW W. The History of the Horn-Book. London, 1898.

TUER, ANDREW W. Pages and Pictures from Forgotten Children's Books. London, 1898-9.

Virginia State Library Bulletin. A Bibliography of Virginia. By Earl G. Swem. Richmond, 1916.

WEGELIN, OSCAR. Early American Poetry. New York, 1930.

WEISS, HARRY B. Joseph Yeager. Early American Engraver, Publisher of Children's Books, Railroad President. New York, 1932.

WEISS, HARRY B. Various articles in *The American Book Collector*, edited by Charles F. Heartman and Harry B. Weiss.

WEISS, HARRY B. William Charles. Early Caricaturist, Engraver and Publisher of Children's Books. New York, 1932.

WELSH, CHARLES. A Bookseller of the Last Century, Being some account of the Life of John Newbery. London, 1885.

WROTH, LAWRENCE C. A History of Printing in Colonial Maryland. Baltimore, 1922.

ERRATUM

No. 784. MOTHER GOOSE'S MELODIES, printed by C. S. Francis and Company [1833].

The firm of C. S. Francis was not formed into a Company until the year 1842. This item is therefore wrongly dated, and is outside the limits of this catalogue.

A CATALOGUE OF SELECTED DOVER BOOKS
IN ALL FIELDS OF INTEREST

A CATALOGUE OF SELECTED DOVER BOOKS
IN ALL FIELDS OF INTEREST

AMERICA'S OLD MASTERS, James T. Flexner. Four men emerged unexpectedly from provincial 18th century America to leadership in European art: Benjamin West, J. S. Copley, C. R. Peale, Gilbert Stuart. Brilliant coverage of lives and contributions. Revised, 1967 edition. 69 plates. 365pp. of text.

21806-6 Paperbound $2.75

FIRST FLOWERS OF OUR WILDERNESS: AMERICAN PAINTING, THE COLONIAL PERIOD, James T. Flexner. Painters, and regional painting traditions from earliest Colonial times up to the emergence of Copley, West and Peale Sr., Foster, Gustavus Hesselius, Feke, John Smibert and many anonymous painters in the primitive manner. Engaging presentation, with 162 illustrations. xxii + 368pp.

22180-6 Paperbound $3.50

THE LIGHT OF DISTANT SKIES: AMERICAN PAINTING, 1760-1835, James T. Flexner. The great generation of early American painters goes to Europe to learn and to teach: West, Copley, Gilbert Stuart and others. Allston, Trumbull, Morse; also contemporary American painters—primitives, derivatives, academics—who remained in America. 102 illustrations. xiii + 306pp. 22179-2 Paperbound $3.00

A HISTORY OF THE RISE AND PROGRESS OF THE ARTS OF DESIGN IN THE UNITED STATES, William Dunlap. Much the richest mine of information on early American painters, sculptors, architects, engravers, miniaturists, etc. The only source of information for scores of artists, the major primary source for many others. Unabridged reprint of rare original 1834 edition, with new introduction by James T. Flexner, and 394 new illustrations. Edited by Rita Weiss. 6⅝ x 9⅝.

21695-0, 21696-9, 21697-7 Three volumes, Paperbound $13.50

EPOCHS OF CHINESE AND JAPANESE ART, Ernest F. Fenollosa. From primitive Chinese art to the 20th century, thorough history, explanation of every important art period and form, including Japanese woodcuts; main stress on China and Japan, but Tibet, Korea also included. Still unexcelled for its detailed, rich coverage of cultural background, aesthetic elements, diffusion studies, particularly of the historical period. 2nd, 1913 edition. 242 illustrations. lii + 439pp. of text.

20364-6, 20365-4 Two volumes, Paperbound $5.00

THE GENTLE ART OF MAKING ENEMIES, James A. M. Whistler. Greatest wit of his day deflates Oscar Wilde, Ruskin, Swinburne; strikes back at inane critics, exhibitions, art journalism; aesthetics of impressionist revolution in most striking form. Highly readable classic by great painter. Reproduction of edition designed by Whistler. Introduction by Alfred Werner. xxxvi + 334pp.

21875-9 Paperbound $2.25

How to Know the Wild Flowers, Mrs. William Starr Dana. This is the classical book of American wildflowers (of the Eastern and Central United States), used by hundreds of thousands. Covers over 500 species, arranged in extremely easy to use color and season groups. Full descriptions, much plant lore. This Dover edition is the fullest ever compiled, with tables of nomenclature changes. 174 full-page plates by M. Satterlee. xii + 418pp. 20332-8 Paperbound $2.50

Our Plant Friends and Foes, William Atherton DuPuy. History, economic importance, essential botanical information and peculiarities of 25 common forms of plant life are provided in this book in an entertaining and charming style. Covers food plants (potatoes, apples, beans, wheat, almonds, bananas, etc.), flowers (lily, tulip, etc.), trees (pine, oak, elm, etc.), weeds, poisonous mushrooms and vines, gourds, citrus fruits, cotton, the cactus family, and much more. 108 illustrations. xiv + 290pp. 22272-1 Paperbound $2.00

How to Know the Ferns, Frances T. Parsons. Classic survey of Eastern and Central ferns, arranged according to clear, simple identification key. Excellent introduction to greatly neglected nature area. 57 illustrations and 42 plates. xvi + 215pp. 20740-4 Paperbound $1.75

Manual of the Trees of North America, Charles S. Sargent. America's foremost dendrologist provides the definitive coverage of North American trees and tree-like shrubs. 717 species fully described and illustrated: exact distribution, down to township; full botanical description; economic importance; description of subspecies and races; habitat, growth data; similar material. Necessary to every serious student of tree-life. Nomenclature revised to present. Over 100 locating keys. 783 illustrations. lii + 934pp. 20277-1, 20278-X Two volumes, Paperbound $6.00

Our Northern Shrubs, Harriet L. Keeler. Fine non-technical reference work identifying more than 225 important shrubs of Eastern and Central United States and Canada. Full text covering botanical description, habitat, plant lore, is paralleled with 205 full-page photographs of flowering or fruiting plants. Nomenclature revised by Edward G. Voss. One of few works concerned with shrubs. 205 plates, 35 drawings. xxviii + 521pp. 21989-5 Paperbound $3.75

The Mushroom Handbook, Louis C. C. Krieger. Still the best popular handbook: full descriptions of 259 species, cross references to another 200. Extremely thorough text enables you to identify, know all about any mushroom you are likely to meet in eastern and central U. S. A.: habitat, luminescence, poisonous qualities, use, folklore, etc. 32 color plates show over 50 mushrooms, also 126 other illustrations. Finding keys. vii + 560pp. 21861-9 Paperbound $3.95

Handbook of Birds of Eastern North America, Frank M. Chapman. Still much the best single-volume guide to the birds of Eastern and Central United States. Very full coverage of 675 species, with descriptions, life habits, distribution, similar data. All descriptions keyed to two-page color chart. With this single volume the average birdwatcher needs no other books. 1931 revised edition. 195 illustrations. xxxvi + 581pp. 21489-3 Paperbound $3.25

AMERICAN FOOD AND GAME FISHES, David S. Jordan and Barton W. Evermann. Definitive source of information, detailed and accurate enough to enable the sportsman and nature lover to identify conclusively some 1,000 species and sub-species of North American fish, sought for food or sport. Coverage of range, physiology, habits, life history, food value. Best methods of capture, interest to the angler, advice on bait, fly-fishing, etc. 338 drawings and photographs. 1 + 574pp. 6⅝ x 9⅜.
22383-1 Paperbound $4.50

THE FROG BOOK, Mary C. Dickerson. Complete with extensive finding keys, over 300 photographs, and an introduction to the general biology of frogs and toads, this is the classic non-technical study of Northeastern and Central species. 58 species; 290 photographs and 16 color plates. xvii + 253pp.
21973-9 Paperbound $4.00

THE MOTH BOOK: A GUIDE TO THE MOTHS OF NORTH AMERICA, William J. Holland. Classical study, eagerly sought after and used for the past 60 years. Clear identification manual to more than 2,000 different moths, largest manual in existence. General information about moths, capturing, mounting, classifying, etc., followed by species by species descriptions. 263 illustrations plus 48 color plates show almost every species, full size. 1968 edition, preface, nomenclature changes by A. E. Brower. xxiv + 479pp. of text. 6½ x 9¼.
21948-8 Paperbound $5.00

THE SEA-BEACH AT EBB-TIDE, Augusta Foote Arnold. Interested amateur can identify hundreds of marine plants and animals on coasts of North America; marine algae; seaweeds; squids; hermit crabs; horse shoe crabs; shrimps; corals; sea anemones; etc. Species descriptions cover: structure; food; reproductive cycle; size; shape; color; habitat; etc. Over 600 drawings. 85 plates. xii + 490pp.
21949-6 Paperbound $3.50

COMMON BIRD SONGS, Donald J. Borror. 33⅓ 12-inch record presents songs of 60 important birds of the eastern United States. A thorough, serious record which provides several examples for each bird, showing different types of song, individual variations, etc. Inestimable identification aid for birdwatcher. 32-page booklet gives text about birds and songs, with illustration for each bird.
21829-5 Record, book, album. Monaural. $2.75

FADS AND FALLACIES IN THE NAME OF SCIENCE, Martin Gardner. Fair, witty appraisal of cranks and quacks of science: Atlantis, Lemuria, hollow earth, flat earth, Velikovsky, orgone energy, Dianetics, flying saucers, Bridey Murphy, food fads, medical fads, perpetual motion, etc. Formerly "In the Name of Science." x + 363pp.
20394-8 Paperbound $2.00

HOAXES, Curtis D. MacDougall. Exhaustive, unbelievably rich account of great hoaxes: Locke's moon hoax, Shakespearean forgeries, sea serpents, Loch Ness monster, Cardiff giant, John Wilkes Booth's mummy, Disumbrationist school of art, dozens more; also journalism, psychology of hoaxing. 54 illustrations. xi + 338pp.
20465-0 Paperbound $2.75

THE PRINCIPLES OF PSYCHOLOGY, William James. The famous long course, complete and unabridged. Stream of thought, time perception, memory, experimental methods—these are only some of the concerns of a work that was years ahead of its time and still valid, interesting, useful. 94 figures. Total of xviii + 1391pp.
20381-6, 20382-4 Two volumes, Paperbound $6.00

THE STRANGE STORY OF THE QUANTUM, Banesh Hoffmann. Non-mathematical but thorough explanation of work of Planck, Einstein, Bohr, Pauli, de Broglie, Schrödinger, Heisenberg, Dirac, Feynman, etc. No technical background needed. "Of books attempting such an account, this is the best," Henry Margenau, Yale. 40-page "Postscript 1959." xii + 285pp. 20518-5 Paperbound $2.00

THE RISE OF THE NEW PHYSICS, A. d'Abro. Most thorough explanation in print of central core of mathematical physics, both classical and modern; from Newton to Dirac and Heisenberg. Both history and exposition; philosophy of science, causality, explanations of higher mathematics, analytical mechanics, electromagnetism, thermodynamics, phase rule, special and general relativity, matrices. No higher mathematics needed to follow exposition, though treatment is elementary to intermediate in level. Recommended to serious student who wishes verbal understanding. 97 illustrations. xvii + 982pp. 20003-5, 20004-3 Two volumes, Paperbound $5.50

GREAT IDEAS OF OPERATIONS RESEARCH, Jagjit Singh. Easily followed non-technical explanation of mathematical tools, aims, results: statistics, linear programming, game theory, queueing theory, Monte Carlo simulation, etc. Uses only elementary mathematics. Many case studies, several analyzed in detail. Clarity, breadth make this excellent for specialist in another field who wishes background. 41 figures. x + 228pp. 21886-4 Paperbound $2.25

GREAT IDEAS OF MODERN MATHEMATICS: THEIR NATURE AND USE, Jagjit Singh. Internationally famous expositor, winner of Unesco's Kalinga Award for science popularization explains verbally such topics as differential equations, matrices, groups, sets, transformations, mathematical logic and other important modern mathematics, as well as use in physics, astrophysics, and similar fields. Superb exposition for layman, scientist in other areas. viii + 312pp.
20587-8 Paperbound $2.25

GREAT IDEAS IN INFORMATION THEORY, LANGUAGE AND CYBERNETICS, Jagjit Singh. The analog and digital computers, how they work, how they are like and unlike the human brain, the men who developed them, their future applications, computer terminology. An essential book for today, even for readers with little math. Some mathematical demonstrations included for more advanced readers. 118 figures. Tables. ix + 338pp. 21694-2 Paperbound $2.25

CHANCE, LUCK AND STATISTICS, Horace C. Levinson. Non-mathematical presentation of fundamentals of probability theory and science of statistics and their applications. Games of chance, betting odds, misuse of statistics, normal and skew distributions, birth rates, stock speculation, insurance. Enlarged edition. Formerly "The Science of Chance." xiii + 357pp. 21007-3 Paperbound $2.00

PLANETS, STARS AND GALAXIES: DESCRIPTIVE ASTRONOMY FOR BEGINNERS, A. E. Fanning. Comprehensive introductory survey of astronomy: the sun, solar system, stars, galaxies, universe, cosmology; up-to-date, including quasars, radio stars, etc. Preface by Prof. Donald Menzel. 24pp. of photographs. 189pp. 5¼ x 8¼.
21680-2 Paperbound $1.50

TEACH YOURSELF CALCULUS, P. Abbott. With a good background in algebra and trig, you can teach yourself calculus with this book. Simple, straightforward introduction to functions of all kinds, integration, differentiation, series, etc. "Students who are beginning to study calculus method will derive great help from this book." Faraday House Journal. 308pp.
20683-1 Clothbound $2.00

TEACH YOURSELF TRIGONOMETRY, P. Abbott. Geometrical foundations, indices and logarithms, ratios, angles, circular measure, etc. are presented in this sound, easy-to-use text. Excellent for the beginner or as a brush up, this text carries the student through the solution of triangles. 204pp.
20682-3 Clothbound $2.00

TEACH YOURSELF ANATOMY, David LeVay. Accurate, inclusive, profusely illustrated account of structure, skeleton, abdomen, muscles, nervous system, glands, brain, reproductive organs, evolution. "Quite the best and most readable account," Medical Officer. 12 color plates. 164 figures. 311pp. 4¾ x 7.
21651-9 Clothbound $2.50

TEACH YOURSELF PHYSIOLOGY, David LeVay. Anatomical, biochemical bases; digestive, nervous, endocrine systems; metabolism; respiration; muscle; excretion; temperature control; reproduction. "Good elementary exposition," The Lancet. 6 color plates. 44 illustrations. 208pp. 4¼ x 7.
21658-6 Clothbound $2.50

THE FRIENDLY STARS, Martha Evans Martin. Classic has taught naked-eye observation of stars, planets to hundreds of thousands, still not surpassed for charm, lucidity, adequacy. Completely updated by Professor Donald H. Menzel, Harvard Observatory. 25 illustrations. 16 x 30 chart. x + 147pp. 21099-5 Paperbound $1.25

MUSIC OF THE SPHERES: THE MATERIAL UNIVERSE FROM ATOM TO QUASAR, SIMPLY EXPLAINED, Guy Murchie. Extremely broad, brilliantly written popular account begins with the solar system and reaches to dividing line between matter and nonmatter; latest understandings presented with exceptional clarity. Volume One: Planets, stars, galaxies, cosmology, geology, celestial mechanics, latest astronomical discoveries; Volume Two: Matter, atoms, waves, radiation, relativity, chemical action, heat, nuclear energy, quantum theory, music, light, color, probability, antimatter, antigravity, and similar topics. 319 figures. 1967 (second) edition. Total of xx + 644pp.
21809-0, 21810-4 Two volumes, Paperbound $4.00

OLD-TIME SCHOOLS AND SCHOOL BOOKS, Clifton Johnson. Illustrations and rhymes from early primers, abundant quotations from early textbooks, many anecdotes of school life enliven this study of elementary schools from Puritans to middle 19th century. Introduction by Carl Withers. 234 illustrations. xxxiii + 381pp.
21031-6 Paperbound $2.50

MATHEMATICAL PUZZLES FOR BEGINNERS AND ENTHUSIASTS, Geoffrey Mott-Smith. 189 puzzles from easy to difficult—involving arithmetic, logic, algebra, properties of digits, probability, etc.—for enjoyment and mental stimulus. Explanation of mathematical principles behind the puzzles. 135 illustrations. viii + 248pp.
20198-8 Paperbound $1.25

PAPER FOLDING FOR BEGINNERS, William D. Murray and Francis J. Rigney. Easiest book on the market, clearest instructions on making interesting, beautiful origami. Sail boats, cups, roosters, frogs that move legs, bonbon boxes, standing birds, etc. 40 projects; more than 275 diagrams and photographs. 94pp.
20713-7 Paperbound $1.00

TRICKS AND GAMES ON THE POOL TABLE, Fred Herrmann. 79 tricks and games— some solitaires, some for two or more players, some competitive games—to entertain you between formal games. Mystifying shots and throws, unusual caroms, tricks involving such props as cork, coins, a hat, etc. Formerly *Fun on the Pool Table*. 77 figures. 95pp.
21814-7 Paperbound $1.00

HAND SHADOWS TO BE THROWN UPON THE WALL: A SERIES OF NOVEL AND AMUSING FIGURES FORMED BY THE HAND, Henry Bursill. Delightful picturebook from great-grandfather's day shows how to make 18 different hand shadows: a bird that flies, duck that quacks, dog that wags his tail, camel, goose, deer, boy, turtle, etc. Only book of its sort. vi + 33pp. 6½ x 9¼. 21779-5 Paperbound $1.00

WHITTLING AND WOODCARVING, E. J. Tangerman. 18th printing of best book on market. "If you can cut a potato you can carve" toys and puzzles, chains, chessmen, caricatures, masks, frames, woodcut blocks, surface patterns, much more. Information on tools, woods, techniques. Also goes into serious wood sculpture from Middle Ages to present, East and West. 464 photos, figures. x + 293pp.
20965-2 Paperbound $2.00

HISTORY OF PHILOSOPHY, Julián Marías. Possibly the clearest, most easily followed, best planned, most useful one-volume history of philosophy on the market; neither skimpy nor overfull. Full details on system of every major philosopher and dozens of less important thinkers from pre-Socratics up to Existentialism and later. Strong on many European figures usually omitted. Has gone through dozens of editions in Europe. 1966 edition, translated by Stanley Appelbaum and Clarence Strowbridge. xviii + 505pp.
21739-6 Paperbound $2.75

YOGA: A SCIENTIFIC EVALUATION, Kovoor T. Behanan. Scientific but non-technical study of physiological results of yoga exercises; done under auspices of Yale U. Relations to Indian thought, to psychoanalysis, etc. 16 photos. xxiii + 270pp.
20505-3 Paperbound $2.50

Prices subject to change without notice.
Available at your book dealer or write for free catalogue to Dept. GI, Dover Publications, Inc., 180 Varick St., N. Y., N. Y. 10014. Dover publishes more than 150 books each year on science, elementary and advanced mathematics, biology, music, art, literary history, social sciences and other areas.